TREASURES
FROM AN OLD
Book

Volume 1

Ancient Wisdom for a
Modern World

LORIN BRADBURY, PH.D.

WESTBOW
PRESS®
A DIVISION OF THOMAS NELSON
& ZONDERVAN

WestBow Press books may be ordered through booksellers or by contacting:

WestBow Press
A Division of Thomas Nelson & Zondervan
1663 Liberty Drive
Bloomington, IN 47403
www.westbowpress.com
1 (866) 928-1240

ISBN: 978-1-9736-9445-8 (sc)
ISBN: 978-1-9736-9447-2 (hc)
ISBN: 978-1-9736-9446-5 (e)

Library of Congress Control Number: 2020911909

Print information available on the last page.

WestBow Press rev. date: 8/6/2020

This book is affectionately dedicated to my wife, Bonnie, who has stood beside me for the past 49 years through thick and thin. While we could have been doing something else, she demonstrated patience throughout the many hours I spent working and reworking the manuscript that became this book. As with all my undertakings—pastoring churches far from where we grew up, going to graduate school with five children, and patiently waiting for me to complete this project, she has been right beside me and provided the support I needed. If she were a selfish person, this book would never have come into existence. Instead, I have always felt her love, support, and encouragement. "Thank you, Sweetheart! You truly are the woman written about in Proverbs 31."

CONTENTS

ACKNOWLEDGMENTS

The apostle Paul taught that credit should be given where credit is due. There are so many people who have impacted my life and the writing of this volume that I fear overlooking some. First, I would like to express my appreciation to the congregation of Bethel United Pentecostal Church for allowing me to minister to them for the past twenty-seven years. They faithfully attend three services a week and encourage me to continue teaching and preaching week after week. Thank you to everyone who has encouraged me by showing up Wednesday after Wednesday evenings to hear me expound the book of Proverbs.

Several years ago, I turned my notes from the first nine chapters of the book of Proverbs into text and thought it was ready for publishing. However, I had Diane Lamas review some of the lessons, and the feedback she provided resulted in a total rewrite of the manuscript. Her critique led to a great improvement in my editing skills. Later, Kelsey Fuentes took on the process of editing many of these lessons and provided excellent critique. She was not afraid to challenge my writing and provided very helpful suggestions. As a result, in some instances, I rewrote total sections. Then my wife, Bonnie Bradbury, became involved in the editing process and read the entire manuscript in detail and provided not only written feedback but verbal dialogue as well.

A dear friend, Rev. Mitchell Glover, read an earlier version of this manuscript and suggested I highlight key points by creating boxes around those key points, either further down the page or on the next page. Another minister friend, Rev. Tad Lindley, read some of the lessons and suggested highlighting words and phrases that introduced certain paragraphs. This led to using subheadings as segues throughout the book. Last but not least, I would like to express my appreciation to Dr. Paul Baumeister, whose keen eyesight spotted errors the rest of us missed.

Again, there were many others who read various lessons. I apologize if your name is not listed above. To all who took the time to read even one chapter and provide me with feedback, I say thank you!

PREFACE

A pastor preaching through an entire book of the Bible could benefit any church. This could be done expositorily or topically. Either way, a practical application can be made by taking the flour of the Word, mixing it with the oil of the Spirit, and producing bread for the congregation. Even though I made an attempt to cover every verse in the book of Proverbs, these lessons are topical in nature. That is the reason for such variety, ranging from establishing a sure foundation on the Word of God to the fear of the LORD to parental instruction to warnings against enticement from the world, all within the first nineteen verses of the first chapter. By doing this, the people of God are not only exposed to every verse in every chapter, but they learn to make practical application to their lives.

I have chosen to refer to these writings as lessons, rather than chapters, because that is what they were originally. August 18, 1999, I, along with the congregation of United Pentecostal Church in Bethel, Alaska, began the long journey through the book of Proverbs. The goal was to teach one lesson each Wednesday evening. But there have been starts and stops, times when a different a topic seemed necessary to meet specific needs, times when I was unable to complete preparation on a lesson in time for a service, holidays, vacations, and special speakers. However, at the writing of this preface, 382 lessons have been produced—enough material for more than seven volumes—and we plod on.

It has been said that wisdom is the ability to apply knowledge. However, even wisdom without a practical application does little to benefit the individual. Steven Showalter (2017) provides the following insight: "One of the most important lessons we can learn is that having wisdom does not prevent us from making foolish mistakes if we do not apply it. We need to take the Word of God and apply it to our daily lives" (pp. 135–136). These lessons are an attempt to apply wisdom to everyday living.

INTRODUCTION

Why study Proverbs? I suppose we could come up with the same answer for every book in the Bible: it's the Word of God! But to be more specific, the book of Proverbs is power packed with wisdom that will guide God's people in daily living. Rev. Ron Mullings taught a lesson titled "The Wonderful Word of God." He described the preached Word—the taught Word as reconstituted. In other words, as some products can be condensed for purpose of shipping and storage, and then reconstituted at a later date, every verse of scripture is condensed but ready to be reconstituted through preaching and teaching. And as that is true for every verse in the Bible, it is especially true for the book of Proverbs. To avoid redundancy, I will allow the first lesson in this book to further provide an introduction.

LESSON 1

A SURE FOUNDATION

PROVERBS 1:1-6

¹ The proverbs of Solomon son of David, king of Israel: ² for gaining wisdom and instruction; for understanding words of insight; ³ for receiving instruction in prudent behavior, doing what is right and just and fair; ⁴ for giving prudence to those who are simple, knowledge and discretion to the young—⁵ let the wise listen and add to their learning, and let the discerning get guidance—⁶ for understanding proverbs and parables, the sayings and riddles of the wise.

WHAT ARE PROVERBS?

The Hebrew word translated *proverbs* comes from a word that signifies *to rule or have dominion over* (Henry, n.d., Vol. 3, p. 790) because of the dominant influence these teachings can have upon those who hear them and apply them to their lives. The book of Proverbs is widely recognized as a source of sound, practical wisdom. Whether one is looking for advice on getting along with other people, planning for the future, rearing children, building a lasting marriage, succeeding financially, or developing spiritual maturity, the book of Proverbs is a rich fountain of profound but simple insight.

Many people have found it helpful to include the book of Proverbs in their daily Bible reading. Since the book has thirty-one chapters, if you were to read one chapter each day of the month, you would read through the entire book twelve times in one year. After you have done this faithfully for a few months, you will find yourself beginning to think in terms of the wisdom of Proverbs. Inevitably, the counsel found in this book will begin to influence your decisions. A study in Proverbs has the potential to improve how you relate to your children, spouse, neighbors, and coworkers. But most importantly, it will affect how you relate to God.

> A study in Proverbs has the potential to improve how you relate to your children, spouse, neighbors, and coworkers. But most importantly, it will affect how you relate to God.

THE AUTHOR

Solomon is credited with gathering the proverbs into what we now know as the book of Proverbs. He went down in history as the wisest man ever. It has been said Solomon "addicted himself to the study of divine things" (Henry, n.d., Vol. 3, p. 790). And God gave him wisdom in response to a humble prayer:

> Now, O LORD my God, you have made me king instead of my father, David, but I am like a little child who doesn't know his way around. And here I am in the midst of your own chosen people, a nation so great and numerous they cannot be counted! Give me an understanding heart so that I can govern your people well and know the difference between right and wrong. For who by himself is able to govern this great people of yours? (1 Kings 3:7–9 NLT)

Imagine a world in which every leader from husband and parent to president and prime minister prayed that same prayer as sincerely as Solomon prayed it. Imagine how orderly the world would be, and righteousness would be the rule of the day.

By praying the prayer he prayed, Solomon put the kingdom of God ahead of personal gain, and the LORD honored him for it:

> So God replied, "Because you have asked for wisdom in governing my people with justice and have not asked for a long life or wealth or the death of your enemies—I will give you what you asked for! I will give you a wise and understanding heart such as no one else has had or ever will have! And I will also give you what you did not ask for—riches and fame! No other king in all the world will be compared to you for the rest of your life! And if you follow me and obey my decrees and my commands as your father, David, did, I will give you a long life." (1 Kings 3:11–14 NLT)

Considering the fact that God has not changed and that He still desires to reward those who humble themselves before Him, a simple promise of Jesus is at our fingertips: "Seek ye first the kingdom of God, and his righteousness; and all these things shall be added unto you" (Matthew 6:33 KJV).

THE REASON FOR THE BOOK OF PROVERBS

The first four verses of the book of Proverbs tell us why Solomon gathered together these proverbs: attaining wisdom, learning discipline, obtaining insight, and acquiring a disciplined and prudent life.

Attaining wisdom. According to H. A. Ironside (1908), the word translated *wisdom* means *skillfulness* or *the ability to use knowledge right* (p. 13). This wisdom provides us with guidance in developing the proper notions concerning life. By reading and meditating on these proverbs, we are filling our minds with clear and distinct principles for righteous living that will result in knowing how to speak and act wisely, and it will aid in giving instruction to others. "Blessed is the man who finds wisdom, the man who gains understanding, for she [wisdom] is more profitable than silver and yields better returns than gold. She is more precious than rubies; nothing you desire can compare with her" (Proverbs 3:13–15). These proverbs are not just fanciful sayings of yesteryear; they are for attaining wisdom today—ancient wisdom for a modern world.

> By reading and meditating on these proverbs, we are filling our minds with clear and distinct principles for righteous living that will result in knowing how to speak and act wisely, and it will aid in giving instruction to others.

Learning discipline. Though not of much comfort to Job, Eliphaz spoke words that in another context are pregnant with truth: "Happy *is* the man whom God correcteth: therefore despise not thou the chastening of the Almighty" (Job 5:17 KJV). Thank God for correction! However, it's much better if we can learn discipline through the study of the Word of God. Learning through instruction prevents the necessity of the rod. How many times have you heard the words, "Do you always have to learn the hard way?" The book of Proverbs provides guidance in disciplining one's self—avoiding having to learn the hard way.

Obtaining insight. Insight develops as a result of instruction, and the book of Proverbs provides that instruction. To survive spiritually, we must possess the insight necessary to discern between truth and falsehood. The apostle John cautioned his readers, "Believe not every spirit, but try the spirits whether they are of God: because many false prophets are gone out into the world" (1 John 4:1 KJV). And the apostle Paul wrote: "I want you to understand what really matters, so that you may live pure and blameless lives until the day of Christ's return" (Philippians 1:10 NLT).

It would be a terrible thing to arrive at heaven's gate only to be turned away because we failed to utilize the wisdom at our fingertips. Though many have attempted to minimize the possibility of such an event happening, Jesus warned that not every person who calls Him

"Lord" will enter into the kingdom of heaven, but only those who do the will of our heavenly Father:

> Many will say to me in that day, Lord, Lord, have we not prophesied in thy name? and in thy name have cast out devils? and in thy name done many wonderful works? And then will I profess unto them, I never knew you: depart from me, ye that work iniquity! (Matthew 7:21–23 KJV)

> It would be a terrible thing to arrive at heaven's gate only to be turned away because we failed to utilize the wisdom at our fingertips.

Acquiring a disciplined and prudent life. The word translated *prudent* is rarely used in the scriptures and means *to be circumspect* and *intelligent* (Strong 1990, *Hebrew/Chaldee Dictionary*, #7919, p. 116). A prudent life will result in doing what is *right and just and fair*. Examining the words translated *right* and *just* and *fair* provides a picture of behaviors that naturally flow from the exercise of prudence. The word *right* refers to right conduct, *just* has to do with decision-making, and *fair* refers to uprightness of moral character. Right conduct, just decisions, and upright moral character are essential to the practice of our faith. It's one thing to declare our faith; it's quite another to practice it. Profession without practice is nothing more than "sounding brass, or a tinkling cymbal" (1 Corinthians 13:1 KJV).

Jesus epitomized a disciplined and prudent life. Power and prestige had no influence upon him. Even the Jewish leaders recognized this strength of character about Him:

> They came to him and said, "Teacher, we know you are a man of integrity. You aren't swayed by others, because you pay no attention to who they are; but you

teach the way of God in accordance with the truth."
(Mark 12:14)

Also, a Christian must be *intelligent* in decision-making and passing judgment. Many incorrectly believe it is a sin to judge others. Jesus condemned judging unrighteously and self-righteously, but He did not condemn making a prudent judgment. While teaching in the temple courts, he plainly stated, "Do not judge according to appearance, but judge with righteous judgment" (John 7:24 NASB). A study of the book of Proverbs provides insight necessary to make prudent judgments.

SOLOMON'S TARGET AUDIENCE

Solomon's audience was described in verse 4 as *the simple* and *the young*. The intent is not to disparage either group but to provide knowledge and guidance.

The simple. *The simple* as used here is not describing the feebleminded or someone with a mental defect but unregenerate people. Humanity in its unregenerate state is very vulnerable to sin—very simple. Until enlightened by the Word of God, fallen mankind lives in a very dark state. The human nature (the flesh) is bent on satisfying its base desires, and without godly principles as an internal guide, an individual can be led like a bull with ring in its nose to the slaughter. Internalizing godly principles will prevent being led astray.

Though not a rocket scientist or a neurosurgeon, a marginally intelligent person can become wise through the study of the Word of God. These proverbs provide a basis for common sense. A person with common sense is often thought of as intelligent, but really, common sense is an expression of internalized principles. You may not yet have a diploma from an institution of higher learning on your wall, but if you internalize the principles embodied within these proverbs, you will, at a minimum, appear intelligent. Someone may comment, "My, that was a brilliant decision." But it was not a brilliant decision of human origin; it was the result of following internalized godly principles.

> Though not a rocket scientist or a neurosurgeon, a marginally intelligent person can become wise through the study of the Word of God.

These proverbs are for giving prudence to the simple. Here, the word translated *prudence* in the original language means *craftiness*. Jesus used a very similar word in speaking to his disciples; "Behold, I send you forth as sheep in the midst of wolves: be ye therefore wise (crafty) as serpents, and harmless as doves" (Matthew 10:16 KJV, word in parentheses added). How do you recognize enticements that lead to sin and know how to avoid them? By internalizing the principles embodied within the Word of God. Matthew Henry (n.d.) summarized it this way: "Those who receive these instructions … though they be simple, will hereby be made subtle, graciously crafty to know the sin they should avoid and the duty they should do, and to escape the tempter's woes" (Vol. 3, p. 792).

The young. "The proverbs of Solomon … for giving … knowledge and discretion to the young" (Proverbs 1:1, 4). The Hebrew word translated *knowledge* contains a sense of *cunning*. To survive, young people need spiritual wit to outmaneuver the devil. They need the Word of God etched into their hearts. The Hebrew word translated *discretion* contains the idea of *thoughtfulness*. Whereas youthfulness is often characterized by impulsivity, these proverbs gathered by Solomon are intended to become so much a part of the decision-making process of a young person that thoughtfulness and carefulness replace impulsivity and recklessness. In essence, the stage of life called adolescence can be eradicated, and young adults can take their places alongside older adults.

IN CLOSING

Reading, memorizing, and meditating on the wise sayings Solomon included in the book of Proverbs will result in the development of wisdom and spiritual growth. The book of Proverbs provides milk for babies but strong meat for the full-grown. A study of this book will not only make the foolish wise, but it will make the wise wiser and the good better. No one ever gets to a place too wise to learn. "Readiness to learn is ever characteristic of the truly wise" (Ironside 1908, p 15). Like Matthew Henry (n.d.), "I am ignorant of many things, but not of my own ignorance" (Vol. 3, p. 792). And like the apostle Paul, we must continually press toward the next spiritual level. (See Philippians 3:12.)

> The book of Proverbs provides milk for babies but strong meat for the full-grown.

Jesus described the preeminent characteristic of the truly wise: "Everyone who hears these words of mine and puts them into practice is like a wise man who built his house on the rock" (Matthew 7:24). A wise person is teachable and welcomes instruction and reproof. Solomon, on the other hand, described not putting instruction into practice as folly, and folly leads to lower quality of life. If you want an abundant life, get wisdom, get instruction, accept correction, and accept reproof. Always remain teachable!

LESSON 2

THE FEAR OF THE LORD

PROVERBS 1:7

⁷ The fear of the LORD is the beginning of knowledge, but fools despise wisdom and instruction.

"Moses said to the people, 'Do not be afraid. God has come to test you, so that the fear of God will be with you to keep you from sinning'" (Exodus 20:20). Interestingly, we are instructed "not to fear" and "to fear" in the same verse. As Matthew Henry (n.d.) explained, this is not a contradiction:

> We must not fear with amazement—with that fear which has torment, which … sets us a trembling, genders to bondage, betrays us to Satan, and alienates us from God; but we must always have in our minds a reverence of God's majesty, a dread of his displeasure, and an obedient regard to his sovereign authority over us: this fear will quicken us to our duty and make us circumspect in our walking. (Vol. 1, p. 363).

KINDS OF FEAR OF THE LORD

There are several kinds of fear of the LORD that will be explored in this lesson: a tyrannical fear of God, a zealous-religious fear of God, and a filial fear of God.

A *tyrannical fear of God* springs from the idea that God is cruel and oppressive. It has potential to immobilize people—to keep them from taking even the slightest risk for fear of reprisal. Jesus described this kind of individual in his parable of the talents:

> Then the man who had received the one bag of gold came. "Master," he said, "I knew that you are a hard man, harvesting where you have not sown and gathering where you have not scattered seed. So I was afraid and went out and hid your gold in the ground. See, here is what belongs to you." (Matthew 25:24–25)

This type of fear results in the desire for removal of the tyrannical agent. Very few people will ever surrender their lives to God with this view of Him as the Master.

Then there is a *zealous-religious fear of God*. The Pharisees feared the scorn of their peers; they feared they might appear to violate their religious traditions. Jesus denounced that behavior, stating, "But all their works they do for to be seen of men" (Matthew 23:5 KJV). Though this kind of fear of God is not a balanced view of God, it might, in some cases, be instrumental in leading especially religious people to the Lord. Paul was one of those zealous-religious people, a Pharisee, and God was able to capitalize on his zealous-religious fear and bring him to his knees. On the road to Damascus, the Lord struck Saul to the ground. And in fear, he asked, "Who art thou, Lord?" (Acts 9:5 KJV). The Lord responded, "I am Jesus whom thou persecutest" (Acts 9:5 KJV).

Once converted, the love of God tempered his religious zeal. Paul came to serve the Lord out of love, rather than out of zealous-religious fear. He let go of the fear of man and became consumed with the heartbeat of the Lord. Paul developed love and compassion for all lost humankind. He acknowledged, "If I preach voluntarily, I have a reward; if not voluntarily, I am simply discharging the trust committed to me" (1 Corinthians 9:17). It would be a waste to go through life doing nothing more than discharging one's duty.

A third kind of fear of God has been described as a *filial fear of God,* or the fear a child would have for a parent. In this type of fear, there is the addition of love and faithfulness: By "love and faithfulness iniquity is atoned for, and by the fear of the LORD one turns away from evil" (Proverbs 16:6 ESV). This kind of fear understands the grace of God. In the parent-child relationship, when appropriate fear of a parent is present, movement of the hand toward the child doesn't elicit a flinch; instead, it anticipates a touch or being picked up and held. Even in moments of correction, filial fear doesn't lead to anger and bitterness but an understanding that the parent's discipline or correction is in the child's best interest. This kind of fear results in admiration for the parent and a desire to please. The same is true of the relationship with our heavenly Father. The child of God stands in awe of the Father's love and kindness. Correction is accepted as an act of love and faithfulness on the part of Father. The child of God anticipates being loved and protected by their heavenly Father. It results in a reverence for the Father and everything He loves. The child of God develops a healthy fear and stands in awe of the Father. It has been said that we view God much like our father. If our father was a pushover, we may view our heavenly Father as weak and impotent; and if our father was a tyrant, we may view our heavenly Father as a tyrant; but if our father was loving, firm, and fair, we likely will develop a proper view of our heavenly Father.

> If our father was a pushover, we may view our heavenly Father as weak and impotent; and if our father was a tyrant, we may view our heavenly Father as a tyrant; but if our father was loving, firm, and fair, we likely will develop a proper view of our heavenly Father.

THE RELATIONSHIP BETWEEN KNOWLEDGE AND THE FEAR OF THE LORD

As the fear of the LORD diminishes, so does true knowledge. Proverbs 1:7 KJV states, "The fear of the LORD is the beginning of knowledge." The fear of the LORD is the foundation of all true knowledge. When the foundation is compromised by a lack of the fear of the LORD, wisdom also is diminished because "the fear of the LORD is the beginning of wisdom" (Psalm 111:10 KJV). Matthew Henry (n.d.) described the truly wise: "These know enough who know how to fear God, who are careful in every thing to please him and fearful of offending him in anything; this is the Alpha and Omega of knowledge" (Vol. 3, p. 793). We cannot profit from God's Word unless we reverence Him. "Of all things that are to be known this is most evident, that *God is to be feared,* to be reverenced, served, and worshipped" (Henry, n.d., Vol. 3, p. 793).

> As the fear of the LORD diminishes, so does true knowledge.

Moses stated; "The fear of God will be with you to keep you from sinning" (Exodus 20:20)." The fear of the LORD results in submission to His will, irrespective of fairness. A loving reverence for God leads to submission to His lordship. This is beautifully illustrated by a discussion between Jesus and Peter. After a satisfying meal, Jesus and Peter were off by themselves. Jesus questioned Peter three times concerning his love for Him. After receiving a heartfelt commitment from Peter, the Lord described the death Peter would die and again stated, "Follow me!" Immediately, Peter saw John coming and asked Jesus, "What about him?"

Jesus's response was straightforward and succinct, "Never mind John. You follow me!" If Peter were to become what the Lord had in mind for him, it would be essential he learn that following isn't about fairness; it's about faithfulness. (See John 21:15–22.) That's a picture of the wise follower of the Lord, but what are the characteristics of a fool?

CHARACTERISTICS OF A FOOL

"Fools despise wisdom and instruction" (Proverbs 1:7 KJV). A fool maintains that he is comfortable just the way he is. And fools will perish because they choose to remain willingly ignorant. (See 2 Peter 3:5 KJV.) "They perish because they refused to love the truth and so be saved" (2 Thessalonians 2:10). In other words, a fool does not want to change. In fact, "The fool hath said in his heart, *There is* no God" (Psalm 14:1 KJV).

The teaching of the theory of evolution over the past one hundred twenty-five years has eroded faith in the foundation of true knowledge. Atheism is not just the sin of rebellion; it is the sin of deliberately discounting God—making God a nonentity. Matthew Henry (n.d.) elaborated on this: The fool "cannot satisfy himself that there is [no God], but he wishes there were none, and pleases himself with the fancy that it is possible there may be none. He cannot be sure there is one, and therefore he is willing to think there is none" (Vol. 3, p. 283).

> Atheism is not just the sin of rebellion; it is the sin of deliberately discounting God—making God a nonentity.

Atheism leaves the mind in universal doubt and distress in regard to all existences and events. Truth is the natural element of the mind. It can by no possibility be at peace without it. To overthrow all evidence—all knowledge—all confidence, is to render the happiness of mind impossible, and to deliver it over to mourning, lamentation, and woe. (Finney, 2005, p. 47)

It is unnatural for humankind—God's supreme creation, made in His image and likeness—to say to the Creator, "You do not exist!" In fact, "No man will say, 'There is no God' till he is so hardened in sin that it has become his interest there should be none to call him to an account" (Henry, n.d., Vol. 3, p. 284). Such a person is among the vilest of sinners and deserves the title "fool."

The Bible clearly reveals that God controls this world:

- He controls the course of world events; he removes kings and sets up other kings. He gives wisdom to the wise and knowledge to the scholars. He reveals deep and mysterious things and knows what lies hidden in darkness, though He is surrounded by light. (Daniel 2:21–22 NLT)
- The heavens proclaim the glory of God. The skies display his craftsmanship. Day after day they continue to speak; night after night they make him known. They speak without a sound or word; their voice is never heard. Yet their message has gone throughout the earth, and their words to all the world. (Psalm 19:1–4 NLT)

> The Bible clearly reveals that God controls this world.

IN CLOSING

There are many foolish things a person can do in this life, but the most foolish of all is to deny the existence of God! To acknowledge and fear the LORD is to recognize that He truly is in control of this world and the world to come. When the time arrives to make the journey into eternity, and we are ushered across that great divide by our Lord, at that moment, we will recognize that living for Jesus in this world has been a wonderful blessing, but to die will result in even greater gain. The fear of the LORD is tied directly to that hope, and as a result, like the apostle Paul, we too can declare, "To live *is* Christ, and to die *is* gain" (Philippians 1:21 KJV).

LESSON 3

BENEFITS OF PARENTAL INSTRUCTION

PROVERBS 1:8–9

8 Listen, my son, to your father's instruction and do not forsake your mother's teaching. 9 They will be a garland to grace your head and a chain to adorn your neck.

A policeman noticed a boy with a lot of stuff packed on his back, riding a tricycle around and around the block. Finally he asked him where he was going.

"I'm running away from home," the boy said.

The policeman then asked him, "Why do you keep going around and around the block?"

The boy answered, "My mother won't let me cross the street." (Teach in Doan, 1968, p. 277)

THE WEIGHT OF PARENTING

We usually don't have to look too far to see a bit of humor in parenting. But there are weights and burdens associated with the task. Job is an example of a parent who carried the weight of his children on his shoulders:

15

His sons used to go to each other's homes, where they would have parties. ... They would send someone to invite their three sisters to eat and drink with them.

When they finished having their parties, Job would send for them in order to cleanse them from sin. He would get up early in the morning and sacrifice burnt offerings for each of them. Job thought, "My children may have sinned and cursed God in their hearts." Job offered sacrifices for them all the time." (Job 1:4–5 GW)

Though many children are oblivious to their parents' concern for them, good parents spend time in prayer for their children. In the book, *Teaching Your Children Responsibility*, Eyre and Eyre (1984) describe the weight on the shoulders of most contemporary parents:

We share a certain bond as parents, and, unfortunately, part of that bond is worry. We worry about our children's physical safety. We worry about their emotional and social safety. We worry about the adequacy of their education. We worry about the effect of the indulgent, convenience-oriented, leisure-emphasizing society we live in. We worry about the amorality and the increasing absence of standards surrounding our children. We worry about the whole range of uncertainties that lie in their future. (p. 1)

It's one thing to be able to conceive and bear a child; it's quite another to be a good parent. Good parents don't just bear children; they bear a burden for their children.

> Good parents don't just bear children; they bear a burden for their children.

MORAL DEVELOPMENT

There are two things to consider in the moral development of a child. The first is the importance of parental instruction and guidance. This cannot be understated. Without parental instruction and teaching, there would be no values to internalize and therefore no moral development. The second is the responsibility of the child to internalize those values and live them out. "Listen, my son, to your father's instruction and do not forsake your mother's teaching" (Proverbs 1:8).

Parents must love God, and they must love God enough to teach their children the Word of God. God directs parents to:

> Write these commandments that I've given you today on your hearts. Get them inside of you and then get them inside your children. Talk about them wherever you are, sitting at home or walking in the street; talk about them from the time you get up in the morning to when you fall into bed at night. Tie them on your hands and foreheads as a reminder; inscribe them on the doorposts of your homes and on your city gates. (Deuteronomy 6:7–9 MSG)

In other words, make certain that everywhere your children look, they see the Word of God.

> Make certain that everywhere your children look, they see the Word of God.

Though it is essential to get the teachings and commands of God inside children's hearts, parents must first love God and obey Him themselves. Notice the sequence—the LORD commanded parents to love and obey Him, and then instruct their children:

Love God, your God, with your whole heart: love him with all that's in you, love him with all you've got! Write these commandments that I've given you today on your hearts. Get them inside of you and then get them inside your children. (Deuteronomy 6:5–6, MSG)

How shall a child learn to refrain from cursing if a parent turns to cursing under stress? It is never acceptable to excuse yourself by telling the child, "See what you made me do!" or "Now you know how I feel!" A parent has the responsibility to be disciplined before trying to discipline his or her children.

> A parent has the responsibility to be disciplined before trying to discipline his or her children.

Parents must love their children enough to instruct them and then enforce godly limits. Abraham was chosen of the LORD because of special qualities he possessed and exercised as a parent. The LORD thought, "For I know him, that he will command his children and his household after him, and they shall keep the way of the LORD" (Genesis 18:19 KJV). In contrast, the LORD was not pleased with Eli's parenting:

And the LORD said to Samuel, Behold, I will do a thing in Israel, at which both the ears of every one that heareth it shall tingle. In that day I will perform against Eli all things which I have spoken concerning his house: when I begin, I will also make an end. For I have told him that I will judge his house for ever for the iniquity which he knoweth; because his sons made themselves vile, and he restrained them not. And therefore I have sworn unto the house of Eli, that the iniquity of Eli's house shall not be purged with sacrifice nor offering for ever. (1 Samuel 3:11–14 KJV)

The role of parents in teaching obedience is essential to the happiness of their children. Again, Eyre and Eyre (1984) explain:

> The world we live in requires obedience—not conformity, not stereotype, but obedience to the laws of nature, the laws of society, the laws of morality and higher values. Obedience does not diminish freedom; it increases it. By teaching our children to obey, we open channels through which we can teach them everything else. (p. 14)

Our children must come to see obedience as desirable and as a route to happiness as well as responsibility. And in addition to happiness and maturity, the Word of God promises a long life to the one who listens to and obeys his parents: "Children, obey your parents in the Lord: for this is right. Honour thy father and mother; (which is the first commandment with promise;) That it may be well with thee, and thou mayest live long on the earth" (Ephesians 6:1–3 KJV).

> The role of parents in teaching obedience is essential to the happiness of their children.

The cry of the teacher in Proverbs 1:8 is that of responsibility. "Don't forget what I taught you—it was given to help you." Eyre and Eyre (1984) wrote that responsibility means to become mature in the sense of being responsible to family, to self, to society. "It means being responsible for all aspects of our lives and our situations: for our talents, for our potential, for our feelings, for our thoughts, for our actions for our freedom" (p. 4). Further, "Responsibility is not the result of maturity, but the cause of it" (p. 4). As we teach our children responsibility, maturation occurs. Children who do not learn responsibility do not mature as God intended. That's why we find forty-year-old adults who are still dependent on their parents and have never assumed responsibility for their own economic self-sufficiency.

When I facilitated substance-abuse treatment groups, I would tell group members, "You are not forty years old; you are fourteen years old." People do not mature until they learn to take responsibility for their actions. People do not mature until they learn to treat others responsibly.

SPIRITUAL ADORNMENTS

Solomon instructed his son to assimilate his parents' instruction and teaching as treasured adornments. Father's instructions and Mother's teachings are to "be a garland to grace your head and a chain to adorn your neck" (Proverbs 1:9). There are three very important adornments: reverence for the things of God, respect for authority, and respect for others.

Reverence for the things of God. Before children are taught that God loves them, they need to know that God is holy. How a child respects and honors their parents and other authority figures is a good indication of how they honor God. There is no better garland to grace a young person's head than reverence for the things of God. Holy living is a manifestation of the fear of God in one's heart: "By the fear of the LORD one turns away from evil" (Proverbs 16:6 ESV). And reverence for the things of God—the fear of God—is an adornment that can be seen by all.

> Before children are taught that God loves them, they need to know that God is holy.

Respect for authority. The fear of God is demonstrated by obedience to God's authority, earthly authorities, and laws of human government. Paul urged his readers to be subject to the all governing authorities. "For there is no authority except from God, and those that exist have been instituted by God. Therefore whoever resists the authorities resists what God has appointed, and those who resist will incur judgment" (Romans 13:1–2 ESV). When a child learns to submit to parental authority, that child is learning to submit to other authorities external to the family, including God. Submission to various levels of authority is a beautiful chain to adorn the neck of a young person.

Respect for others. A third very important adornment is respect for others. Yes, we are our brother's keeper. John was emphatic, "If a man say, I love God, and hateth his brother, he is a liar: for he that loveth not his brother whom he hath seen, how can he love God whom he hath not seen" (1 John 4:20 KJV)? How else can I show my respect for someone I have not seen (i.e., God) than by respecting the ones I am able to see? Not only is this virtue manifest by respecting others; it is manifest by respecting other people's things. A teacher and her husband visited our church. The next day, while in the restroom, a young lady (a ninth-grade girl) from our church happened to be in the restroom and stated, "You were in church last night." The teacher acknowledged that she had been. Then the young lady did something the teacher did not expect: she began picking up all the paper on the floor around the garbage can. That young lady demonstrated maturity by taking responsibility for respecting the property of others.

INTERGENERATIONAL TRANSMISSION OF VALUES

When children internalize their parents' values, those values become "a garland to grace their heads and a chain to adorn their necks." Solomon instructed his son to listen to his father's instruction and his mother's teaching. His intent was to accomplish what is called intergenerational transmission of values. For this to become a reality, both accommodation and assimilation must occur. Before any value can be transmitted to the next generation, that child or young adult must accommodate or make room for that value. No value can be transmitted until there is an openness to at least consider the teaching. Once accommodation occurs, assimilation can become a reality. Assimilation is the process whereby the value becomes a part of the child's paradigm. This means that a young person must continually be making room for their parents' values (accommodation), eventually making them their own (assimilation).

Amy Zietlow (2013), a scholar with the Institute for American Values, interviewed Vern Bengtson, a longtime scholar at the University of Southern California, about this subject. Dr. Bengston began studying intergenerational transmission of values in 1970, and after more than forty years, he has concluded there are two factors critical to the transmission of values. The first critical factor is consistent modeling of values by parents.

> If the parents aren't consistent, the kids won't have religious role models to emulate. In other words, don't just send your children to church, bring them!
>
> The second thing we found was that the quality of the relationship between the child and the parent affects the success or lack of success in transmission. Warm, affirming parents, especially fathers, tend to be the most successful. (pp. 1–2)

Parents must remain totally committed to bringing up godly children by intentionally taking time to be with them, talking with them about the things of God, and living a good example of committed Christianity before them. If the father is a good worker, the son will often be a good worker. If the mother is a good housekeeper, the daughter will often be a good housekeeper. If the parents are honest, the children will tend to be honest, pay their bills, and not cheat. If children see their parents respect the Bible, they are likely to respect the Bible. One writer put it very simply, "Our children cannot see how we think, but they can see the results of our thoughts demonstrated in our actions" (Davis 2013, summer, p. 9). The parents who constantly are worried about measuring up to the world's standards of beauty, fashion, and success are teaching their children the world is the final arbiter of perfection. However, those who set a pattern of living a separated life of righteousness, peace, and joy in the Holy Spirit model the message that pleasing Jesus Christ is the primary focus of their lives.

If the father is a good worker, the son will often be a good worker. If the mother is a good housekeeper, the daughter will often be a good housekeeper. If the parents are honest, the children will tend to be honest, pay their bills, and not cheat. If children see their parents respect the Bible, they are likely to respect the Bible.

IN CLOSING

When God created man and told him to go forth and fill the earth, He planned that parents would instruct and teach their children, and that their children would take to heart that teaching, rather than every generation having to learn the hard way. Yes, the most certain way for children to become wise and avoid life's pitfalls is to heed their parents' instructions and teachings. Returning to where this lesson began, we have considered two processes that must work in concert to bring about the moral development of a child. The first is the importance of parental instruction and guidance. If that doesn't occur, children left to themselves to try to find their way in life. Without parental instruction and teaching, there would be no values to internalize and therefore no moral development. "A child left *to himself* bringeth his mother to shame" (Proverbs 29:15 KJV). Therefore, the benefits of parental instruction cannot be overemphasized. The second process is the responsibility of the child to internalize those values and live them out. As we have learned, that comes about by a process of accommodation and assimilation. Therefore, "Listen, my son, to your father's instruction and do not forsake your mother's teaching!" (Proverbs 1:8). Listen! And do not forsake! Take advantage of parental instruction.

LESSON 4

WARNING AGAINST ENTICEMENT

PROVERBS 1:10-19

10 My son, if sinful men entice you, do not give in to them. 11 If they say, "Come along with us; let's lie in wait for innocent blood, let's ambush some harmless soul; 12 let's swallow them alive, like the grave, and whole, like those who go down to the pit; 13 we will get all sorts of valuable things and fill our houses with plunder; 14 cast lots with us; and we will share in the loot"—15 my son, do not go along with them, do not set foot on their paths; 16 for their feet rush into evil, they are swift to shed blood. 17 How useless to spread a net where every bird can see it! 18 These men lie in wait for their own blood; they ambush only themselves! 19 Such is the end of all who go after ill-gotten gain; it takes away the life of those who get it.

These instructions, though written to "My Son," are applicable to all ages—man, woman, boy, or girl. It is more a parable than a proverb, and though it targets those who go after ill-gotten gain, the moral of the story applies to all temptations. The word translated *sinners* is one of the mildest Hebrew words for sin. It means *to miss the mark, to stumble or fall.* It refers to falling short morally and includes thoughts, words, and deeds. It refers to choice, not inherited sin.

THE LURE OF TEMPTATION

"Come along with us; let's lie in wait for innocent blood, let's ambush some harmless soul" (Proverbs 1:11). Sinners love company in their sin. The angels that fell immediately became tempters, and most often, they do not threaten or argue; they entice. So stay away from places you know will lead to temptation. The Spirit of God helps us overcome temptation, but you have to want to overcome temptation. Jesus is not going to do surgery on your human nature and take away your desire; He expects you to place it on the altar and crucify it. It would be foolish to purposefully walk into a place that holds a lot of temptation for you and expect God to bail you out. You have to choose to do what is right, and sometimes that choice includes avoiding certain places altogether. If the internet has become a temptation, unhook it or use a public internet service, such as the library. And if traveling away from your hometown results in spiritual failure, limit your trips and build safety nets in the city you are visiting ahead of time. Contract with your pastor that you will go to church while away and report back when you return. Call the pastor in the city where you are going and make a commitment to him to attend church services. If bingo is a temptation, don't drive by the bingo hall on bingo nights, wishing you were inside. If pull tabs or other forms of gambling are a weakness, avoid those settings.

> Jesus is not going to do surgery on your human nature and take away your desire; He expects you to place it on the altar and crucify it.

THE SUBTLETY OF SATAN

Knowing humankind's weaknesses, including pride, Satan entices humans by putting high price tags on things of little value and devaluing those things that really matter in life. A story is told of two thieves who broke into a clothing store.

After rifling the safe and looting the clothes racks of all articles they could either use or sell, they decided to have a bit of fun. After stripping the price tags from the remaining merchandise, they then "re-priced" everything in the store. Expensive suits became give-away bargains. Handkerchiefs and hatpins increased in value a thousandfold. For months after the burglars were gone confusion reigned. (Brown 1976, fall, p. 63)

That's exactly what Satan has done in our world. He entices the unsuspecting to believe that spiritual things are of little value, while expensive price tags are attached to things that will quickly pass away. Jude warned of the subtlety of sin:

For certain individuals whose condemnation was written about long ago have secretly slipped in among you. They are ungodly people, who pervert the grace of our God into a license for immorality and deny Jesus Christ our only Sovereign and Lord. (Jude 1:4)

> Satan entices humans by putting high price tags on things of little value and devaluing those things that really matter in life.

Further, he described their characteristics:

On the strength of their dreams these ungodly people pollute their own bodies, reject authority and heap abuse on celestial beings … These people are blemishes at your love feasts, eating with you without the slightest qualm—shepherds who feed only themselves. They are clouds without rain, blown along by the wind; autumn trees, without fruit and uprooted—twice dead. They are wild waves of the sea, foaming up their

shame; wandering stars, for whom blackest darkness
has been reserved forever ... These men are grumblers
and faultfinders; they follow their own evil desires;
they boast about themselves and flatter others for their
own advantage ... These are the people who divide
you, who follow mere natural instincts and do not have
the Spirit. (Jude 1:8, 12–13, 16, 19)

Be wary of an invitation to wrongdoing. Verses 11 and 12 describe
this enticement: "Come along with us; let's lie in wait for innocent
blood, let's ambush some harmless soul; let's swallow them alive, like
the grave, and whole, like those who go down to the pit" (Proverbs
1:11–12). Jesus bluntly described Satan's goals: "To steal, and to kill,
and to destroy" (John 10:10 KJV). And the apostle Paul cautioned his
readers to not give the devil a foothold (Ephesians 4:27), or he will
worm his way into your life.

> Be wary of an invitation to wrongdoing.

THE COMMONALITY OF TEMPTATION

Temptation is a reality in this life. If Jesus experienced temptations
throughout His lifetime, we can expect temptation whenever Satan
has the opportunity. Immediately following forty days of temptation
in the wilderness, an angel came and comforted Him. (See Matthew
4:11.) But note this, "When the devil had ended every temptation, he
departed from him until an opportune time" (Luke 4:13 ESV). From
this verse, it appears we can be assured the devil will be back.

Temptation is a common human experience. (See 1 Corinthians
10:13.) Because of the commonality of temptation, some teach that
grace, in contrast to the law, overlooks sin. Nothing could be further
from the truth. Paul confronted the Romans concerning this belief:
"Shall we continue in sin, that grace may abound? God forbid. How

shall we, that are dead to sin, live any longer therein?" (Romans 6:1–2 KJV). E. M. Bounds (1990) so eloquently made the same point:

> God's commandments, then, can be obeyed by all who seek supplies of grace which enable them to obey. These commandments must be obeyed. God's government is at stake. God's children are under obligation to obey him; disobedience cannot be permitted. The spirit of rebellion is the very essence of sin. It is repudiation of God's authority, which God cannot tolerate. (p. 54)

The key to overcoming temptation is simply learning to say, "No!" In fact, the apostle Paul emphasized that the grace of God teaches us to reject sin: "For the grace of God ... teaches us to say 'No' to ungodliness and worldly passions, and to live self–controlled, upright and godly lives in this present age" (Titus 2:11–12).

> The key to overcoming temptation is simply learning to say, "No!"

Joseph is one of the best biblical examples of resisting temptation. John Phillips (1995) described Joseph's situation:

> He was a lonely slave. His visions had not come true. His father was far away and doubtless thought him dead. The moral climate of Egypt was utterly worldly and carnal. Immorality was rampant. An offer of love and passion was his for the taking and the cost of refusal was high. (p. 35)

But what did Joseph say when he was tempted? "How then can I do this great wickedness, and sin against God?" (Genesis 39:9 KJV). He did not think twice; his mind was already made up; his response was quick. To contemplate the invitation to sin is a slippery slope. Matthew Henry (n.d.) warned, "The way of sin is down-hill; men not only cannot stop themselves, but, the longer they continue in it, the faster they run" (Vol. 3, p. 795). Solomon wisely stated, "Do not set foot on their paths" (Proverbs 1:15). Stay as far away as possible. Abstain from even the appearance of evil. (See 1 Thessalonians 5:22.) David wrote, "Blessed *is* the man that walketh not in the counsel of the ungodly, nor standeth in the way of sinners, nor sitteth in the seat of the scornful" (Psalm 1:1 KJV).

Yes, the slope of sin is slippery and always downward. Take note of James's warning: "Then when lust hath conceived, it bringeth forth sin: and sin, when it is finished, bringeth forth death" (James 1:15 KJV). Like courtship, the end result is more than a casual friendship. Courtship with sin, or sinners, will take you further and cost you more than you ever imagined.

> Courtship with sin, or sinners, will take you further and cost you more than you ever imagined.

TWO GATES AND TWO WAYS

Jesus taught that life offers two gates from which to choose, each at the beginning of a road. One leads to eternal life, the other to eternal damnation. He urged His followers:

> Enter through the narrow gate; for the gate is wide and the way is broad that leads to destruction, and there are many who enter through it. For the gate is small and the way is narrow that leads to life, and there are few who find it. (Matthew 7:13–14 NASB)

Enter through the narrow gate! John Phillips (1995) described these two gates and two ways:

Two "ways" run through history. The way of Cain runs via the judgment of the flood, past the tower of Babel and the confusion of tongues, by the way of the murder of Christ, to the lake of fire. It is the way of the world, the flesh, and the devil. It has its roll call of colorful characters, consummate villains, and giant intellects. Its sidewalks are lined with establishments offering power, pleasure, prosperity, promotion, and even piety. Its grand capital is Babylon; its most popular resort is Vanity Fair; its final destination is Hell.

The other way is the way of Abel, Seth, Melchizedek, Abraham, Moses, David, and Christ. It runs by Gethsemane, Gabbatha, and Golgotha to glory. Those fleeing the City of Destruction look for the Celestial City and go home by the way of the cross. This way has a roll call of giants. (See Hebrews 11.) Its steep slopes are not wanting in attractions: at the place of prayer, the table of the Lord, and the daily quiet time, the Lord of that way draws especially near to His own. Its grand capital is the new Jerusalem; its most popular resorts are the local church and the house of the "Interpreter"; its end is an eternity of bliss. (Vol. 1, p. 38)

The sinner misses out on the real pleasures of life that come by serving the LORD and living in His presence. David wrote, "In thy presence is fulness of joy; at thy right hand there are pleasures for evermore" (Psalm 16:11 KJV). And Jesus promised, "I am come that they might have life, and that they might have *it* more abundantly" (John 10:10 KJV).

> The sinner misses out on the real pleasures of life that come by serving the LORD and living in His presence.

AVOIDING HELL AT ALL COST

The Jehovah's Witnesses teach that hell is a place where the soul is annihilated. In truth, it would not be so bad if your soul suddenly came to an end and all remembrances were gone. But the Word of God contradicts annihilation theology:

- The citizens of that kingdom will be thrown outside into the darkness. People will cry and be in extreme pain there. (Matthew 8:12 GW)
- The Son of Man will send out his angels, and they will gather out of his kingdom all who cause sin and all who do evil. The angels will throw them into the blazing furnace, where the people will cry and grind their teeth with pain. (Matthew 13:41–42 NCV)
- But he shall say, I tell you, I know you not whence ye are; depart from me, all *ye* workers of iniquity. There shall be weeping and gnashing of teeth, when ye shall see Abraham, and Isaac, and Jacob, and all the prophets, in the kingdom of God, and you *yourselves* thrust out. (Luke 13:27–28 KJV)
- And in hell he lift[ed] up his eyes, being in torments, and seeth Abraham afar off, and Lazarus in his bosom. And he cried and said, Father Abraham, have mercy on me, and send Lazarus, that he may dip the tip of his finger in water, and cool my tongue; for I am tormented in this flame. (Luke 16:23–24 KJV)

Wide is the gate and broad is the way that leads to eternal destruction, and many will be snared by the world, the desires of the flesh, and the inborn human tendency to sin. Solomon declared that even the birds can see and avoid the snare of the net set in full view, but humans often plunge headlong toward eternal damnation. It is important to never forget that the slope on the road of sin is very slippery. And once you begin to slide, it's difficult to regain your footing before you crash at the bottom. The following story illustrates this slippery slope well. Unfortunately, it has been repeated over and over again.

As I watched you tonight, I wished for an opportunity to talk with you. I watched your beautiful face as you sang and worshipped. You reminded me of myself seven years ago. And then, after church, I watched you as you got into that car with a boy who does not know God. Oh, yes, he was at church tonight. He even went to the altar and shed a few tears. I am sure that you would not accept the idea that, for him, this is just a means to an end.

Seven years ago I was in your shoes. I had known God since my early teens, and had grown up under God-anointed preaching and teaching. I didn't lack boy friends or dates, as is so often the case with ... girls in churches where girls outnumber the boys. Some very wonderful, consecrated young men came my way. But Satan, who watches diligently and waits patiently to ensnare a soul, saw me one day as I was lukewarm. Oh, I was still going to church and playing my accordion and singing and doing all the right things outwardly. But I had never really had that special moment with God when His will and mine were made one.

I met him at work. And before long, without anyone else's knowing it, I felt I couldn't live without him. He ... went to church with me, he went to the altar and cried.

And so I married him, while my family and those who loved me wept and agonized.

It was six months later that I realized my soul was in danger and that I had to have a touch from God. I prayed through and got a grip on God. Then the battle began. No, he wasn't going to church anymore. I could count on my fingers the number of times he went during the last seven years. Before I married him, the thought of living without him was unbearable. 'How lonely it would be!' I thought. But now I know what loneliness really is, and I'd like to tell you about it.

Loneliness is receiving a blessing from God and going home to a man you can't share it with. He isn't interested; he's watching television.

Loneliness is going to a church social alone and watching the young couples enjoy God's blessings together. You can go alone or stay home alone; he has other interests.

Loneliness is feeling the urgency of Christ's coming and knowing that the one you love most on this earth is not ready, and shows no sign of caring.

Loneliness is seeing two children born and knowing that if your influence is to outweigh his, it will be a miracle.

Loneliness is going to a General Conference and seeing young couples everywhere who are truly one and dedicated to God's work. And there goes the young man who loved you once and wanted to marry you. He's preaching the gospel now, and he has never married. Oh God! Help me! I mustn't think of it!

Loneliness is lying awake struggling with the suspicion that he's unfaithful. Then comes the unbelievable pain of knowing for sure. He doesn't care if I know. She even calls me on the phone. After a time, he makes an effort to break it off. I vow to do everything humanly possible to keep this marriage together. I will love him more and pray for him more. Seven years of my life are involved in this! There's a little girl and a little boy!

Loneliness is now. My children and I will go home to a dark, empty apartment that will be my home until the lawyer says it's all over. I, who have always been afraid to stay alone, now welcome the peace and solitude.

As I look in the mirror; I see that seven years haven't changed my face so much. But inside I am old, and something that was once alive and beautiful is now dead.

Of course, this is not an unusual story. The remarkable thing about it is that I am still living for God. I am thankful for my family and their prayers of intercession for me.

Oh, I am praying for you ...! Please believe me when I tell you that no matter how wonderful he is, how loving, how tender—you cannot build a happy life upon disobedience to God's word. You see, no matter what the future holds for me, I have missed His perfect will for my life. I will never stop paying for breaking a commandment of God! Don't let it happen to you!

This is the story of my sister, and the tragic mistake she made. It ended ... in the divorce court this week. There is no way to put her suffering into words, but perhaps this will save some girl from making the same mistake. (Anonymous 1976, p. 17)

IN CLOSING

The principles of God's Word are true and eternal. They have been tried and tested for thousands of years, and they have proven to be beneficial for both individuals and society as a whole. The way of the righteous, with its consistency and discipline, contrasts greatly with the way of the sinner. "Blessed is the man who does not walk in the counsel of the wicked or stand in the way of sinners or sit in the seat of mockers" (Psalm 1:1 KJV).

Anyone who encourages another to disobey God—"Come along with us … join in with us"—is not a friend. The offer may sound exciting and even rewarding—"we will share the loot"—but it only leads to destruction. "My son, if sinners entice you, do not give in to them" (Proverbs 1:10). This passage is a clear warning against negative peer pressure. Those who would entice attempt to make it easy to sin and disobey God; this makes them enemies, not friends. They want you to join with them in their evil schemes, not in righteousness. A clear line must be drawn between the godly and the ungodly when it comes to associations and friendships. A break with worldly friends is necessary in order to avoid shipwreck. When you face Christ at the Judgment Seat, you will not be able to say that you didn't know it wasn't right to walk in the counsel of the wicked or stand in the way of sinners or sit in the seat of mockers. You will not be able to excuse your behavior by saying you didn't know that it would lead to spiritual and moral failure. If sinners entice you, "do not give in to them."

LESSON 5

WISDOM'S CRY

PROVERBS 1:20-33

²⁰ Out in the open wisdom calls aloud, she raises her voice in the public square; ²¹ on top of the wall she cries out, at the city gate she makes her speech: ²² "How long will you who are simple love your simple ways? How long will mockers delight in mockery and fools hate knowledge? ²³ Repent at my rebuke! Then I will pour out my thoughts to you, I will make known to you my teachings. ²⁴ But since you refuse to listen when I call and no one pays attention when I stretch out my hand, ²⁵ since you disregard all my advice and do not accept my rebuke, ²⁶ I in turn will laugh when disaster strikes you; I will mock when calamity overtakes you—²⁷ when calamity overtakes you like a storm, when disaster sweeps over you like a whirlwind, when distress and trouble overwhelm you.

²⁸ "Then they will call to me but I will not answer; they will look for me but will not find me, ²⁹ since they hated knowledge and did not choose to fear the LORD. ³⁰ Since they would not accept my advice and spurned my rebuke, ³¹ they will eat the fruit of their ways and be filled with the fruit of their schemes. ³² For the waywardness of the simple will kill them, and the complacency of fools will destroy them; ³³ but whoever listens to me will live in safety and be at ease, without fear of harm."

In this portion of scripture, Wisdom is personified as a woman who is not hard to find. Even in the streets where common people mingle with one another, her voice can be heard. She is available not only "beneath the high-vaulted ceilings of research libraries or in the conclave of scholars. She is available for all" (Segraves 1990, p. 31).

THE CRY OF GOD'S SPIRIT

Before Wisdom can impact the heart, the Spirit of God must prepare the heart. It is the Spirit that draws individuals to a place where they desire to make a change. Jesus let us know, "No man can come to me, except the Father which hath sent me draw him" (John 6:44 KJV). Though we are undeserving, He keeps drawing us along the path toward righteousness. Thank God He does not give up easily! Thank God He is "not willing that any should perish, but that all should come to repentance" (2 Peter 3:9 KJV). God is long-suffering! The cry of His heart is for every soul to listen to Wisdom. How many times did the Lord say, "He who has ears to hear, let him hear, and he who has eyes to see, let him see"? How many times did you feel convicted before you finally yielded to the Spirit? How many times did you hear the cry of His voice before you surrendered your heart to the Lord? The working of God's Spirit brings conviction that leads to repentance. And real repentance brings about real change. (See 2 Corinthians 7:10.) "Therefore if any man *be* in Christ, *he is* a new creature: old things are passed away; behold, all things are become new" (2 Corinthians 5:17 KJV).

A HAUNTING VOICE

Reject Wisdom, and all that remains is a haunting voice. "I also will laugh at your calamity; I will mock when your fear cometh; When your fear cometh as desolation, and your destruction cometh as a whirlwind; when distress and anguish cometh upon you" (Proverbs 1:26–27 KJV). It is not God who laughs and mocks but knowledge of what should have been done—"If only I had listened; if only I had walked in the ways of God." Wisdom declares up front:

Then shall they call upon me, but I will not answer; they shall seek me early, but they shall not find me: For that they hated knowledge, and did not choose the fear of the Lord: They would none of my counsel: they despised all my reproof. Therefore shall they eat of the fruit of their own way, and be filled with their own devices. (Proverbs 1:28–31 KJV)

Rejection of God's mercy and grace puts Him in a helpless position. He prefers to bless, but his ability to bless is based on the principle of submission to His will, submission to the cry of Wisdom. People who reject Wisdom often find that when they need Wisdom, it is too late.

> People who reject Wisdom often find that when they need Wisdom, it is too late.

THE RESULTS OF REJECTING WISDOM

With a voice of sorrow, Wisdom explained, "If you respond to my warning, then I will pour out my spirit on you and teach you my words" (Proverbs 1:23 CHSB). It is foolish to spurn reproof. Whether reproof comes from God or a person, the intent is the same—for learning and for growth. "The person who is never reproved, or who never accepts reproof, never grows. He can only deteriorate" (Segraves 1990, p. 32). It must be remembered that correction is not rejection. "For the commandment is a lamp and the teaching a light, and the reproofs of discipline are the way of life" (Proverbs 6:23).

Just as there are natural laws created by God, there are spiritual laws. One of these laws is the law of sowing and reaping. We are warned, "Be not deceived; God is not mocked: for whatsoever a man soweth, that shall he also reap" (Galatians 6:7 KJV). The rejection of wisdom is deadly. John Phillips (1995) illustrated this by drawing upon John Bunyan's *Pilgrim's Progress*:

There is a striking picture of Atheist volubly deriding Christian. Atheist is dressed like a dandy. His face is hard and a sneer twists his lips. One arm is outstretched in a scornful gesture and his other hand holds a walking stick on which he is about to lean. He is so concerned with making fun of Christian that he does not notice that the stick is poised over the edge of a precipice. Christian's horrified countenance conveys a warning but Atheist ignores it. (p. 45)

It's imperative that we heed the words of Wisdom, "For waywardness kills the simple, and the complacency of fools destroys them" (Proverbs 1:32).

Wisdom desires involvement in the life of every Christian. She is often no more than a prayer away. In fact, when the child of God gets too close to sin, Wisdom, along with her sister, Grace, waves her arms and tries to prevent a fall. She "calls aloud, she raises her voice in the public square; on top of the wall she cries out, at the city gate she makes her speech" (Proverbs 1:20–21). Wisdom's cry is this: "Accept my reproof and live."

> When the child of God gets too close to sin, Wisdom, along with her sister, Grace, waves her arms and tries to prevent a fall.

WISDOM'S REWARD

Though Solomon spent considerable time warning his son and us of the dire consequences of rejecting the voice of Wisdom, he concluded his teaching with the promise of Wisdom's reward: "Whoever listens to me will live in safety and be at ease, without fear of harm" (Proverbs 1:33). The Bible, as well as church history, is replete with examples of God working with and for those who heed the voice of Wisdom. For example, Noah lived in a wicked, sinful society, but he saved his family by heeding the words of Wisdom: "By faith Noah, being warned of God of things not seen as yet, moved with fear, prepared an ark to the saving of his house ... and became heir of the righteousness which is by faith" (Hebrews 11:7 KJV).

Another good illustration of the benefits of heeding the cry of Wisdom is seen in the life of Jonathan Edwards and his descendants.

> His father was a preacher and before him his mother's father. Trace the history of the offspring of this godly man. More than 400 of them have been traced, and they include 14 college presidents, and 100 professors, 100 of them have been ministers of the Gospel, missionaries, and theological teachers. More than 100 of them were lawyers and judges. Out of the whole number 60 have been doctors, and as many more, authors of high rank, or editors of journals. In fact, almost every conspicuous American industry has had as its promoters one or more of the offspring of the Edward's stock since the remote ancestor was married in the closing half of the seventeenth century. (Tan 1979, p. 962)

Compare the progeny of Jonathan Edwards with the Jukes family, which did not practice the principles of righteousness. The name *Jukes* is a pseudonym given by the author Robert L. Dugdale for a family that lived in rural New York whose family line reached back to early colonists (McCaghy 1985).

> A total of 1,200 descendants have been traced of this prolific family tree. Some 400 of these were physically self-wrecked, 310 professional paupers, 130 convicted criminals, 60 habitual thieves and pick-pockets, and 7 murderers; while out of the whole 1,200 only 20 ever learned a trade, and of these half of them owed it to prison discipline. (Tan 1979, p. 961)

IN CLOSING

The evidence is overwhelming. The outcome of the individual guided by Wisdom is so much better off than the one who attempts to go it alone. Listen to Wisdom's cry! Build your life on the solid rock of godly principles! The outcome is guaranteed by Jesus Himself:

> Therefore whosoever heareth these sayings of mine, and doeth them, I will liken him unto a wise man, which built his house upon a rock: And the rain descended, and the floods came, and the winds blew, and beat upon that house; and it fell not: for it was founded upon a rock. (Matthew 7:24–25 KJV)

LESSON 6

IF

PROVERBS 2:1-9

¹ My son, if you accept my words and store up my commands within you, ² turning your ear to wisdom and applying your heart to understanding—³ indeed, if you call out for insight and cry aloud for understanding, ⁴ and if you look for it as for silver and search for it as for hidden treasure, ⁵ then you will understand the fear of the LORD and find the knowledge of God. ⁶ For the LORD gives wisdom; from his mouth come knowledge and understanding. ⁷ He holds success in store for the upright, he is a shield to those whose walk is blameless, ⁸ for he guards the course of the just and protects the way of his faithful ones. ⁹ Then you will understand what is right and just and fair—every good path.

As chapter 2 of Proverbs opens, we hear Solomon speaking to his son concerning the importance of listening to and benefiting from instruction. In speaking to his son, Solomon used conditional if-then statements to instruct his son. He knew that if his son would listen to him, he could avoid many pitfalls and much suffering in this life, and the outcome would be much better. It's a fact, the wise listen and obey, but the foolish don't. As Solomon wrote, "Stop listening to instruction, my son, and you will stray from the words of knowledge" (Proverbs 19:27). In like manner, if we will listen to the instruction of our heavenly Father and accept the guidance of His wisdom, our journey through this life will be much more fulfilling and result in a much better outcome.

IF

If you accept my words. Wisdom is acquired by listening to someone older and wiser. If you believe you are already wise, you will see no need to humble yourself to learn from another. A teachable spirit is necessary for learning. One of the bits of wisdom I have clung to through my years of pastoral ministry, which I received from my pastor while I was still young, was his statement to me, "Always remain teachable!" Unfortunately, many ignore valuable teaching and resent correction. I am very aware of the discomfort one feels when receiving correction. Early in my walk with God, I arranged for someone to teach my Sunday school class without consulting my pastor. When he learned that I had asked someone without first clearing it with him, he confronted me. My initial internal reaction was to become defensive. However, the Spirit of God checked me and reminded me that someday I would be a pastor, and I would reap what I sowed. So how I reacted in that situation would likely come back to me at a later date. What is relevant is that I weighed the costs and accepted correction. In retrospect, I am grateful for what I learned by my pastor's corrective action.

Throughout the first seven chapters of the book of Proverbs, Solomon exhorted his son over and over again to humble himself and receive the instruction of his father. Every son today who is wise will heed the same exhortation. It is foolish for any generation not to build on the wisdom of the previous generations. All learning requires an openness to instruction, yet many find it difficult to accommodate corrective information and assimilate it into their paradigms. It is the folly of youth that leads to each generation committing the same mistakes, rather than building on the accumulated knowledge and wisdom of the past. Only a few are noble enough to listen and receive instruction.

> It is foolish for each generation not to build on the wisdom of the previous generations.

Cornelius was not only a devoted, praying, God-fearing Roman military leader, he was wise. When an angel instructed him to go to Joppa and find a man named Simon Peter who would tell him how to be saved, Cornelius immediately obeyed and sent for Peter. When Peter arrived, Cornelius and his household were ready to accept the Word of God brought by the man of God. His statement to Peter is an expression of the wisdom that made him a good leader: "Now we are all here in the presence of God to listen to everything the Lord has commanded you to tell us" (Acts 10:33). That's wisdom!

The apostle Paul found the members of the church in Thessalonica to be equally open to receive instruction. They "received *it* not *as* the word of men, but as it is in truth, the word of God" (1 Thessalonians 2:13 KJV). Those men and women believed they had heard from God, even though it was spoken by the voice of a preacher of the Gospel.

If you store up my commands within you. Solomon's father, King David, declared how he avoided sin: "Thy word have I hid in mine heart, that I might not sin against thee" (Psalm 119:11 KJV). Very likely, it was teaching such as that Solomon wanted to pass on to his son. There are many benefits to storing the commands of God in our hearts.

David began the second stanza of Psalm 119 with a question: "How can a young man keep his way pure?" (Psalm 119:9 ESV). Immediately, he gave the answer—"By living according to God's word." Jesus assured his disciples, "When you are brought before synagogues, rulers and authorities, do not worry about how you will defend yourselves or what you will say, for the Holy Spirit will teach you at that time what you should say" (Luke 12:11–12). I truly believe the Lord will only anoint what has already been stored up in the heart. Whether facing synagogue rulers, enemies of the Gospel, or the devil himself, the Word stored in our hearts will be anointed by the Holy Spirit to say exactly the right thing at the right moment. Then you can expect to experience the Lord's promise: "Open thy mouth wide, and I will fill it" (Psalm 81:10 KJV).

> Whether facing synagogue rulers, enemies of the Gospel, or the devil himself, the Word stored in our hearts will be anointed by the Holy Spirit to say exactly the right thing at the right moment.

If you call out for insight. The most important kind of seeing is the seeing of spiritual realities. Many people are blind to these. They see well enough with their physical eyes, but their inward eyes are blind, so their perception of this world is faulty. Even today, if you were to visit the city of Rome, it is evident that, as a culture, the Romans of the apostle Paul's day had a natural eye for beauty; however, their spiritual eyes failed them. They failed in the realm of spiritual insight. Paul was emphatic: if they were to be saved, they must do more than open their natural eyes; they must open their spiritual eyes, because God made it plain to them. (See Romans 1:19.) There was no problem with their natural eyes; the problem was with their spiritual eyes.

It is amazing that people can have such insight from what they see with their eyes when they look at a drop of blood under a microscope, a company balance sheet on the computer terminal, a cloud pattern in the sky, an animal's footprint in the dust, or a thousand such things. But it is sad that many of these same individuals often have no depth of spiritual insight. There's really no excuse for an absence of spiritual insight. "For the invisible things of him from the creation of the world are clearly seen, being understood by the things that are made, *even* his eternal power and Godhead; so that they are without excuse" (Romans 1:20 KJV).

If you cry aloud for understanding. If you pray for understanding, you will find answers to your most perplexing problems. When you ask for the right things, the Lord is more than willing to respond. And that's exactly what Solomon did when he became king. He recognized his youth and inexperience, so he turned to the Lord and asked for the right things:

> "Now, O Lord my God, you have made me king instead of my father, David, but I am like a little child who doesn't know his way around. And here I am in the midst of your own chosen people, a nation so great and numerous they cannot be counted! Give me an understanding heart so that I can govern your people well and know the difference between right and wrong. For who by himself is able to govern this great people of yours?"
>
> The Lord was pleased that Solomon had asked for wisdom. So God replied, "Because you have asked for wisdom in governing my people with justice and have not asked for a long life or wealth or the death of your enemies—I will give you what you asked for! I will give you a wise and understanding heart such as no one else has had or ever will have! And I will also give you what you did not ask for—riches and fame! No other king in all the world will be compared to you for the rest of your life! And if you follow me and obey my decrees and my commands as your father, David, did, I will give you a long life." (1 Kings 3:7–12 NLT)

When you ask for the right things, the Lord is more than willing to respond.

If you look for it as for silver and search for it as for hidden treasure. The mysterious Money Pit of Nova Scotia's Oak Island supposedly contains hidden treasure at the bottom of an ingenious man-made shaft. At the cost of at least six lives, millions of dollars, and countless disappointments over a period of more than two hundred years, men have sought to find the presumed treasure. It is with this kind of intensity that we ought to search for the knowledge and wisdom of God. We must hunger after godly knowledge, "as someone that is ready to perish for hunger begs hard for bread. Faint desires will not prevail; we must be importunate, as those that know the worth of knowledge and our own want of it" (Henry, n.d., Vol. 3, p. 799). Peter understood this, and he urged his readers, "Like newborn babies, you must crave pure spiritual milk so that you will grow into a full experience of salvation" (1 Peter 2:2 NLT).

The kingdom of God is life's greatest priority, and Jesus illustrated this by teaching parables of those selling all they had to buy a field or a valuable pearl (see Matthew 13:44–46). In both parables, the individual who found the treasure sold everything to obtain the treasure. If you are willing to give up everything in this world, then you too can have the treasure.

THEN

Then you will understand the fear of the LORD. Wisdom will not simply fall into your lap; it is a reward to those who ask and seek for it. God will not give wisdom to those who are only half-hearted or lazy, but He will reward zealous seekers. "Ye shall seek me, and find *me*, when ye shall search for me with all your heart" (Jeremiah 29:13 KJV). We have only begun to tap into an almost limitless supply of insight and instruction available to provide wisdom and guidance. Ordinary men amazed the Jewish leadership in Jerusalem with their command of scripture and wisdom. Leaders and priests "marvelled; and they took knowledge of [Peter and John], that they had been with Jesus" (Acts 4:13 KJV). These common men had been walking with and listening to the source of all knowledge and wisdom. "For the LORD gives wisdom, and from his mouth come knowledge and understanding" (Proverbs 2:6). And if you recognize that you lack wisdom in any area of life, or in any situation, you can turn at any moment to the Author of Wisdom and ask for assistance. James declared, "If any of you lacks wisdom, you should ask God, who gives generously to all without finding fault, and it will be given to you" (James 1:5).

God will not give wisdom to those who are only half-hearted or lazy, but He will reward zealous seekers.

Then you will find the knowledge of God. Just as Solomon wanted his son to understand the fear of the LORD and to find the knowledge of God, the LORD commanded parents to talk to their children about His covenant with them while sitting, walking, reclining, or rising, in the privacy of the home and in public:

> And these words, which I command thee this day, shall be in thine heart: And thou shalt teach them diligently unto thy children, and shalt talk of them when thou sittest in thine house, and when thou walkest by the way, and when thou liest down, and when thou risest up. (Deuteronomy 6:6–7 KJV)

In other words, whenever possible, make a connection between the world around them and the God who created it. The purpose of those talks was to impress these commandments into the hearts of their children. These were to be conversations, not a set of lectures.

> Children were to learn the commandments through hearing them recited at public feasts, new moons, and holy days. These blunt recitations were to be sharpened by discussing them with their parents. In other words, parents were to sharpen their children by repeated and continual interaction that, depending on the maturity of the child, would increasingly become a reciprocal discussion about living in covenant as opposed to a recitation of requirements and restrictions of the law. This continually brought the parent's attention back to the child and encouraged interaction that treated the child as valuable and worthy to be listened to as well as spoken to. Such interaction fills a child's heart

as well as his head. It produced a love for the Word of God rather than just a memory of the words. (Davis 2013, summer, pp. 8–9)

It is this relationship between a father and a son, parents and their children, and God and His people that brings about a transmission and assimilation of values from one generation to the next.

The story is told of a great painter who had three scholars studying under him at a particular time. They all seemed very eager to learn the secret of his power and to become great painters themselves. The first student spent all the time in the master's studio studying his paintings and copying them one after the other. He tried to imitate their beauty with his own brush and was the last to leave the studio at night and the first to arrive in the morning. He spent little time with the master painter nor attended any of his lectures. He wanted to be his own director, make his own discoveries and find himself a self-made man. He lived and died and never expressed on canvas the noble characteristics of the master.

The second scholar spent little time in the studio. He seldom used his brush. He attended every lecture and asked all kinds of questions about theory, coloring, light, etc. After all of his study he too died, without producing a single work that resembled the master's.

The third student was zealous in the practical work of the first student, and he sought to find out the theory as well as did the second, but he did one thing that neither of the first two thought of doing. He came to know and love the master. They were together often and spent much time in communion. They grew to talk alike, think alike, and some said, look alike. It was inevitable that before long they began to paint alike. The canvas of the third student began to produce the beauty and majesty that shone from the canvas of the great master. (Kloepper 1972, fall, p. 12)

Then you will understand what is just and fair. The Holy Spirit can and will provide wisdom and guidance when judgment is required and decisions have to be made. That is why the apostle Paul could instruct the Corinthian church to trust the judgment of peers within the church:

> Dare any of you, having a matter against another, go to law before the unjust, and not before the saints? Do ye not know that the saints shall judge the world? and if the world shall be judged by you, are ye unworthy to judge the smallest matters? Know ye not that we shall judge angels? how much more things that pertain to this life? If then ye have judgments of things pertaining to this life, set them to judge who are least esteemed in the church. (1 Corinthians 6:1–4 KJV)

Solomon assures his readers not only of wisdom and understanding if they take the words of God to heart, but He will also be a shield to them. The LORD "is a shield to those whose walk is blameless, for he guards the course of the just and protects the way of his faithful ones" (Proverbs 2:7–8).

IN CLOSING

If you seek the LORD, then you will find wisdom. For those living under the New Covenant, James promised that God will generously give wisdom to His people if they ask. (See James 1:5.) Wisdom should be desired ahead of wealth, fame, education, and power "because the only wisdom by which you can handle everyday things in conformity with their nature is the wisdom by which they were divinely made and ordered" (Kidner 1964, p. 32). Simply put, you have to know the LORD to possess true wisdom. Your search for wisdom in this life is really a search for God. And God is the source of all wisdom. When you really know the LORD, then you will possess wisdom.

LESSON 7

THE BETTER THINGS

PROVERBS 2:10-11

¹⁰ For wisdom will enter your heart, and knowledge will be pleasant to your soul. ¹¹ Discretion will protect you, and understanding will guard you.

Though missing from the paradigm of a godless generation, "The fear of the LORD is the beginning of wisdom, and knowledge of the Holy One is understanding" (Proverbs 9:10). Secular humans have attempted to find wisdom in the absence of God because God can't be quantified. How do you measure omnipotent, omniscient, and omnipresent? So, in this futile search, secular humans move through life "ever learning, and never able to come to the knowledge of the truth" (2 Timothy 3:7 KJV). What secular humans do not recognize is that "the gates of Knowledge and Wisdom are closed, and they are opened only to the knock of Reverence" (Horton 1903, p. 17). There are four words—wisdom, knowledge, discretion, and understanding—that are at the heart of the two verses above.

> Secular humans have attempted to find wisdom in the absence of God because God can't be quantified.

Wisdom. More significant than the wisdom required to send a man to the moon and back again, and more significant than the wisdom to catalogue all the genes in the human body is the wisdom that comes from fearing God and making Him the center of one's life. True wisdom will keep you from sin. "Wisdom is better than weapons of war" (Ecclesiastes 9:18 KJV). Matthew Henry (n.d.) noted that wisdom will save you from "men of corrupt principles, atheistical profane men, who make it their business to debauch young men's judgments, and instill into their minds prejudices against religion and arguments for vice" (Vol. 3, pp. 800–801). When wisdom entirely possesses you, it will keep you.

> More significant than the wisdom required to send a man to the moon and back again, and more significant than the wisdom to catalogue all the genes in the human body is the wisdom that comes from fearing God and making Him the center of one's life.

WHEN WISDOM POSSESSES YOU

There's a story about a proud young man who came to Socrates asking for knowledge. He walked up to the philosopher and said, "O great Socrates, I come to you for knowledge."

In response Socrates led the young man through the streets, to the sea, and chest deep into the water. Then he asked the young man, "Now tell me, what is it that you want?"

"Knowledge, O wise Socrates," said the young man with a smile.

Socrates put his hands on the man's shoulders and pushed him under the water. Thirty seconds later the wise philosopher lifted his pupil out of the water. "What is it again that you want?" he asked.

"Wisdom, O great and wise Socrates," the young man said under labored breathing.

Socrates again took the man and held him under water, this time longer. Thirty seconds passed, thirty-five, forty, forty-five. Finally, Socrates let him up. The man gasped for air as Socrates asked him, "What do you want, young man?"

He labored to answer. "Knowledge, O wise and wonderful …"

To this response, Socrates then plunged the man under water, this time holding him for close to a minute. As the young man came up panting for oxygen, Socrates asked him, "What do you want?"

"Air!" the young man screamed. "I need air!"

"When you desire wisdom as you have just desired air, then you will have it." (Leak, n.d.)

So when does the desire for wisdom become as strong as the desire for air? When it fills your heart as well as your head. When it sits on the throne of your heart and it has dominion over your thoughts. When it gives law to your affections and passions. When it permeates the heart as leaven permeates the dough. And when it changes you into its own image. So when does the desire for wisdom have possession of your entire being?

When thou beginnest to relish it as the most agreeable entertainment, and art subject to its rules, of choice, and with satisfaction,—when thou callest the practice of virtue, not a slavery and a task, but liberty and pleasure, and a life of serious godliness the most comfortable life a man can live in this world,—then thou wilt find the benefit of it. (Henry, n.d., Vol. 3, p. 800)

TRUE KNOWLEDGE WILL SAVE YOU

Knowledge. Knowledge is gained through instruction, experience, and/or association. Ignorance concerning God is not bliss, but the truth of God's Word will save you. The LORD declared through the prophet, "My people are destroyed for lack of knowledge: because thou hast rejected knowledge, I will also reject thee" (Hosea 4:6 KJV). In fact, without the knowledge that comes from the Word of God, you cannot be born again. Peter stated that we are "born again ... by the word of God, which liveth and abideth for ever" (1 Peter 1:23 KJV). It is knowledge from God's Word that teaches us how to be born again. Not only were you saved through the Word of God by being born again, you remain in a state of salvation by the Word of God. Only through the Word of God will you know "how ye ought to walk and to please God" (1 Thessalonians 4:1 KJV).

"Knowledge will be pleasant to your soul" (Proverbs 2:10). The truths of God are pleasant to your soul because they set you free. That is a promise from Jesus Himself: "Ye shall know the truth, and the truth shall make you free" (John 8:32 KJV). The more time you spend with Jesus, the greater your knowledge of Him and His will, and the greater the freedom that will be attained.

Only "the fool hath said in his heart, *There is* no God" (Psalm 14:1 KJV). Atheism is not knowledge; it is foolishness. True knowledge emanates from God. That is exactly what Solomon asked for and received. Are you seeking an understanding of the world around you through the paradigm of God as the sole creator and sustainer, or are you looking for a way around God? "What shall it profit a man, if he shall gain the whole world, and lose his own soul?" (Mark 8:36 KJV).

> Atheism is not knowledge; it is foolishness.

DISCRETION WILL PROTECT YOU

Discretion. "Discretion will protect you" (Proverbs 2:11). Discretion is counting the cost before you commit to a project. It is looking before you leap. Discretion is the ability to make responsible decisions, guided by godly principles. David's prayer for Solomon was, "May the LORD grant you discretion and understanding, that when he gives you charge over Israel you may keep the law of the LORD your God" (1 Chronicles 22:12 ESV).

Those who do not live by well-established biblical principles are not likely to make good decisions. As long as Solomon kept the law of the LORD and made decisions in accordance with the Word of the LORD, he did well. But his decision-making ability waned when the Word of God was no longer his guide. Foolishly, he acquired "seven hundred wives of royal birth and three hundred concubines, and his wives led him astray. As Solomon grew old, his wives turned his heart after other gods" (1 Kings 11:3–4).

Discretion will protect you, and it would have protected Solomon had he exercised it. It's important to remember that God has not promised to keep you from the evil man, but discretion will keep you from the evil man's ways.

> For the grace of God has appeared that offers salvation to all people. It teaches us to say "No" to ungodliness and worldly passions, and to live self-controlled, upright and godly lives in this present age, while we wait for the blessed hope—the appearing of the glory of our great God and Savior, Jesus Christ. (Titus 2:11–13)

God has not promised to keep you from the evil man, but discretion will keep you from the evil man's ways.

UNDERSTANDING WILL GUARD YOU

Understanding. "Understanding will guard you" (Proverbs 2:11). Putting faith in God as the Creator of all things and fearing God for who He is leads to an understanding of the Spirit realm. "The fear of the Lord, that *is* wisdom; and to depart from evil *is* understanding" (Job 28:28 KJV). All we have to do for understanding to flood our hearts is to look around at what has been created and acknowledge Him who made all things.

Our Lord never expected humans to believe in something that is incomprehensible. "For the invisible things of him from the creation of the world are clearly seen, being understood by the things that are made, *even* his eternal power and Godhead; so that they are without excuse" (Romans 1:20 KJV). If that is true, how much more will we be without excuse if we have the Word of God at our fingertips and don't build our lives upon its principles? Remember the solemn words of our Lord, "Not everyone who says to me, 'Lord, Lord,' will enter the kingdom of heaven, but only the one who does the will of my Father who is in heaven" (Matthew 7:21).

The ability to reason and understand is something God afforded humans. The LORD, when He broke the silence and spoke to Job, described the ostrich as lacking in understanding: "She deals cruelly with her young, as if they were not hers; though her labor be in vain, yet she has no fear, because God has made her forget wisdom and given her no share in understanding" (Job 39:16–17 ESV). Animals are driven by instinct rather than understanding. David issued a warning to not to be like "the horse, *or* as the mule, *which* have no understanding: whose mouth must be held in with bit and bridle" (Psalm 32:9 KJV). God provided humankind with the ability to understand, and He gave humans free will. It is here that we run into trouble. The fallen human nature tends toward the pleasure of sin and self-satisfaction, rather than submission to God. But if we will seek true wisdom, knowledge, and discretion, which come from God, understanding will follow. There are commands and dictates in the Word of God that may make little sense to the carnal nature, but recognizing that God knows best and submitting to those commands will result in heartfelt understanding. Just as believing is seeing, obedience to God's Word brings understanding.

> Just as believing is seeing, obedience to God's Word brings understanding.

IN CLOSING

If you will crave wisdom as your body craves air, you will find it, and it will keep you from sin. And the more time you spend with Jesus, the greater your knowledge of Him and His plan for your life will be. Discretion and understanding will guard and protect you. The Lord wants nothing more than for you to have a blessed life. Jesus declared, "I am come that they might have life, and that they might have *it* more abundantly" (John 10:10 KJV).

WISDOM'S PROTECTION

PROVERBS 2:12-15

¹² Wisdom will save you from the ways of wicked men, from men whose words are perverse, ¹³ who have left the straight paths to walk in dark ways, ¹⁴ who delight in doing wrong and rejoice in the perverseness of evil, ¹⁵ whose paths are crooked and who are devious in their ways.

The ability to negotiate one's way through the world without being tainted by the world requires the work of the Spirit. Unless the Lord returns the moment you are born again, it will take more than the new birth to keep you saved; it will take godly wisdom, and it will require building your life on godly principles.

DEFINING WISDOM

The *Random House Dictionary* (1968) defines *wisdom* as "the quality or state of being wise; knowledge of what is true or right coupled with good judgment" (p. 1511). Further, it defines wisdom as "scholarly knowledge or learning, wise sayings and teachings." *Webster's Seventh New Collegiate Dictionary* (1970) defines wisdom as "accumulated philosophic or scientific learning: Knowledge, ability to discern inner qualities and relationships: Insight, Good sense: Judgment, a wise attitude or course of action, or the teachings of ancient wise men" (p. 1025).

Probably *Random House*'s definition, "knowledge of what is true or right coupled with good judgment" is a good place to begin in understanding the meaning of wisdom as used in the book of Proverbs. One weakness of any of these definitions is that they say very little about action. From a biblical perspective, wisdom is associated with action (i.e., the ability to apply knowledge or make good decisions). The intent is for those wise sayings to govern a person's life. Therefore, it is the responsibility of every child of God to meditate frequently on the words of wisdom put forth in the book of Proverbs. The wisdom derived from these proverbs is not simply theoretical knowledge. It is practical, and it will guide the reader in discerning between good and evil and right and wrong. These wise sayings are a divinely created system of rules that are meant to govern the moral fiber of the life of a child of God. So the best place to discover wisdom is the Bible—God's Word. "The fear of the LORD *is* the beginning of wisdom: a good understanding have all they that do *his commandments*" (Psalm 111:10 KJV). The outcome of "wisdom living" is found in the last sentence of that verse, and it speaks of action: "A good understanding have all they that do his commandments."

> It is the responsibility of every child of God to meditate frequently on the words of wisdom put forth in the book of Proverbs.

PROTECTION FROM THE WICKED

The exercise of wisdom provides protection from the ways of wicked people. The wicked as described in Proverbs, chapter 2, are characterized by using "perverse words." *Random House Dictionary* defines *perverse* as "willfully determined not to do what is expected or desired; contrary;" or "persistent or obstinate in what is wrong;" or "turned away from what is right, good, or proper; wicked" (*Random House Dictionary* 1968, p. 992). Satan is the master of perverse words, and we don't have to read far into the Bible before we see perverseness played out:

Now the serpent was more subtil than any beast of the field which the LORD God had made. And he said unto the woman, Yea, hath God said, Ye shall not eat of every tree of the garden? And the woman said unto the serpent, We may eat of the fruit of the trees of the garden: But of the fruit of the tree which is in the midst of the garden, God hath said, Ye shall not eat of it, neither shall ye touch it, lest ye die. And the serpent said unto the woman, Ye shall not surely die. (Genesis 3:1–4 KJV)

There is no doubt that the ministry of Satan challenges the ministry of godliness. All you have to do is look at the values promoted and supported by television, the movie industry, and the internet to understand that Satan is in the business of dispensing perversity. Satan has never lost his desire to control the hearts of men. Consider how he tempted our Lord:

The devil taketh him up into an exceeding high mountain, and sheweth him all the kingdoms of the world, and the glory of them; And saith unto him, All these things will I give thee, if thou wilt fall down and worship me. (Matthew 4:8–9 KJV)

Jesus's response—"Get out of here, Satan" (Matthew 4:10 NLT)—should be our response. If Satan would tempt the Lord, you can rest assured he will tempt you.

> If Satan would tempt the Lord, you can rest assured he will tempt you.

It is unfortunate that any Christian would even consider following Satan's lead to "leave the straight paths to walk in dark ways," but it is a reality. It is very important that, as children of God, we recognize that we have the potential to turn our backs on the light and walk away from salvation. If we allow ourselves to go places or engage in activities that expose us to danger, we are tempting God and giving Satan an opportunity to cause spiritual shipwreck. These unwholesome activities can weaken our resistance and may cause us to fall. Hear the following two verses: "The Spirit speaketh expressly, that in the latter times some shall depart from the faith, giving heed to seducing spirits, and doctrines of devils" (1 Timothy 4:1 KJV). And "Watch your life and doctrine closely. Persevere in them, because if you do, you will save both yourself and your hearers" (1 Timothy 4:16). Paul was instructing Timothy to be cognizant of the false doctrines he might encounter that could deceive him and cause him to be lost. Two words in these passages are especially important: *abandon* and *persevere*. Clearly, we cannot abandon something we never had, nor can we persevere in something we have not begun. Therefore, Paul was writing to Timothy about those already saved who had the potential to wander away from truth.

DRIFTING FROM WISDOM

In the book of Revelation, Jesus was speaking to those who at one time had put the Lord first in their lives. However, over time, they had allowed themselves to lose their love for God. Jesus sent them a love letter that included the following words: "You have forsaken the love you had at first. Consider how far you have fallen! Repent and do the things you did at first" (Revelation 2:4–5).

Not only do we need to be careful that we are not deceived by others, we must be careful that spiritual self-confidence does not deceive us. "Wherefore let him that thinketh he standeth take heed lest he fall!" (1 Corinthians 10:12 KJV). In addition to the danger of feeling too confident in Christ, we must not get distracted by the things of this world, thinking we can handle things we can't. Unfortunately, there will be believers who will be seduced to turn away from Christ and return to sin. Peter grieved over those who had turned away, and he described their behaviors:

With eyes full of adultery, they never stop sinning; they seduce the unstable; they are experts in greed— an accursed brood! They have left the straight way and wandered off to follow the way of Balaam son of Bezer, who loved the wages of wickedness. (2 Peter 2:14–15)

> Not only do we need to be careful that we are not deceived by others, we must be careful that spiritual self-confidence does not deceive us.

If you do not make choices based upon godly principles, it is likely you will flow with the desires of the flesh or the thinking of the group—"men whose words are perverse." We do not live in a protective bubble. There are relentless forces—both internal and external—that will come against the child of God. James taught that humans are persuaded to sin by internal desires. "But every man is tempted, when he is drawn away of his own lust, and enticed" (James 1:14 KJV). And the Old Testament is replete with examples of those who were drawn into sin by their own desires—the way of Cain, Balaam's error, and Korah's rebellion. (See Jude 1:11.) Cain *desired* to be accepted by God but without complying with God's commands. Balaam's *desire* drove him to ask the LORD to change His mind, even after the LORD clearly told him His will. And Korah *desired* a leadership role and was willing to rebel against God's established leadership to get it.

Though Korah desired or coveted (inner force) something that was not his, the group (external force) also supported him in his rebellion:

Now Korah the son of Izhar, son of Kohath, son of Levi, and Dathan and Abiram the sons of Eliab, and On the son of Peleth, sons of Reuben, took men. And they rose up before Moses, with a number of the people of Israel, 250 chiefs of the congregation, chosen from the assembly, well-known men. They assembled themselves together against Moses and against Aaron and said to them, 'You have gone too far! For all in the congregation are holy, every one of them, and the LORD is among them. Why then do you exalt yourselves above the assembly of the LORD? (Numbers 16:1–3 ESV)

Unfortunately, there are many "who delight in doing wrong and rejoice in the perverseness of evil" (Proverbs 2:14), and the group provides support for their behavior. While Moses was on the mountain communing with the LORD, the Israelites persuaded Aaron to make them a golden calf to worship. When Moses confronted Aaron, he blamed the group (diffusion of responsibility):

You yourself know how evil these people are. They said to me, "Make us gods who will lead us. We don't know what happened to this fellow Moses, who brought us here from the land of Egypt." So I told them, "Whoever has gold jewelry, take it off." When they brought it to me, I simply threw it into the fire— and out came this calf! (Exodus 32:22–24 NLT)

Though Aaron excused his behavior by blaming the group, it didn't take much for him to be persuaded by the group.

> Though Aaron excused his behavior by blaming the group, it didn't take much for him to be persuaded by the group.

IN CLOSING

If the wisdom that comes from the Word of God is allowed to rule and reign in an individual's life, it will save that person from untold pain and suffering, and it will protect them from evil people. David declared, "I will never forget your precepts, for by them you have preserved my life" (Psalm 119:93).

The Bible does not consist of merely human words. These words come from the mouth of God: "No prophecy of the scripture is of any private interpretation. For the prophecy came not in old time by the will of man: but holy men of God spake *as they were* moved by the Holy Ghost" (2 Peter 1:20–21 KJV). God is a God of order, and following the inspired Words of God is guaranteed to protect the hearer from a chaotic end.

Can you imagine the world today completely devoid of the Word of God? Most people have at one time or another stood gazing at the heavens in absolute amazement, wondering how all the stars and planets could stay in place without colliding. The answer is found in the Word of God. "By God's word, the present heaven and earth are ... being kept until the day ungodly people will be judged and destroyed" (2 Peter 3:7 GW). They are kept in place by God's Word. And just as the Word of God maintains order in the heavens, so it does on the earth.

> Just as the Word of God maintains order in the heavens, so it does on the earth.

On the other hand, the scriptures are clear; wicked people abound. Their words are perverse, their paths are dark, they delight in doing wrong, and they rejoice in the perverseness of evil. Their paths are crooked, and their ways are devious. However, we have assurance; wisdom will protect the saint of God from being persuaded to do evil that comes from internal and external forces. Following God's precepts will not only keep people from falling into Satan's trap, but those already in Satan's snare will be set free when they climb back on the straight and narrow way that leads to the Celestial City. The Word of God must be our guiding principle. Jesus warned us that the tempter is often subtle: "Beware of false prophets, which come to you in sheep's clothing, but inwardly they are ravening wolves" (Matthew 7:15 KJV). Further, He warned of the subtle influence of the expert, the doubting theologian, or the philosopher. "Be careful! Watch out for the yeast of the Pharisees and Sadducees!" (Matthew 16:6 GW).

A little yeast (untruth or unrighteousness) will permeate the whole lump of dough; a little false teaching will tarnish the pure doctrine of God. "See to it that no one takes you captive through philosophy and empty deception, according to the tradition of men, according to the elementary principles of the world, rather than according to Christ" (Colossians 2:8 NASB). Through it all, the guiding principle must be the same; "Fear God, and keep his commandments: for this *is* the whole *duty* of man" (Ecclesiastes 12:13 KJV).

LESSON 9

WISDOM AND THE SPOUSE OF YOUR YOUTH

PROVERBS 2:16-19

16 Wisdom will save you also from the adulteress woman, from the wayward woman with her seductive words, 17 who has left the partner of her youth and ignored the covenant she made before God. 18 Surely her house leads down to death and her paths to the spirits of the dead. 19 None who go to her return or attain the paths of life.

The scriptures are replete with examples of the destructiveness of infidelity. "Wisdom hidden in the heart is ... the most effectual deliverance; restraining even the eye from the hurtful object" (Bridges 1846/1968, p. 19). In medicine, an object that is not meant to be in the human body is referred to as a foreign body. Two Hebrew words were used to translate *adulteress*. The literal meanings of the words are "foreigner" and "female." The two words *wayward woman* come from a single Hebrew word meaning "strange, stranger, or foreigner." Probably the reason the translators rendered that word *wayward woman* is because of the context of the remainder of the sentence, "who has left the partner of her youth and ignored the covenant she made before God" (Proverbs 2:17).

THE PENALTY OF PROMISCUITY

Promiscuity is not something that arrived with the flower children and free love of the 1960s. It's been around nearly as long as humanity. In Noah's day, men's thoughts were evil continually, and it resulted in the judgment of God. Ignoring God's Word concerning morality leads to death: "Surely her house leads down to death and her paths to the spirits of the dead. None who go to her return or attain the paths of life" (Proverbs 2:18–19).

Those who defend promiscuity would like you to believe that any restraint upon sexual activity is to limit living. Sexual promiscuity does not prolong life or promote living; it is degrading, and it leads to death. Paul made that point clear when writing the church in Rome:

> People knew God perfectly well, but when they didn't treat him like God, refusing to worship him, they trivialized themselves into silliness and confusion so that there was neither sense nor direction left in their lives. They pretended to know it all, but were illiterate regarding life. They traded the glory of God who holds the whole world in his hands for cheap figurines you can buy at any roadside stand.
>
> So God said, in effect, "If that's what you want, that's what you get." It wasn't long before they were living in a pigpen, smeared with filth, filthy inside and out. And all this because they traded the true God for a fake god, and worshiped the god they made instead of the God who made them—the God we bless, the God who blesses us. Oh, yes!
>
> Worse followed. Refusing to know God, they soon didn't know how to be human either—women didn't know how to be women, men didn't know how to be men. Sexually confused, they abused and defiled one another, women with women, men with men—all lust, no love. And then they paid for it, oh, how they

paid for it—emptied of God and love, godless and loveless wretches. (Romans 1:21–27 MSG)

The theme of Proverbs 2:16–19 is "follow God's Word and live." "Wisdom will save you from the adulteress" (Proverbs 2:16). There is no better life than a life lived in Jesus Christ. Jesus stated simply, "I am come that they might have life, and that they might have *it* more abundantly" (John 10:10 KJV). You will never be cheated out of the fullness of life as long as you live by God's Word.

> You will never be cheated out of the fullness of life as long as you live by God's Word.

THE SACREDNESS OF THE MARRIAGE COVENANT

Before going further, I would like to focus on the spouse of your youth and the sacredness of the covenant made before God in marriage. Marriage is not an institution concocted by humans but a plan established by God. Jesus referenced the sacredness of this institution:

> From the beginning of the creation God made them male and female. For this cause shall a man leave his father and mother, and cleave to his wife; And they twain shall be one flesh: so then they are no more twain, but one flesh. What therefore God hath joined together, let not man put asunder. (Mark 10:6–9 KJV)

When someone creates a machine or product, they usually provide a book of instructions. Failing to follow the instructions may result in damage to the machine or risk to the user of the product. God gave us explicit instructions in His Word concerning the marriage relationship. The scriptures depict God's intent for oneness in the relationship between the couple, commitment to each other for life, and the awfulness of an affair. Though these are very serious topics, there are several nursery rhymes that can help illustrate some of these truths.

APPRECIATING DIFFERENCES

Jack Sprat could eat no fat, his wife could eat no lean; but betwixt the two of them, they licked the platter clean.

One of the first things we learn from the Bible is that God recognized man was not complete by himself. "Then the Lord God said, 'It is not good for the man to be alone. I will make a helper who is just right for him'" (Genesis 2:18 NLT). In marriage, each is to be a complement to the other. Jack and his wife were complete with each other. The weakness in each was made up by the strength in the other. Consider the following:

> If you plan to marry it is certain that you have a preconceived fantasy of your ideal mate or the perfect marriage. After a while you will begin to realize that your fantasy and the person you have married will begin to diverge sharply. At that point you may embark upon a reform program ... You misconstrued the words of the wedding ceremony "and the two shall become one" to mean that your mate should become like you and your fantasy. You would become one in likes, preferences, interests, hobbies, ideas, even reactions and feeling: YOURS! The oneness in marriage is not similarity or sameness in matters relating to ideas or feelings but to the oneness of understanding. Any attempt to mold our mates in an effort to match them to our fantasies is arrogance on our part and an insult to them. While it is true that we can never mold or remake another person, we can "allow" him to change. (Tanner 1973, pp. 92–93)

The Amplified Bible beautifully illustrates this: "[Living as becomes you] with complete lowliness of mind (humility) and meekness (unselfishness, gentleness, mildness), with patience, bearing with one another and making allowances because you love one another" (Ephesians 4:2 AMPC).

Even if your spouse is an unbeliever, it is not your job to mold the other person to your fantasy. However, you may aid in the change by being a living example. This is what Paul meant when he wrote the Corinthians:

> If a believing woman has a husband who is not a believer and he is willing to continue living with her, she must not leave him. For the believing wife brings holiness to her marriage, and the believing husband brings holiness to his marriage. (1 Corinthians 7:13–14 NLT)

Even if your spouse is an unbeliever, it is not your job to mold the other person to your fantasy.

Differences provide an opportunity for growth, and marriage is an opportunity to grow together.

> Every person who marries has characteristics similar to the one he marries. But he also has many that are different. Different ways of perceiving, thinking, feeling, and behaving are part of marital adjustment. Differentness is important because it holds out the promise of need fulfillment for each person. It is important to remember that one of the main motivating factors toward marriage is the person's need to feel complete because of what the other person has to offer. Consciously or unconsciously people choose others who can help them feel complete. On

the other hand this innate differentness contains the seeds for hurt and disruption. Why? The answer is quite simple. We are threatened by the differences in our spouse. We are afraid that we might have to adjust our way or thinking and doing things. We also believe that "If it's different, it's wrong!" Many problems occur because of the lack of tolerance for differences of attitude or opinions in the marital relationship. Problems occur because we do not allow the other person to be different. (Roberts & Wright 1978, p. 10)

Not appreciating different character traits is nothing short of selfishness. It is disregarding the fact that God created an array of different personality characteristics, and they are not bad just because they are different. Not allowing for these differences can open the door for discontent that results in looking beyond the marital relationship for sexual and relational fulfillment. On the other hand, allowing for differences in your relationship strengthens your marital bond. Sydney Smith so beautifully describes the strength of these differences: "Marriage resembles a pair of shears, so joined that they cannot be separated; often moving in opposite directions, yet always punishing anyone who comes between them" (cited in *The Living Marriage* by H. Norman Wright, 1975, p. 17).

> Differences provide an opportunity for growth, and marriage is an opportunity to grow together.

RECOGNIZING THE SANCTITY OF THE MARRIAGE COVENANT

Many do not appreciate the fact that marriage is a covenant between two people made before God. As a result, the divorce rate is high. The absence of the fear of God and self-centeredness results in abandonment of the sacred covenant whenever some act, or lack thereof, does not please one or the other. There is little longsuffering and patience in our contemporary culture. Nevertheless, it is God's intent for marriage to be for life. Though He provided the possibility for divorce in the event of infidelity by one party or the other, we see the Lord's feelings about the breaking of the covenant in the book of Malachi:

> You cover the LORD's altar with tears, weeping and groaning because he pays no attention to your offerings and doesn't accept them with pleasure. You cry out, "Why doesn't the LORD accept my worship?" I'll tell you why! Because the LORD witnessed the vows you and your wife made when you were young. But you have been unfaithful to her, though she remained your faithful partner, the wife of your marriage vows.
>
> Didn't the LORD make you one with your wife? In body and spirit you are his. And what does he want? Godly children from your union. So guard your heart; remain loyal to the wife of your youth. "For I hate divorce!" says the LORD, the God of Israel. "To divorce your wife is to overwhelm her with cruelty," says the LORD of Heaven's Armies. "So guard your heart; do not be unfaithful to your wife." (Malachi 2:13–16 NLT)

It is the LORD's intent for marriage to be "until death us do part." If only couples would fully comprehend the vows they make when they enter into that sacred commitment. They are committing to God, to each other, and to those present that they will remain faithful to each other "for richer or for poorer, for better or for worse, in sickness and in health." Once that covenant is made, a couple is to be in it together forever. Consider our childhood friends—Jack and Jill.

> Jack and Jill went up the hill to fetch a pail of water.
> Jack fell down and broke his crown, and Jill came tumbling after.

For better or for worse, they were in it together. Jack tripped and tumbled down that hill, but when he dusted himself off, there was Jill right beside him. "For better or for worse, in sickness and in health." There is nothing in the traditional marriage vow that suggests limitations on commitment, such as, "if he provides all I need to spend," or "as long as she can perform sexually at the level of my perceived need," or "until I lose interest in him."

- Marriage is a covenant of responsible love, a fellowship of repentance and forgiveness. (Wayne Oats in *The Living Marriage* by H. Norman Wright, 1975, p. 17)
- Marriage is a total commitment of the total person for the total life. (Robert Sharper in *The Living Marriage* by H. Norman Wright, 1975, p. 17)

> There is nothing in the traditional marriage vow that suggests limitations on commitment, such as, "if he provides all I need to spend," or "as long as she can perform sexually at the level of my perceived need," or "until I lose interest in him."

THE SHALLOWNESS OF AN AFFAIR

Contrast God's idea of commitment with the shallowness of an affair. The writer of the book of Proverbs cautioned:

> Drink water from your own cistern, running water from your own well. Should your springs overflow in the streets, your streams of water in the public squares? Let them be yours alone, never to be shared with strangers. May your fountain be blessed, and may you rejoice in the wife of your youth. A loving doe, a graceful deer— may her breasts satisfy you always, may you ever be intoxicated with her love. (Proverbs 5:15–19)

It's so sad to see the end result of an affair and adultery. This is portrayed so well in another nursery rhyme.

> Humpty Dumpty sat on a wall; Humpty Dumpty had a great fall. All the king's horses and all the king's men couldn't put Humpty together again.

"All the king's horses and all the king's men couldn't put Humpty together again." Some claim their relationships are stronger after an affair than they were before. But not as strong as it could have been had the covenant with the spouse of one's youth not been broken! You may find forgiveness from God and from your spouse, but Humpty Dumpty will never look the same again. That's why Paul declared, "Flee from sexual immorality. Every other sin a person commits is outside the body, but the sexually immoral person sins against his own body" (1 Corinthians 6:18 ESV).

> Some claim their relationships are stronger after an affair than they were before. But not as strong as they could have been had the covenant with the spouse of one's youth not been broken!

IN CLOSING

The following excerpt delivered by James Dobson Sr. to his bride to be demonstrates what God had in mind when He created the marriage covenant:

> I want you to understand and be fully aware of my feelings concerning the marriage covenant which we are about to enter. I have been taught at my mother's knee, and in harmony with the Word of God, that the marriage vows are inviolable, and by entering into them, I am binding myself absolutely and for

life. The idea of estrangement from you through divorce for any reason at all (although God allows one—infidelity) will never at any time be permitted to enter into my thinking. I'm not naive in this. On the contrary, I'm full aware of the possibility, unlikely as it now appears, that mutual incompatibility or other unforeseen circumstances, could result in extreme mental suffering. If such becomes the case, I am resolved for my part to accept it as a consequence of the commitment I am now making, and to bear it, if necessary, to the end of our lives together.

I have loved you dearly as a sweetheart and will continue to love you as my wife. But over and above that, I love you with a Christian love that demands that I never react in any way toward you that would jeopardize our prospects of entering heaven, which is the supreme objective of both our lives. And I pray that God Himself will make our affection for one another perfect and eternal. (cited in Dobson 1980, pp. 14–15)

I personally saw that kind of commitment lived out by a physician who came to Juneau, Alaska, in 1940—the late Dr. Joseph Rude. When I knew him, he was in his late eighties but still practicing medicine and still skiing at Eaglecrest. It is my recollection that his wife was afflicted with dementia and had resided in St. Ann's Nursing Home for some time. I observed Dr. Rude on many occasions sitting beside his wife, he in a chair and she in a wheelchair. He would put his arms around her, hold her, and talk to her, though she could not respond to his words of affection, and he would even feed her, because she no longer could feed herself. One night, around nine o'clock, as I was leaving St. Ann's, Dr. Rude came bounding through the doors with a piece of cake on a paper plate. He smiled at me, and with feeling in his voice, he stated, "I was at a birthday party and thought my wife would like a piece of cake." "For better or for worse, for richer or for poorer, in sickness and in health," committed to the spouse of his youth.

LESSON 10

LESSONS FROM A FALLEN KING

PROVERBS 2:20–22

20 Thus you will walk in the ways of the good and keep to the paths of the righteous. 21 For the upright will live in the land, and the blameless will remain in it; 22 but the wicked will be cut off from the land, and the unfaithful will be torn from it.

Solomon spoke with confidence that his son would "walk in the ways of good men and keep to the paths of the righteous." He reminded him of the consequences of not heeding wisdom. If there was a need for a reminder in Solomon's day, how much more is there a need for a reminder in our day?

LIVING IN A WORLD OF SENSUALITY

One need turn on the television for only a few minutes to feel the heat of the oppressive sensuality of our day. Most of the oppression is crude. A boring trip around the TV channels at midday invariably reveals at least one couple wrapped in bed sheets and much sensual monotony. But the heat has become increasingly artful, especially if its purpose is to sell. The camera focuses close up, in black and white, on an intense, lusting male face, over which is superimposed an amber flame, which then becomes a glowing bottle of Calvin Klein's Obsession as the face intones its desire. (Hughes 1991, p. 21)

In the thirty years since those words were penned, the internet has come into being, making available at the push of a button filth and degradation unseen, and even unthought-of by previous generations. If there was ever a need for godly instruction, it is today. In 1991, R. Kent Hughes made the following observation that is just as true today:

The contemporary evangelical Church ... is "Corinthian" to the core. It is being stewed in the molten juices of its own sensuality ... No wonder the Church has lost its grip on holiness. No wonder it is so slow to discipline its members. No wonder it is dismissed by the world as irrelevant. No wonder so many of its children reject it. No wonder it has lost its power in many places. (p. 22)

Godliness and depravity are incompatible. It's impossible to be a Christian and live like the devil. As long as one remains in the grip of sin and debauchery, they will never produce true godliness.

It's impossible to be a Christian and live like the devil.

The apostle Paul, like Solomon, speaking words of guidance, cautioned the young man Timothy, "Train yourself to be godly" (1 Timothy 4:7 NLT). To live a holy, godly life requires attention to the will of God as written in the Word of God. "See then that ye walk circumspectly, not as fools, but as wise, Redeeming the time, because the days are evil. Wherefore be ye not unwise, but understanding what the will of the Lord *is*" (Ephesians 5:15–17 KJV). One must walk circumspectly, as though walking through a field of landmines. And Paul provides us with the key to remaining unspotted from the world: "Be filled with the Spirit" (Ephesians 5:18 KJV). Be filled and stay filled with the Spirit of God.

THE SLIPPERY SLOPE OF SIN

Solomon's father is considered the greatest king in Israel's history, yet he forgot his heavenly Father's instructions and yielded to the seductive desires of his flesh. From his earliest appearance in scripture, David was a passionate lover of the LORD. The LORD liked what He saw—a heart that was focused on Him. David was so in love with God that yet today his Psalms move individuals and whole congregations in worship of God, and they are a comfort in times of distress. He was at the pinnacle of his reign, and no one expected him to fail morally, but he was vulnerable. Like every living soul, there were character defects that left him open to a great fall. The following steps that led to his moral failure are taken from Hughes's (1991) provocative book, *Disciplines of a Godly Man*.

Desensitization. "David took *him* more concubines and wives out of Jerusalem, after he was come from Hebron" (2 Samuel 5:13 KJV). Though it may have been acceptable within the culture of David's day to take additional wives, God's Word, with which David was very familiar, calls polygamy sin. Moses clearly stated:

> When you enter the land the LORD your God is giving you and have taken possession of it and settled in it, and you say, "Let us set a king over us like all the nations around us ..." The king ... must not take many wives, or his heart will be led astray. (Deuteronomy 17:14, 16–17)

Hughes (1991) described David's first step downward:

> A progressive desensitization to sin and a consequent inner descent from holiness had taken root in David's

life. ... King David's sensual indulgence desensitized him to God's holy call in his life, as well as to the danger and consequences of falling" (p. 23).

There are behaviors accepted by society but disapproved of by God that can take a person from the pinnacle to the pit. It's the old frog in the kettle syndrome. Being cold-blooded, the frog doesn't notice the increase in heat as its body temperature rises relative to the surrounding temperature, even as it is cooked to death. Exposing oneself to vulgar language, off-colored jokes, and ungodly values through hours of indiscriminate TV watching and internet surfing guarantees desensitization. And as desensitization sets in, what would have caused you to blush yesterday is hardly noticed today.

> There are behaviors accepted by society but disapproved of by God that can take a person from the pinnacle to the pit.

Relaxation. After the death of Saul and the return of allegiance to David by all of the tribes of Israel, David's kingdom appeared secure. He could relax from the rigors and discipline of war that had been so much a part of his life. It was no longer necessary for him to spend weeks and months in the field leading the army. External threats to his kingdom had been subdued. For the first time since the days of his youth with a harp on the hillside, he could truly relax. The problem was his relaxation extended to his moral life. Beware! Just when you think you are the safest and you no longer need to keep your guard up, temptation will come. "Wherefore let him that thinketh he standeth take heed lest he fall" (1 Corinthians 10:12 KJV). Remember, even when chased off by Jesus, Satan was waiting for an opportune time to return. (See Luke 4:13.)

Fixation. It was during this time of relaxation that David forgot the God who had made it possible for him to relax, and he became fixated on another man's wife. One evening, "David arose from off his bed, and walked upon the roof of the king's house: and from the roof he saw a woman washing herself; and the woman *was* very beautiful to look upon" (2 Samuel 11:2 KJV). "His look became a sinful stare and then a burning libidinous sweaty leer. In that moment David, who had been a man after God's own heart, became a dirty, leering old man" (Hughes 1991, p. 24). And David sent one of his loyal household servants to take the wife of Uriah from her house and bring her into his bedroom. When fixation on an object of lust sets in, "God disappears to lust-glazed eyes" (Hughes 1991, p. 25). When that occurs, "Satan does not fill us with hatred of God, but with forgetfulness of God" (Bonhoeffer 1955, p. 33). Not only did David's awareness of God diminish, but he "lost awareness of who he was—his holy call, his frailty, and the certain consequence of sin" (Hughes 1991, p. 25). Relaxation and forgetfulness of God led to fixation on that which was not his and that which would tarnish the glory of his legacy. The next step on the slippery slope of sin is rationalization.

Rationalization. When coveting sets in, a person is able to rationalize nearly anything. David's rationalizations may have sounded something like this:

> Uriah is a great soldier but he's probably not much of a lover—years older than she is—and he'll be away for a long time. This girl needs a little comfort in her loneliness. This is one way I can help her. No one will get hurt. I do not mean anything wrong by it. This is not lust—I have known that many times. This is love. This is not the same as finding a prostitute on the street. God knows that. And to the servant "Bring her to me." (Peterson 1983, p. 29)

Consider the following modern rationalizations:

- How can something that has brought such enjoyment be wrong?
- God's will for me is to be happy, certainly He would not deny me anything which is essential to my happiness!

- My marriage was never God's will in the first place.
- You Christians and your narrow judgmental attitudes make me sick. You are judging me. You are a greater sinner than I'll ever be! (Hughes 1991, p. 25)

> When coveting sets in, a person is able to rationalize nearly anything.

Desensitization removes the conviction of God, relaxation allows for a feeling of comfort in the midst of sin, and fixation is blind to all the danger signs along the way. Desensitization and rationalization deafen one's ears to verbal warnings. For example, one of David's servants took his life into his own hands in an attempt to keep David from sin—"She is Bathsheba, the daughter of Eliam and the wife of Uriah the Hittite" (2 Samuel 11:3 NLT).

Degeneration. Once rationalization sets in, degeneration is the next checkpoint on the slippery slope. "So David sent messengers and took her, and she came to him, and he lay with her" (2 Samuel 11:4 ESV). David was unaware the man after God's own heart was degenerating into a thief, an adulterer, a deceiver, and a murderer. He stole Uriah's wife, committed adultery with her, and concocted devious ways to cover his tracks, including getting Uriah drunk and eventually murdering him.

> The breaking of the Tenth Commandment, coveting his neighbor's wife, led to his breaking the seventh and committing adultery. Soon, in order to break the eighth, stealing what did not belong to him, he broke the sixth and committed murder. He broke the ninth by bearing false witness against his neighbor. He brought dishonour to his parents and thus broke the fifth. Thus he broke all the commandments which refer to loving one's neighbour as one's self. And of course, in its very nature, his sin dishonoured God as well. (Sanders 1965, p. 123)

It probably is true that at that point in David's life, "Uriah was a better man drunk than David was sober" (Hughes 1991, p. 26).

A year later, David repented in response to the convicting words of Nathan the prophet, but the consequences of his act could never be undone. If David had recognized the pain and suffering he and everyone connected with him would experience, he never would have given more than a fleeting glance at Bathsheba. Though he was eventually restored over Israel, the glory associated with the slaying of Goliath was tarnished, and his throne never regained its former glory. The child of his illicit relationship with Bathsheba died. Incest blighted his household when Amnon raped his half sister, Tamar. David's tarnished moral character prevented him from properly addressing Amnon's sin. As a result, Absalom, Tamar's full brother, murdered Amnon and eventually led a rebellion against his father, David.

STEPS TO KEEP YOUR WAY PURE

God left the history of the fall of King David for all to know, and every man and woman of God must recognize the ever-present potential for moral failure. Desensitization can easily occur through daily contact with our sex-oriented culture; moral relaxation is a by-product of spiritual apathy; sensual fixation blinds the beholder; and rationalization becomes easy on the slippery slope of lust. To avoid that slippery slope, it is essential that every Christian take steps to maintain purity of heart and mind. We hear this warning in the admonition of Paul to the Thessalonians:

> It is God's will ... that each of you should learn to control
> your own body in a way that is holy and honorable, not
> in passionate lust like the pagans, who do not know
> God; ... For God did not call us to be impure, but to
> live a holy life. (1 Thessalonians 4:3–5, 7)

Considering how easy it is to slide down the slippery slope from desensitization to degeneration, it is imperative that we put preventive measures in place.

Make yourself accountable to someone. It is deception to believe that you are answerable to no one but God. Everyone needs to be a part of a local congregation and to be accountable to a pastor and to other members of that congregation. When sin occurs, it is very important to have someone to whom you can confess that sin. In fact, having a process in place for such confession can benefit an entire church. Though not popular and rarely practiced today, requiring public confession from those who backslide or disgrace the church before being received back into fellowship of that congregation benefits both the one being restored and those receiving the person. In well-ordered homes, children are accountable to both parents. The scriptures teach that God is our Father (Malachi 2:10) and the church is our mother (Galatians 4:26). That being true, we need to not only repent and ask our Father for forgiveness, we need to ask our mother to forgive us for bringing shame and reproach upon her.

> We need to not only repent and ask our Father for forgiveness, we need to ask our mother to forgive us for bringing shame and reproach upon her.

Many contemporary Christians seem to believe they have matured to a level where they need nothing more than an individual relationship with Christ. These same individuals often commit sin and bring reproach upon the church, believing they are accountable to no one but God. As a result, some establish a cycle of sin … confess … sin … confess … sin … confess. This leads to spiritual weakness both in the individual and in the body of Christ.

Making oneself accountable to one another within the body of Christ helps break this cycle. The founders of Alcoholic Anonymous found the practice of confessing one's wrongdoing to another person was essential to deliverance from addiction to alcohol. Though each individual was taught to rely on a power higher than self—that is, on God—each individual also was expected to confess past misdeeds to another person. Accountability is essential to spiritual growth and overcoming character defects and moral failings. Unfortunately, many so strongly emphasize the power of the Holy Ghost to keep them from sinning that they are fearful of being rejected from their "heavenly places" if they admit to another that they struggle with sin. In truth, pastors need others in whom to confide and hold them accountable. Men need other men in the church to listen carefully, prayerfully, and with compassion. Women need other women who will go to the grave without repeating the words that have been entrusted to them. The apostle James urged, "Confess *your* faults one to another, and pray one for another, that ye may be healed" (James 5:16 KJV).

> Unfortunately, many so strongly emphasize the power of the Holy Ghost to keep them from sinning that they are fearful of being rejected from their "heavenly places" if they admit to another that they struggle with sin.

Pray daily for personal moral purity. Jesus made this a part of his model prayer: "And lead us not into temptation, but deliver us from evil" (Matthew 6:13 KJV). We may be great prayer warriors in petitioning God, but after making all those requests, we must make sure we remain in a right relationship with God. David concluded one of his psalms with "Search me, O God, and know my heart: try me, and know my thoughts: And see if *there be any* wicked way in me" (Psalm 139:23–24 KJV).

Memorize and meditate on God's Word. "How can a young person stay pure? By obeying your word. … I have hidden your word in my heart, that I might not sin against you" (Psalm 119:9, 11 NLT). We can maintain pure hearts and minds by filling them with God's Word. And we fill our hearts and minds with God's Word by memorizing scriptures. But we must do more. We must meditate on those scriptures. By doing so, we overcome temptation and sin.

> This book of the law shall not depart out of thy mouth; but thou shalt meditate therein day and night,

that thou mayest observe to do according to all that
is written therein: for then thou shalt make thy way
prosperous, and then thou shalt have good success.
(Joshua 1:8 KJV)

I have to believe that becoming prosperous and successful is much
more than becoming rich and famous. There's a spiritual prosperity
that fills one's life with the good things of God, and there is spiritual
success that cannot be measured by the number of diplomas on one's
wall or the number of accolades one receives over a lifetime. Spiritual
prosperity has to do with the development of virtues, and spiritual
success has to do with battles fought and victories won over the enemy
of our souls.

Control your environment. "It is impossible for you to maintain
a pure mind if you are a television-watching 'couch potato.' In one
week you will watch more murders, adulteries, and perversions than
our grandfathers read about in their entire lives" (Hughes 1991, p. 29).
And by throwing caution to the wind, men and women who profess
Christianity have become addicted to pornography, chat rooms, and
even exhibitionism for the pleasure of voyeurs. But there is a simple
solution to all of that—control your environment. Jesus said, "If thine
eye offend thee, pluck it out: it is better for thee to enter into the
kingdom of God with one eye, than having two eyes to be cast into
hell fire" (Mark 9:47 KJV). Since it's a sin to defile the temple of God,
Jesus did not intend for you to literally pluck out your eye. He intended
for you to pluck your eye out by controlling your environment. Control
your environment by turning off the television, putting filters on your
computers, placing them in public areas, and turning in electronic
devices at night. Some may see this as legalism, but it is nothing more
than controlling your environment. And you have a responsibility to
control your environment. Solomon asked a rhetorical question, "Can a
man scoop fire into his lap without his clothes being burned?" (Proverbs
6:27). No! If you handle fire, you will get burned.

We need to be like Job, "I made a covenant with my eyes not to
look lustfully at a young woman" (Job 31:1).

Job's covenant forbids a second look. It means treating all women with dignity—looking at them respectfully. If their dress or demeanor is distracting, look them in the eyes, and nowhere else, and get away as quickly as you can! (Hughes 1991, pp. 29–30)

Establish boundaries and live by them. Refrain from intimate conversations with the opposite sex other than your spouse. Do not bare your heart to someone of the opposite sex, unless it's a counselor in a professional setting. Many affairs begin by talking about personal, intimate matters to the wrong person. Other than members of your family, do not treat the opposite sex with casual affection. If you are married, never travel or dine out alone with someone of the opposite sex who is not your spouse. Further, never flirt with anyone but your spouse; and if you are not married, don't flirt with another person's spouse.

> Never flirt with anyone but your spouse; and if you are not married, don't flirt with another person's spouse.

In 1948, the young evangelist Billy Graham knew that two things had taken down the ministries of previous evangelists—money and sex. In Modesto, California, his team gathered in a hotel room and drew up a pact that became known as the Modesto Manifesto. It included provisions on how to distribute money raised during crusades and the use of official estimates of crowds so as to avoid exaggeration. But the most well-known provision of the manifesto called for each man on the Graham team never to be alone with a woman other than his own wife.

Graham, from that day forward, pledged not to eat, travel, or meet with a woman other than Ruth unless other people were present. This pledge guaranteed Graham's sexual probity and enabled him to dodge accusations that have waylaid evangelists before and since. (Dowland 2014, p. 40)

Always be aware of your vulnerability. Every Christian must establish boundaries—a Modesto Manifesto—and live by them. But even with well-defined boundaries in place, be careful of statements like "I would never do such a thing." Never forget, as long as you wear this flesh, you are not above sin. King David slew a giant while he was still a shepherd lad, but power, prestige, and privilege resulted in desensitization to the God who elevated him to the mountaintop, and there—on the mountaintop—not in the valley—the giant slew David.

IN CLOSING

The credibility of God's Word lies in the fact that not every hero lived happily ever after. It is here in the unadulterated, unredacted rawness of the scriptures that we learn lessons from a fallen king. We must take every step possible to avoid a fall like David's. We must make ourselves accountable to someone other than just God. We must pray for personal moral purity, and we must memorize and meditate on the Word of God. We must do whatever we can to control the environment in which we immerse ourselves, we must establish boundaries and live by them, we must be aware of our vulnerability as human beings, and we must never forget God. The awareness of God's presence is what sustained Joseph during temptation: "How then can I do this great wickedness, and sin against God?" (Genesis 39:9 KJV). It's better to lose your cloak and your position than to lose your soul. Before you take a second look, before you allow lust to attach itself to the womb of your heart, and before you consider giving in to sin, "Feet do your thing!" The apostle Paul's advice is just as pertinent today as it was the day he instructed his son, Timothy, "Flee also youthful lusts: but follow righteousness, faith, charity, peace, with them that call on the Lord out of a pure heart" (2 Timothy 2:22 KJV). And that brings us full circle to where we began—Solomon's warning to his son, "Walk in the ways of the good and keep to the paths of the righteous" (Proverbs 2:20).

LESSON 11

WHEN YOUR HEAD AND HEART GET IT TOGETHER

PROVERBS 3:1-2

¹ My son, do not forget my teaching, but keep my commands in your heart, ² for they will prolong your life many years and bring you peace and prosperity.

As in the two previous chapters, Solomon continues his instruction to his son. But let's assume for the next few moments that these words are not just the words of Solomon but the words of the Lord spoken through Solomon to us—kind words of our heavenly Father. In commenting on the above verses, Charles Bridges (1846/1968) made the following observation:

> This is not the stern language of command. It is our Father's voice in all the endearing persuasiveness of promise—My son—He had before instructed us to seek and search after wisdom, and set out before us its invaluable blessings. Now he calls us to bring it into practical exercise—Forget not my law. (p. 21)

DOERS—NOT JUST HEARERS

We must be doers and not just hearers of the Word of God. "For it is not the hearers of the law who are righteous before God, but the doers of the law who will be justified" (Romans 2:13 ESV). James was emphatic. "Do not merely listen to the word, and so deceive yourselves. Do what it says" (James 1:22).

It is insufficient to have the Word of the Lord in our minds alone; it must be kept in our hearts. You will never be able to please God until your understanding of His will reaches the level of your heart. David knew this: "Thy word have I hid in mine heart, that I might not sin against thee" (Psalm 119:11 KJV).

> The danger of simply storing God's Word in our heads is that our treacherous memories will fail to call it to mind when it is most needed. But if we hide God's Word in our hearts, it will remain there and it will control our response to the vicissitudes of life. (Phillips 1995, pp. 74–75)

> You will never be able to please God until your understanding of His will reaches the level of your heart.

God gave a command to Israel that is still applicable today:

> Hear, O Israel: The LORD our God, the LORD is one. Love the LORD your God with all your heart and with all your soul and with all your strength. These commandments that I give you today are to be on your hearts. (Deuteronomy 6:4–6)

> It was not easy for an Old Testament Jew to forget God's Word. He was required by law to write Bible texts on the doorposts of his house. When he went

out, the texts on his doorposts called after him: "Where are you going? With whom will you be? What business are you transacting? Be mindful of your conduct. Guard your conversation. Watch out for your character. Listen to your conscience. God never sleeps." When he returned home, the texts on his doorposts cross-examined him: "Where have you been? What have you been doing? Examine yourself. You cannot get away from God." (Phillips 1995, p. 75)

THE NEED FOR CONVICTIONS

When God's Word is truly in our hearts, it will always hold center stage. Daniel was a man who truly had the Word of the Lord in his heart. His captivity in Babylon could have been a time of shattered faith. Jerusalem lay in ruins, its former glory was a distant memory, and future leaders were slaves in Babylon. No deliverance could be seen on the horizon, yet he retained his integrity.

One of the Seven Wonders of the World lay before him. In the Great Temple of Marduk, or Bel, there was a golden image of Bel and a golden table, which together is estimated to have weighed fifty thousand pounds. Also, at this temple in the "city of gold" were two golden lions, a solid golden human figure eighteen feet high, and a golden table forty feet long and fifteen feet wide. There were fifty-three temples in Babylon. Ishtar, the goddess of love, whose worship included immoral practices, had one hundred and eighty altars in the city.

In this city, Daniel's convictions were put to the test. He was a long way from home, and obeying God's law had not spared him from captivity. Subtle temptations were everywhere. He was not required to worship heathen gods, nor was he required to kill anyone. The concern was eating ceremonially unclean meats. The great danger in this type of temptation is that it could have been very easy to find grounds to justify compromising his convictions. Occasionally, we all are tested to see if we will lower our standards just a little.

But Daniel purposed in his heart that he would not defile himself with the portion of the king's meat, nor with the wine which he drank: therefore he requested of the prince of the eunuchs that he might not defile himself. (Daniel 1:8 KJV)

The trouble with many is that in their own hearts, they have not settled just exactly what is right or wrong. For Daniel, it was settled; he had determined that he would not allow himself to be defiled. And God honored the faith and conviction of Daniel and the three young men with him. "At the end of the ten days, Daniel and his three friends looked healthier and better nourished than the young men who had been eating the food assigned by the king" (Daniel 1:15 NLT).

> The trouble with many is that in their own hearts, they have not settled just exactly what is right or wrong.

"God gave these four young men an unusual aptitude for understanding every aspect of literature and wisdom. And God gave Daniel the special ability to interpret the meanings of visions and dreams" (Daniel 1:17 NLT). As a result, Daniel became ruler over the province of Babylon and chief of the governors over all the wise men of the province. One of the last official acts of Belshazzar was to proclaim Daniel the third ruler in the kingdom. And under Darius, Daniel was appointed the first of three presidents over 120 princes who oversaw the kingdom. This is a good example of how God honors faithfulness to convictions. Some believe they have to lower their standards to get ahead. Repeatedly, in the history of God interacting with humankind, we find blessing and honor and reward as a direct result of commitment and conviction.

THE PROMISE OF A LONG LIFE

Solomon wrote, "Do not forget my teaching, but keep my commands in your heart, for they will prolong your life many years" (Proverbs 3:1–2). Throughout the book of Proverbs, he made it clear that if you will hold to godly convictions, the LORD will add years to your life:

- Fear of the LORD lengthens one's life. (Proverbs 10:27 NLT)
- The fear of the LORD leads to life. (Proverbs 19:23 ESV)
- For through wisdom your days will be many, and years will be added to your life. (Proverbs 9:11)

Keeping the Lord's teaching will not only prolong your life, but those years will be enriched by the blessings of God. Jesus stated, "I am come that they might have life, and that they might have *it* more abundantly" (John 10:10 KJV). When Solomon asked for the better things, the Lord stated to him that he would receive more than he ever imagined:

> I will also give you what you did not ask for—riches and fame! No other king in all the world will be compared to you for the rest of your life! And if you follow me and obey my decrees and my commands as your father, David, did, I will give you a long life. (1 Kings 3:13–14 NLT)

> Keeping the Lord's teaching will not only prolong your life, but those years will be enriched by the blessings of God.

It is the Lord who promised humans a long and abundant life. It is one of the promises of obedience to God's commands. This association is embedded in the fifth commandment: "Honour thy father and mother; (which is the first commandment with promise;) That it may be well with thee, and thou mayest live long on the earth" (Ephesians

6:2–3 KJV). It only makes sense that those who live godly avoid the kinds of behaviors that cut lives short.

PEACE AND PROSPERITY

Solomon informed his son that obedience to his teaching and commands would prolong his life many years and bring him peace and prosperity. (See Proverbs 3:2.) In the King James Version, the Hebrew word *shalowm* was translated *peace* 175 times and *prosperity* four times. It is a word that cannot be expressed fully in the English language by either *peace* or *prosperity*. Its overarching meaning is that of *completeness, soundness, welfare, and peace*. The inclusion of both *peace* and *prosperity* by the translators of the New International Version captures the greater meaning of the original word.

The psalmist wrote, "Great peace have they which love thy law: and nothing shall offend them" (Psalm 119:165 KJV). The one who has the teachings and commands of the Lord in their heart can live in peace, has nothing to fear, and has no need to be offended. "The work of righteousness shall be peace; and the effect of righteousness quietness and assurance for ever" (Isaiah 32:17 KJV). That person will experience completeness, fullness of life, and protection. Paul assured that if we will truly trust in the Lord and follow His commands, we do not have to live with fear and anxiety:

> Do not be anxious about anything, but in everything by prayer and supplication with thanksgiving let your requests be made known to God. And the peace of God, which surpasses all understanding, will guard your hearts and your minds in Christ Jesus. (Philippians 4:6–7 ESV)

The one who has the teachings and commands of the Lord in their heart can live in peace, has nothing to fear, and has no need to be offended.

LORIN BRADBURY, PH.D.

The peace of God does not guarantee peace in this world; instead, it assures peace in the heart even when there isn't peace in the world. This peace might be described as "the settled quiet of the heart." It can only occur when the commands of God stored in your head make their way into your heart.

IN CLOSING

Almost all Christians know the importance of prayer and will often declare the same. However, if you polled those same Christians who declare prayer is a priority, only a small percentage would be found to actually make time to pray more than a few moments at mealtimes and before they go to bed. In other words, they have a command of God—"Pray without ceasing"—in their heads but not in their hearts. As a result, Christians, including preachers, become prayerless. One writer posed the following questions, "Did you spend time with the Boss today? How about yesterday? Is there peace in your heart from that daily recharging of the spiritual batteries that makes your inner man strong? Is your heart being guarded?" (Bell 2012, p. 100). It's very possible that we know in our heads the importance of finding time to spend with the Boss, but until that knowledge moves from the head to the heart, prayer of any significance will remain elusive. We must know in our hearts that prayer is important enough to give up a predetermined amount of time daily if it is ever going to happen. We must exercise faith and dare to give up that time, trusting that when we do, the Lord will provide enough time during the remaining hours to accomplish those things that really matter.

> We must know in our hearts that prayer is important enough to give up a predetermined amount of time daily if it is ever going to happen.

Like prayer, the Sabbath principle must make its way from our heads to our hearts, and we must exercise faith that God will allow us to accomplish all that needs to be accomplished during the remaining six. We may know that it is important to set a part a day unto the Lord, but until the sacredness of that command moves from the head to the heart, we will find work to fill that day. Consider the following quote: "The most melancholy thing about human nature, is, that a man may guide others in the path of salvation, without walking in it himself; that he may be a pilot and yet a castaway" (Augustus William in Bell 2012, p. 84). It is insufficient to have the Word of the Lord in our minds alone; it must become embedded in our hearts.

LESSON 12

LOVE AND FAITHFULNESS

PROVERBS 3:3-4

³ Let love and faithfulness never leave you; bind them around your neck, write them on the tablet of your heart. ⁴ Then you will win favor and a good name in the sight of God and man.

The Hebrew words *checed* and *emeth* are translated *love* and *faithfulness* in the above verse. The most frequent use of those words paired together is in contexts referring to the character traits of God as they are demonstrated in the relationship between God and humans. Moses discovered these character traits when he met God on Mount Sinai:

> The LORD descended in the cloud and stood with him there, and proclaimed the name of the LORD. The LORD passed before him and proclaimed, "The LORD, the LORD, a God merciful and gracious, slow to anger, and abounding in steadfast love and faithfulness." (Exodus 34:5–6 ESV)

Psalmists repeatedly praised the LORD for manifesting this pair of attributes:

- Righteousness and justice are the foundation of your throne; steadfast love and faithfulness go before you. (Psalm 89:14 ESV)
- All the paths of the LORD are steadfast love and faithfulness, for those who keep his covenant and his testimonies. (Psalm 25:10 ESV)
- But you, O Lord, are a God merciful and gracious, slow to anger and abounding in steadfast love and faithfulness. (Psalm 86:15 ESV)
- For great is his steadfast love toward us, and the faithfulness of the LORD endures forever. (Psalm 117:2 ESV)

God's people are to respond to His great love and faithfulness by demonstrating the same. Jesus clearly stated, "By this shall all *men* know that ye are my disciples, if ye have love one to another" (John 13:35 KJV). This was not a suggestion but an expectation.

> To love one another was not a suggestion but an expectation.

LOVE DEFINED

Writing to the Corinthian Church, the apostle Paul put forth what stands yet today as the classic description of love. Love is like a beautiful tapestry made up of many different color threads. In I Corinthians 13, Paul examines each thread that makes up that beautiful tapestry:

> Love is patient, love is kind. It does not envy, it does not boast, it is not proud. It does not dishonor others, it is not self-seeking, it is not easily angered, it keeps no record of wrongs. Love does not delight in evil but rejoices with the truth. It always protects, always trusts, always hopes, always perseveres. (1 Corinthians 13:4–7)

Love is patient (suffereth long). Long-suffering allows one to tolerate unbearable people and situations. While himself a prisoner for the sake of the Gospel, the apostle Paul urged the church members in Ephesus to live a life worthy of their calling as Christians "with all lowliness and meekness, with longsuffering, forbearing one another in love" (Ephesians 4:2 KJV). And when it is necessary to correct someone, Paul instructed Timothy to "reprove, rebuke, exhort with all longsuffering and doctrine" (2 Timothy 4:2 KJV).

Love is kind. Kindness is love in action, and Jesus was the epitome of love. Peter observed that Jesus went about doing good and healing those who were oppressed of the devil (Acts 10:38). Phillips (1972) translated "love is kind" as "it looks for a way of being constructive." Henry Drummond (2007) wrote, "The greatest thing a man can do for his Heavenly Father is to be kind to some of his other children" (p. 19).

Love does not envy. Love is never jealous—it always is generous. Envy and bitterness go hand in hand, and if left unchecked, like cancer, they will consume one's entire being. Instead of envy and jealousy, a Christian must develop a spirit of contentment. Paul wrote that through much suffering, he had "learned the secret of being content in any and every situation" (Philippians 4:11).

Love does not boast; it is not proud. It is humble. Love places others ahead of self. "It does not dishonor others" (1 Corinthians 13:5). Love is courteous. It is a gentleman. Lyman Abbot described courtesy as "the eye which overlooks your friend's broken gateway but sees the rose which blossoms in his garden" (Doan 1968, p. 107). The ability to recognize and overlook another's faults and shortcomings will prevent many arguments and hurt feelings.

Love is not selfish. "It does not demand its own way" (1 Corinthians 13:5 NLT). You can never take love or force someone to love you; you can only give love and receive it. To attempt to force someone to love you corrupts the whole concept of love, even if the person responds in a loving manner. A forced response can never be love, because love is something offered freely.

> To attempt to force someone to love you corrupts the whole concept of love, even if the person responds in a loving manner.

It is not easily angered. Love is not touchy, irritable, resentful, or easily offended. It has a good temper. There are two great classes of sins—sins of the body and sins of the disposition. Because they are so easily denied, Jesus expressed great concern about the sins of the disposition. The prodigal in Luke 15 is an example of the sins of the body. His older brother, on the other hand, displayed sins of the disposition. In that parable, the older brother represented the Pharisees. Outwardly, they appeared righteous, but pertaining to their disposition—guilty!

Love keeps no record of wrongs. This is the basis for forgiveness. If forgiveness is absent, whenever stress arises, past insults are remembered and thrown at the other person like stones. But love is uninterested in keeping score. "Love does not delight in evil but rejoices with the truth" (1 Corinthians 13:6). It finds a way to simultaneously tolerate the sinner and despise the sin. "Love never stops being patient, never stops believing, never stops hoping, never gives up" (1 Corinthians 13:7 GW). Love believes the best of all even when there might be some dark appearances. It strives to always give the benefit of the doubt.

LOVE DEMONSTRATED

As can be seen from Paul's description of love, it is more than a feeling; love must be demonstrated. "Beloved, if God so loved us, we ought also to love one another" (1 John 4:11 KJV). Our love for God is not complete just by believing in Him; we must show it by our works of love. James was emphatic that faith must be demonstrated by works: "Faith without works is dead" (James 2:26 KJV). In the same manner, love must be demonstrated.

LORIN BRADBURY, PH.D.

> Our love for God is not complete just by believing in Him; we must show it by our works of love.

One writer so wisely stated, "It is no chore for me to love the whole world. My only real problem is my neighbor next door" (Davis 1995, spring, p. 18). After declaring that the first and greatest commandment is to love the Lord with all your heart, soul, mind, and strength, Jesus reminded His hearers that there is a second commandment to which he seems to give equal weight: "Thou shalt love thy neighbour as thyself" (Matthew 22:39 KJV). Further, He declared, "A new commandment I give unto you, That ye love one another; as I have loved you" (John 13:34 KJV). "Love may not make the world go around, but it sure makes the trip worthwhile" (Davis 1995, spring, p. 18).

Something that is rarely talked about is the fact that if you dare to truly love, you will get hurt. But if you want to experience love, you must take the risk to love. If you dare to fall in love and marry, sometime, somehow, that person you fall in love with will hurt you, though hopefully not on purpose. If you have children and you love them unconditionally, you will get hurt. On the other hand, it would be possible to minimize the risk of getting hurt by isolating yourself from as many relationships as possible. But who really wants to live without love? How horrible to go through this life without giving and receiving love. "The loneliest place in the world is the human heart when love is absent" (Davis 1995, spring p. 18). If you want love in your life, you have to be willing to take the risk.

> "We become vulnerable when we love people and go out of our way to help them," the wealthy industrialist Charles Schwab declared after going to court and winning a nuisance suit at age seventy. Given permission by the judge to speak to the audience, he made the following statement: "I'd like to say here in a court of law, and speaking as an old man, that nine-tenths of my troubles are traceable to my being

kind to others. Look, you young people, if you want to steer away from trouble, be hard-boiled. Be quick with a good loud 'NO' to anyone and everyone. If you follow this rule, you will seldom be bothered as you tread life's pathway. Except you'll have no friends, you'll be lonely, and you won't have any fun!" (Davis 1995, spring, p. 18)

FAITHFULNESS DEMONSTRATED

Then there's faithfulness. Being a slave did not excuse Joseph from being faithful to the LORD and to his master. Though sold into slavery by the hatefulness of his brothers, he remained faithful to the LORD, and the LORD stood beside him throughout his years of slavery:

> And the LORD was with Joseph, and he was a prosperous man; and he was in the house of his master the Egyptian. And his master saw that the LORD *was* with him, and that the LORD made all that he did to prosper in his hand. And Joseph found grace in his sight, and he served him: and he made him overseer over his house, and all *that* he had he put into his hand. (Genesis 39:2–4 KJV)

If slavery wasn't bad enough, remaining faithful to the LORD through temptation resulted in him being thrown into prison. When Potiphar heard the accusations of his wife—"That Hebrew slave raped me!"—he felt betrayed and angry—and understandably so. In anger, Potiphar locked Joseph in the king's prison. But even being unjustly accused and unjustly punished did not change the character of Joseph; he remained faithful. And since God's character is unchanged by our situations, the LORD remained faithful to Joseph. Just as before, the LORD was with Joseph, showed him mercy, and gave him favor in the eyes of the warden. (See Genesis 39:22–23.) Just as love can be risky business, the scriptures seem to reveal that faithfulness can be risky business but only if your perspective is from outside the kingdom of God. But from inside the kingdom of God, it is perceived as an opportunity to bless and to be blessed.

> Just as love can be risky business, the scriptures seem to reveal that faithfulness can be risky business but only if your perspective is from outside the kingdom of God.

A faithful servant by the name of Caleb was one of only two over the age of twenty when they left Egypt who were allowed to enter the Promised Land. In his forty-year march through the desert, he had seen no more of God than the others, but what he saw he retained. Caleb was not so focused on today's problems that he forgot tomorrow's promises. He was sent by Moses as a member of a delegation to spy out the Promised Land. The report of the other ten spies was simply this, "We are nothing, we will not be able to possess it." Caleb's report was not based on what he saw at the moment; it was based on the promise of the LORD. So, instead of shrinking to the size of a grasshopper, he sounded a battle cry, "Let us go up at once, and possess it; for we are well able to overcome it" (Numbers 13:30 KJV). However, because of the lack of faith among the others, he would have to wait to claim his promise. And he would have to remain faithful when the promise seemed elusive.

Caleb's confidence was anchored in a God who cannot lie. And his faithfulness did not go unnoticed: "But my servant Caleb—this is a different story. He has a different spirit; he follows me passionately. I'll bring him into the land that he scouted and his children will inherit it" (Numbers 14:24 MSG). With those words of assurance, we too can know that our God takes note of our faithfulness.

The highest point a believer ever reaches in this life is when they are faithfully walking with God. But never get ahead of God. Many times, faithfulness includes waiting. From what we can tell at this distant perspective, Caleb followed the LORD fully, and he followed the LORD cheerfully. What a combination! Faithfulness often includes enduring, and "he that shall endure to the end, the same shall be saved" (Matthew 24:13 KJV). It also may require walking all alone. It's refreshing to see someone stand for convictions, even if it is a lone vote. Are you willing to faithfully stand alone for Christ's sake? As you take a stand for God's truths and God's cause—whatever the cost—God's kingdom will be advanced. Put your trust in God and faithfully walk before Him with courage!

THE REWARD OF FAITHFULNESS

That having been said, our concept of faithfulness needs to be reexamined. We sometimes believe that the more active we are, the more spiritual we are.

> There is a breed of mice that is so hyper-tense that it never quits moving. Pet store owners put the little creatures in mazes to delight their customer. The mice will run bumping into this wall and that and only gaining an opening by sheer chance. (Hall 1977, fall, p. 30)

It takes no great imagination to see the similarity between the nervous mice and some people. Faithfulness is not taking on every job in the church; faithfulness is finding your calling and doing it to the very best of your ability.

Caleb was faithful to the LORD, and the LORD was faithful to Caleb. Caleb was faithful throughout the forty years of wandering in the desert, and he lived to receive his reward. Hebron was worth waiting for. You can detect the enthusiasm in his voice when he came to claim his prize:

> Now then, just as the LORD promised, he has kept me alive for forty-five years since the time he said this to Moses, while Israel moved about in the wilderness. So here I am today, eighty-five years old! I am still as

strong today as the day Moses sent me out; I'm just as vigorous to go out to battle now as I was then. Now give me this hill country that the LORD promised me that day. You yourself heard then that the Anakites were there and their cities were large and fortified, but, the LORD helping me, I will drive them out just as he said. (Joshua 14:10–12)

You too have a reward awaiting at the end of your journey in this life if you remain faithful.

IN CLOSING

Just as our Lord is a God of love and faithfulness, we are instructed to demonstrate the same: "Let love and faithfulness never leave you; bind them around your neck, write them on the tablet of your heart" (Proverbs 3:3). Love and faithfulness are two sides of the same coin. Both are character traits of God. And it's God's will that these character traits become our character traits. You will never go wrong by practicing love and faithfulness. If you are to emulate anyone, you should emulate the Lord. "Then you will win favor and a good name in the sight of God and man" (Proverbs 3:4).

LESSON 13

TRUST IN THE LORD

PROVERBS 3:5-6

⁵ Trust in the Lᴏʀᴅ with all your heart and lean not on your own understanding; ⁶ in all your ways submit to him, and he will make your paths straight.

Trust is the key word in the above verses. God's character makes it impossible for Him to lie; therefore, He is utterly dependable. His wisdom is so great He can never make a mistake. He has high and holy purposes and no ulterior motives. But modern humans have tried desperately to reinvent God. They have done so by minimizing or ignoring many of those facets of God's character.

A GOD WHO CAN BE TRUSTED

The fingerprints of an incredible God mark the orderliness, complexity, diversity, and immensity of nature. God's greatness is evident in the heavens. According to NASA'S (2014) webpage, our galaxy alone has been estimated to contain more than two hundred billion stars. It is only one of hundreds of billions of galaxies estimated to exist as a result of the far reaches into space by the Hubble telescope. "Hubble observed a tiny patch of sky (one-tenth the diameter of the moon) for one million seconds (11.6 days) and found approximately 10,000 galaxies, of all sizes, shapes, and colors" (NASA 2014). NASA (2009) estimates that from our position in our universe, we are about fourteen billion light-years from its farthest reaches. A light-year is how far light travels in one year at the speed of slightly more than 186,000 miles per second. This is approximately 5.878 trillion miles a year. If the universe were only sixteen billion light years in diameter, and we multiply 5.878 trillion by sixteen billion, the universe would be some ninety-four billion trillion miles in diameter. However, this still would not be the measurement of God. God is greater than the universe and the infinite space that surrounds it. Thousands of tiny pinpricks of glowing light in the night sky offer testimony to God's creative power.

> The fingerprints of an incredible God mark the orderliness, complexity, diversity, and immensity of nature.

Again, God's greatness is seen in creation as a whole. Scientists with a creation worldview recognize the improbability of life forming without a creator.

> The calculation which supports the creationist argument begins with the probability of a 300-molecule-long protein forming by total random chance. This would be approximately 1 chance in 10^{390}. This number is astoundingly huge. By comparison, the number of all the atoms in the observable universe is 10^{80}. So, if a simple protein has that unlikely chance of forming, what hope does a complete bacterium have? (Peacock, n.d.)

And by extension, what hope does a galaxy have of forming by chance? "By faith we understand that the universe was formed at God's command, so that what is seen was not made out of what was visible" (Hebrews 11:3).

Why is the earth the exact size it is? If it were larger, the increased gravitational pull would crush us into the earth's surface. If it were smaller, the gravitational pull would be insufficient. Why is the surface of the earth no more than 71 percent water? It has been estimated that if it were made up of 10 percent more water than it is, only the highest mountain peaks would be above sea level. The amount of moisture, temperature, wind patterns, soil composition, and hundreds of other factors interact in very specific ways, revealing the work of an intelligent Creator. Out on the hillside under the canopy of a cloudless sky, David lifted his voice and acknowledged his Creator:

> When I look at your heavens, the work of your fingers,
> the moon and the stars, which you have set in place,
> what is man that you are mindful of him, and the son
> of man that you care for him? (Psalm 8:3–4 ESV)

The same creative mind that spoke the galaxies into existence lovingly crafted the complex cells that make up the human body. David didn't need a microscope or a class in anatomy and physiology to recognize the work of his Creator. All he had to do was look in the mirror. That's why he declared, "I will praise thee; for I am fearfully *and* wonderfully made: marvellous *are* thy works" (Psalm 139:14 KJV).

The same creative mind that spoke the galaxies into existence lovingly crafted the complex cells that make up the human body.

TRUST IN THE LORD WITH ALL YOUR HEART

The writer of the book of Proverbs stated, "Trust in the LORD with all your heart" (Proverbs 3:5). Considering only a few of the facts noted above concerning the greatness of our LORD, it should not be a problem to trust in Him. And that is significant because our walk with God is based on trust. "'Trust' steps unto the bridge of God's loving power and leaves the shoreline of our own abilities and ambitions behind. Such belief means literally to 'bet your life' on God's truth and wisdom" (Hubbard 1989, p. 71). Job is the classic example of trust. "Though he slay me, yet will I hope in him" (Job 13:15). Job trusted! He trusted even when heaven was silent. Phillips (1995) wrote this concerning Job:

> He lost everything. Once he had been rich; now he was poor. Once he had been blessed with a lovely family of attractive boys and girls; now he was utterly bereaved. Once he had enjoyed good health; now he was afflicted by a horribly disfiguring and incurable disease. Once his wife had stood by him; now she advised him to curse God and die. Once his integrity had been unquestioned; now even his friends accused him of secret sin. Once he walked in communion with God; now he appealed passionately to a silent Heaven. (p. 78)

God's knowledge, God's wisdom, and God's plans for our lives are beyond our comprehension. "For my thoughts *are* not your thoughts, neither *are* your ways my ways, saith the LORD. For *as* the heavens are higher than the earth, so are my ways higher than your ways, and my thoughts than your thoughts" (Isaiah 55:8–9 KJV). Paul summed it up as follows:

> Oh, the depth of the riches of the wisdom and knowledge of God! How unsearchable his judgments, and his paths beyond tracing out! "Who has known the mind of the Lord? Or who has been his counselor?" "Who has ever given to God, that God should repay him?" For from him and through him and for him are all things. To him be the glory forever! (Romans 11:33–36)

Yes. All we can do is stand in awe and worship Him for what we can see and acknowledge there is much we will never see.

His attributes we may name, His benefits we can claim, His help we can receive, His love we can experience, His salvation we can appropriate, His Word and promises we can believe, but His being will still remain behind the mysterious curtain of infinity. When we encounter Him, we can only bow ourselves before Him in worship and adoration. (Davis 1995, fall, p. 14)

> All we can do is stand in awe and worship Him for what we can see and acknowledge there is much we will never see.

IN ALL YOUR WAYS ACKNOWLEDGE HIM

In all your ways acknowledge him, and he will make your paths straight. Hubbard (1989) noted that *acknowledge* and *fear* are terms of personal bonding that result in changes of behavior. "They combine the senses of awe, intimacy, and obligation which mark sound relationships. They suggest that God's people want to know Him so well that they do his bidding virtually without having to be reminded" (p. 71). We should not have to be reminded, yet there is strong evidence that humans continually run the risk of failing to acknowledge and consult God in making decisions. The strength of a person's relationship with God is positively correlated with one's reverence for God.

Once, during the time of Joshua's leadership, he and the elders failed to consult the LORD before making a covenant with the enemy. He and his men sat down and ate the enemy's musty bread but did not inquire of the LORD as to who these people were. In the process, he made a peace treaty with the enemy and ratified it by oath. (See Joshua 9:14–15.) By failing to consult the LORD, the enemy became "snares and traps" for the nation of Israel, "whips on their backs and thorns in their eyes." (See Joshua 23:12–13.)

There is no situation that is too insignificant about which to consult the Lord. Instead of dividing our lives into spiritual and secular, all areas must be dedicated to God. Acknowledge Him in all your ways, and He will make your paths straight. A visual example of God's presence, day and night, was seen by the Israelites as they left the bondage of Egypt. When they arose in the morning, there was that pillar of cloud to guide them through the day, and when darkness of night settled in, there was the pillar of fire to remind God's people He had not left them. (See Exodus 13:22.) Whether visible or not, just as the LORD led Israel through the desert to the Promised Land, He continues to lead those who will acknowledge Him.

> There is no situation that is too insignificant about which to consult the Lord.

God never intended for humans to direct their own way—to be in charge of their own destiny! This is a fact acknowledged by Jeremiah: "LORD, I know that people's lives are not their own; it is not for them to direct their steps" (Jeremiah 10:23). The Lord not only makes his will known to us, he gives us the power to accomplish it, "for it is God who is at work in you, both to will and to work for *His* good pleasure" (Philippians 2:13 NASB).

IN CLOSING

During the days of the kings of Israel, there was a little Israelite girl, captured by the Arameans and forced into slavery, who still put her faith and trust in the LORD. Though a slave to Naaman, a commander in the Aramean army, she acknowledged the LORD. Her master, Naaman, possessed great prestige and authority, but he was a leper. This young lady served Naaman's wife, and she had compassion on him. She mentioned to his wife that a prophet in Israel could heal him. Naaman's wife went to her husband with the message of hope, and he, in turn, went to the king of Aram. The king of Aram sent a letter to the king of Israel, and when Elisha heard of the man's plight, he requested the king send Naaman to him:

So Naaman came with his horses and with his chariot, and stood at the door of the house of Elisha. And Elisha sent a messenger unto him, saying, Go and wash in Jordan seven times, and thy flesh shall come again to thee, and thou shalt be clean. But Naaman was wroth, and went away, and said, Behold, I thought, He will surely come out to me, and stand, and call on the name of the Lord his God, and strike his hand over the place [of leprosy], and recover the leper. (2 Kings 5:9–11 KJV)

As a result of his refusal to acknowledge the Lord's way, his leprosy clung to him. This is a good example of the difference between God's ways and humankind's ways. It made no sense to him, but Naaman's servants went to him and asked, "My father, *if* the prophet had bid thee *do some* great thing, wouldest thou not have done *it*? how much rather then, when he saith to thee, Wash, and be clean?" (2 Kings 5:13 KJV). Having nothing to lose, he went and "dipped himself seven times in Jordan, according to the saying of the man of God: and his flesh came again like unto the flesh of a little child, and he was clean" (2 Kings 5:14 KJV).

What do you have to lose by turning the remainder of your life over to the guidance and direction of the Lord? "Trust in the Lord with all your heart and lean not on your own understanding; in all your ways submit to him, and he will make your paths straight" (Proverbs 3:5–6).

LESSON 14

WALKING IN HUMILITY AND THE FEAR OF THE LORD

PROVERBS 3:7-8

*⁷ Do not be wise in your own eyes; fear the L*ORD *and shun evil.*
⁸ This will bring health to your body and nourishment to your bones.

The Roman philosopher Seneca once stated, "I suppose that many might have attained to wisdom, had they not thought they already attained it" (Bridges 1846/1968, footnotes, p. 26). Murphy (1998) posed the following question, "When does wisdom cease to be wisdom?" And then answered it, "When you think you are wise" (p. 21). Isaiah warned, "Woe to those who are wise in their own eyes and clever in their own sight" (Isaiah 5:21). The apostle Paul warned the Galatians, "If a man think himself to be something, when he is nothing, he deceiveth himself" (Galatians 6:3 KJV). And the apostle Peter, who knew what it was to eat humble pie, was emphatic, "Humble yourselves therefore under the mighty hand of God, that he may exalt you in due time" (1 Peter 5:6 KJV).

NAVIGATING THE WALK OF HUMILITY

The scriptures must be our guide. Humbling oneself requires purposeful action. "Boasters and braggarts must learn a new vocabulary if they are to pursue humility. They must change their sentence structures. They need to learn to speak and live in ways that exalt the Lord Jesus Christ rather than themselves" (Johnson 2010, winter, p. 34). It's difficult to hide pride for very long. Even if the proud individual doesn't recognize pride, others are quick to identify it. A person's expressions tend to show one's level of arrogance.

There is a fine line between humility and pride masquerading as humility. When I was a young minister and someone complimented my preaching, I would deflect the compliment by crediting the Lord for any good that was accomplished. I was disingenuous because I enjoyed the compliment but rejected it outwardly. It would have been more honest and a greater expression of humility to simply have said, "Thank you," rather than, "Don't thank me; thank the Lord." In deflecting the compliment, I was rejecting the expression of gratitude from the one caring enough to express it, yet I was receiving the affirmation I desired.

> There is a fine line between humility and pride masquerading as humility.

Unfortunately, when you give in to pride, you create a barrier between God and yourself. And while humility in itself cannot purchase the blessings of God, it opens the channel to His blessings.

> If my people, which are called by my name, shall humble themselves, and pray, and seek my face, and turn from their wicked ways; then will I hear from heaven, and will forgive their sin, and will heal their land. (2 Chronicles 7:14 KJV)

When a Roman centurion approached Jesus with a need, humility opened the way for an answer:

> The centurion replied, "Lord, I do not deserve to have you come under my roof. But just say the word, and my servant will be healed. For I myself am a man under authority, with soldiers under me. I tell this one, 'Go,' and he goes; and that one, 'Come,' and he comes. I say to my servant, 'Do this,' and he does it." (Matthew 8:8–9)

The Lord responded to the combination of faith and humility, and the centurion received an answer to his petition: "Go! Let it be done just as you believed it would" (Matthew 8:13).

God's ways often seem paradoxical to the human mind; they seem illogical. For example, "Those who exalt themselves will be humbled, and those who humble themselves will be exalted" (Matthew 23:12 NLT). Logic often keeps people from receiving what God desires to give them. Logic says, "Be strong and overpower your opponent. Conquer by might, deception, and manipulation." God says, "Humble yourself, and I will lift you up. I will cause you to excel. Humble yourself and your gift will make room for itself because I have the power to place you in positions you never dreamed were possible." Therefore, there is no need to envy another's gift. "A man's gift maketh room for him, and bringeth him before great men" (Proverbs 18:16 KJV).

> God's ways often seem paradoxical to the human mind; they seem illogical.

The church is described in scriptures as the body of Christ. All that is said about our natural bodies can be said about the body of Christ. The apostle Paul emphasized this when writing to the church at Rome. He stated that just as each member of our natural body has a purpose and function, so do the members of the body of Christ. There are different gifts, and whatever your gift is, it should be used for the glory of God. (See Romans 12:4–8.) But no one gift is more significant than another:

> The eye cannot say to the hand, "I have no need of you," nor again the head to the feet, "I have no need of you." On the contrary, the parts of the body that seem to be weaker are indispensable, and on those parts of the body that we think less honorable we bestow the greater honor, and our unpresentable parts are treated with greater modesty, which our more presentable parts do not require. But God has so composed the body, giving greater honor to the part that lacked it, that there may be no division in the body, but that the members may have the same care for one another. (1 Corinthians 12:21–25 ESV)

Since these gifts are God-given, a superior attitude or self-righteousness only becomes an impediment to a person's usefulness in the kingdom of God.

FEARING GOD—ACKNOWLEDGING GOD IS RIGHT

"Do not be wise in your own eyes; fear the LORD and shun evil. This will bring health to your body and nourishment to your bones" (Proverbs 3:7–8). The scriptures are replete with examples of those who were benefited by fearing God. For example, "The midwives, however, feared God and did not do what the king of Egypt had told them to do; they let the boys live" (Exodus 1:17). They stood for their convictions because they feared God. When Moses's father-in-law, Jethro, spoke to him about the art of delegation, among the characteristics Moses considered essential to leadership was the fear of God: "Select capable men from all the people—men who fear God, trustworthy men who hate dishonest gain" (Exodus 18:21).

The law of God cites fear of God as a reason to treat the disabled well: "Thou shalt not curse the deaf, nor put a stumblingblock before the blind, but shalt fear thy God" (Leviticus 19:14 KJV). Likewise, it is given as a reason to respect the elderly: "Stand up in the presence of the elderly, and show respect for the aged. Fear your God" (Leviticus 19:32 NLT). In the New Testament, the apostle Paul commanded the Corinthians to "cleanse [themselves] from all filthiness of the flesh and spirit, perfecting holiness in the fear of God" (2 Corinthians 7:1 KJV).

To be God-fearing, you need to stop fearing what the world thinks of you and can do to you and start fearing the one who judges you for all eternity. Jesus declared that humankind would be better off to enter heaven missing parts than to continue through this life whole and end up in hell:

> If your hand or your foot causes you to stumble, cut it off and throw it away. It is better for you to enter life maimed or crippled than to have two hands or two feet and be thrown into eternal fire. And if your eye causes you to stumble, gouge it out and throw it away. It is better for you to enter life with one eye than to have two eyes and be thrown into the fire of hell. (Matthew 18:8–9)

If you are God-fearing, you need to stop fearing what the world thinks of you and can do to you and start fearing the one who judges you for all eternity.

William D. Eisenhower (1986), writing in *Christianity Today*, made the following observation:

> Unfortunately, many of us presume that the world is the ultimate threat and that God's function is to offset it. How different this is from the biblical position that God is scarier than the world by far …

When we assume that the world is the ultimate threat, we give it unwarranted power, for in truth, the world's threats are temporary. When we expect God to balance the stress of the world, we reduce him to the world's equal.

… As I walk with the Lord, I discover that God poses an ominous threat to my ego, but not to me; that he stands over against my delusions, but not against the truth that sets me free; that he casts me down, but only to lift me up; that he sits in judgment of my sin, but forgives me nevertheless. The fear of the Lord is the beginning of wisdom, but love is its completion. (p. 34)

FEARING GOD AND SHUNNING EVIL

"Do not be wise in your own eyes; fear the LORD and shun evil. This will bring health to your body and nourishment to your bones" (Proverbs 3:7–8). Joseph is one of the greatest examples of a man shunning sin as a direct result of fearing God. Imagine the setting. He was rejected by his brothers and sold into slavery. Any future he would have had in his father's house was gone. As a slave, it was unlikely he would ever have a wife, but that did not diminish the desire for a romantic relationship with the opposite sex. The opportunity to yield to the lust of the flesh lay before him when, on more than one occasion, his master's wife attempted to seduce him. Joseph had complete control of the affairs of the household. How easy it would have been to reason that he was just a slave and had no choice but to do what she demanded. Or how easy it would have been to have allowed entitlement thinking to take advantage of the moment. But "No!" Joseph feared God, and his fear of God drove him to shun evil.

Unfortunately, godly behavior in the face of Satan's seductions did not keep him from prison, but it kept him from eternal destruction, and eventually it resulted in his elevation to a position of power, second only to the king. When tempted, he declared the following:

"No one is greater in this house than I am. My master has withheld nothing from me except you, because you are his wife. How then could I do such a wicked thing and sin against God?" And though she spoke to Joseph day after day, he refused to go to bed with her or even be with her. (Genesis 39:9–10)

Like Joseph, Job maintained his integrity in the midst of great trial. Utter despair may have filled Job's heart, but he didn't give up on God. He was steadfast in his convictions. Likewise, we must avoid falling prey to the temptation to give up on God when He seems so far away. "He that endureth to the end shall be saved" (Matthew 10:22 KJV).

With his wealth taken and all his children dead, Job had only his wife. And then, as he sat on an ash heap in pain from the boils covering his body, his wife mocked his integrity. Instead of standing by his side and encouraging him to press on, she railed on him, "Are you maintaining your integrity? Curse God and die!" (Job 2:9) It's difficult to imagine the intensity of the temptation to quit, to give up on God. However, Job's integrity was greater than his discouragement. He did not allow her criticism to destroy his own sense of personal integrity. We, too, must learn to do the same.

Like Joseph, giving into temptation was not an option. The thought of it was foolishness, and to discuss it would have been foolish talk. His response to the voice of temptation was simply this, "Should we accept only good things from the hand of God and never anything bad?" (Job 2:10 NLT).

> Job's integrity was greater than his discouragement.

Job had learned a secret to maintaining his faith and his integrity in the face of temptation. He worshiped:

> Then Job arose, and rent his mantle, and shaved his head, and fell down upon the ground, and worshipped, And said, Naked came I out of my mother's womb,

and naked shall I return thither: the LORD gave, and the LORD hath taken away; blessed be the name of the LORD. In all this Job sinned not, nor charged God foolishly. (Job 1:20–22 KJV)

"Give thanks in all circumstances, for this [the giving of thanks] is God's will for you in Christ Jesus" (1 Thessalonians 5:18). Some folks drop out of relationship with God the first time adversity hits them. Job, on the other hand, trusted God to see him through the best of times and the worst of times. Regardless of his suffering, his faith was fixed in God:

But [God] knows where I am and what I've done. He can cross-examine me all he wants, and I'll pass the test with honors. I've followed him closely, my feet in his footprints, not once swerving from his way. I've obeyed every word he's spoken, and not just obeyed his advice—I've treasured it. (Job 23:10–12 MSG)

HEALTH TO YOUR BODY—A TESTIMONY OF THE GOODNESS OF GOD

"Do not be wise in your own eyes; fear the LORD and shun evil. This will bring health to your body and nourishment to your bones" (Proverbs 3:7–8). Yes! Fearing God and shunning evil will bring health to your body and nourishment to your bones! Peace of mind, a cheerful attitude, a good temper, and choosing not to be anxious but trusting in the Lord are the fruit of fearing God and shunning evil. And all these are highly correlated with longevity. Insurance companies have made this discovery, and actuarial tables validate that the children of God possess the earth, while the lives of the wicked are cut short.

Though both Joseph and Job went through trying times for very specific reasons, generally it is not the Lord's desire for His people to live miserable lives. Jesus Himself declared, "My purpose is to give them a rich and satisfying life" (John 10:10 NLT). When you reap the benefits of fearing God and shunning evil, it is a testimony to those not yet converted: "The people of the world will see all the good I do for my people, and they will tremble with awe at the peace and prosperity I provide for them" (Jeremiah 33:9 NLT).

It's unfortunate that some church bodies have chosen "to be wise in their own eyes" and violate the Word of God. This human wisdom touted under the guise of Christianity has wormed its way into a culture that was once Christian. Some have accepted such ungodly philosophies as abortion on demand, euthanasia, no-fault divorce, premarital sex, and homosexual lifestyle. A church body can be the salt of the earth and the light of the world only when it follows God's Word and lives out His teachings. To fail to do so results in being nothing more than another social club or get-together. "Professing themselves to be wise, they became fools" (Romans 1:22 KJV).

> A church body can be the salt of the earth and the light of the world only when it follows God's Word and lives out His teachings.

When you are enjoying the fruit of God's blessings don't get careless and forget the source of those blessings. Those blessings remain a testimony of the goodness of God only as long as they are associated with righteousness. Korah wrote a song to remind Israel: "Oh yes. God gives Goodness and Beauty; our land responds with Bounty and Blessing. Right Living strides out before him, and clears a path for his passage" (Psalm 85:12–13 MSG). In all of your enjoying the blessings of the Lord, you must stride in "right living" and be prepared for His coming at any moment.

NOURISHMENT TO YOUR BONES—
INTEGRITY OF CHARACTER

"Do not be wise in your own eyes; fear the Lord and shun evil. This will bring health to your body and nourishment to your bones" (Proverbs

3:7–8). It might seem that health to your body and nourishment to your bones could have been covered under a single heading, but I believe there is a distinct difference. Bones make up the skeleton of the body, and without the skeleton, the body would be nothing more than a blob of soft tissue. It is possible for a person to live in the blessings of God but lack integrity because there are dark secrets within that no one but God can see. However, just as a building or a bridge will eventually collapse when the integrity of the structure is compromised, so will the Christian.

Power and prestige present additional risks to the life of every Christian. They are seductive, and if you are not careful, these forces will become a threat to the integrity of your Christian walk. Achieving or inheriting honor and power increases your vulnerability to becoming wise in your own eyes. When that occurs, it is easy to lose the fear of God, and at that point, evil is only a step away. In fact, at that point, evil is already present because sins of omission have taken up residence. Don't be deceived; omission of humility and the fear of God is sin.

> Achieving or inheriting honor and power increases your vulnerability to becoming wise in your own eyes.

Integrity is the quality of being of sound moral principle; uprightness; honesty; and sincerity. Job stands out as one of the greatest examples of integrity, so much so that the LORD put confidence in Job's sound moral principles. Because of his integrity, the LORD allowed Satan to test him twice. The LORD believed Job possessed internal braces sufficient to withstand Satan's outer forces thrown against him:

> Then the LORD asked Satan, "Have you noticed my servant Job? He is the finest man in all the earth. He is blameless—a man of complete integrity. He fears God and stays away from evil. And he has maintained his integrity, even though you urged me to harm him without cause." (Job 2:3 NLT).

Humility, fear of God, and resisting evil when it first appears brings health to the bones. These characteristics provide soundness to your entire being. A good indicator of these characteristics is the willingness to be proven. Job went so far as to put himself on the line with God: "Let God weigh me in honest scales and he will know that I am blameless" (Job 31:6).

When Job came out on the other side of that terrible trial, he still possessed his integrity. And the LORD took note of it and commended Job when He spoke to Job's accusers, "I am angry with you and your two friends, because you have not spoken the truth about me, as my servant Job has" (Job 42:7). The health of Job's body may have been weakened for a time, but his integrity was still intact. He possessed internal fortitude sufficient to withstand all the outer forces Satan could throw against him. In fact, Job went so far as to declare that if he died and his body decomposed, he still would someday see God in a new body: "And after my body has decayed, yet in my body I will see God!" (Job 19:26 NLT). One may wonder how Job held up under such testing, but it was quite simple; he was humble in spirit, he feared God, and he shunned evil.

IN CLOSING

"Do not be wise in your own eyes; fear the LORD and shun evil. This will bring health to your body and nourishment to your bones" (Proverbs 3:7–8). It all begins with humility and the willingness to confront pride whenever it raises its ugly head. To truly fear God and maintain pride in one's heart at the same time is quite impossible. But "humility opens the door to allow the grace of God to operate within the life of a believer" (Johnson 2010, winter, p. 38).

Jesus taught humility as the gate into the kingdom of God: "Great blessings belong to those who know they are spiritually in need. God's kingdom belongs to them" (Matthew 5:3 ERV). That's a great way to describe the humble: "They are spiritually in need of God." Unless you recognize that you are spiritually in need of God, you are not going to fear God. And if you don't fear God, it is unlikely that you will shun evil when challenging times arise. If a person fears God, they have no reason to fear anything else. On the other hand, if a person does not fear God, then fear becomes a way of life. Job feared God, so he did not fear the opinions of others when put on trial.

Oh, yes, Job felt the pressure of being on trial. His wife told him to plead no contest and accept the death penalty. But Job refused; he was entitled to his day in court. Three skilled prosecutors sat at the table a few feet away from his table. He sat alone at his table. The judge remained silent throughout the proceedings. Each prosecutor—Eliphaz, Bildad, and Zophar—put forth their best evidence of Job's guilt. No longer being able to even afford an attorney, he attempted to defend himself alone. Each prosecutor spoke, and Job put forth his rebuttal:

> So hold your tongue while I have my say, then I'll take whatever I have coming to me. Why do I go out on a limb like this and take my life in my hands? Because even if he killed me, I'd keep on hoping. I'd defend my innocence to the very end. Just wait, this is going to work out for the best—my salvation! If I were guilt-stricken do you think I'd be doing this—laying myself on the line before God? You'd better pay attention to what I'm telling you, listen carefully with both ears. Now that I've laid out my defense, I'm sure that I'll be acquitted. Can anyone prove charges against me? I've said my piece. I rest my case. (Job 13:13–19 MSG)

You too can rest your case. Aspire to live a life of humility, always fear God more than humankind, and shun evil regardless of the situation. Situational ethics is another of those ungodly philosophies that has wormed its way into the thinking of modern Christianity. Instead, like Job, be prepared to lay your life on the line before God and trust Him, even if it seems that death is imminent. Rest your case. The Judge is listening, even if He hasn't said a word. This will bring health to your body and nourishment to your bones.

LESSON 15

THE BLESSING OF GIVING

PROVERBS 3:9-10

⁹ Honor the LORD with your wealth, with the firstfruits of all your crops; ¹⁰ then your barns will be filled to overflowing, and your vats will brim over with new wine.

Jesus gave a simple principle concerning giving:

> Give, and it shall be given unto you; good measure, pressed down, and shaken together, and running over, shall men give into your bosom. For with the same measure that ye mete withal it shall be measured to you again. (Luke 6:38 KJV)

THE HISTORY OF TITHING

This principle of giving did not suddenly appear when Jesus arrived upon the earth. It was woven into the fabric of the Old Testament as well. For example, the first mention of tithes was in the days of Abraham, after he returned from defeating Kedorlaomer and his allies.

And Melchizedek king of Salem brought forth bread and wine: and he was the priest of the most high God. And he blessed him, and said, Blessed *be* Abram of the most high God, possessor of heaven and earth: And blessed be the most high God, which hath delivered thine enemies into thy hand. And [Abram] gave [Melchizedek] tithes of all. (Genesis 14:18–20 KJV)

Moses urged the Israelites, "Bring the best of the firstfruits of your soil to the house of the Lord your God" (Exodus 23:19). Concerning this Old Testament command, Matthew Henry (n.d.) wrote, "God, who is the first and best, must have the first and best of everything; his right is prior to all other, and therefore he must be served first" (Vol. 3, p. 804). Scripturally, the tithe is the firstfruits of one's increase. According to the law, the tithe belongs to the Lord even before it is given. "And all the tithe of the land, *whether* of the seed of the land, *or* of the fruit of the tree, *is* the Lord's: *it is* holy unto the Lord" (Leviticus 27:30 KJV). Therefore, tithes are not paid or given to the Lord; they are returned to the Lord. It is a matter of lordship. It is honoring the Lord with the firstfruits of one's crops, or the increase of one's wealth.

> Tithes are not paid or given to the Lord; they are returned to the Lord.

OUR ATTITUDE TOWARD GIVING

Our attitude toward all giving, whether tithes or offerings, is of utmost importance. "Each one must give as he has decided in his heart, not reluctantly or under compulsion, for God loves a cheerful giver" (2 Corinthians 9:7 ESV). The word translated *cheerful* in this verse is derived from the Greek word *hilaros*, from which the English language derives the word *hilarious*. When we give, we are not to give "reluctantly, or under compulsion" but "cheerfully." Though the tithe is a command of God, it must never be perceived as a tax. When the first tenth is returned to the Lord, attitude is of utmost importance. One's willingness to give to God is a good indication of the condition of the heart. "For where your treasure is, there will your heart be also" (Luke 12:34 KJV). The following illustration speaks of the deceitfulness of the heart:

> A man … came to Peter Marshall, former chaplain of the Unites States Senate, with a concern about tithing. He said: "I have a problem. I have been tithing for some time. It wasn't too bad when I was making $20,000 a year. I could afford to give the $2,000. But you see, now I am making $500,000, and there is just no way I can afford to give away $50,000 a year."
>
> Dr. Marshall reflected on this wealthy man's dilemma but gave no advice. He simply said: "Yes, sir. I see that you do have a problem. I think we ought to pray about it. Is that alright?"
>
> The man agreed, so Dr. Marshall bowed his head and prayed with boldness and authority. "Dear Lord, this man has a problem, and I pray that you will help him. Lord, reduce his salary back to the place where he can afford to tithe." (Harney 2005, p. 200)

One's willingness to give to God is a good indication of the condition of the heart.

THE IMPORTANCE OF TITHING

The importance God places on tithing is seen in the conquering of the city of Jericho. Jericho was the first of ten cities the Israelites were to capture upon entering Canaan. It was to be God's tithe of the land they were conquering. They were told, "Jericho and everything in it…

made from silver, gold, bronze, or iron is sacred to the LORD and must be brought into his treasury" (Joshua 6:17, 19 NLT).

When Achan violated God's tithe principle by taking that which belonged to the LORD, a curse came upon the Israelites in their next battle. The men of Ai, a very small community, drove the Israelites back and killed about sixteen Israelite soldiers. Joshua was distraught, and he sought the LORD. The LORD informed him that there was sin in the camp. It was discovered that Achan had put his hand upon the tithe that belonged to the LORD. When Joshua sought the LORD, he learned a very important principle: "Israel has sinned and broken my covenant! They have stolen some of the things that I commanded must be set apart for me" (Joshua 7:11 NLT).

It's frightening to consider using, or even withholding, the things devoted to the Lord when you realize how strongly the Lord feels about it: "And all Israel stoned him with stones, and burned them with fire, after they had stoned them with stones" (Joshua 7:25 KJV). You will never gain by taking from or withholding from the Lord.

GIVEN TO SUSTAIN THE MINISTRY

Under the law, the tithe was given to sustain the ministry. It's important to note that it was to sustain not a minister but the ministry:

> And, behold, I have given the children of Levi all the [tithe] in Israel for an inheritance, for their service which they serve ... *it shall be* a statute for ever throughout your generations ... the tithes of the children of Israel, which they offer ..., I have given to the Levites to inherit. (Numbers 18:21, 23–24 KJV)

Under the law, the tithe was given to sustain the ministry. It's important to note that it was to sustain not a minister but the ministry.

LORIN BRADBURY, PH.D.

According to the apostle Paul, the New Testament ministry, as well as the Old Testament ministry, was granted permission by the law to receive a living from the firstfruits:

> What soldier has to pay his own expenses? What farmer plants a vineyard and doesn't have the right to eat some of its fruit? What shepherd cares for a flock of sheep and isn't allowed to drink some of the milk? ... For the law of Moses says, "You must not muzzle an ox to keep it from eating as it treads out the grain." Was God thinking only about oxen when he said this? Wasn't he actually speaking to us? Yes, it was written for us, so that the one who plows and the one who threshes the grain might both expect a share of the harvest.
>
> Since we have planted spiritual seed among you, aren't we entitled to a harvest of physical food and drink? If you support others who preach to you, shouldn't we have an even greater right to be supported? (1 Corinthians 9:7, 9–12 NLT)

In the Old Testament, the Levites who derived their living from the tithe were required to return a tithe of what they received, just like everyone else. The LORD instructed Moses:

> When ye take of the children of Israel the tithes which I have given you from them for your inheritance, then ye shall offer up an heave offering of it for the LORD, *even* a tenth *part* of the tithe. (Numbers 18:26 KJV).

So, when it came to tithing, no one was exempt. Based on this principle, it is reasonable to conclude that those who derive their living from the tithe today must also tithe.

> When it came to tithing, no one was exempt.

AN OPEN DOOR OF BLESSING

Tithing is an open door of blessing. You cannot out give God. In the book of Malachi, the LORD challenged Israel to tithe with the promise that they could not out give Him:

> Will a man rob God? Yet ye have robbed me. But ye say, Wherein have we robbed thee? In tithes and offerings. Ye *are* cursed with a curse: for ye have robbed me, *even* this whole nation. Bring ye all the tithes into the storehouse, that there may be meat in mine house, and prove me now herewith, saith the LORD of hosts, if I will not open you the windows of heaven, and pour you out a blessing, that *there shall not be room* enough to receive it. And I will rebuke the devourer for your sakes, and he shall not destroy the fruits of your ground; neither shall your vine cast her fruit before the time in the field, saith the LORD of hosts. (Malachi 3:8–11 KJV)

I am reminded of the following illustration:

> A generous and greatly blessed Christian … once was asked how he could give so much to the Lord's work and still possess great wealth. The man replied, "Oh, as I shovel it out, He shovels it in. The Lord has a bigger shovel." (Johnson 2009, fall, p. 79)

Israel was robbing God by not tithing, and they didn't even realize it. This principle is just as real in the New Testament. Many rob God by failing to return to Him what belongs to Him, and as a result, they miss out on His bountiful blessings. Therefore, "Honor the LORD with your wealth, with the firstfruits of all your crops; then your barns will be filled to overflowing, and your vats will brim over with new wine" (Proverbs 3:9–10). This is "the way to make a little much, and much more; it is the surest and safest method of thriving" (Henry, Vol. 3, p. 804). The more God gives us, the more we should strive to honor him with our substance. Paul wrote that God blesses you so that you can bless someone else: "You will be enriched in every way so that you can be generous on every occasion" (2 Corinthians 9:11).

> God blesses you so that you can bless someone else.

J. B. Phillips (1995) wrote the following personal testimony:

> My father taught me the grace of giving. He had a small automobile business in southern Wales. He bought, fixed, and sold cars. One of a handful of craftsmen in our hometown who were licensed to work on Rolls Royce cars, he was generous and consistent giver to the Lord's work all his life ...
>
> His small business survived the hard times of the great depression but when World War II broke out, my father faced ruin. Food was heavily rationed and gasoline even more so. The government commandeered all private cars; only individuals doing essential war business could own one. No new cars were made for the civilian market; factories were turned over to production of tanks and guns. My father laid off his employees and paced the floor of his workshop as he prayed. He faced certain bankruptcy.
>
> Just then he heard a footstep behind him. He turned and recognized the manager of a large Austin car dealership that owned a fleet of several hundred rental cars. The man said, "How are you, Leonard?"
>
> "I'm not sure, Mr. Brooks," responded my father. "I think I'm going to have to close." Little did my father realize that God had sent him an angel unawares.

The Austin dealer was in a similar squeeze. He could not buy any new cars either. Another problem was how to keep his fleet of rental cars running throughout the war years. He had no mechanics; all the men he had were in the armed services.

"Len," he said, "I'd like to bring you an engine to be rebored and rebuilt. We can get the parts. What do you say?" The next day an engine along with pistons, rings, valves, and spark plugs was delivered to my father's workshop. Two days later my father returned the rebored and rebuilt engine to the dealer.

A week passed. Then once more Mr. Brooks appeared in my father's empty shop. ... "Now how many engines can you rebore and rebuild in a week? We will keep you supplied until the war ends." Mr. Brooks was as good as his word, and God was as good as His Word. (p. 85)

IN CLOSING

God is as good as His Word, and His Word says, "Prove me and see if I will not open the windows of heaven." He desires to bless His people, but His hands are tied when His people sin by stealing from Him by withholding tithes and offerings. As a child of God, it is a privilege to give to God. It is an honor to be trusted with that which belongs to God, and it is an honor to return it to its rightful owner. "Honor the LORD with your wealth, with the firstfruits of all your crops" (Proverbs 3:9).

LESSON 16

DISCIPLINE OF THE LORD

PROVERBS 3:11-12

¹¹ My son, do not despise the LORD's discipline, and do not resent his rebuke, ¹² because the LORD disciplines those he loves, as a father the son he delights in.

INTRODUCTION

Discipline is not a bad word, and it should not be thought of as something painful. Correction is not rejection. If one remains open to discipline, it can be a positive experience. The writer of Hebrews reminded his readers of that fact with a question:

> Have you forgotten the encouraging words God spoke to you as his children? He said, "My child, don't make light of the Lord's discipline, and don't give up when he corrects you. For the Lord disciplines those he loves, and he punishes each one he accepts as his child." (Hebrews 12:5–6 NLT)

Charles Bridges (1846/1968) wrote, "We need [the rod] as much as our daily bread. Children of God are still children of Adam; with Adam's will, pride, independence, and waywardness" (pp. 27–28).

DISCIPLINE—THE GRACE OF GOD

Before the rod is ever considered, the Lord gives a gentle nudge in the direction of righteousness. In fact, it's likely He gives a series of nudges before the rod is ever applied. We see this in the LORD's dealings with Cain. At the end of the harvest season, Cain brought a sampling of his crops to the LORD as a sacrifice. Abel, in turn, brought a blood sacrifice. No doubt, Adam and Eve had carefully instructed both boys concerning the essentiality of a blood sacrifice. But Cain chose to do it his own way. "The LORD accepted Abel and his gift, but he did not accept Cain and his gift. This made Cain very angry, and he looked dejected" (Genesis 4:4–5 NLT).

> Before the rod is ever considered, the Lord gives a gentle nudge in the direction of righteousness.

Consider how the LORD could have dealt with Cain. He could have terminated any further communication with him, or worse yet, He could have destroyed him. Instead, we see a concerned father approaching him with grace:

> "Why are you so angry?" the LORD asked Cain. "Why do you look so dejected? You will be accepted if you do what is right. But if you refuse to do what is right, then watch out! Sin is crouching at the door, eager to control you. But you must subdue it and be its master." (Genesis 4:6–7 NLT)

The LORD didn't rail on him; instead, He provided fatherly direction—a gentle nudge in the right direction. He approached Cain with words of confidence. "Son, sin is crouching at your door, but you must master it. Son you can do it."

But as the story goes, Cain rejected the correction and the grace of God. We learn that "Cain suggested to his brother, 'Let's go out into the fields.' And while they were in the field, Cain attacked his brother, Abel, and killed him'" (Genesis 4:8 NLT).

However, grace is not easily discouraged, and one more time the LORD tried to reach him with a gentle nudge: "Where *is* Abel thy brother? And he said, I know not: *Am* I my brother's keeper? And he said, What hast thou done? the voice of thy brother's blood crieth unto me from the ground" (Genesis 4:9–10 KJV).

> Grace is not easily discouraged.

The LORD had nothing but good in mind for Cain. Instead of responding to the grace offered by the hand of the LORD, we find an angry man, rejecting loving correction. No doubt, this has been repeated untold times. "Often do we see the child of God ... He is irritated by looking at the rod, rather than the hand that inflicts it. He shrinks from searching into the cause. He disregards his Father's loving voice and purpose" (Bridges 1846/1968, p. 28). Consider Asa's response to the corrective word that came through the prophet Hanani. Asa was king of Judah, and out of fear, he entered into a treaty with Ben-Hadad of Aram. The prophet Hanani came to him and gently rebuked him for allowing the king of Aram to slip through his fingers. Instead of falling on his face before the LORD and repenting, "Asa became so angry with Hanani for saying this that he threw him into prison and put him in stocks" (2 Chronicles 16:10 NLT). He refused to look into the need for correction and disregarded the grace of his heavenly Father.

LIMITATIONS OF GRACE

Some perceive that the grace of God is limitless, but there seems to be a limit to grace, though it's unclear as to exactly where that line of demarcation lies. Cain crossed that line and never again experienced the tender voice of the LORD. The last words he heard from the LORD were these:

Now *art* thou cursed from the earth, which hath opened her mouth to receive thy brother's blood from thy hand; When thou tillest the ground, it shall not henceforth yield unto thee her strength; a fugitive and a vagabond shalt thou be in the earth. (Genesis 4:11–12 KJV)

And in response, "Cain said unto the LORD, My punishment *is* greater than I can bear" (Genesis 4:13 KJV).

Very possibly the greatest example of the Lord's attempt to steer someone away from sin and toward the path of righteousness is the story of Judas Iscariot. How many times had the Lord offered him the hand of grace before that critical moment when he crossed the line of no return? On the night of the Last Supper, Jesus stated, "One of you which eateth with me shall betray me" (Mark 14:18 KJV). They were shocked and began to question who it might be. Jesus responded, "*It is* one of the Twelve" (Mark 14:20 KJV). Then he dropped another hint, "One who dips bread into the bowl with me … But woe to that man who betrays the Son of Man! It would be better for him if he had not been born'" (Mark 14:20–21). Judas failed to respond to this last offer of grace, and in doing so, he moved beyond the reach of the arm of grace: "Judas threw the money into the temple and left. Then he went away and hanged himself" (Matthew 27:5). As abundant as grace is, Judas could not find a place of repentance. What a horrible state to be in! It was an unnecessary state because the will of God will never lead you where the grace of God cannot keep you.

> The will of God will never lead you where the grace of God cannot keep you.

KEPT BY THE GRACE OF GOD

I wonder how many times we have been kept by the grace of God when we didn't do the will of God. Balaam was one of those infamous individuals who heard the voice of God but seemed to pick and choose what he wanted to obey. Initially, he appeared to follow the LORD by obeying the voice of God:

> And God said unto Balaam, Thou shalt not go with them; thou shalt not curse the people: for they *are* blessed. And Balaam rose up in the morning, and said unto the princes of Balak, Get you into your land: for the LORD refuseth to give me leave to go with you. (Numbers 22:12–13 KJV)

When the Lord places limitations in our lives, they are for our benefit and should never be thought of as offensive. Sometimes when the Lord speaks, the answer is simply, "No!" That doesn't mean Satan accepts the answer of "No!" and goes off to never return. Additionally, the flesh continues its longing to be satisfied. For example:

> Balak sent yet again princes, more, and more honourable than they. And they came to Balaam, and said to him, Thus saith Balak the son of Zippor, Let nothing, I pray thee, hinder thee from coming unto me: For I will promote thee unto very great honour, and I will do whatsoever thou sayest unto me: come therefore, I pray thee, curse me this people. And Balaam answered and said unto the servants of Balak, If Balak would give me his house full of silver and gold, I cannot go beyond the word of the LORD my God, to do less or more. (Numbers 22:15–18 KJV)

> When the Lord places limitations in our lives, they are for our benefit and should never be thought of as offensive.

So far, so good. Except for the fact that Balaam shouldn't have gone with Balak once he knew the will of God. All seemed well up to this point, but Satan knows the pathways to a person's heart. John wrote that there are three avenues that Satan uses to tempt people—"The lust of the flesh, and the lust of the eyes, and the pride of life" (1 John 2:16 KJV). Seeing the offer of glitter and gold, Balaam returned to the LORD in prayer, hoping the LORD would change His mind. Balaam's attempt to negotiate with the LORD was a manifestation of fleshly lust. Given his propensity to fleshly lusts, Balaam was nothing more than a prophet for hire.

IGNORING CORRECTION— REJECTING GRACE

Is there a price at which you can be bought? Balaam's rejection of God's command not to go with Balak was a demonstration of his unrestrained sinful nature. It was greed, and it was pride. Notice the deceptiveness of the human heart. Seeing the more distinguished princes and the more handsome rewards, Balaam instructed his tempters, "Now spend the night here so I can find out what else the LORD will tell me" (Numbers 22:19). He even made it a matter of prayer, and God seemed to respond: "That night God came to Balaam and said, 'If these men have come to summon you, go with them, but do only what I tell you'" (Numbers 22:20 GW). "Wow! Maybe God *will* change His mind!" Do you ever try to convince the Lord to change His mind? The truth is you don't want the Lord to change His mind once He has told you "No." To do so puts you in a category with "those who follow the corrupt desire of the flesh and despise authority" (2 Peter 2:10). It is interesting to note how Peter described those individuals: "They have left the straight way and wandered off to follow the way of Balaam son of Bezer, who loved the wages of wickedness" (2 Peter 2:15). Balaam was bent on personal gain, and he wanted the LORD to help him accomplish it. But the LORD corrected Balaam: "A donkey, which normally can't talk, spoke with a human voice and wouldn't allow the prophet to continue his insanity" (2 Peter 2:16 GW). How much better off he would have been had he simply accepted "No" as an answer.

> You don't want the Lord to change His mind once He has told you "No."

Balaam's pleading with God to change His mind raises a question. Is there ever a time to plead with God for Him to change His mind? Yes! When Abraham pleaded for the lives of his family living in Sodom, his pleading was selfless. Also, in that case, the Lord had not previously said, "No." Instead, He said, "Yes," every time Abraham lowered the number necessary to spare the city.

THE STING OF CONVICTION—GRACE

Leaving behind the renegade prophet, we will consider a man after God's own heart. David is known as Israel's greatest king and as a man who truly loved God. But at the pinnacle of his career, he failed to listen to the grace of God. And God left the story of David's great sin in the Bible for all to learn from. It seems that David was in his palace relaxing when he should have been out on the front lines with his army. He arose from his bed and began to walk around on the flat roof of his palace. Looking down into the courtyard of his neighbor, he saw a beautiful young lady bathing. He sent someone to inquire as to who she was. The man he sent returned and put his life on the line by raising the question, "*Is* not this Bathsheba, the daughter of Eliam, the wife of Uriah the Hittite?" (2 Samuel 11:3 KJV). But at that point, even the knowledge of who she was didn't restrain David. "David sent messengers to go and bring Bathsheba to him. … She went to David, he had sexual relations with her, and then she went back to her house" (2 Samuel 11:4 ERV).

Sometime within the next couple of months, David received a note from Bathsheba informing him that she was pregnant and he was the father. David immediately went to work trying to cover his tracks. When he could not cover his dirty deed, he went a step further and had her husband murdered on the battlefield. After she completed the thirty-day mourning ritual, David sent for her, and she became his wife. "But the thing that David had done displeased the LORD" (2 Samuel 11:27 KJV).

The law allowed capital punishment for the crimes of adultery and murder, but grace provided a way of restoration. The prophet Nathan was the voice of God in David's day. He brought a word of conviction at the behest of the LORD. He began with a story:

> There were two men in a certain town. One was rich, and one was poor. The rich man owned a great many sheep and cattle. The poor man owned nothing but one little lamb he had bought. He raised that little lamb, and it grew up with his children. It ate from the man's own plate and drank from his cup. He cuddled it in his arms like a baby daughter. One day a guest arrived at the home of the rich man. But instead of killing an animal from his own flock or herd, he took the poor man's lamb and killed it and prepared it for his guest. (2 Samuel 12:1–4 NLT)

Upon hearing the story, David was furious. "'As surely as the LORD lives,' he vowed, 'any man who would do such a thing deserves to die! He must repay four lambs to the poor man for the one he stole and for having no pity'" (2 Samuel 12:5–6 NLT). He could see the awfulness of another's sin but not his own. It was at this point that the prophet delivered a convicting blow, "You are the man!" Through the voice of the prophet, the LORD brought a thundering rebuke. Yes, through the grace of God, David found forgiveness, but the penalty for his disobedience would be high:

> Because of what you have done, I will cause your own household to rebel against you. I will give your wives to another man before your very eyes, and he will go to bed with them in public view. You did it secretly, but I will make this happen to you openly in the sight of all Israel. (2 Samuel 12:11–12 NLT)

The sting of conviction brought David to his knees, and he penned the fifty-first psalm. The introductory note to the psalm explains why he wrote it: "To the chief Musician, A Psalm of David, when Nathan the prophet came unto him, after he had gone in to Bathsheba." It is far more important to save your soul than to save face. David fully understood that by writing out his confession, the world would forever talk about his great sin. What concerned him most was finding forgiveness from God and restoration of relationship with God: "Have mercy upon me, O God, according to thy lovingkindness: according unto the multitude of thy tender mercies blot out my transgressions. Wash me throughly from mine iniquity, and cleanse me from my sin" (Psalm 51:1–2 KJV).

> It is far more important to save your soul than to save face.

THE GRACE OF FATHER'S CORRECTION

Bridges (1846/1968) offers insight into the relationship between the correction of the Lord and the grace of the Lord: "But [the Lord's] rules imply much more than their negative meaning. Instead of *despising*, reverence *the chastening of the Lord*. Let it be a solemn remembrance to thee, that thou art under thy Father's *correction*" (p. 29). The discipline of the Lord can be heavy, and David experienced that heavy hand during the year between the night he slept with Bathsheba and the day God sent His rod in the hand of Nathan:

> When I refused to confess my sin, my body wasted away, and I groaned all day long. Day and night your hand of discipline was heavy on me. My strength evaporated like water in the summer heat.
>
> Finally, I confessed all my sins to you and stopped trying to hide my guilt. I said to myself, "I will confess my rebellion to the LORD." And you forgave me! All my guilt is gone. (Psalm 32:3–5 NLT)

David wrote, "Remove your scourge from me; I am overcome by the blow of your hand" (Psalm 39:10). But the discipline of the Lord will never be as heavy as the weight of sin and guilt. For the remainder of his days, David never forgot his sin and the mercy the LORD granted him. As a result, he was cautious in bringing judgment on others, and he saw affliction as possible correction from the LORD. When David was driven from his kingdom, he did not pass judgment on Shimei when he mocked him and threw stones at him. Instead, he looked inward to see if God might be disciplining him. When one of David's men wanted to kill the man, David looked inward and said, maybe "the LORD has told him to curse me" (2 Samuel 16:10 NLT).

> The discipline of the Lord can be heavy but never as heavy as the weight of sin and guilt.

When the kingdom finally was restored and David returned to Jerusalem, he demonstrated what it meant to be "a man after God's own heart":

> When Shimei son of Gera crossed the Jordan, he fell prostrate before the king and said to him, "May my lord not hold me guilty. Do not remember how your servant did wrong on the day my lord the king left Jerusalem. May the king put it out of his mind. For I your servant know that I have sinned, but today I have come here as the first from the tribes of Joseph to come down and meet my lord the king." (2 Samuel 19:18–20)

David forgave Shimei!

LORIN BRADBURY, PH.D.

IN CLOSING

When the still, small voice whispers in your ear, give heed! Listening to the Lord will save you a lot of pain, heartache, or embarrassment. When the Lord says, "No," accept it gracefully. Remember, Father knows best! If you ever see the bony finger of the prophet pointed in your face and hear his voice, don't become angry; instead, run to the altar. The grace of God may be administering the discipline of the Lord.

LESSON 17

MEET LADY WISDOM

PROVERBS 3:13-18

13 Blessed are those who find wisdom, those who gain understanding, 14 for she is more profitable than silver and yields better returns than gold. 15 She is more precious than rubies; nothing you desire can compare with her. 16 Long life is in her right hand; in her left hand are riches and honor. 17 Her ways are pleasant ways, and all her paths are peace. 18 She is a tree of life to those who embrace her; those who lay hold of her will be blessed.

Here, wisdom is portrayed as a lady everyone should want to meet and no one would want to live without. Lady Wisdom is worth more than all the money you could possibly acquire throughout a lifetime upon this earth. Eugene Peterson has a wonderful way of bringing scriptures to life through paraphrase:

> You're blessed when you meet Lady Wisdom, when you make friends with Madame Insight. She's worth far more than money in the bank; her friendship is better than a big salary. Her value exceeds all the trappings of wealth; nothing you could wish for holds a candle to her. With one hand she gives long life, with the other she confers recognition. Her manner is beautiful, her life wonderfully complete. She's the

very Tree of Life to those who embrace her. Hold her tight—and be blessed! (Proverbs 3:13–18 MSG)

We are living in what has come to be known as the information age. Copious quantities of information are literally at our fingertips, but information is not wisdom. Information is a collection of data; wisdom is the ability to make meaning out of those data and apply them to everyday living.

> Those who find wisdom are fortunate; they will be blessed when they gain understanding. Profit that comes from wisdom is better than silver and even the finest gold. Wisdom is worth more than fine jewels. Nothing you desire has more value. (Proverbs 3:13–15 ERV)

LADY WISDOM GUIDES

Lady Wisdom provides guidance in navigating the seas of life, conducting oneself in the affairs of everyday life, making right choices in relation to others, and providing insight into the true nature of things. She provides the ability to apply God's Word to your daily walk, not merely understanding but doing—acting on the truth of God's Word. Lady Wisdom guides in the art of Christian living. That being true, what sort of things does Lady Wisdom tell you about life?

- She warns you about the destructiveness of sexual promiscuity: "For the lips of an adulteress drip honey, and her speech is smoother than oil; but in the end she is bitter as gall, sharp as a double-edged sword. Her feet go down to death; her steps lead straight to the grave" (Proverbs 5:3–5).
- Lady Wisdom will "keep you from making wrong turns, or following the bad directions of those who are lost themselves" (Proverbs 2:12–13 MSG).

- Lady Wisdom teaches the virtue of hard work: "Go to the ant, you sluggard; consider its ways and be wise!" (Proverbs 6:6).

- She cautions you to be careful about the friends you choose: "He that walketh with wise *men* shall be wise: but a companion of fools shall be destroyed" (Proverbs 13:20 KJV).

- Lady Wisdom gives you guidance concerning speech: "Careful words make for a careful life; careless talk may ruin everything" (Proverbs 13:3 MSG).

- She tells you to be honest and upright in all your ways: "The LORD detests the use of dishonest scales, but he delights in accurate weights" (Proverbs 11:1 NLT).

- Lady Wisdom cautions you concerning the danger of starting a quarrel: "Starting a quarrel is like opening a floodgate, so stop before a dispute breaks out" (Proverbs 17:14 NLT).

- She is the greatest source of parental instruction: "Whoever spares the rod hates his son, but he who loves him is diligent to discipline him" (Proverbs 13:24 ESV).

When you follow the advice of Lady Wisdom, your life will be full, and your home will be a place of joy, laughter, and fulfillment. But how do you get this wisdom? How do you make Lady Wisdom a part of your home, your family, and your marriage? Do you come to know her by reading and studying? No! Do you come to know her by being smart or by being blessed with a high IQ? No! Is she the equivalent of common sense? No! Listen to what she says: "The fear of the LORD is the beginning of wisdom, and knowledge of the Holy One is understanding" (Proverbs 9:10). You come to know Lady Wisdom by acknowledging the Lord is sovereign and by obeying His commandments. Long life is in her right hand, and it is God's reward for obedience. "The teaching of the wise is a fountain of life, turning a person from the snares of death" (Proverbs 13:14). If you reject Lady Wisdom, you have increased your likelihood of dying early: "Those who fail to find me harm themselves; all who hate me love death" (Proverbs 8:36).

LONG LIFE IS IN HER RIGHT HAND

How can Lady Wisdom extend life?

- She can save you from infidelity and moral failure: "Drink water from your own cistern, running water from your own well. Should your springs overflow in the streets, your streams of water in the public squares? Let them be yours alone, never to be shared with strangers. May your fountain be blessed, and may you rejoice in the wife of your youth. A loving doe, a graceful deer—may her breasts satisfy you always, may you ever be intoxicated by her love" (Proverbs 5:15–19).
- Lady Wisdom can save you from a dangerous lifestyle: "The prudent see danger and take refuge, but the simple keep going and pay the penalty" (Proverbs 22:3).
- She can save you from the need to take revenge: "Do not say, 'I'll pay you back for this wrong!' Wait for the Lord, and he will avenge you" (Proverbs 20:22).
- Lady Wisdom can save you from the sin of drunkenness. You will never have to worry about becoming an alcoholic if you never start drinking alcohol: "Do not gaze at wine when it is red, when it sparkles in the cup, when it goes down smoothly! In the end it bites like a snake and poisons like a viper. Your eyes will see strange sights and your mind imagine confusing things" (Proverbs 23:31–33).

You will never have to worry about becoming an alcoholic if you never start drinking alcohol.

RICHES AND HONOR ARE
IN HER LEFT HAND

In Lady Wisdom's left hand are riches, and she provides guidance in the acquisition of material and monetary wealth. The book of Proverbs is replete with instruction in the care and use of financial blessings.

- Lady Wisdom preaches hard work as a means to acquiring and accumulating material and financial wealth: "Lazy hands make for poverty, but diligent hands bring wealth" (Proverbs 10:4).
- Along with hard work, she urges you to save: "Go to the ant, you sluggard; consider its ways and be wise! It has no commander, no overseer or ruler, yet it stores its provisions in summer and gathers its food at harvest" (Proverbs 6:6–8).
- Likewise, Lady Wisdom teaches the benefit of giving. By giving, you become a conduit from the Source of All Things to others: "One person gives freely, yet gains even more; another withholds unduly, but comes to poverty. A generous person will prosper; he who refreshes others will be refreshed" (Proverbs 11:24–25).
- She warns against the accumulation of debt: "The rich ruleth over the poor, and the borrower is servant to the lender" (Proverbs 22:7 KJV).
- Lady Wisdom warns against cosigning for another's debt: "My son, if you have put up security for your neighbor, if you have shaken hands in pledge for a stranger, you have been trapped by what you said, ensnared by the words of your mouth. So do this, my son, to free yourself, since you have fallen into your neighbor's hands: Go—to the point of exhaustion—and give your neighbor no rest! Allow no sleep to your eyes, no slumber to your eyelids. Free yourself, like a gazelle from the hand of the hunter, like a bird from the snare of the fowler" (Proverbs 6:1–5).

- She cries with a loud voice to those who might get caught up in get-rich-quick schemes: "A hard worker has plenty of food, but a person who chases fantasies ends up in poverty" (Proverbs 28:19 NLT).
- Also in her left hand is honor. "Cherish her, and she will exalt you; embrace her, and she will honor you" (Proverbs 4:8).
- Lady Wisdom declares: "With me are riches and honor, enduring wealth and prosperity" (Proverbs 8:18).

IN CLOSING

To have a blessed life, a life filled with joy, a heart filled with laughter, and a soul fully satisfied, you need Lady Wisdom. You can meet her only through a right relationship with the Lord. That right relationship begins by developing a healthy fear of the Lord. Fear, in this case, is the kind of awe you might have for the president or a visiting dignitary. It is a deference you express toward one who is infinitely greater and higher and more important than you. The fear of the Lord is reverence for the Lord and a desire to submit to Him, to love Him, and to obey Him.

The writer of Proverbs says you are blessed if you make Lady Wisdom your companion. Those who embrace her call her the Tree of Life. (See Proverbs 3:18). By eating her fruit, you gain life and health and happiness. No wonder we are told to "hold her tight!"

LESSON 18

A CASE FOR DESIGN

PROVERBS 3:19-20

¹⁹ *By wisdom the* Lord *laid the earth's foundations, by understanding he set the heavens in place;* ²⁰ *by his knowledge the depths were divided, and the clouds let drop the dew.*

The holy scriptures are replete with references concerning a case for design by a great and mighty Creator. People can only bow their heads in recognition of the magnificence of God's creation:

- "By the word of the Lord were the heavens made, their starry host by the breath of his mouth" (Psalm 33:6).
- "For the Lord is a great God, and a great King above all gods. In his hand *are* the deep places of the earth: the strength of the hills *is* his also. The sea *is* his, and he made it: and his hands formed the dry *land*" (Psalm 95:3–5 KJV).

> People can only bow their heads in recognition of the magnificence of God's creation.

ATTENTION TO DETAIL

Some have discounted the importance of a case for design, but God "made the earth, whose wisdom gave shape to the world, who crafted the cosmos. He thunders, and rain pours down. He sends the clouds soaring. He embellishes the storm with lightnings, launches wind from his warehouse" (Jeremiah 10:12–13 MSG). If you do not accept this verse without question, how can you accept any other verse in the Bible?

Wernher von Braun was the leading figure in the development of rocket technology in Germany and the father of rocket technology and space science in the United States. On September 14, 1972, Dr. John Ford read the following letter, written by Dr. von Braun, to the California State Board of Education:

> Dear Mr. Grose:
>
> In response to your inquiry about my personal views concerning the "Case for DESIGN" as a viable scientific theory for the origin of the universe, life and man. I am pleased to make the following observations. For me, the idea of a creation is not conceivable without invoking the necessity of design. One cannot be exposed to the law and order of the universe without concluding that there must be design and purpose behind it all. In the world around us, we can behold the obvious manifestations of an ordered, structured plan or design. We can see the will of the species to live and propagate. And we are humbled by the powerful forces at work on a galactic scale, and the purposeful orderliness of nature that endows a tiny and ungainly seed with the ability to develop in to a beautiful flower. The better we understand the intricacies of the universe and all it harbors, the more reason we have found to marvel at the inherent design upon which it is based.

... Many men who are intelligent and of good faith say they cannot visualize a Designer. Well, can a physicist visualize an electron? The electron is materially inconceivable and yet, it is so perfectly known through its effects that we use it to illuminate our cities, guide our airliners through the night skies and take the most accurate measurements. What strange rationale makes some physicists accept the inconceivable electron as real while refusing to accept the reality of a Designer on the ground that they cannot conceive Him? I am afraid that, although they really do not understand the electron either, they are ready to accept it because they managed to produce a rather clumsy mechanical model of it borrowed from rather limited experience in other fields, but they would not know how to begin building a model of God.

... We in NASA were often asked what the real reason for the amazing string of successes we had with our Apollo flights to the Moon. I think the only honest answer we could give was that we tried to never overlook anything. It is in that same sense of scientific honesty that I endorse the presentation of alternative theories for the origin of the universe, life and man in the science classroom. It would be an error to overlook the possibility that the universe was planned rather than happening by chance.

With Kindest regards,
(signed) Wernher von Braun. (Segraves 1973, pp. 7–10)

The attention to detail found in creation points to the work of an intelligent being and provides evidence for a case for design. The size of the earth is just right, and the atmosphere possesses the perfect composition of life-sustaining elements to support its creation.

Essential factors include moisture, temperature, wind patterns, and soil composition, just to name a few. They all point to the existence of a designer.

One writer expressed his amazement at the wonder of God's creation: "Splashes of starlight, color-filled balls floating in space, blue waters and green plains, yellow fish and red parrots, and one creature crafted from dust—all these comprise God's universe" (Johnson 2009, winter, p. 6). The Great Eternal Designer did not just create random splotches on the canvas of space, nor did He haphazardly throw living beings together. He designed the universe and all within it with an intricate and detailed master plan in mind. "God is not an abstract artist. He is an engineer, architect, builder, and contractor all at once. The beauty of the created world came from the mind of the greatest inventor—the Eternal Developer" (Johnson 2009, winter, p. 6).

Job described the grandeur of this omnipotent God:

> God stretches the northern sky over empty space and hangs the earth on nothing. He wraps the rain in his thick clouds, and the clouds don't burst with the weight. He covers the face of the moon, shrouding it with his clouds. He created the horizon when he separated the waters; he set the boundary between day and night. (Job 26:7–10 NLT)

Wow! What a great God! Our galaxy alone has been estimated to contain more than two hundred billion stars (NASA 2014). It is only one of hundreds of billions of galaxies known to exist. Our universe is about sixteen billion light-years in diameter. But God is greater than the universe and the infinite space that surrounds it. "Through faith we understand that the worlds were framed by the word of God, so that things which are seen were not made of things which do appear" (Hebrews 11:3 KJV). The complexity, diversity, immensity, and orderliness of all that exists represent the fingerprints of an incredibly intelligent Creator.

Creation starts with absolutely nothing and ends with everything. God did not need a paintbrush or a hammer to create His masterpiece. He used one tool—His spoken Word. When God spoke, matter miraculously emerged. When He spoke again, matter obeyed His command and organized into tiny particles, dense compounds, and intricate cells. God did not need millions of years to perfect His ideas. He did not need thousands of years to bring forth planets, animals, and humankind. The LORD simply spoke creation into existence. The same creative mind that spoke the galaxies into existence lovingly crafted the complex cells that make up the human body. Reflecting on all of this, David exclaimed, "I will praise thee; for I am fearfully *and* wonderfully made: marvellous *are* thy works" (Psalm 139:14 KJV).

REDEMPTION—A CONTINUATION OF CREATION

The day Adam awoke in that beautiful newly created garden, the LORD gave him these simple instructions: "Of every tree of the garden thou mayest freely eat: But of the tree of the knowledge of good and evil, thou shalt not eat of it: for in the day that thou eatest thereof thou shalt surely die" (Genesis 2:16–17 KJV). The day Adam and Eve transgressed God's command and ate of that fruit, a spiritual death settled upon them. Guilt, shame, and fear were experienced for the first time. "Adam and his wife hid themselves from the presence of the

LORD God amongst the trees of the garden. ... And he said, I heard thy voice in the garden, and I was afraid, because I *was* naked" (Genesis 3:8, 10 KJV). Adam and Eve had violated God's law, and they could not save themselves from the consequences of death. They were helpless to remove the guilt, the shame, and the fear, so God provided a cover for their sin. It was at this juncture that we see the first evidence of a case for design in the plan of redemption. Though the fullness of the plan would not come to fruition for another four thousand years, the Designer/Creator rolled out a type of the plan. Just prior to banishing Adam and Eve from the garden, "The LORD God made for Adam and for his wife garments of skins and clothed them" (Genesis 3:21 ESV). The LORD provided a covering. Adam and Eve's attempt to cover their sin would not do then, and anyone who attempts to cover their sin will do no better today.

Unlike the god of the deist, the God of the Bible has remained involved with His creation. When humans sinned, the LORD wasn't caught off guard. Redemption wasn't an afterthought or something God came up with as time progressed. Instead, we learn that Jesus was the Lamb of God slain from the creation of the world. (See Revelation 13:8.) And in the book of Romans, Paul wrote that Adam was "a pattern of the one to come" (Romans 5:14). "The one to come" was none other than the Lord Jesus Christ. As the LORD scraped the dirt together that would form His greatest creation, He imagined what He would look like when He came to redeem that creature. And with that pattern in mind, "God created man in his *own* image" (Genesis 1:27 KJV).

> Redemption wasn't an afterthought or something God came up with as time progressed.

Today, we face a similar dilemma: "There is none righteous, no, not one" (Romans 3:10 KJV). "For all have sinned, and come short of the glory of God" (Romans 3:23 KJV). We are unable in any way to redeem ourselves from the consequences of inherited sin. "But God [demonstrated] his love toward us, in that, while we were yet sinners,

Christ died for us" (Romans 5:8 KJV). He provided His own sacrifice sufficient to satisfy the demand of the law. It was His creative power that brought forth the design for righteousness, and it was His creative power that satisfied the demand for righteousness.

Notice the attention to detail not only in the creation of the world and in the creation of every living thing but in the plan of salvation. As you study the Old Testament, a theme develops, and you see the elements—blood, water, and fire (Spirit). Leaving Egypt, there was the Passover Lamb (blood), the Red Sea (water), and Mount Sinai (Spirit). Each correlated with something greater in the future. We find the tabernacle plan of worship laid out the requirements of blood, water, and fire (Spirit) in an orderly fashion. And when we reach the time of the ushering in of the New Covenant, we find its fulfillment. John asked the question, "Who is it that overcomes the world" (1 John 5:5)? Then he goes on to answer his question, "This is the one who came by water and blood—Jesus Christ. He did not come by water only, but by water and blood. And it is the Spirit who testifies, because the Spirit is the truth. For there are three that testify: the Spirit, the water and the blood; and the three are in agreement" (1 John 5:6–8). Notice the three elements incorporated into his answer—blood, water, and Spirit! And on the first day of the New Testament church, in response to a sincere question—"Men and brethren, what shall we do?" (Acts 2:37 KJV)—Peter replied, "Repent (blood), and be baptized (water) every one of you in the name of Jesus Christ for the remission of sins, and ye shall receive the gift of the Holy Ghost (Spirit)" (Acts 2:38 KJV, words in parentheses added). The thread of blood, water, and Spirit runs through the entire Bible.

> The thread of blood, water, and Spirit runs through the entire Bible.

Every time a soul is born again, the case for design is manifest. Millions of times since the New Testament church was born on the Day of Pentecost in Acts chapter 2, men and women, young and old, have been blessed by the Designer. Coming to the foot of the cross, bearing their guilt, shame, and fear, they find a design sufficient to cover that guilt and shame. There they find a design sufficient to replace fear with confidence. And when they have been born again of the water and the Spirit, they rejoice: "He saved us through the washing of rebirth and renewal by the Holy Spirit" (Titus 3:5).

SANCTIFICATION—A CONTINUATION OF CREATION

Again, unlike the god of the deist, the God of the Bible is still actively creating in the lives of His people. We call it sanctification. Darkness yields to light, hatred turns to love, fears to faith, problems to peace, and gloom to gladness. As a result, "if any man *be* in Christ, *he is* a new creature: old things are passed away; behold, all things are become new" (2 Corinthians 5:17 KJV).

> The alcoholic is no longer an alcoholic; the person who is guilty of fornication and adultery has his past pardoned and a new life to live; the idolater becomes a worshiper of the one true God; the thief no longer steals; envy, jealousy, and covetousness no longer claw the blood from a person's heart; and the violent man will practice peace. (Hall 1980, fall, p. 39)

Unlike the god of the deist, the God of the Bible is still actively creating in the lives of His people.

The Spirit of God creates a new heart and brings new life to the one who will yield to Him. As the Spirit works, the redeemed lay aside attitudes, thoughts, and lifestyles of carnality, and they become more like Christ. Since our bodies are temples of the Holy Ghost, our dress, speech, conduct, thoughts, and habits—everything about us—must be set apart and reserved solely for the Master's use and service. The overwhelming importance of sanctification in the life of a believer is expressed in Hebrews 12:14: "*Continually* pursue peace with everyone, and the sanctification without which no one will [ever] see the Lord" (AMP).

"The belief that God is the Creator of the universe lifts the meaning of life from chaos to cosmos, from defeatism to optimism, from fatalistic thoughts to a future hope" (Hall 1980, fall, p. 40). The truth of God as our Creator is the foundation upon which human hope and dignity are built. It supports the thesis that humankind is more than happenstance of an endless and meaningless sequence of mindless accidents. Human beings are not merely a higher form of evolved animal; they are the crowning achievement of God's creation, having been made in the image of God.

> The truth of God as our Creator is the foundation upon which human hope and dignity are built.

It is God's desire to turn every living soul into a new creation. The same Designer that spoke the earth into existence—the same Designer that hung the universe in space—is the same force that comes to take up residence within you by filling you with His Spirit. And it was our great God, the Lord and Savior, Jesus Christ, who masterminded the intricacies of the world, of human life, and of salvation.

> He made the things we can see and the things we can't see—such as thrones, kingdoms, rulers, and authorities in the unseen world. Everything was created through him and for him. He existed before anything else, and he holds all creation together."
> (Colossians 1:16–17 NLT)

That same God offers to us an overcoming life with overcoming power. As a result, "We are more than conquerors through him that loved us" (Romans 8:37 KJV)—evidence of a case for design lived out in shoe leather.

IN CLOSING

Creation starts with absolutely nothing and ends with everything. Someone stated, "To think that life originated by accident is comparable to believing the dictionary resulted from an explosion in a printing press" (Davis 1990, winter, p. 6). And no intelligent person would ever believe that such a thing could actually occur. Yet those same intelligent people choose to believe that all nonliving and living things came about by some mysterious big bang followed by a very slow evolutionary process. As noted earlier, Dr. Werner von Braun cautioned, "It would be an error to overlook the possibility that the universe was planned rather than happening by chance." However, the evolutionist would like you to believe that it is an error to even consider the possibility of a creative force that had anything to do with a planned, orderly universe and all living things. G. D. Chesterton whimsically wrote, "The evolutionists seem to know everything about the missing link except the fact that it's missing" (Rhodes 2011, p. 82).

The evidence of a case for design is so strong that it is inconceivable to consider that all, or even any of it, happened by chance. For the child of God, there is no mystery to the age-old question, "Which came first, the chicken or the egg?" Putting faith in the Word of God, which reveals the Creator of everything, provides the answer to that question. God created the chicken—male and female—and He put the seed for all future chickens within those first two chickens. "God said, 'Let the earth produce every sort of animal, each producing offspring of the same kind—livestock, small animals that scurry along the ground, and wild animals. And that is what happened'" (Genesis 1:24 NLT).

> The evidence of a case for design is so strong that it is inconceivable to consider that all, or even any of it, happened by chance.

When given to sincere and honest contemplation, mankind must conclude there is a power far superior to himself. Creation itself is a constant witness to the omnipotence and omniscience of God. Who can make a tree such as a living gigantic oak? From where did the animals come? How did mankind come into existence? Who fashioned the sun, moon, and the starry heavens? Who designed fish in their various sizes and shapes to live in the watery depths? There can be only one answer to these questions, and that is God who is infinite in wisdom, knowledge, and power. (Davis 2012, fall, p. 28)

Considering all the evidence, the case for design is beyond reasonable doubt. You only have to look as far as yourself to realize that God not only designed you, but through the plan of salvation, He performed a creative miracle within your life, changing you from who you were to who you are—a new creation in Christ.

LESSON 19

IT'S A TREASURE— GUARD IT!

PROVERBS 3:21-26

²¹ My son, do not let wisdom and understanding out of your sight, preserve sound judgment and discretion; ²² they will be life for you, an ornament to grace your neck. ²³ Then you will go on your way in safety, and your foot will not stumble. ²⁴ When you lie down, you will not be afraid; when you lie down, your sleep will be sweet. ²⁵ Have no fear of sudden disaster or of the ruin that overtakes the wicked, ²⁶ for the LORD will be at your side and will keep your foot from being snared.

Once again, Solomon addresses his son and urges him to "preserve" sound judgment and discretion. Solomon understood the importance of repetition as a teacher. Similarly, Paul explained to the Philippian church, "To write the same things *again* is no trouble to me, and it is a safeguard for you" (Philippians 3:1 NASB). Likewise, Peter wrote, "Therefore, I will always be ready to remind you of these things, even though you *already* know *them*, and have been established in the truth which is present with *you*" (2 Peter 1:12 NASB).

PRACTICE MAKES PERFECT

Overlearning skill sets is what airplane pilots do in training, so in an emergency, they don't have to pull out an instruction manual. Those overlearned skills immediately spring into action, safely bringing a plane out of a spin or landing on a makeshift airstrip. Likewise, emergency responders rely on overlearned skill sets. They don't have time to pull out a training manual at the site of an emergency. Christians must do the same. Sound judgment and discretion are developed through the process of overlearning, thus a good reason for memorizing the Word of God. When important decisions must be made or when temptation looms, the overlearned skills will safeguard you. In those moments, sound judgment and discretion will save the day.

> When important decisions must be made or when temptation looms, the overlearned skills will safeguard you.

The word translated *preserve* was translated *keep* in the KJV. Both are acceptable renderings of the original Hebrew *naw-tsar*, but it also means *to guard*. Given the context of the above verses, *to guard* may be a better rendering: "My son, *guard* sound judgment and discretion, do not let them out of your sight." Sound judgment and discretion are gifts from God, and they are a treasure that must be guarded. Sound judgment and discretion come only by understanding biblical principles that in turn provide guidance when addressing issues that seem complicated. For example, the apostle Paul, though a single man, was able to give sound judgment and discretion to those who had written to him about marital relationships. (See 1 Corinthians 7:10–17.)

Sound judgment and discretion "will be life for you." If sound judgment and discretion are present, then one can anticipate a much richer life. In fact, sound judgment and discretion teach God's people to number their days and to order their lives by principles that have been tried and tested. Psalm 90 is a prayer of a psalmist by the name of Moses: "Teach us to number our days aright, that we may gain a heart of wisdom" (Psalm 90:12 KJV). Too many people live out their Christian faith from event to event—Easter Sunday, Christmas Eve candlelight service, a revival, a praise concert, or a special church dinner. But in between, they fail to manifest a Christian lifestyle. They live for the earthly benefits of being a Christian, not for fellowship with Jesus Christ and the life He brings.

Jesus stated, "The words that I speak unto you, *they* are spirit, and *they* are life" (John 6:63 KJV). When Walter Scott was dying, he said to his secretary, "Bring me the Book." Looking over at the library, she saw thousands of books, so she returned and asked, "Dr. Scott, which book?" He responded, "The Book, the Bible, the only book for a dying man" (cited in Macarthur 1979). And if the Bible is the only book for a dying man, it's the only book for a living man, because it is the Word of life, as well as the Word of hope in death.

> If the Bible is the only book for a dying man, it's the only book for a living man, because it is the Word of life, as well as the Word of hope in death.

"Sound judgment and discretion … they will be … an ornament to grace your neck" (Proverbs 3:21–22). Literally, the phrase "to grace to your neck" is "grace to your jaws." "Jaw" in this case refers to what you say. Sound judgment and discretion give grace to the words you speak. In reference to this verse, Matthew Henry (n.d.) wrote, "It shall infuse grace into all thou sayest, shall furnish thee with acceptable words, which shall gain thee credit" (Vol. 3, p. 807). "Anyone who is never at fault in what they say is perfect, able to keep their whole body in check" (James 3:2). Praise is given not to the strong person who takes a city but to a stronger person who rules their own spirit and ultimately their tongue. The stronger person is the one who, by discipline, exercises a constant control over their speech. Someone has said, "The tongue being in a wet place is prone to slip" (Doan 1968, p. 360). Another remarked, "Some can't help having false teeth, but everyone can have a true tongue" (Doan 1968, p. 360). Therefore, "Let your speech always be gracious, seasoned with salt, so that you may know how you ought to answer each person" (Colossians 4:6 ESV). If we hide the Word of the Lord in our hearts, the Spirit of God will provide us with sound judgment and discretion when we speak.

If we hide the Word of the Lord in our hearts, the Spirit of God will provide us with sound judgment and discretion when we speak.

BENEFITS OF SOUND JUDGMENT AND DISCRETION

Solomon described for his son the many benefits of sound judgment and discretion:

A safe journey through this life. "Then you will go on your way in safety" (Proverbs 3:23). This is not to say that you never again will be ill or injure yourself. The Lord never promised we would be free of trouble or problems in this life, even while serving Him. In fact, trials and suffering often are an integral part of the development of one's faith. However, He promised that He would never leave us nor forsake us: "I am with you alway, even unto the end of the world" (Matthew 28:20 KJV). David declared, "Though I walk through the valley of the shadow of death, I will fear no evil: for thou *art* with me; thy rod and thy staff they comfort me" (Psalm 23:4 KJV).

Sure-footedness in dangerous terrain. Many people walk in a moral fog without a compass to guide them. For many, the media has taken the place of the church in providing ethical and moral guidance. Today, societal mores lack absolutes. Grossly sinful individuals who scorn and deride righteous people as archaic and ignorant are held up as glamorous icons. However, the principles Jesus taught are true and eternal. They have been tried and tested for thousands of years and have proven to be beneficial for both individuals and society as a whole.

When your feet are planted solidly upon the Rock, you need not fear stumbling. Jesus told a parable about two builders; one built his house upon the sand, and the other built upon the Rock. When the storms of life came, the one built on the sand washed away and was destroyed. However, during the same storms, the other "did not fall, because it had its foundation on the rock" (Matthew 7:25). Solomon assured that if you develop sound judgment and discretion, "then you will go on your way in safety, and your foot will not stumble" (Proverbs 3:23).

> When your feet are planted solidly upon the Rock, you need not fear stumbling.

There has always been a tendency for humans to play as close to the edge of the cliff as possible without falling over. However, sound judgment and discretion will keep you on safe ground, far back from the edge of the cliff. The way of the righteous, with its consistency and discipline, contrasts greatly with situational ethics. Blessed is the person who develops sound judgment and discretion, for they shall not stumble. Solomon could assure that this person will not stumble. Why? This person doesn't "walk in the counsel of the ungodly" (Psalm 1:1 KJV).

The Bible provides many examples of those who failed to develop sound judgment and discretion. As a result, they listened to the counsel of the wicked and suffered the consequences of wrong choices. Eve listened to the serpent and was cast out of the garden. Rehoboam listened to the inexperienced counsel of his peers, oppressed God's people, and lost the kingdom. An unnamed prophet of God listened to a false prophet and was eaten by a lion. Aaron listened to the people and built a golden calf. In every one of these examples, had they turned to the LORD for guidance, sound judgment and discretion would have kept them safe, and they would not have stumbled.

Freedom from fear. "When you lie down, you will not be afraid" (Proverbs 3:24). Drug and alcohol use have become a modern-day scourge. Many turn to such remedies in an attempt to find peace of mind and freedom from fear. The truth is they cannot and never will find the peace they are looking for through the mind-altering effects of drugs or alcohol. Sound judgment and discretion, on the other hand, provide freedom from fear as one rests in the assurance that there is someone much greater who never slumbers or sleeps. Paul wrote to the Philippian Church, "Do not be anxious about anything" (Philippians 4:6 ESV). He followed that statement with an explanation as to how to have that assurance: "In everything by prayer and supplication with thanksgiving let your requests be made known to God" (Philippians 4:6 ESV). And when you do those things, you can rest free from fear because "the peace of God, which surpasses all understanding, will guard your hearts and your minds in Christ Jesus" (Philippians 4:7 ESV). Similarly, Peter encouraged his readers to cast all their anxieties and cares upon him because he cared for them. (See 1 Peter 5:7.) And He cares for you!

When you exercise sound judgment and discretion by trusting your heavenly Father to keep you safe and meet your needs, you will lie down, and you will not be afraid.

> When you exercise sound judgment and discretion by trusting your heavenly Father to keep you safe and meet your needs, you will lie down, and you will not be afraid.

Restful sleep. Solomon declared that as a result of sound judgment and discretion, you can live under the umbrella of God's protective assurance. "When you lie down, your sleep will be sweet" (Proverbs 3:24). A sweet peace will overcome you. Sound judgment and discretion eliminate the need to fear disaster. That does not mean you will never experience disaster, but if your God cannot keep you, then no one can keep you. If you have ordered your life according to God's Word, exercising sound judgment and discretion, you will be able to close out each day with a simple prayer, "I pray the Lord my soul to keep and close my eyes in restful sleep."

Security. "The LORD is your security. He will keep your foot from being caught in a trap" (Proverbs 3:26 NLT). The reason you can sleep so restfully is that the Lord is your security force protecting you while you sleep. One can only wonder how many wars have been fought in the heavens for your soul while you slept secure under the watchful eye and the protection of the Lord. The Lord has always provided a place of security or refuge for His people. David expressed, "Trust in him at all times ... God *is* a refuge for us" (Psalm 62:8 KJV). Placing trust in the Lord is much like anchoring a boat in a secure harbor. He is the only perfect and suitable anchorage for a person's soul. Other forces and conditions influence everything else in the universe, but the Lord is immovable by any force or object!

> One can only wonder how many wars have been fought in the heavens for your soul while you slept secure under the watchful eye and the protection of the Lord.

Protection from the enemy. The military intelligence corps plays a vital part in army warfare because it enables the officers to know and understand the enemy. Unless a Christian has insight into how the enemy of their soul operates, they will have a difficult time avoiding being snared by the enemy. When David faced Goliath, he not only faced a big man, but he faced the opposing forces of evil. Goliath bellowed, "Give me a man, that we may fight together" (1 Samuel 17:10 KJV). Satan always wants to keep the battle at the level of humans. Sound judgment and discretion raised the battle to the level of God, preventing the whole nation of Israel from being snared by the devil:

> Then said David to the Philistine, Thou comest to me with a sword, and with a spear, and with a shield: but I come to thee in the name of the LORD of hosts, the God of the armies of Israel, whom thou hast defied. This day will the LORD deliver thee into mine hand; and I will smite thee, and take thine head from

thee; and I will give the carcases of the host of the Philistines this day unto the fowls of the air, and to the wild beasts of the earth; that all the earth may know that there is a God in Israel. (1 Samuel 17:45–46 KJV)

David knew that if he raised the battle to the realm of the Spirit, his God would not let him down. To maintain spiritual victory, you must raise the battle to the realm of the Spirit. Exercise sound judgment and discretion.

> To maintain spiritual victory, you must raise the battle to the realm of the Spirit.

IN CLOSING

Guard sound judgment and discretion; it is a treasure. For by sound judgment and discretion, God's purpose for your life will be revealed. Jesus said, "I am come that they might have life, and that they might have *it* more abundantly" (John 10:10 KJV). And Paul knew that if he was going to be effective in the work of evangelism, he would need guidance from above to direct his speech: "Rather than using clever and persuasive speeches, I relied only on the power of the Holy Spirit" (1 Corinthians 2:4 NLT).

Treasure sound judgment and discretion, for by them you will walk securely upon the path, and your feet will not stumble. And when you lie down at night, you will not fear and your sleep will be sweet, "For God hath not given us the spirit of fear; but of power, and of love, and of a sound mind" (2 Timothy 1:7 KJV). All this is yours because you have given your cares and concerns to the Lord, and He has promised to provide you with protection and to keep you from being snared by the enemy.

LESSON 20

BEING A GIVER INSTEAD OF A TAKER

PROVERBS 3:27-28

27 Do not withhold good from those to whom it is due, when it is in your power to act. 28 Do not say to your neighbor, "Come back tomorrow and I'll give it to you"—when you already have it with you.

Selfishness is a lonely state in which to live. The more one focuses on self, the less one is able to enjoy others. Selfish individuals spend untold energy trying to dam up the natural flow from themselves to others. Selfishness is a form of control. People who are selfish often are quick to resist any form of perceived control by another because they are guarding their own turf. But generous people have learned that when they give, more is given in return.

> Give, and it shall be given unto you; good measure, pressed down, and shaken together, and running over, shall men give into your bosom. For with the same measure that ye mete withal it shall be measured to you again. (Luke 6:38 KJV)

For those who practice this principle, their barrels of meal and jars of oil will never run out. (See 1 Kings 17:7–16.)

> The more one focuses on self, the less one is able to enjoy others.

THE PROFILE OF A SELFISH PERSON

Selfishness can manifest itself in a variety of ways, some of which are noted below:

Not producing good works. As Christians, we are called upon to take advantage of every opportunity to do good. In fact, every opportunity to do good is our call to do good. That may sound circular and redundant, but it is the truth. The Lord provides opportunities to do good works so He may receive the glory. "Let your light so shine before men, that they may see your good works, and glorify your Father which is in heaven" (Matthew 5:16 KJV). The Word of God (both Old and New Testaments) demands good works on the part of God's people. The writer of Ecclesiastes asserted, "Whatever your hand finds to do, do it with all your strength" (Ecclesiastes 9:10 NLV).

> Every opportunity to do good is our call to do good.

Jesus spoke of a golden rule: "Treat others the same way you want them to treat you" (Luke 6:31 NASB). Yet a thorough reading of the entire Bible finds the golden rule is not a New Testament revelation but has been a concept interwoven throughout the whole Bible. When God gave the law to Moses, you find the golden rule embedded in it: "Thou shalt not avenge, nor bear any grudge against the children of thy people, but thou shalt love thy neighbour as thyself" (Leviticus 19:18 KJV).

The principle of the golden rule is fulfilled through our neighbors, as they are the real possessors of our good. Most of the blessings you will receive from God will come through your neighbors. And since blessings are reciprocal, you choke the blessings of God when you are selfish. Jesus taught that how you treat others is directly related to eternal rewards:

Then he will say to those on his left, "Depart from me, you cursed, into the eternal fire prepared for the devil and his angels. For I was hungry and you gave me no food, I was thirsty and you gave me no drink, I was a stranger and you did not welcome me, naked and you did not clothe me, sick and in prison and you did not visit me." Then they also will answer, saying, "Lord, when did we see you hungry or thirsty or a stranger or naked or sick or in prison, and did not minister to you?" Then he will answer them, saying, "Truly, I say to you, as you did not do it to one of the least of these, you did not do it to me. (Matthew 25:41–45 ESV)

Withholding affection. In the marital relationship, selfishness sometimes is manifest when one member withholds affection from the other. This should not be. Do not withhold affection from the one who deserves it when it is in your power to act. "The husband should fulfill his wife's sexual needs, and the wife should fulfill her husband's needs" (1 Corinthians 7:3 NLT). There are only two things you can do with love—give it and receive it. Love can never be forced, and true love will never be withheld. Any attempt to force love turns the response into a duty, and though duty is one of the characteristics of love, duty does not equal love. Genuine love flows as naturally as water runs downhill. It flows uninhibited from the one who loves. And that is not to be confused with lust. Lust thinks only of self, whereas love always puts others first. "It always protects, always trusts, always hopes, always perseveres" (1 Corinthians 13:7). The greedy partner is never full because fullness comes only by giving.

> The greedy partner is never full because fullness comes only by giving.

Keeping back a laborer's wages. James declared, "Behold, the wages of the laborers who mowed your fields, which you kept back by fraud, are crying out against you, and the cries of the harvesters have reached the ears of the Lord of hosts" (James 5:4 ESV). The Lord seems to pay special attention to any who are taken advantage of. Just as the Lord hears the cry of the harvester, He sees exactly how we treat our neighbor. The LORD condemned King Jehoiakim for the way he treated subordinates: "What sorrow awaits Jehoiakim, who builds his palace with forced labor. He builds injustice into its walls, for he makes his neighbors work for nothing. He does not pay them for their labor" (Jeremiah 22:13 NLT). He may have been king, but he still was not above the law. The law clearly declared that no one was to withhold wages owed:

> Never take advantage of poor and destitute laborers, whether they are fellow Israelites or foreigners living in your towns. You must pay them their wages each day before sunset because they are poor and are counting on it. If you don't, they might cry out to the LORD against you, and it would be counted against you as sin. (Deuteronomy 24:14–15 NLT).

Just as the Lord hears the cry of the harvester, He sees exactly how we treat our neighbor.

Borrowing with no intent to repay. "The wicked borrows and does not pay back" (Psalm 37:21 NASB). If you borrow knowing you cannot pay the debt, you are a thief. As a child, you learned about the sin of shoplifting. No doubt, your parents taught you about paying for things before exiting a store, and you learned to not take toys from other children. It is just as important to keep the eighth commandment as it is to keep any of the other nine. "Anyone who has been stealing must steal no longer, but must work, doing something useful with their own hands, that they may have something to share with those in need" (Ephesians 4:28). Unfortunately, unless individuals are arrested and charged with theft or robbery, they do not think of themselves as thieves. But the eighth commandment is not just about taking something that doesn't belong to you. Other behaviors that violate this commandment include cheating on a test, failing to disclose money earned on income tax returns, driving customers away from your place of employment by a bad attitude, overcharging customers, false advertising, being careless with something borrowed, not returning borrowed items, or wasting a teacher's class time by being unruly. These are all sinful actions that God forbids under the commandment "Thou shalt not steal."

> If you borrow knowing you cannot pay the debt, you are a thief.

Not returning tithes. We often speak of giving tithes, but in truth, we return tithes to the Lord. The Lord trusts us with 100 percent of our earnings with the understanding that we will return the first 10 percent to Him. When Israel failed to return the first tenth to the Lord, He called them "robbers" (thieves). "Will a man rob God? Yet ye have robbed me. But ye say, Wherein have we robbed thee? In tithes and offerings" (Malachi 3:8 KJV). No doubt, many churchgoers fall far short the Lord's expectation in this area. And whether they realize it or not, they are missing out on untold blessings. In fact, the LORD informed the Israelites they were cursed as the result of not bringing the entire tithe into the storehouse—the house of God:

> Ye *are* cursed with a curse: for ye have robbed me, *even* this whole nation. Bring ye all the tithes into the storehouse, that there may be meat in mine house, and prove me now herewith, saith the LORD of hosts, if I will not open you the windows of heaven, and pour you out a blessing, that *there shall* not *be room* enough *to receive it.* And I will rebuke the devourer for your sakes, and he shall not destroy the fruits of your ground; neither shall your vine cast her fruit

before the time in the field, saith the LORD of hosts. And all nations shall call you blessed: for ye shall be a delightsome land, saith the LORD of hosts. (Malachi 3:9–12 KJV)

With a promise and a warning such as that, no one should even consider not returning the first tenth of everything earned to the house of the Lord.

> The Lord trusts us with 100 percent of our earnings with the understanding that we will return the first 10 percent to Him.

Withholding offerings. This brings us to the subject of offerings to God. Tithes are not offerings. The tithe—the first tenth—already belongs to the Lord. An offering is anything given beyond the tithe. Offering to God a portion of the blessings He has so graciously given to you is a wonderful opportunity. Not only does the Lord give you the means to make a living, but He also blesses you financially. Don't take that for granted. David testified of God's ability to always provide: "I have been young, and *now* am old; yet have I not seen the righteous forsaken, nor his seed begging bread" (Psalm 37:25–26 KJV). So be ready to give when the need arises, and you will be blessed in return.

An unnecessary delay. How important it is not to delay in dispensing your obligation to another. An unnecessary delay in meeting the needs of others also is a form of selfishness. How many times have you submitted an application and it could have moved through the system more quickly were it not for the disregard of some worker? How many times have you been responsible to make something happen and you allowed other things to take priority? "Do not say to your neighbor, 'Come back tomorrow and I'll give it to you'—when you already have it with you" (Proverbs 3:28). Consider the following:

A little given in time of need is more than a larger sum when the time is gone by. We should cultivate a quick sensibility of the wants and sufferings of others; putting ourselves as much as possible in their place; not only "doing good," but "ready to every good work." (Bridges 1846/1968, p. 38)

> An unnecessary delay in meeting the needs of others also is a form of selfishness.

Ignoring the gospel debt. Even if we owe no one a monetary debt, we owe everyone a gospel debt. As with all the other characteristics noted above, the selfish person overlooks the debt they owe to others—the debt to touch another person for Jesus. Selfish people never have time for others unless it will benefit them in some way. Jesus was emphatic, "When you give a banquet, invite the poor, the crippled, the lame, the blind, and you will be blessed. Although they cannot repay you, you will be repaid at the resurrection of the righteous" (Luke 14:13–14). Though we can never pay Jesus back for what He has done for us, we must recognize that He intended for us to be His hands and feet upon this earth, making time for others. The apostle Paul is the greatest example in this area. Throughout the years of his life as a Christian, he bore the weight of the need to carry the gospel to everyone. He wrote passionately, "I am debtor both to the Greeks, and to the Barbarians; both to the wise, and to the unwise" (Romans 1:14 KJV). Though that debt will always remain, we must attempt to pay it. In fact, Paul urged his readers, "Pay your debts as they come due. However, one debt you can never finish paying is the debt of love that you owe each other" (Romans 13:8 GW).

RECOGNIZING YOUR NEIGHBOR

A Pharisee, wanting to justify himself, asked Jesus, "Who is my neighbor?" (Luke 10:29 KJV). From that question came the parable of the Good Samaritan. In that parable, both the priest and the Levite were selfish with their time and turned their heads away from the need of a wounded brother. To increase the impact of the story, Jesus told how a hated Samaritan did what the other two religious people failed to do. He made time for and showed compassion to the wounded man. Not only was he selfless with his time, he invested his monetary resources in seeing that the man was cared for. We too have the potential to be like the good religious people Jesus described in that parable. It is just as easy for us to turn our heads or walk on the other side of the street to avoid expending energy or resources on another. But Jesus made it clear that everyone is our neighbor—even those we dislike. "As we have therefore opportunity, let us do good unto all *men*" (Galatians 6:10 KJV).

> It is just as easy for us to turn our heads or walk on the other side of the street to avoid expending energy or resources on another.

IN CLOSING

We have heard of dead people, dead beasts, dead trees and dead flowers, but is there such a thing as a dead sea? There is and they call it dead because it receives all and gives nothing. This body of water—the most remarkable in the world—is at the southern end of the Jordan Valley in Palestine. It is 47 miles long and ten miles wide, 1292 feet below the sea level and is in one of the hottest regions on earth. It receives 5,000,000 tons of water daily into its bosom from the Jordan River, but gives none out to refresh and nourish the valley below, which has become an arid desert on account of the close fistedness of the sea. Its water is five times as salty as the ocean, is bitter to the taste, oily to the touch and leaves a yellow stain. No

LORIN BRADBURY, PH.D.

fish live in the water, no flowers bloom or fruits grow
on its shores, no birds sing in its neighborhood. Its
barkless driftwood and shores are incrusted with salt.
Its setting is a scene of desolation and gloom, looking
as if the curse of God rested on all the region. (Gospel
Herald in Knight 1956, p. 614)

What a picture of selfishness. If you want freshness in your life, begin
by giving out and not worrying about taking in. And as you give out,
abundance will flow back in.

> If you want freshness in your life, begin by giving out and
> not worrying about taking in.

We live in the most affluent nation in the world, where the average
American has more material blessings than at any previous time in
history. It is unfortunate that so many are missing the opportunity to
be a channel of blessing to others. The LORD posed a scenario to the
people of Ezekiel's day that we should consider:

Suppose a certain man is righteous and does what
is just and right ... He is a merciful creditor, not
keeping the items given as security by poor debtors.
He does not rob the poor but instead gives food to the
hungry and provides clothes for the needy. (Ezekiel
18:5, 7 NLT)

Just suppose those who claim to be righteous lived a life of
generosity. What might our world be like? It would be a world of givers
rather than takers.

Remember the teaching of Jesus. The givers did not realize they
had done anything out of the ordinary. They simply did it out of the
generosity of their hearts. Getting a reward, or even an honorable
mention, was not their reason for giving. They just did it:

Then the righteous will answer him, saying, "Lord, when did we see you hungry and feed you, or thirsty and give you drink? And when did we see you a stranger and welcome you, or naked and clothe you? And when did we see you sick or in prison and visit you?" And the King will answer them, "Truly, I say to you, as you did it to one of the least of these my brothers, you did it to me." (Matthew 25:37–40 ESV)

Jesus assures that no one will lose out when they give to one in need. "Whosoever shall give you a cup of water to drink in my name, because ye belong to Christ, verily I say unto you, he shall not lose his reward" (Mark 9:41 KJV). Jesus provides the blessing, and you are the conduit. Somewhere above you, the Lord has a giant reservoir filled with all that you or anyone else could ever need. Regardless of how large and how full it is, it remains only a reservoir until someone is willing to take the step of faith and become a conduit by sharing what they already have. Much like the loaves and fishes blessed by Jesus, as you share, more suddenly appears in your hands. Go ahead. Take the step of faith. Share what you have and see if the Lord won't give you more than you had to start with.

LESSON 21

NO MORE SOUP, PLEASE

PROVERBS 3:29-30

²⁹ Do not plot harm against your neighbor, who lives trustfully near you. ³⁰ Do not accuse anyone for no reason—when they have done you no harm.

Death was a common experience in the Old Testament. War was a fact of life. Man was allowed to defend himself and his family. Capital punishment was prescribed for certain crimes. However, to plot against and kill an unsuspecting neighbor was considered a terrible crime: "May anyone who kills his neighbor secretly be under the Lord's curse" (Deuteronomy 27:24 NIrV).

MALICIOUS DECEPTION

There's a story in the Old Testament that runs contrary to Solomon's words above. Jacob's daughter, Dinah, being probably fifteen or sixteen years of age, went to visit the ladies of Shechem. We might assume that she went, possibly unbeknown to her parents, to a public event, such as a dance. Before the evening was over, she and Shechem had committed the sin of fornication. It appears Dinah did not return home the following morning. Instead, Shechem sent his father to negotiate a price for the girl. They agreed on one condition—that the Shechemites enter into a covenant with Jehovah: "The sons of Jacob answered

Shechem and Hamor his father deceitfully, and said ... we consent unto you: If ye will be as we *be*, that every male of you be circumcised" (Genesis 34:13, 15 KJV). But after agreeing to become family with the Shechemites, Jacob's sons deceitfully trapped them, eventually killing them all and taking their sister home:

> Three days later, while all of them were still in pain, two of Jacob's sons, Simeon and Levi, Dinah's brothers, took their swords and attacked the unsuspecting city, killing every male. They put Hamor and his son Shechem to the sword and took Dinah from Shechem's house and left. (Genesis 34:25–26)

When Jacob heard the news, he was shocked and grieved over the behavior of his own flesh and blood. "Jacob said to Simeon and Levi, Ye have troubled me to make me to stink among the inhabitants of the land" (Genesis 34:30 KJV). Though Solomon's words had not yet been written, Jacob understood the gravity of the principle, "Do not plot harm against your neighbor, who lives trustfully near you" (Proverbs 3:29).

SAUL'S MALICE AGAINST DAVID

Not only are we not to plot harm against our neighbors who live trustfully near us; we must not accuse falsely or act maliciously toward anyone who has done us no harm. King Saul is an example of one who acted impulsively and recklessly in response to jealous thoughts urged on by an evil spirit.

Saul's malicious acts toward David began when his relationship with the LORD grew cold. The first indication of a growing spiritual coldness was when he overstepped the bounds of kingship and stepped into the role of priest by offering a sacrifice, rather than waiting for Samuel the priest. His excuse was that Samuel had not shown up on time to offer the sacrifice and his army was scattering. When Samuel arrived—on time—he rebuked Saul:

"You have done a foolish thing," Samuel said. "You have not kept the command the LORD your God gave you; if you had, he would have established your kingdom over Israel for all time. But now your kingdom will not endure; the LORD has sought out a man after his own heart and appointed him ruler of his people, because you have not kept the LORD's command." (1 Samuel 13:13–14)

> Saul's malicious acts toward David began when his relationship with the Lord grew cold.

Saul continued his disobedience, and the LORD rejected him as king. Samuel admonished Saul, "Because you have rejected the word of the LORD, he has rejected you as king" (1 Samuel 15:23). As a result of rebellion, "the Spirit of the LORD had departed from Saul, and an evil spirit from the LORD tormented him" (1 Samuel 16:14). Only the presence of God could relieve the insanity brought on by the evil spirit. Whenever that evil spirit was upon Saul, David took his harp and played under the anointing of God until "Saul was refreshed, and was well, and the evil spirit departed from him" (1 Samuel 16:23 KJV).

Whether Saul was yet aware of it or not, David already had been anointed king, and the power of God rested upon him. This was demonstrated when Saul's army was pinned down for forty days by a Philistine giant named Goliath. No one dared accept his challenge to fight until David came on the scene. David could not tolerate seeing God's army cowering in response to the threats of the enemy of God's people. Taking five stones (though he only needed one) and a sling, he faced off against the giant. In the name of the LORD of Hosts, David ran toward the giant and killed him with a single stone. Using the giant's own sword, David decapitated him, and the word of this feat spread. David became an idol among all the young ladies of the land: "As they danced, they sang: 'Saul has slain his thousands, and David his tens of thousands'" (1 Samuel 18:7). Saul's jealousy became so intense that for seven years he pursued David, attempting to kill him at every turn. Ignoring the Word of God, he plotted harm against his neighbor who lived trustfully near him, accusing him of wrongdoing when he had done him no wrong. There was no one more loyal to King Saul than David, and yet he sought to destroy him.

MURDER IN THE TONGUE

In the Sermon on the Mount, Jesus explained that murder was more than taking another person's life, forcing us to consider the possibility that we all have committed murder with our tongues. It is a fact, "Death and life *are* in the power of the tongue" (Proverbs 18:21 KJV).

> For every kind of beasts, and of birds, and of serpents, and of things in the sea, is tamed, and hath been tamed of mankind: But the tongue can no man tame; *it is* an unruly evil, full of deadly poison. (James 3:7–8 KJV)

Jesus explained that murder was more than taking another person's life, forcing us to consider the possibility that we all have committed murder with our tongues.

The interpreters of the law in Jesus's day had gutted the law of its meaning. Jesus contrasted the true spirit of the law with the corrupted version of the teachers of that day:

> Ye have heard that it was said by them of old time, Thou shalt not kill; and whosoever shall kill shall be in danger of the judgment [of the local council]: But I say unto you, That whosoever is angry with his brother without a cause shall be in danger of the judgment [of God]: and whosoever shall say to his brother, Raca, shall be in danger of the council [judgment of the local council]: but whosoever shall say, Thou fool,

shall be in danger of hell fire [judgment of God]. (Matthew 5:21–22 KJV)

Though I cannot prove it from a physiology textbook, I find in the scriptures the tongue is connected to the heart:

> A good man out of the good treasure of his heart bringeth forth that which is good; and an evil man out of the evil treasure of his heart bringeth forth that which is evil: for of the abundance of the heart his mouth speaketh. (Luke 6:45 KJV)

Envy, jealousy, and feelings of inferiority are often at the root of a murderous tongue. There is a personality disorder, which out of selfishness often kills that which it cannot have rather than allow another to have it. In fact, the personality-disordered person often smothers and kills its object of affection.

> The personality-disordered person often smothers and kills its object of affection.

LEARN FROM GOD'S CREATION AND BE WISE

A female spider is often a widow for embarrassing reasons—she regularly eats those who come her way. Lonely suitors and visitors alike quickly become corpses, and her dining room is a morgue. A visiting fly, having become captive, will appear to be whole, but the spider has drunk his insides so that he has become his own hollow casket.

... The reason for this [gruesome] procedure is that she has no stomach and so is incapable of digesting anything within her. Through tiny punctures she injects her digestive juices into a fly so that his insides are broken down and turned into warm soup. (Hughes 1991, p. 138)

Is not this a picture of what human beings often do to one another? Yet the Word of God teaches to do no harm to your neighbor who lives peacefully near you, and to never falsely accuse a person who has done you no harm.

First-degree murder—a malicious tongue. The uncontrolled dagger of a tongue is an abomination to the Lord:

And the tongue is a fire, a world of iniquity: so is the tongue among our members, that it defileth the whole body, and setteth on fire the course of nature; and it is set on fire of hell. ... Out of the same mouth proceedeth blessing and cursing. My brethren, these things ought not so to be" (James 3:6, 10 KJV)

James described the uncontrolled tongue in three ways—a fire, a world of iniquity, and deadly poison. Though the tongue is a very small member among the members of the body, it has the potential to destroy the entire body. James reminds us that it takes only a spark to create a great forest fire. Further, malicious words can turn a home, a church, or a workplace into a world of iniquity. Behind most problems created by the tongue is a troubled heart. "For out of the abundance of the heart the mouth speaketh" (Matthew 12:34 KJV). And it is a deadly poison. It is impossible to have a peaceful heart and a malicious tongue in the same body. The destruction that an uncontrolled tongue can produce is beyond measure.

> It is impossible to have a peaceful heart and a malicious tongue in the same body.

LORIN BRADBURY, PH.D.

King David revealed in the Psalms that on more than one occasion he felt the sharp blade of a dagger tongue:

- They are glad now that I am in trouble; they gleefully join together against me. I am attacked by people I don't even know; they slander me constantly. ... They don't talk of peace; they plot against innocent people who mind their own business. (Psalm 35:15, 20 NLT)
- [My best friend] has betrayed his friends. He has broken his solemn promise. His speech is smoother than butter, but there is war in his heart. His words are more soothing than oil, but they are like swords ready to attack. (Psalm 55:20–21 GW)

Second-degree murder—a careless tongue. This often occurs when people are in a group. Negative talk is infectious:

A Farmer's wife had spread a slanderous story about her pastor through the village and soon the whole countryside had heard it. Some time later the woman became sick and confessed the story was untrue. After her recovery she came to the pastor and craved his pardon. The old pastor said, "Of course I will gladly pardon you if you will comply with a wish of mine."

"Gladly," replied the woman.

"Go home, kill a black hen, pluck the feathers, and put them in a basket, and bring them here."

In half an hour she was back. "Now," said the pastor, "go through the village and at each street corner scatter a few of these feathers, the remaining ones take to the top of the bell tower and scatter them to the winds, then return."

She did so.

"Now go through the village and gather the feathers again, and see that not one is missing."

The woman looked at the pastor in astonishment and said, "Why that is impossible! The wind has scattered them over the fields everywhere!"

"And so," said he, "while I forgive you gladly, do not forget that you can never undo the damage your untrue words have done." (Tan 1979, pp. 1172–1173)

"Do not plot harm against your neighbor, who lives trustfully near you. Do not accuse anyone for no reason—when they have done you no harm" (Proverbs 3:29–30).

IN CLOSING

The following poem by Walter Wangerin Jr. (1984), titled "Modern Hexameron—DAranea," provides the conclusion and the title for this lesson.

The spider's the spinner, the spinster, the busy web-weaver, often a widow—for embarrassing reasons—and a homemaker generally careless of her children. Most commonly she swaddles her eggs together with a stunned bit of food against the day of the children's emergence, and then she takes her leave before she has taken their measure, or seen their faces, or named them.

Little of love in most of the spinsters. Personal survival, rather, and a life, though lasting, lonely: suitors and visitors alike fast become corpses. Her dining room's a morgue.

Plainly: she eats them that come to her.

She's very much like the rest of us: she allows a little fly his shape and the illusion of wholeness; but she has drunk his insides, and he is hollow, in fact; has become his own casket, as it were; his own memorial.

It is a neat, deceptive way to eat. But she has no stomach of her own, you see. She can digest nothing within her. Therefore her prey must also be her stomach. Through tiny punctures she injects into a bounden fly digestive juices; inside his body his organs and nerves and tissues are broken down, dissolved, and turned to warm soup. This soup she swills—

—even as the most of us swill souls of one another after having cooked them in various enzymes: guilt, humiliations, subjectivities, cruel love—there are a number of fine, acidic mixes. And some among us are so skilled with the hypodermic word that our dear ones continue to sit up and to smile, quite as though they were still alive. But the evidence of eating is in our own fatness. Neither we nor the spinster can conceal fatness.

But (and this *but* is no ordinary conjunction: it is graceful altogether!) there is one species of spider different from all the others. Not that she has a stomach. She is a spider, after all, with all the external properties of her genus; with them, she lacks a stomach.

No it is her manner that makes her wonderful. A man might almost weep to see how she behaves.

For this one does not leave her eggs to chance.

She stays. She protects the eggs in incubation. By the hundreds she gathers her brood upon her back so that she seems a grotesque sort of lump, rumpled and swollen. But she is love: it makes the lover ugly.

And when the children emerge, she feeds them. Her juices soften the meat to their diminutive snorkels. Yet even this care, peculiar among the spinsters, does not give her a name above all other names. Many mothers mother their children; that is not uncommon.

Rather, it is the last supper which she reserves against necessity that astonishes the watcher and makes him wonder to see heaven in a tiny thing …

Sometimes food grows scarce, and no amount of netting can snare the fly that isn't there. Sometimes tiny famine descends upon the mother and her spiderlings, and then they starve, and then they may die, if they do not eat.

But then, privately, she performs the deed unique among the living.

Into her own body this spinster releases the juices that digest. Freely they run through her abdomen while she holds so still, digesting not some other meat, but her own, breaking down the parts of her that kept her once alive, until her eyes are flat.

She dies.

She becomes the stomach for her children, and she herself the food.

And Jesus said to those who stood around him, "I am the bread of life. I am the living bread which came down from heaven; if any one eats of this bread, he will live forever; and the bread which I will give for the life of the world is my flesh."

Take—and eat.

This one was different from all the rest of us: cooked on a cross. (pp. 25–27)

Cooked on the cross that we might have life. Cooked on the cross that we might have His Spirit within us. It's interesting that just as the tongue is connected to the heart, it's the heart that receives the Spirit and the tongue that manifests it. "Do not kill and eat your neighbor—I am the bread of life, take and eat."

LESSON 22

A SECRET GARDEN

PROVERBS 3:31-32

³¹ Do not envy the violent or choose any of their ways. ³² For the Lord detests the perverse but takes the upright into his confidence.

The King James Version translates *the violent* as *oppressor*. The word means "someone who oppresses in a violent way." The word translated *perverse* comes from a root word meaning "to turn aside or depart from." The idea is that of turning aside from all that is good and righteous, a departing from godliness. The word translated *confidence* is translated *secret* in the King James Version, and it means "in the company of persons (in close deliberation); intimacy; consultation; a secret assembly, or counsel; it refers to something inward, or secret; confidential" (Strong 1990, *Hebrew/Chaldee Dictionary*, #5475, p. 82).

According to these verses, the Lord takes the upright into His confidence. We see this played out in the life of Abraham. The Lord along with two angels paid him a visit. After communing and eating with Abraham, the Lord sent the angels on to Sodom to do what ultimately had to be done. But the Lord questioned, "Shall I hide from Abraham what I am about to do?" (Genesis 18:17). The Lord lingered near Abraham, and then He took him into His confidence. He took Abraham into that secret garden to share with him His plans.

> The LORD lingered near Abraham, and then He took him into His confidence.

THE LORD CONFIDES IN
THE RIGHTEOUS

David wrote, "The LORD confides in those who fear him; he makes his covenant known to them" (Psalm 25:14). And in the New Testament, Jesus described the same kind of relationship with His believers when he stated, "No longer do I call you servants, for the servant does not know what his master is doing; but I have called you friends, for all that I have heard from my Father I have made known to you" (John 15:15 ESV). We see this played out in the life of Peter. Though Peter had been given the keys to the kingdom years earlier, shortly before Jesus would ascend into heaven, He took Peter into that secret garden and spoke very intimately with him. And when Peter left that secret garden, he knew God's plans for his life. For our benefit, the Lord Jesus allows us to eavesdrop on that meeting:

> So when they had dined, Jesus saith to Simon Peter, Simon, son of Jonas, lovest thou me more than these? He saith unto him, Yea, Lord; thou knowest that I love thee. He saith unto him, Feed my lambs. He saith to him again the second time, Simon, son of Jonas, lovest thou me? He saith unto him, Yea, Lord; thou knowest that I love thee. He saith unto him, Feed my sheep. He saith unto him the third time, Simon, son of Jonas, lovest thou me? Peter was grieved because he said unto him the third time, Lovest thou me? And he said unto him, Lord, thou knowest all things; thou knowest that I love thee. Jesus saith unto him, Feed my sheep. Verily, verily, I say unto thee, When thou wast young, thou girdedst

thyself, and walkedst whither thou wouldest: but when thou shalt be old, thou shalt stretch forth thy hands, and another shall gird thee, and carry thee whither thou wouldest not. This spake he, signifying by what death he should glorify God. And when he had spoken this, he saith unto him, Follow me. (John 21:15–19 KJV)

> Jesus took Peter into that secret garden and spoke very intimately with him. And when Peter left that secret garden, he knew God's plans for his life.

Peter would never be the same when he left that secret garden. Many commentators refer to the last chapter of John as a time when Jesus reinstated Peter's apostleship. There is no indication in the scriptures that Jesus ever rescinded that call. Instead of a time of reinstatement, those moments Jesus spent alone with Peter, speaking in a muted tone, apparently no more than a few feet away from the other apostles, were a time in which the call to a life of ministry began to take form in Peter. It was a moment when the Lord took him into His confidence. There was no discussion about calling fire down from heaven. Instead, he was informed that his job would be to feed the flock of God over which Jesus was making him an overseer. The call would be lonely, and he must not compare it with others. He was informed that to accept the call and do the will of God would cost him his life.

Times really have not changed. Jesus still takes men and women aside, speaks to them in muted tones, and calls them to a life of servitude. He still is looking for Peters who are willing to feed the flock, walk alone, and even die for Him if necessary. But only those who are willing to step aside from the crowd and go into the secret garden with the Lord hear the call. Any honor the world could bestow upon a person pales in comparison to the honor of being taken into the confidence of our Lord.

WHERE HAVE ALL THE HEROES GONE?

Today, honor often is given to a worldly hero, an actor, or a sports team—hero worship. Frequently, the hero is someone who is violent, self-seeking, or works contrary to what God's Word depicts as righteous. The older generation often asks, "Where have all the heroes gone?" Oh, heroes still exist, but they often have names like Sylvester Stallone, the Terminator, Darryl Strawberry, Hannah Montana, Rihanna, Beyoncé, Justin Bieber, or Ice-T.

The reason our fathers and grandfathers ask, "Where have all the heroes gone?" is because these individuals don't look like heroes. They glorify evil rather than good. J. B. Phillips (1995) described this modern-day hero. "Often the oppressor seems to ride high, wide, and handsome. He swaggers through life. He always has his coterie of sycophants who toady to him" (p. 104).

> The reason our fathers and grandfathers ask, "Where have all the heroes gone?" is because these individuals don't look like heroes.

Solomon advises us to beware of seeing anything glamorous or desirable about an oppressor's lifestyle. Unfortunately, far too often, only oppressors appear to win. But God's Word urges, "Don't envy evil people or desire their company" (Proverbs 24:1 NLT). One of the greatest oppressors in history was the pharaoh who kept the Hebrew people in bondage. Moses grew up in his court as his adopted grandson, and he had every opportunity to become an oppressive and violent man. Moses received the finest education in the world at that time. As royalty, he had all the pleasures anyone could want; the treasures of a wealthy king were at his fingertips, and yet that did not tempt him to remain in Pharaoh's household. When Moses became a man, he chose to suffer affliction with the people of God, and he turned his back on all the benefits of royalty. (See Hebrews 11:24–26.) As a result, Moses went down in history as one of the greatest leaders ever—a true hero.

THE NEED FOR A SECRET
PLACE WITH THE LORD

The rewards of an oppressor are short-lived. "Disaster will overtake him in an instant; he will suddenly be destroyed—without remedy" (Proverbs 6:15). Asaph came to understand this truth when he went into the sanctuary of God. While in prayer in that secret garden, God shared with him the outcome of the wicked: They will "stumble, never to get up again. They will be terrified, suddenly swept away and no longer there" (Psalm 73:18–19 CEV). Like Asaph, it's easy to fix our eyes on what seem to be the advantages of the wicked. "For I was envious at the foolish, *when* I saw the prosperity of the wicked" (Psalm 73:3 KJV). However, "The LORD detests the way of the wicked, but he loves those who pursue godliness" (Proverbs 15:9 NLT).

> The rewards of an oppressor are short-lived.

It's amazing how fickle humans can be. After the nation of Israel was delivered from the bondage of Egypt and walked through the Red Sea on dry ground, it was easy to pick up the tambourine and sing the song of Moses. But "They soon forgat his works; they waited not for his counsel: But lusted exceedingly in the wilderness, and tempted God in the desert. And he gave them their request; but sent leanness into their soul" (Psalm 106:13–15 KJV). Fix your eyes upon the bounty of the wicked and leanness of the soul results. What the Israelites needed, what Asaph needed, and what we really need is a secret place with the Lord.

An unknown psalmist wrote, "He that dwelleth in the secret place of the most High shall abide under the shadow of the Almighty" (Psalm 91:1 KJV). Charles Spurgeon (1988), commenting on this verse, made the following observation: "The blessings here promised are not for all believers, but for those who live in close fellowship with God" (Vol. 2, Part 2, p. 88). David asked, "Who shall ascend into the hill of the LORD? or who shall stand in his holy place?" (Psalm 24:3 KJV). Then he answered his own questions, "He that hath clean hands, and a pure heart; who hath not lifted up his soul unto vanity, nor sworn deceitfully. He shall receive the blessing from the LORD, and righteousness from the God of his salvation" (Psalm 24:4–5 KJV). Those who abide in God's presence become possessors of rare and special blessings that are missed by those who follow afar off.

In the New Testament, we have been provided heavenly places in which to sit. God "hath raised *us* up together, and made *us* sit together in heavenly *places* in Christ Jesus" (Ephesians 2:6 KJV). Those who have never experienced being taken into God's confidence know little of what occurs in that secret garden. Oh, the pleasure of being taken into the confidence of the Lord.

> Those who have never experienced being taken into God's confidence know little of what occurs in that secret garden.

IN CLOSING

"Do not envy the violent or choose any of their ways, for the LORD detests a perverse but takes the upright into his confidence" (Proverbs 3:31–32). The following is a story of a young man who admired the violent man and even chose to walk in his ways for a time. But through a turn of events that only God could orchestrate, he discovered the secret garden and was taken into the confidence of the Lord:

> At Providence College [Adoniram] Judson met a classmate named Jacob Eames, an avowed unbeliever who was brilliant, witty, and daringly outspoken. He fascinated Judson, who was flattered by the attention Eames paid to him. Spurred on by charismatic Eames, Judson abandoned the faith of his fathers, followed Eames along the slippery path of unbelief, and became an outspoken and aggressive unbeliever.

During a tour of the northern states, nineteen-year-old Judson stopped one night at a wayside inn. The landlord, full of apologies explained that the only vacant room he had left was next to one in which a young man lay ill. The sick man, it was feared, might be dying. Judson didn't care and assured the landlord that death meant nothing to him.

The partition between the two rooms was thin. During the night the most terrible cries awakened Judson. The heart-rending sounds shook him, unbelieving though he was, but he tried to pull himself together. What would his companions say? What would Jacob Eames say if he knew of this weakness just because a fellow was dying next door? But it was no use. The awful sounds continued as the dying man screamed his way into eternity. He poured out the most frightful blasphemies and then the most pitiful wails. Judson hid his head beneath the blankets and stopped his ears. Finally all was quiet. The man next door had died.

Shattered, Judson rose with the dawn. He sought out the landlord and asked about the young man next. "He's Dead," the landlord said.

"Dead!" exclaimed Judson. "Who was he?"

"He was a student from Providence College." the landlord explained. "A very fine fellow. His name was Jacob Eames." (Phillips 1995, pp. 105–106)

That night, Adoniram Judson came face-to-face with death, and he learned what happens to a violent person who is an abomination to the Lord. He also found that secret garden where he was taken into the confidence of the Lord. It was there he dedicated the next forty years of his life to taking the Word of God to the country of Burma.

LESSON 23

BUILDING A RIGHTEOUS HOME

PROVERBS 3:33

³³ The Lᴏʀᴅ's curse is on the house of the wicked, but he blesses the home of the righteous.

To ignore the Word of God is to invoke a curse. Rank does not have privilege when it comes to living for God. His principles apply equally. Rich or poor, famous or infamous, if you build your house on sand, that house is destined to collapse. We see this principle borne out in Eli's day when he failed to discipline his sons:

> And the Lᴏʀᴅ said to Samuel ... I will perform against Eli all *things* which I have spoken concerning his house ... For I have told him that I will judge his house for ever for the iniquity which he knoweth; because his sons made themselves vile, and he restrained them not. And therefore I have sworn unto the house of Eli, that the iniquity of Eli's house shall not be purged with sacrifice nor offering for ever. (1 Samuel 3:11–14 KJV)

The wicked have a house, a stately house perhaps, but the curse of the LORD is upon it. Though the affairs of the family may prosper, even the blessings are cursed. The result is leanness to the soul. The psalmist described that condition: God "gave them their request; but sent leanness into their soul" (Psalm 106:15 KJV). It is possible to be blessed of God and yet have that blessing turn into a curse. There are grown men and women today who were raised in church and they appear blessed in life, but they have turned their backs on the one who bestows the blessings. They may have money in their bank accounts but leanness in their souls.

HOME—A LITTLE COLONY OF HEAVEN ON EARTH

The challenge of today's Christian families is to have daily interaction with the world yet establish and maintain a home that is separate from the world and dedicated to the Lord. Christian homes ought to stand out in sharp contrast to those of this world. It is here that many Christian homes come up short, but they don't have to. T. F. Tenney (n.d.) wrote:

> If you will open your heart to the Holy Spirit today, He can show you how to make your home a little colony of heaven right here on the terra firma called earth … This is His perfect will. The home may be earth's hardest school, but it is also its highest heaven. … a little heaven on earth … He wants us to live together as families with righteousness peace and joy; not with unrighteousness, chaos and despair. (pp. 22–22)

> The challenge of today's Christian families is to have daily interaction with the world yet establish and maintain a home that is separate from the world and dedicated to the Lord.

Consider the following excerpt from R. E. Ballman's *How Your Family Can Flourish: A Guide to Christian Living in a Post-Christian Culture* (1991):

> It is time we realize that having a home "just as Christian as the next" does not necessarily go far enough. Let's face it—many Christian homes have been polluted by the world. If there was ever an area where Christians need to get out of step with cultural mores, it is in those areas which tempt families towards moral impurity.
>
> If there was ever a time to break ranks, now is the time. You can't change the whole world, but you can avoid exposure to some of its vices. It takes real leadership and spiritual courage to act in defense of your family's moral decency and purity. Some hope the problems won't affect their children. Others talk about how bad things are, but do little more than wink at the issues. Uncompromising Christians don't just wish for a solution—they act. We need more Christians with backbone—believers who will take the offensive, put greater moral safeguards in place, and speak out for Jesus Christ. (pp. 40–41)

The ideal Christian family—and I believe it's time to once again put forth a picture of the ideal Christian family—is one that places the home under the authority of Jesus Christ. The ideal Christian family is one in which the husband is the head of the home and loves his wife as Christ loves the church. It is a family in which the wife is both a helper to her husband and homemaker for her family. She submits to her husband as to the Lord, and the children are obedient to both. I realize that due to unfortunate circumstances, many families do not look like God's ideal model of the family. However, that does not mean we should abandon God's model for the family just because His model cannot always be achieved. If you are one who has experienced divorce or borne children out of wedlock prior to conversion, you should not be offended by the presentation of God's model of the family as the ideal. Instead, you should aspire to emulate His model as much as possible.

> The ideal Christian family—and I believe it's time to once again put forth a picture of the ideal Christian family—is one that places its home under the authority of Jesus Christ.

Be it ever so humble, God "blesses the home of the righteous" (Proverbs 3:33). The word translated *home* in that verse means a *poor cottage*. It may be a simple dwelling, but if it is built on righteousness, God will continually bless it. Righteousness affects all that it touches. If you are a convert to Christ, but your spouse has not yet made the conversion, if you do all that is possible to build your home according to the God-given model, you will become a channel of righteousness to those yet unconverted:

> If you are a man with a wife who is not a believer but who still wants to live with you, hold on to her. If you are a woman with a husband who is not a believer but he wants to live with you, hold on to him. The unbelieving husband shares to an extent in the holiness of his wife, and the unbelieving wife is likewise touched by the holiness of her husband. Otherwise, your children would be left out; as it is, they also are included in the spiritual purposes of God. (1 Corinthians 7:12–14, MSG)

THE UNGODLY INFLUENCE OF
TELEVISION AND THE MOVIE INDUSTRY

The media—particularly television, movies, the internet, social media, and advertising—have shaped the culture in which we live. Television and movie producers have done everything possible to change the meaning of family from the God-given model to a picture of brokenness. Instead of putting forth the God-given model as an ideal to aspire toward, they want to display their model, which falls far short of the ideal. As a result, mainstream society moves further and further away from the ideal put forth in the Bible.

> Television and movie producers have done everything possible to change the meaning of family from the God-given model to a picture of brokenness.

Though dated, a poll by the American Enterprise Institute for Public Policy Research in Washington is revealing of some of the values of television writers:

- 45 percent profess no religious service once a month.
- 7 percent profess no religion at all.
- 80 percent do not regard homosexual relations as wrong.
- 97 percent favor abortion on demand.
- 75 percent call themselves political liberals.
- Only 17 percent condemned adultery (Ballmann 1991, p. 36).

Keep in mind those statistics were from 1991. The world has not improved its values. Solomon admonishes us, "Above all else, guard your heart, for everything you do flows from it" (Proverbs 4:23). God's people are called upon to stand strong for godliness. Worldly values must not be assimilated into our homes and churches. As a result of subtle pressure from the media and the unquestioning acceptance of sin, many of today's teenagers and adults accept immorality as a way of life. But can we blame them? Immoral suggestions and temptations are continually being thrown in their faces, often when they least expect it—in the checkout lines at the grocery stores, on billboards, in magazines, and on social media ads. To maintain righteousness, we must choose to avoid activities and environments where immorality is likely to be set before our faces.

> To maintain righteousness, we must choose to avoid activities and environments where immorality is likely to be set before our faces.

AN ANTIDOTE TO WORLDLINESS

What can we do to counteract the onslaught of the world? Living in a cold climate, the only place you want the outside environment coming in is through the door when you selectively choose to open it. As much as possible and within reason, Christian families must insulate themselves from ungodly cultural influences and activities without isolating themselves. There are a number of steps that can be taken to accomplish this, and it begins with parents.

Demonstrate your love for God. "Seek ye first the kingdom of God, and his righteousness" (Matthew 6:33 KJV). The scriptures, particularly the New Testament, teach us—above all else—to love. "Thou shalt love the Lord thy God with all thy heart, and with all thy soul, and with all thy mind" (Matthew 22:37 KJV). But it is not enough to simply say, "I love God"; it must be demonstrated. Your love for God must be demonstrated in hundreds of little ways that your children will quickly perceive. If your love for God is only half-hearted, they will quickly become aware of that also.

Demonstrate your love for family members. The Lord desires that there be a demonstration of true love for spouse and children. Frequently, failure to demonstrate love toward other family members is the result of a faulty relationship with God. To truly yield to the love of God will produce perfect love toward others, including your spouse and children. The greatest thing a man can do for his children is to love their mother. Likewise, the greatest thing a woman can do for her children is to love their father.

> The greatest thing a man can do for his children is to love their mother. Likewise, the greatest thing a woman can do for her children is to love their father.

Develop strong scriptural standards. Develop strong scriptural standards of holiness and teach them to your children. It has been said, "The best defense is a good offense." Committed Christians recognize the importance of spiritual warfare and fight the good fight of faith, relying on the power of God, the Word of God, and the wisdom of God. Peter was well aware of the need to maintain good defenses when he wrote, "Therefore, dear friends, since you already have been forewarned, be on your guard so that you may not be carried away by the error of the lawless" (2 Peter 3:17). To "be on guard" not only means to "watch" out for temptation, but also "to take whatever steps necessary to protect your family's moral purity."

Protect your family's moral purity. Jesus cautioned, "Watch and pray, that ye enter not into temptation" (Matthew 26:41 KJV). Again, to *watch* not only means to watch out for temptation but also to take whatever steps are necessary to protect your family's moral purity. "Lead us not into temptation" (Matthew 6:13 KJV) does not put the responsibility for our victory or defeat our heavenly Father. Rather, it is a request for awareness of those things that might lead us into temptation, so that we can eliminate them from our lives and our homes. For example, Christians need to eliminate morally compromising entertainment from their homes and daily lifestyles. The Old English language has a nice word to describe *lifestyle* (i.e., conversation), because whatever you do speaks loudly to those around you. "Only let your conversation be as it becometh the gospel of Christ" (Philippians 1:27 KJV). And "As he which hath called you is holy, so be ye holy in all manner of conversation" (1 Peter 1:15 KJV). Some need to cancel subscriptions to certain publications that have articles or advertisements that routinely appeal to unhealthy sexual appetites. Still others need to examine their children's classroom activities and values that are being taught contrary to the Word of God. And every parent needs to closely observe the *conversations* they are exhibiting to their children.

> Christians need to eliminate morally compromising entertainment from their homes and daily lifestyles.

Promote courtship in place of dating. Further, the practice that has come to be known as dating needs to be replaced with the concept of courtship. Emerson and April Morris (n.d.) make the following comparison between dating and courting. Dating includes such behaviors and characteristics as "Game play, Eventful, Pleasureful, Ends with another date, Self-centered, and Hormonal Decisions." On the other hand, they describe courting as including the following behaviors: "Intentional, Purposeful, Ends in Marriage, God-centered, Accountability, and Holy decisions."

Dating, by today's definition, often includes an expectation of a sexual encounter outside the bounds of marriage, often on the first date. It is a social encounter that is less goal oriented toward marriage. Today, dating frequently includes moving in together and setting up a household as though married. It includes enjoying many of the benefits of marriage without the commitment. Often, when you ask a dating couple about plans for marriage, they will respond with something like, "We're not ready yet," or "We don't know each other well enough yet," even though they have been living together and have children together. It leaves the door open for an easy exit.

In contrast, courting is an old term that speaks of respect and includes the concept of the man wooing the lady. In a courting relationship, a couple commits to each other and to spending time communicating and doing fun activities together, with marriage as a potential goal. Courtship is a time of getting to know each other without complicating the relationship with sexual intimacy. This way, the courting couple has plenty of time to come to know each other, to build lasting trust, and to allow love to develop.

Be aware of the worldly encroachment. Christians, under the guidance of the Holy Spirit, need to be aware of the encroachment of the world into their daily lives. Paul warned, "Don't copy the behavior and customs of this world, but let God transform you into a new person by changing the way you think" (Romans 12:2 NLT). Don't let the world set the standards for your family; let the Word of God and the guidance of the Holy Spirit establish deep-rooted convictions in your lives and the lives of your family members. Remember, good insulation keeps the chill of the world out. You don't save your family and change the world by becoming like the world; you save your family and change the world around you be being a counterculture shaped by the Word of God.

> Don't let the world set the standards for your family; let the Word of God and the guidance of the Holy Spirit establish deep-rooted convictions in your lives and the lives of your family members.

Maintain separation from the world. Jesus reminded, "If the world hates you, remember that it hated me first. The world would love you as one of its own if you belonged to it, but you are no longer part of the world. I chose you to come out of the world, so it hates you" (John 15:18–19 NLT).

> The radical Christian family goes out of its way to keep its focus on God and to maintain separation from the world. This doesn't come easily. Holy living is rugged and demanding; it exacts a price. Daily we must battle in the trenches of a sinful world, being thankful for every opportunity to serve God. We need to enact safeguards and disciplines that others

may dub unnecessary, overreactive or legalistic. We may have to bear criticism, mockery and scorn for our commitment to God's standards. Sometimes this criticism even comes from those within the church. Sometimes it comes from relatives. This all hurts terribly! But we understand and expect it, for this is the cost of discipleship. (Ballmann 1991, p. 128)

IN CLOSING

Jesus stated that every Christian and, by extension, every Christian family is to be the salt of the earth and the light of the world. (See Matthew 5:13–16.) The choice is ours.

Our lives and our families can be permanent memorials for Almighty God or sand castles whose works are soon erased. We can let our lives and witness etch their eternal marks in God's master plan, or we can expend our effort building short-lived earthly empires. (Ballmann 1991, p. 165)

Ask yourself the following questions: Is your family lukewarm or red-hot for Jesus? What does your lifestyle reveal about your spiritual commitments? If you raise your children with godly values, the probability of them internalizing those values when they become adults is significantly increased. And that, in turn, increases the probability of the next generation building a righteous home.

LESSON 24

THOU SHALT NOT MOCK GOD

PROVERBS 3:34

³⁴ *He mocks proud mockers but shows favor to the humble and oppressed.*

As an introduction, consider the following sayings about pride:

- They that know God will be humble; they that know themselves cannot be proud. (Schmitt 1975, p. 54)
- The true way to be humble is not to stoop until you are smaller than yourself, but to stand at your real height against some higher nature. (Schmitt 1975, pp. 54–55)
- Pride *goeth* before destruction, and an haughty spirit before a fall. (Proverbs 16:18 KJV)

A COMMON HUMAN EXPERIENCE

Pride is universal. We are all in love with ourselves to some degree. Pride and humility are not dichotomous but continuous. All of us fall somewhere on the continuum between pride and humility. An extremely proud person is unlikely to be aware of their pride, and only arrogance would lead someone to proclaim, "I am humble." The moment you boast of your humility is the moment you slide back into pride.

> The moment you boast of your humility is the moment you slide back into pride.

PRIDE IS INSIDIOUS

Nebuchadnezzar was a man who was great in his own eyes, and that pride brought about his destruction. Nebuchadnezzar dreamed a dream that so troubled him he called upon all his magicians, enchanters, sorcerers, and astrologers. To test their veracity, he not only demanded they provide him an interpretation of the dream but that they tell him what he had dreamed. When the king was about to execute the wise men of the kingdom for their inability to tell him his dream, Daniel pleaded their cause: "No wise man, enchanter, magician or diviner can explain to the king the mystery he has asked about, but there is a God in heaven who reveals mysteries" (Daniel 2:27–28). Daniel acknowledged the source of the dream and went to the source for the answer. He took no credit for being able to interpret the dream. He explained, "It is not because I am wiser than anyone else that I know the secret of your dream, but because God wants you to understand what was in your heart" (Daniel 2:30 NLT).

Impressed by the omniscience of Daniel's God, Nebuchadnezzar acknowledged the source of both the dream and the interpretation: "The king answered unto Daniel … your God *is* a God of gods, and a Lord of kings, and a revealer of secrets, seeing thou couldest reveal this secret" (Daniel 2:47 KJV). But Nebuchadnezzar struggled with pride. When Shadrach, Meshach, and Abednego did not bow down and worship the image of gold he set up, Nebuchadnezzar flew into a rage, sending them to the fiery furnace. But when God delivered them, Nebuchadnezzar again acknowledged the one true God: "Blessed *be* the God of Shadrach, Meshach, and Abednego, who hath sent his angel, and delivered his servants that trusted in him!" (Daniel 3:28 KJV).

Pride is insidious, and unless rooted out and destroyed, it will spring to life and reemerge:

> At the end of twelve months [King Nebuchadnezzar] walked in the palace of the kingdom of Babylon. The king spake, and said, Is not this great Babylon, that I have built for the house of the kingdom by the might of my power, and for the honour of my majesty? (Daniel 4:29–30 KJV)

> Pride is insidious, and unless rooted out and destroyed, it will spring to life and reemerge.

Immediately, Nebuchadnezzar "was driven from men, and did eat grass as oxen, and his body was wet with the dew of heaven, till his hairs were grown like eagles' *feathers*, and his nails like birds' *claws*" (Daniel 4:33 KJV). By Nebuchadnezzar's own words, he remained that way until he humbled himself and acknowledged the true God:

> At the end of that time, I, Nebuchadnezzar, raised my eyes toward heaven, and my sanity was restored ... Now I, Nebuchadnezzar, praise and exalt and glorify the King of heaven, because everything he does is right and all his ways are just. And those who walk in pride he is able to humble. (Daniel 4:34, 37)

One would think that anyone who knew the story of Nebuchadnezzar would learn vicariously. But his grandson, Belshazzar, apparently was not a student of history. He mocked God by desecrating the sacred vessels that belonged to the temple of the LORD:

> King Belshazzar gave a great banquet for a thousand of his nobles and drank wine with them. While Belshazzar was drinking his wine, he gave orders to bring in the

gold and silver goblets that Nebuchadnezzar his father had taken from the temple in Jerusalem, so that the king and his nobles, his wives and his concubines might drink from them. So they brought in the gold goblets that had been taken from the temple of God in Jerusalem, and the king and his nobles, his wives and his concubines drank from them. As they drank the wine, they praised the gods of gold and silver, of bronze, iron, wood and stone.

Suddenly the fingers of a human hand appeared and wrote on the plaster of the wall, near the lampstand in the royal palace. The king watched the hand as it wrote. His face turned pale and he was so frightened that his knees knocked together and his legs gave way. (Daniel 5:1–6 NLT)

Again, Daniel was called to interpret the writing on the wall, and it was not good news: "O Belshazzar, [thou] hast not humbled thine heart, though thou knewest all this; But hast lifted up thyself against the Lord of heaven" (Daniel 5:22–23 KJV). God mocks the mocker. "That very night Belshazzar, king of the Babylonians, was slain, and Darius the Mede took over the kingdom" (Daniel 5:30–31).

YOU CAN MOCK GOD, BUT YOU CAN'T GET AWAY WITH IT.

Voltaire, who died in 1778, proclaimed, "One hundred years from now the Bible will be an obsolete book, relegated to the dusty shelves of the antiquarian" (Barton 1914, p. 454). A wise peasant responded to the thinking of those who lived during the time of Voltaire—the Age of Enlightenment:

French revolutionaries ... tore the cross from the cathedral of Notre Dame and promoted atheism, hatred, and violence. One of them said to a peasant,

"We are going to pull down all that reminds you of God." The peasant was not impressed. He replied, "Well, citizen, then pull down the stars." (Phillips 1995, pp. 106–107)

Though Voltaire and the enlightened French Revolutionaries went by the way of the grave, mockers of godliness have not gone away. "Christian values, according to Hollywood, are dangerous and no child should be exposed to them without their parents' consent" (Wildmon 1985, p. 23). Donald Wildmon (1985) dared to challenge the secularists of his day when he wrote the book *The Home Invaders*. In it, he made the following observation:

To the humanist mind and mentality, all influence of Christian faith must be removed from society. To achieve this end, the humanist feels obligated and duty-bound to use whatever methods available, particularly the media. It also means establishing humanism as the rule for law and justice in our society—the establishing of a system of law undergirded and guided by the humanist religion.

... This definite shifting of the foundation of our society from a Christian view of man to a humanist view naturally brings about changes. One of the most fundamental changes is that the church loses its ability to influence society ... And this is precisely what the national media elite desire. (p. 25)

While the media reports chaos in our schools and in our streets, they fail to recognize that you can't destroy the foundation and expect the building to stand. And marriage is the foundation of any society, but it is under attack by humanistic thinkers who have given birth to the postmodern post-Christian era. However, the Bible still remains the standard in defining moral behavior. And in the Bible, the writer of Hebrews declared boldly, "Give honor to marriage, and remain faithful to one another in marriage. God will surely judge people who are immoral and those who commit adultery" (Hebrews 13:4 NLT). Popenoe and Whitehead (1999) describe the demise of biblical morals in contemporary culture:

> Cohabitation is replacing marriage as the first living together experience for young men and women. When blushing brides walk down the aisle ..., more than half have already lived together with a boyfriend.
>
> For today's young adults, ... living together seems like a good way to achieve some of the benefits of marriage and avoid the risk of divorce. Couples who live together can share expenses and learn more about each other. They can find out if their partner has what it takes to be married. If things don't work out, breaking up is easy to do. Cohabiting couples do not have to seek legal or religious permission to dissolve their union. Not surprisingly, young adults favor cohabitation. According to surveys, most young people say it is a good idea to live with a person before marrying.
>
> But a careful review of the available social science evidence suggests that living together is not a good way to prepare for marriage or to avoid divorce. What's more, it shows that the rise in cohabitation is not a positive family trend. Cohabiting unions tend to weaken the institution of marriage and pose clear and present dangers for women and children. Specifically, the research indicates that: Living together before marriage increases the risk of breaking up after marriage. Living together outside of marriage increases the risk of domestic violence for women, and the risk of physical and sexual abuse for children. Unmarried couples have lower levels of happiness and well-being than married couples.

> While the media reports chaos in our schools and in our streets, they fail to recognize that you can't destroy the foundation and expect the building to stand.

Will God stand by and be mocked? Rome fell because of immorality and promiscuity. By the time Paul wrote to the Roman church, the nation of Rome was already in its decline. Sexual perversion had permeated their culture. God will not be mocked; He will mock the mocker:

> So God abandoned them to do whatever shameful things their hearts desired. As a result, they did vile and degrading things with each other's bodies. They traded the truth about God for a lie. ... That is why God abandoned them to their shameful desires. Even the women turned against the natural way to have sex and instead indulged in sex with each other. And the men, instead of having normal sexual relations with women, burned with lust for each other. Men did shameful things with other men, and as a result of this sin, they suffered within themselves the penalty they deserved. (Romans 1:24–27 NLT)

God will not be mocked; He will mock the mocker. Sexually transmitted diseases (STDs) are at record highs: the US Centers for Disease Control (CDC 2013) reports that there are more than 110 million sexually transmitted infections (STIs) overall among men and women nationwide. This estimate includes both new and existing infections. That is one in three Americans. "Young people (ages 15–24) are particularly affected, accounting for half (50 percent) of all new STIs, although they represent just 25 percent of the sexually experienced population" (CDC 2013). Contraception is far from foolproof. "Currently, about half (51%) of the 6.6 million pregnancies in the United States each year (3.4 million) are unintended" (Guttmacher

Institute, 2013). There are between 1.3 and 1.4 million abortions each year in the United States (Trupin et al. 2014). Illegitimate births went from 5 percent of all births in 1960 to 40.7 percent in 2014 (CDC 2014).

Is it possible that when the world has tried everything, and everything has failed, it will turn to Jesus? Will they at least acknowledge the principles undergirding Christianity to be true? Is it possible that the world in despair might turn to the Word of God for instruction?

GOD HONORS THE HUMBLE

"He mocks proud mockers but shows favor to the humble" (Proverbs 3:34). Humility involves freedom from arrogance or pride. Those who are humble do not view others as inferior to themselves, nor do they view themselves as inferior to others. When looking for an example of humility, Moses is a good place to begin. Moses received great authority, yet he never let that authority go to his head. Receiving a position of authority is a real test of humility. Often when an individual receives a little authority, their humility—or lack thereof—quickly becomes evident. Robert G. Ingersoll (1888) cautioned: "Most people can bear adversity. But if you wish to know what a man really is, give him power." This may be what the LORD saw in Moses. "Moses was very humble—more humble than any other person on earth" (Numbers 12:3 NLT).

> Those who are humble do not view others as inferior to themselves, nor do they view themselves as inferior to others.

Moses did not jealously guard his authority. He rejoiced when the LORD allowed other Israelites to act as prophets alongside him:

> Eldad and Medad, had stayed behind in the camp. They were listed among the elders, but they had not

gone out to the Tabernacle. Yet the Spirit rested upon them as well, so they prophesied there in the camp. A young man ran and reported to Moses, "Eldad and Medad are prophesying in the camp!"

Joshua son of Nun, who had been Moses' assistant since his youth, protested, "Moses, my master, make them stop!"

But Moses replied, "Are you jealous for my sake? I wish that all the LORD's people were prophets and that the LORD would put his Spirit upon them all!" (Numbers 11:26–29 NLT)

And toward the end of his life, although still physically strong, Moses asked the LORD to appoint a successor. In doing so, he demonstrated that he did not put his authority ahead of the welfare of others:

Please appoint a new man as leader for the community. Give them someone who will guide them wherever they go and will lead them into battle, so the community of the LORD will not be like sheep without a shepherd. (Numbers 27:16–17 NLT)

When the LORD selected Joshua, Moses wholeheartedly supported the younger man, urging the people to follow Joshua's lead into the Promised Land.

HUMILITY ISN'T FASCINATED WITH STATUS

Moses's example also teaches us not to place too much importance on our status or authority. We must never let power, authority, or natural ability go to our heads. Many years after Moses had passed off the scene, Samuel reminded King Saul that when his humility exceeded his ability, the LORD was able to use him: "Although you were once small in your own eyes, did you not become the head of the tribes of Israel? The LORD anointed you king over Israel" (1 Samuel 15:17). In order to be useful to God, our humility should always exceed our ability.

> In order to be useful to God, our humility should always exceed our ability.

Would we benefit from imitating Moses's example of humility? Without question! When we cultivate genuine humility, we make life easier for the people around us, endearing ourselves to them. More importantly, we endear ourselves to the LORD, who himself displays this beautiful quality of humbling Himself, as described by David: "Your right hand upholds me, and your humility exalts me" (Psalm 18:35 HCSB). God "mocks proud mockers but shows favor to the humble" (Proverbs 3:34).

IN CLOSING

God will not be mocked; He will mock the mocker. However, He gives grace to the humble. There are benefits to following the ways of God. There are benefits in acknowledging the LORD and honoring Him with both your spirit and your body. "He guides the humble in what is right and teaches them his way" (Psalm 25:9).

Too often, the only picture we have of humility is the tax collector standing beside the Pharisee: "The publican, standing afar off, would not lift up so much as *his* eyes unto heaven, but smote upon his breast, saying, God be merciful to me a sinner" (Luke 18:13 KJV). Humility is not necessarily characterized by hanging our heads. When Nebuchadnezzar came to himself, in humility, he wrote a song:

> I Nebuchadnezzar lifted up mine eyes unto heaven,
> and mine understanding returned unto me, and I
> blessed the most High, and I praised and honoured him

that liveth for ever, whose dominion *is* an everlasting dominion, and his kingdom *is* from generation to generation: And all the inhabitants of the earth *are* reputed as nothing: and he doeth according to his will in the army of heaven, and *among* the inhabitants of the earth: and none can stay his hand, or say unto him, What doest thou? (Daniel 4:34–35 KJV)

Though a pagan king, this was humility expressing reverence to an all-knowing, all-powerful God. As noted earlier, those who are humble do not view others as inferior to themselves, nor do they view themselves as inferior to others. Humility recognizes one's limitations but also expresses gratefulness to God for one's abilities and accomplishments with those abilities. Humility doesn't deflect compliments but respects others by acknowledging their desire to express thankfulness and gratefulness. Humility recognizes one's accomplishments but is grateful to the God in heaven who grants the ability to accomplish a task well.

LESSON 25

HOW WILL YOU BE REMEMBERED?

PROVERBS 3:35

35 The wise inherit honor, but fools get only shame.

Nearly 200 years ago there were two Scottish brothers named John and David Livingstone. John had set his mind on making money and becoming wealthy, and he did. But under his name in an old edition of the Encyclopedia Britannica John Livingstone is listed simply as "the brother of David Livingstone" (1813–1873).

While John had dedicated himself to making money, David had invested his life as a missionary to Africa. He resolved, "I will place no value on anything I have or possess unless it is in relationship to the kingdom of God." The inscription over his burial place in Westminster Abbey reads, "For thirty years his life was spent in an unwearied effort to evangelize." Two men ... two brothers, yet, both lived very different lives. (Krell 2006)

Similar to John and David Livingstone, Abraham and Lot are biblical examples of two very different men who lived two very different lives. Thirteen chapters in Genesis are devoted to the life and time of Abraham; among these thirteen, five tell the story of Lot. Unlike Abraham's story, Lot's story describes the results of tragic choices.

Given Lot's failure, why is so much space devoted to telling us about Lot's tragedy? As with all biblical narratives, there are lessons to be learned. Lot represents the one who walks by sight, while Abraham represents the individual who walks by faith. Like Abraham, we must "walk by faith, not by sight" (2 Corinthians 5:7 KJV). Lot looked for a city built with human hands; Abraham looked for "a city which hath foundations, whose builder and maker *is* God" (Hebrews 1:10 KJV).

Both men were from the same family; both of them received the call of God, followed God, and were blessed. However, the world remembers one as a great man of God with good values to adopt, whereas the other is remembered for his failures. The Bible tells us, "Abraham believed God, and it was counted unto him for righteousness" (Romans 4:3 KJV). In contrast, Lot made choices that took his family out of the land of promise to what appeared to be a well-watered plain. Looking for even greener grass, he moved from that well-watered plain to a place so consumed with sexual perversion the LORD could not withhold judgment. Only the grace of God led Lot out of the city, but it cost the life of his wife (Genesis 19:26) and the moral integrity of his two daughters (Genesis 19:30–38).

> Lot made choices that took his family out of the land of promise to what appeared to be a well-watered plain.

CHOICES

We all make choices, and every decision we make leads us either closer to or further from our God-given destiny. How are your choices and decisions affecting your life today? Are your choices righteous or evil? Are the choices you make furthering you in His kingdom or leading you to destruction? You have the potential to influence your world for Jesus by the way you order your family. In all that you do, you are making choices for your family. Lot chose to let the world shape his family. He made a choice that determined his future and the future of generations of descendants to come. Tensions between Abraham's herdsmen and Lot's herdsmen led Abraham to offer Lot the choice between the hillsides of Canaan or the well-watered plain of the Jordan:

> Lot looked around and saw that the whole plain of the Jordan toward Zoar was well watered, like the garden of the LORD, like the land of Egypt. ... So Lot chose for himself the whole plain of the Jordan and set out toward the east. (Genesis 13:10–11)

We all make choices, and every decision we make leads us either closer to or further from our God-given destiny.

It was evident that after twelve years in Sodom, Lot had made no impact upon the culture and the world in which he lived. Though not partaking of the sins of Sodom, he had become comfortable living in that environment. The LORD, however, was not comfortable with the condition of Sodom, and with no missionary effort put forth by Lot, "The LORD said, Because the cry of Sodom and Gomorrah is great, and because their sin is very grievous; I will go down now, and see whether they have done altogether according to the cry of it" (Genesis 18:20–21 KJV).

Angels were sent on ahead, seemingly to rescue Lot and his family from wicked Sodom. But as the fire was about to fall, we see Lot demonstrating no leadership for his family, still reluctant to leave that sinful place. Lot embraced the culture of his world, and in turn, the culture influenced both him and his family. When it was almost too late, "Lot rushed out to tell his daughters' fiancés, 'Quick, get out of the city! The LORD is about to destroy it.' But the young men thought he was only joking" (Genesis 19:14 NLT). And even Lot seems to have had a difficult time leaving that city: "When Lot still hesitated, the angels seized his hand and the hands of his wife and two daughters and rushed them to safety outside the city, for the Lord was merciful" (Genesis 19:16 NLT). And then the most horrible of all happened: "Lot's wife looked back, and she became a pillar of salt" (Genesis 19:26).

THE INFLUENCE OF A GODLY FAMILY

In contrast to Lot, Abraham chose to embrace a culture of righteousness. The LORD said, "I know him, that he will command his children and his household after him, and they shall keep the way of the LORD" (Genesis 18:19 KJV). Thus, he became a stepping-stone for generations yet to be born. As you order your family according to the Word of God, you are influencing the world in which you live, and your children will live, and their children after them.

> As you order your family according to the Word of God, you are influencing the world in which you live, and your children will live, and their children after them.

Though it may not be politically correct to speak of being a culture changer, that's exactly what Christians are to be. Believers are the light and salt to whatever culture they are immersed in. Righteousness is the only preserving force in the world in which we live. Society does not have the answer for the crime and severe problems plaguing our world today. The church has the answer because Jesus is the only hope and cure for the world's ills.

Like Lot, Noah also was immersed in a wicked culture. The picture the LORD gives of Noah's day is not a very pretty one: "The LORD observed the extent of human wickedness on the earth, and he saw that everything they thought or imagined was consistently and totally evil" (Genesis 6:5 NLT). However, unlike Lot, Noah attempted to affect the culture of his day. Peter wrote that Noah was "a preacher of righteousness" (2 Peter 2:5 KJV). It is unclear from the scriptures how much Noah influenced the culture in his day, but we do know that the culture didn't influence him. "Noah did everything exactly as God commanded him" (Genesis 6:22 NLT). Too often, we become preoccupied with the threat the culture of the world presents to the church without considering the opposite. The church is supposed to be influencing culture. "Greater is he that is in you, than he that is in the world" (1 John 4:4 KJV). When a Spirit-filled family becomes a part of a community, they have the power to shape culture:

> A pastor related how a teenage Christian girl in his church refused to wear shorts when participating in athletic functions. She was the only one wearing a skirt. Instead of her being tempted to wear shorts, the other girls asked if they could wear skirts. When the teacher gave them permission, all the girls wore skirts instead of shorts. (Davis 2103, summer, p. 89)

> Too often, we become preoccupied with the threat the culture of the world presents to the church without considering the opposite. The church is supposed to be influencing culture.

Satan wants Christians to feel they are oddballs for not conforming to the culture of the world. However, they are the light of their world, and living a godly lifestyle pushes back darkness. Jesus was emphatic:

> Ye are the light of the world. A city that is set on an hill cannot be hid. Neither do men light a candle, and put it under a bushel, but on a candlestick; and it giveth light unto all that are in the house. Let your light so shine before men, that they may see your good works, and glorify your Father which is in heaven. (Matthew 5:14–16 KJV)

As a follower of Jesus, you are to reflect the light of Jesus Christ into this dark world, creating a culture of righteousness. If you fail to do so, the world will be a dark place with little or no hope. Christians often do not realize how much their godly lives are a deterrent to evil. If you think it's dark now, wait until the church is removed. The church is the only factor hindering Satan from doing a complete work of deceiving the world. Thank God for the light of individual Christians in our dark world!

> As followers of Jesus, you are to reflect the light of Jesus Christ into this dark world, creating a culture of righteousness.

Christians are the salt of the world in which they live. They must not lose their saltiness. If they do, in Jesus's own words, they are "good for nothing, but to be cast out, and to be trodden under foot of men" (Matthew 5:13 KJV). Their saltiness is their power and influence. If Christians lose their ability to be a positive influence on earth, they lose their usefulness to God's purpose. For your life to be an effective witness for Christ, your experience with God must remain fresh.

IN CLOSING

When Abraham appealed to the LORD in prayer, it appears the LORD would have held back judgment if the culture of Sodom could have been changed. Abraham began by asking for a stay of execution if he could find fifty righteous people. And God was willing to go as low as ten righteous persons. When Abraham interceded for Lot, the LORD responded, "For the sake of ten, I will not destroy it" (Genesis 18:32). And maybe the LORD would have gone as low as five, but we will never know because Abraham stopped at ten.

Like Abraham, you have great influence on the world in which your grandchildren will live. When your life is over, how will you be remembered? Will your tombstone simply bear a dash between two numbers, or will it note how you influenced your world?

LESSON 26

REMEMBERING DADDY'S WORDS

PROVERBS 4:1-9

¹ Listen, my sons, to a father's instruction; pay attention and gain understanding. ² I give you sound learning, so do not forsake my teaching. ³ For I too was a son to my father, still tender, and cherished by my mother. ⁴ Then he taught me and said to me, "Take hold of my words with all your heart; keep my commands and you will live. ⁵ Get wisdom, get understanding; do not forget my words or turn from them. ⁶ Do not forsake wisdom, and she will protect you; love her, and she will watch over you. ⁷ The beginning of wisdom is this: Get wisdom. Though it cost all you have, get understanding. ⁸ Cherish her, and she will exalt you; embrace her, and she will honor you. ⁹ She will give you a garland to grace your head and present you with a glorious crown."

In the above verses, Solomon urges his sons and all future generations of sons who might read these words to heed his instruction. As he speaks with his sons, he recalls a very intimate moment when he was young and his father, David, instructed him. The warmth and intimacy are clearly displayed. It's likely David had many chats with Solomon, but this one stood out in Solomon's mind as so significant that he dated it to a time before his brothers were born and he was still an only child. He probably was quite young, but he never forgot.

In his instruction, Solomon spelled out several specific points to his sons from which we can learn. First, he urged them to listen to his instruction. Then he encouraged them to get wisdom and never forsake it. Third, he emphasized the supreme value of wisdom.

UNDERSTANDING AUTHORITY

Solomon urged his sons to listen to listen to his instruction. Everyone must learn the reality of authority. A Roman centurion comes to mind as one who understood authority. He stated, "I also am a man set under authority, having under me soldiers, and I say unto one, Go, and he goeth; and to another, Come, and he cometh; and to my servant, Do this, and he doeth *it*" (Luke 7:8 KJV). That centurion recognized the authority he exercised daily was not his but was delegated to him from above. Though a military officer with one hundred men under his charge, he was not exempt from authority; he was part of the chain of command. All of the authority in heaven and earth is positioned above us as a protective and empowering umbrella.

> All of the authority in heaven and earth is positioned above us as a protective and empowering umbrella.

It is necessary to learn obedience to authority if one is to fit harmoniously into society. Young people who don't learn to respect authority don't make good citizens, good businesspeople, good husbands, or good wives. This teaching is not the word of humans but of God:

> Let everyone be subject to the governing authorities, for there is no authority except that which God has established. The authorities that exist have been established by God. Consequently, whoever rebels against the authority is rebelling against what God has instituted, and those who do so will bring judgment on themselves. (Romans 13:1–2)

THE FIFTH COMMANDMENT

In reading Solomon's instructions to his son, the fifth commandment comes to mind: "Honour thy father and mother; (which is the first commandment with promise;) That it may be well with thee, and thou mayest live long on the earth" (Ephesians 6:2–3 KJV). The fifth commandment is for everyone's benefit. It is one of the precepts of the Lord that promises great reward when obeyed. First of all, it's for the child's own good; then it benefits the home, the church, and society. The benefit of respect for authority is attested to by thousands of years of human history.

Obey your parents. It would be interesting to know what David told Solomon and, in turn, what Solomon told his sons. However, considering what we know from the Word of God, it is very likely obeying parents was at the top of the list. Children owe their parents obedience: "Children, obey your parents in the Lord: for this is right" (Ephesians 6:1 KJV). Obedience is a virtue of character. It is a necessary preparation for positions of trust and authority. No one is prepared to lead until they have learned to obey. It is notable how Jesus responded to His earthly parents when they found Him ministering in the temple. At His mother's command, "he went down to Nazareth with them and was obedient to them" (Luke 2:51).

> No one is prepared to lead until they have learned to obey.

An interview with those who are in penal institutions will reveal that many who made shipwreck of their lives did so because they had no respect for parental authority. Disobedience to parents leads to disobedience to other forms of authority. That has led to untold misery in millions of homes. David's cry of anguish when his son, Absalom, died as a result of rebellion has been heard over and over again: "'O my son Absalom! My son, my son Absalom! If only I had died instead of you—O Absalom, my son, my son!'" (2 Samuel 18:33). The matter of obedience should not be taken lightly because it is an important step toward honoring the father and mother.

> Disobedience to parents leads to disobedience to other forms of authority.

Respect your parents. Another word of advice Solomon may have heard from his father was "respect your parents." The LORD was very serious when He commanded, "Each of you must respect your mother and father ... I am the LORD your God" (Leviticus 19:3). To be respectful means one must never talk back. One individual described how he learned that lesson:

> I remember as a boy I went into the kitchen one day to ask permission of my mother to do something. Mother was standing with her back to me, washing dishes. She didn't give me permission to do what I wanted, and I had heard other children "talk back;" so I thought this was one time I could get by. I was a pretty good-sized teenager. I was standing behind my mother, so I sassed her. I do not recall what I said but before I could finish, Mother's wet and soapy hand caught me on the left side of my face. She stood facing me with her eyes looking right into my startled eyes. She said, "Son, if you are forty years old and still live in my house where I put the food on the table, I'll be your boss and you'll like it." I never did forget that; and it made me know, at least in a measure, the reason for such lack of respect for parents is because it is not taught by them. (Kloepper 1972, p. 30)

That illustration may sound harsh by today's standards, but if it troubles you, it may also be an indication of how far as a society we have moved from God's idea of respect. Which should trouble you more, the mother slapping the boy or the boy sassing his mother?

> Which should trouble you more, the mother slapping the boy or the boy sassing his mother?

Speak kindly to your parents. Further, Solomon may have instructed his sons to speak kindly to their parents—"Honour thy father and thy mother" (Exodus 20:12 KJV). One way to honor your parents is to speak kindly to them. The extreme opposite of speaking kindly would be to curse. To curse parents means to be scornful toward, disrespectful of, to speak ill of, or to wish ill upon them. And in the Old Testament, to curse a parent was to invite the penalty of death. (See Leviticus 20:9.) "If someone curses their father or mother, their lamp will be snuffed out in pitch darkness" (Proverbs 20:20).

Treat your parents well. And finally, David and Solomon probably taught their sons to treat their parents well. "Whoever robs their father and drives out their mother is a child who brings shame and disgrace" (Proverbs 19:26). Those who would rob their parents would probably stoop to anything. The law was very clear: "Anyone who attacks their father or mother is to be put to death" (Exodus 21:15). Such behavior toward parents by their children is a severe provocation to God, and if parents don't punish the guilty, God will. If your children are to learn respect and honor, it must be taught in the home. Consider how far our world has slipped from what God intended family relationships to be.

GET WISDOM

Secondly, Solomon wanted his son to "get wisdom." When Solomon says, "Get wisdom, get understanding," he does not mean, "Go to school and take more courses." That might be part of God's plan for you, but that is not what he had in mind. He's talking about wisdom that will develop your character as a child of God. There are likely several lessons that Solomon taught his son to help develop that wisdom.

***Fear the* Lord.** The first lesson in character development is very basic— "Fear the Lord." Why is this so important? "The fear of the Lord is the beginning of wisdom, and knowledge of the Holy One is understanding" (Proverbs 9:10). Therefore, the fear of the Lord is the beginning of wisdom because every other virtue of character flow from the fear of the Lord like a river flows from a spring.

***Humble yourself before the* Lord.** A wise person is characterized by humility. Those who are proud cannot progress in wisdom as long as pride keeps the fear of the Lord out of their lives. Persons who truly fear the Lord will be humble, because they depend on God for everything, and they fear to take credit for what God does. Humility is teachable and open to change and growth. But the proud person does not like to admit shortcomings and a need for growth. Humility, unlike pride, does not recoil when corrected or commanded to do something. And this is essential for the advancement of wisdom.

> Those who are proud cannot progress in wisdom as long as pride keeps the fear of the Lord out of their lives.

***Know and obey the commandments of the* Lord.** Moses taught us that wisdom consists in knowing and obeying the commandments of God:

> I have taught you decrees and laws as the Lord my God commanded me, so that you may follow them in the land you are entering to take possession of it. Observe them carefully, for this will show your wisdom and understanding to the nations, who will hear about all these decrees. (Deuteronomy 4:5–6)

Similarly, Jesus taught, "Therefore whosoever heareth these sayings of mine, and doeth them, I will liken him unto a wise man, which built his house upon a rock" (Matthew 7:24 KJV).

THE APPLICATION OF WISDOM

Third, Solomon wanted his sons to acquire wisdom and to never forsake it. He knew that by saturating their minds and hearts with God's Word, they would gain the spiritual wisdom necessary to guide them through all situations. As previously noted, he wanted his sons to "hear and obey God's Word," but wisdom is more than hearing and obeying God's Word, because God's Word does not specifically address every human dilemma. Wisdom is the application of God's Word and godly principles to those dilemmas. A famous example concerning Solomon's decision-making ability illustrates this point. There was no biblical command to tell Solomon what to do when two prostitutes claim the same baby. Therefore, wisdom had to go beyond "knowing and obeying" the Word of God:

> And the one woman said, O my lord, I and this
> woman dwell in one house; and I was delivered of a
> child with her in the house. And it came to pass the
> third day after that I was delivered, that this woman
> was delivered also: and we *were* together; *there was*
> no stranger with us in the house, save we two in the
> house. And this woman's child died in the night;
> because she overlaid it. And she arose at midnight, and
> took my son from beside me, while thine handmaid
> slept, and laid it in her bosom, and laid her dead child
> in my bosom. And when I rose in the morning to give
> my child suck, behold, it was dead: but when I had
> considered it in the morning, behold, it was not my
> son, which I did bear. (1 Kings 3:17–21 KJV)

Solomon applied wisdom to that human dilemma. He requested a sword be brought, and he gave a most unusual order: "Divide the living child in two, and give half to the one, and half to the other" (1 Kings 3:25 KJV). Love immediately identified the real mother: "Please, my lord, give her the living baby! Don't kill him" (1 Kings 3:26)! "But the other said, 'Neither I nor you shall have him. Cut him in two'" (1 Kings 3:26)! Without need for further investigation, wisdom solved the dilemma. Then the king said, "Give her the living child, and in no wise slay it: she *is* the mother" (1 Kings 3:27 KJV). The story concludes with the following statement: "When all Israel heard the verdict the king had given, they held the king in awe, because they saw that he had wisdom from God to administer justice" (1 Kings 3:28).

> Solomon knew that by saturating their minds and hearts with God's Word, they would gain the spiritual wisdom necessary to guide them through all situations.

THE SUPREMACY OF WISDOM

In speaking to his sons, Solomon emphasized the supremacy of wisdom:

> Wisdom is supreme—so get wisdom. And whatever else you get, get understanding. Cherish her, and she will exalt you; if you embrace her, she will honor you. She will place a garland of grace on your head; and she will give you a crown of beauty. (Proverbs 4:7–9 HCSB)

This is summed up in one verse: "For whoever finds [wisdom] finds life and receives favor from the LORD" (Proverbs 8:35). Wisdom urges you to invest in eternal wealth. But many look for fulfillment in the riches this world has to offer, only to find those riches are of little value when facing the eternal judge. Jesus illustrated this irrational thinking in one of His parables:

> The ground of a certain rich man brought forth plentifully: And he thought within himself, saying, What shall I do, because I have no room where to bestow my fruits? And he said, This will I do: I will

pull down my barns, and build greater; and there will I bestow all my fruits and my goods. And I will say to my soul, Soul, thou hast much goods laid up for many years; take thine ease, eat, drink, *and* be merry. But God said unto him, *Thou* fool, this night thy soul shall be required of thee: then whose shall those things be, which thou hast provided? So is he that layeth up treasure for himself, and is not rich toward God. (Luke 12:16–21 KJV)

This farmer had made every provision possible for this life, but he had made no preparation to face the Lord in eternity. Wisdom cries out, "Life is more than food, and the body more than clothes" (Luke 12:23). Are you allowing Wisdom to lead and guide you? Are you investing in eternal life? Are you making preparations to meet the Lord face-to-face? The rich but foolish man was rich in worldly goods but had not prepared his soul to meet the Lord. "How much better to get wisdom than gold, and good judgment than silver!" (Proverbs 16:16 KJV).

> This farmer had made every provision possible for this life but had made no preparation to face the Lord in eternity.

IN CLOSING

It was Solomon's aspiration as a father that his sons would desire wisdom with all their might. "Cherish her, and she will exalt you; embrace her, and she will honor you" (Proverbs 4:8). These are not frivolous words. To *cherish* something and to *embrace* someone are signs of intense desire and love. We must value wisdom: "Look for it as for silver and search for it as for hidden treasure" (Proverbs 2:4). Since wisdom is found in the Word of God, Solomon knew they must apply themselves to study and meditation of God's Word to assimilate the Word into their thought processes.

The law of the LORD *is* perfect, converting the soul: the testimony of the LORD *is* sure, making wise the simple. The statutes of the LORD *are* right, rejoicing the heart: the commandment of the LORD *is* pure, enlightening the eyes. (Psalm 19:7–8 KJV)

Therefore, we must devote ourselves to know and understand the law of the LORD, the testimony of the LORD, the statutes of the LORD, and the commands of the LORD. It will not be accomplished by randomly opening your Bible and hoping something meaningful will leap out; it will be accomplished when you read with purpose. Solomon was not born a wise man, but he prayed for an "understanding heart." It was a simple, humble request, and as a result, "The Lord was pleased that Solomon had asked for wisdom" (1 Kings 3:10 NLT). And when you pray with the right motive, the compassionate Savior will give you more than you ask for. So seek the Lord through prayer and the Word, and the result will be that wisdom shows up when you need it. Remember Daddy's words!

LESSON 27

DRIVING INSTRUCTIONS

PROVERBS 4:10-17

¹⁰ Listen, my son, accept what I say, and the years of your life will be many. ¹¹ I instruct you in the way of wisdom and lead you along straight paths. ¹² When you walk, your steps will not be hampered; when you run, you will not stumble. ¹³ Hold on to instruction, do not let it go; guard it well, for it is your life. ¹⁴ Do not set foot on the path of the wicked or walk in the way of evildoers. ¹⁵ Avoid it, do not travel on it; turn from it and go on your way. ¹⁶ For they cannot rest until they do evil; they are robbed of sleep till they make someone stumble. ¹⁷ They eat the bread of wickedness and drink the wine of violence.

Driving is one of the more complicated tasks you are going to learn in your lifetime. However, it may not be any more complicated than learning to live. The above verses let you know evil is willing to lose sleep to bring about your destruction. Thus, there is a need for guidance every step of the way in life. Solomon instructed his son, "Listen and accept what I say, and your life will be lengthened." Daniel Segraves (1990) made the following observation:

> There is a way of "wisdom" to follow and "right paths" to take. Clearly, there must also be a "way of ignorance" and "wrong paths," but neither David nor Solomon thought it necessary to teach error in order

to equip their sons to deal with it. They taught what was right. When truth only is taught, error is readily recognized when it presents itself" (p. 59).

Like most parents, Solomon assured his son that he had his best interest at heart. He knew the ways of the LORD were right, so he stressed to his son the importance of accepting his instructions. How many parents around the world, regardless of language or culture, have posed the following question to their children: "Do you always have to learn the hard way?" The truth is it is not necessary to learn the hard way. Solomon was urging his son to do it the easy way. "Accept what I say," and "When you walk, your steps will not be hampered; when you run, you will not stumble" (Proverbs 4:10, 12).

The exhortation, "Hold on to instruction, do not let it go; guard it well, for it is your life" (Proverbs 4:13), speaks of the value that should be placed on parental instruction. Deep inside, most parents want to do what is right and to give their children the best training possible. As a parent, you must seize every opportunity to share scriptural truths with your children. You don't have to preach sermons to your kids, but you can help them learn to think biblically in the course of everyday life.

> You don't have to preach sermons to your kids, but you can help them learn to think biblically in the course of everyday life.

APPLY BIBLICAL PRINCIPLES

Bring biblical principles to bear on situations your children experience throughout their day. Pray with your children regularly. Pray before meals, before your children go to bed, before they go to school, before a big test, and before making big decisions. Teach them to turn to the Lord first. Read the Bible with your children. Make it a regular part of your daily routine. Find ways to teach your children the importance of studying the Bible. Develop some type of family devotion. Memorize

Bible verses together; meditate on them and be careful to do everything written in them. "Then you will be prosperous and successful" (Joshua 1:8).

> Bring biblical principles to bear on situations your children experience throughout their day.

When one of your children talks about another child being bullied, remind him it's their responsibility to show love to that child because the Bible states, "If anyone says, 'I love God,' and hates his brother, he is a liar; for he who does not love his brother whom he has seen cannot love God whom he has not seen" (1 John 4:20 ESV). If any of your children talk about cheating, remind them that God wants everyone to be honest: "The LORD detests lying lips, but he delights in those who tell the truth" (Proverbs 12:22 NLT). And when they fail, remind them God offers forgiveness for their sins: "If we confess our sins, he is faithful and just to forgive us *our* sins, and to cleanse us from all unrighteousness" (1 John 1:9 KJV).

Instruct your children in biblical stewardship by encouraging them to tithe and to give offerings to the Lord. Show them how you decide how much to give and encourage them to follow the same pattern. As you work together on projects around the house or even on school assignments, remind your children to do their best all the time, because they should always work as though they were doing it for the Lord. For the Bible teaches, "Whatsoever ye do, do *it* heartily, as to the Lord, and not unto men" (Colossians 3:23 KJV).

The truths of God's Word—godly principles—must be lived through good times and bad times. These principles must move from our heads to our hearts and be lived out in our daily lives, even when away from the fellowship of other believers. Educators speak of accommodation and assimilation as necessary steps in the process of learning. When a new concept is presented, the individual must first make room for it (accommodation), and in order for that concept to become useful, a paradigm shift must occur (assimilation). Solomon instructed, "My son, do not forget my teaching, but keep my commands in your heart, for they will prolong your life many years and bring you peace and prosperity" (Proverbs 3:1–2). As a father, he was saying, "Make room for what I say; incorporate it into your life, and you can anticipate the favor of God—the assurance of a happy and extended life."

How much greater value is godly instruction than worldly philosophies that change with each passing generation. Matthew Henry (n.d.) wrote the following, "Those that make God's word their rule shall walk at liberty and be at ease in themselves" (Vol. 3, p. 812). David acknowledged the freedom and liberty he experienced by following the LORD's Word. "I will walk at liberty: for I seek thy precepts" (Psalm 119:45 KJV). Just as taking driver's training and listening to your instructor will likely reduce your chance of accidents and extend your life, making room for God's Word and assimilating it into your life will guard you, guide you, and extend your life.

> Just as taking driver's training and listening to your instructor will likely reduce your chance of accidents and extend your life, making room for God's Word and assimilating it into your life will guard you, guide you, and extend your life.

THE TEMPTATION TO VIOLATE BIBLICAL PRINCIPLES

As a warning, Solomon wrote, "Do not set foot on the path of the wicked or walk in the way of evildoers. Avoid it, do not travel on it; turn from it and go on your way" (Proverbs 4:14–15). We must keep in the forefront of our thought processes that sin is not to characterize a Christian's life. John wrote, "No one born of God makes a practice of sinning" (1 John 3:9 ESV). So do not set your foot on the path of the wicked. Paul instructed Timothy to flee from ungodliness. "Flee these things; and follow after righteousness, godliness, faith, love, patience, meekness" (1 Timothy 6:11 KJV). Sometimes a path seems safe enough, but if it's not the path of righteousness, it's not safe. Just because the majority are doing it does not make it right, and we should not follow along just for the sake of unity. Warren Wiersbe (1988) wrote, "Not all unity is good, and not all division is bad. There are times when a servant of God should take a stand against false doctrine and godless practices, and separate himself from them" (p. 81). There are times when running is a mark of cowardice. At other times, fleeing is a mark of wisdom and a means of victory. Joseph is one of the best examples in the Bible:

> Joseph was a very handsome and well-built young man, and Potiphar's wife soon began to look at him lustfully. "Come and sleep with me," she demanded.
>
> But Joseph refused. "Look," he told her, "my master trusts me with everything in his entire household. No one here has more authority than I do. He has held back nothing from me except you, because you are his wife. How could I do such a wicked thing? It would be a great sin against God."
>
> She kept putting pressure on Joseph day after day, but he refused to sleep with her, and he kept out of her way as much as possible. One day, however, no one else was around when he went in to do his work. She came and grabbed him by his cloak, demanding, 'Come on, sleep with me!' Joseph tore himself away, but he left his cloak in her hand as he ran from the house. (Genesis 39:6–12 NLT)

There are times when running is a mark of cowardice. At other times, fleeing is a mark of wisdom and a means of victory.

Situational ethics would have cleared Joseph had he yielded to the temptation. The result of fleeing initially may have seemed like the wrong thing to do, especially when the steel doors of the dungeon clanged behind him. One could reason that his master never would have found out, but Joseph had a higher reason for fleeing. His own words declare his conviction and integrity: "How then can I do this great wickedness, and sin against God?" (Genesis 39:9 KJV).

> Situational ethics would have cleared Joseph had he yielded to the temptation.

The scriptures clearly declare things we must flee from. It's not a matter of if it's *convenient* or *when I feel like it*. We must not even set a foot on the path of the wicked. "Flee from idolatry" (1 Corinthians 10:14 KJV). "Flee fornication" (1 Corinthians 6:18 KJV). "Flee also youthful lusts: but follow righteousness, faith, charity, peace, with them that call on the Lord out of a pure heart" (2 Timothy 2:22 KJV).

SATAN WANTS TO DESTROY THE CHILD OF GOD

There are individuals who operate under the influence of Satan. "For they cannot rest until they do evil; they are robbed of sleep till they make someone stumble. They eat the bread of wickedness and drink the wine of violence" (Proverbs 4:16–17). It's important to understand that Satan has a price on the head of every Christian. John Phillips (1995) tells his own story:

> When I was in the British army I was stationed for two years on Haifa docks in a small detachment of about twenty men. My lifestyle greatly irritated my superior officer. What seemed to irk him most was my refusal to drink even one glass of beer. All the other fellows drank and some of them, including the officer, were almost confirmed drunkards.

The officer had many fine qualities ... But he did everything in his power to get me to drink. Once he even offered me his pay for three months if I would just get drunk once! Whatever made him think that I could be bought so cheaply, I don't know. Drink was abhorrent to me. If he had offered me his pay for ten years, it would not have tempted me ... The point is, my determined sobriety troubled this man's conscience. He lost sleep while he plotted to drag me down to his level ... The Lord protected me, however, and made me invulnerable. (pp. 117–118)

The righteous and the wicked have been the two players throughout the story of the human race. These two sides emerged in the beginning chapters of Genesis. Adam and Even transgressed against the command of God and lost their innocence. Cain slew Abel and continued the succession of yielding to evil. The wicked are always poised to oppose the righteous. "The wicked bend their bows; they set their arrows against the strings to shoot from the shadows at the upright in heart" (Psalm 11:2). They may not always openly attack the child of God, but they secretly work against the principles of righteousness. "For they cannot rest until they do evil; they are robbed of sleep till they make someone stumble" (Proverbs 4:16).

IN CLOSING

In contrast to the highway of error, the path of truth is always narrow. Christians must "strive to enter in at the strait gate: for many, I say unto you, will seek to enter in, and shall not be able" (Luke 13:24 KJV). And Christian parents have to say "No!" to activities that violate godly principles. Just because everybody does it does not make it right. We all must remember, "Strait is the gate, and narrow is the way, which leadeth unto life, and few there be that find it" (Matthew 7:14 KJV).

The following illustration is worthy of consideration:

The narrow way ... broadens out at the end when it takes on the infinite dimensions of eternity. The horizons of the narrow path are lost in the vastness of a boundless shore in a land of fadeless day, where time is not counted by years and where Christ sits on the right hand of the Majesty on high. There for endless ages we will explore the marvels of the mysteries prepared for us by the God of omniscient genius and omnipotent power, the God who will never run out of ideas for making Heaven an exciting place to be. (Phillips 1995, p. 115)

> In contrast to the highway of error, the path of truth is always narrow.

It's an interesting thought that the *strait* and narrow become endlessly broad at heaven's shores. So what appears to be constraint at one end becomes freedom at the other. Like learning to drive, learning to live a godly life requires practice. We never get too old to learn from instruction. Timothy was well along in his walk with God, yet his mentor, apostle Paul, continued to coach him, "Train yourself to be godly. For physical training is of some value, but godliness has value for all things, holding promise for both the present life and the life to come" (1 Timothy 4:7–8). Whether we are the age of Solomon's son or the age of Timothy, we are never too old to learn to be godly. "Hold on to instruction, do not let it go; guard it well, for it is your life" (Proverbs 4:13).

LESSON 28

TOWARD THE FULL LIGHT OF DAY

PROVERBS 4:18-19

¹⁸ The path of the righteous is like the morning sun, shining ever brighter till the full light of day. ¹⁹ But the way of the wicked is like deep darkness; they do not know what makes them stumble.

This portion of scripture paints a picture of someone facing the eastern horizon as the sun is about to appear. The New Living Translation renders the words *the morning sun* as *the first gleam of dawn*. Regardless of the speed at which you are moving, if you are facing the right direction, the full light of day will appear. This is a beautiful picture of spiritual growth—progressing from darkness to light.

> This is a beautiful picture of spiritual growth—progressing from darkness to light.

Before God created light, there was absolute darkness. The darkness was so dark you could not have seen the water that covered the earth. It was the absence of light. This is what Pharaoh and the Egyptians experienced at the time of the exodus: "And the LORD said unto Moses, Stretch out thine hand toward heaven, that there may

241

be darkness over the land of Egypt, even darkness *which* may be felt" (Exodus 10:21 KJV).

JESUS—THE LIGHT OF THE WORLD

Darkness is the state of the sinner. When Adam and Eve fell into sin, they fell into darkness. After being cast out of paradise where the Light visited regularly, every descendent of theirs groped toward the full light of day for the next four thousand years. Throughout the Old Testament, people lived in a state of darkness with only a promise of light. Just as God's first creative act was to dispel the darkness with light, the church exists to dispel darkness with the Gospel. The coming of Jesus into the world brought the first gleam of dawn. Jesus said, "I am the light of the world: he that followeth me shall not walk in darkness, but shall have the light of life" (John 8:12 KJV).

"The first gleam of dawn" is what individuals see at the moment of conversion. Conversion is an interaction between God and an individual. God gives everyone a measure of faith (Romans 12:3), and people put faith into action by taking the first steps toward God. Much like a toddler being coaxed to take their first steps, the Spirit of God says, "Come to Daddy." Jesus stated plainly, "No man can come to me, except the Father which hath sent me draw him" (John 6:44 KJV). People are drawn to the Light, and then the Light dispels darkness. When Light comes, darkness has to leave.

> "The first gleam of dawn" is what individuals see at the moment of conversion.

No matter how wicked you have been in the past, that measure of faith is all that is necessary to get you moving in the right direction. The Spirit of God tugs at your heart, and if you yield to Him, he will bring light "like the first gleam of dawn." The demoniac is a classic example of a man acting upon the measure of faith and moving from darkness into light: "When he saw Jesus afar off, he ran and worshipped him" (Mark 5:6 KJV).

The demoniac was a man without hope. The scriptures describe his condition: "This man lived in the tombs, and no one could bind him anymore, not even with a chain" (Mark 5:3). "Many times [the demon] had seized him, and though he was chained hand and foot and kept under guard, he had broken his chains and had been driven by the demon into solitary places" (Luke 8:29).

When Jesus arrived on his shore, the demoniac saw the "first gleam of dawn." And with that gleam of dawn came life. Not only did he see the light, he became a new creature. Still today, nearly two thousand years later, "If any man be in Christ, he is a new creature: old things are passed away; behold, all things are become new" (2 Corinthians 5:17 KJV). What a change that light made in the demoniac's life. Instead of a frightening-looking insane man, the people saw the man who had been "possessed with the devil, and had the legion, sitting, and clothed, and in his right mind" (Mark 5:15 KJV). What blessings the Light brought! There were no bills from a hospital or a physician for the services rendered. Instead, there was a new lease on life. Jesus said to him, "Go home to your family and tell them how much the Lord has done for you, and how he has had mercy on you" (Mark 5:19).

> When Jesus arrived on his shore, the demoniac saw the "first gleam of dawn."

THE SEDUCTIVENESS OF DARKNESS

"But the way of the wicked is like deep darkness; they do not know what makes them stumble" (Proverbs 4:19). It's always good to remember that people are not sinners because they sin; they sin because they are sinners. David declared, "Surely I was sinful at birth, sinful from the time my mother conceived me" (Psalm 51:5). Therefore, "All have sinned, and come short of the glory of God" (Romans 3:23 KJV). "There is none righteous, no, not one" (Romans 3:10 KJV). But to remain in darkness once the light has dawned is a very bad choice. Had the demoniac not acted upon the measure of faith the Lord placed in his heart and the tug of the Spirit of God upon his heart, he would have remained in darkness—deep darkness.

> To remain in darkness once the light has dawned is a very bad choice.

Darkness lurks ready to engulf and destroy people's lives. Its seduction is everywhere, always attempting to lure the innocent and not so innocent into its grasp so as to kill, steal, and destroy their souls. (See John 10:10.) The fallen human nature has a fascination with the dark side of life, and the internet has made it available at the click of a finger. Satan's forces are continually luring souls to the dark side through the internet, movies, and television. His messengers urge you to say, "Yes!" to the dark side. These enticing spirits tell lies that describe the satisfaction that comes with alcohol, tobacco, and sexual immorality. They promise great rewards to those who indulge in such lifestyles. The dark side says, "Go ahead and have sex whenever and with whomever is willing. And when you talk about it, don't use old-fashioned terms like adultery and fornication; there are much nicer sounding words like 'premarital' and 'extramarital sex.' In fact, skip the word 'marital' altogether." Those are some of the values being promoted by the twisted thinking of the dark side. They promise pleasure and self-indulgence while robbing you of decency and self-respect. Wickedness is not a respecter of age. It lures and entices the young, the middle-aged, and the old.

Darkness will corrupt you; darkness will control you; and darkness will destroy you. Darkness is not a friend; it is a fiend bent on destroying you because you were created in the image of God. Darkness hates God and anything that looks like Him. Because light dispels darkness, it drives darkness away. The Word of God repeatedly warns us not to listen to the dark side. It cautions us to be careful of the influence darkness has on our thinking: "Woe unto them that call evil good, and good evil; that put darkness for light, and light for darkness; that put bitter for sweet, and sweet for bitter!" (Isaiah 5:20 KJV).

> Darkness will corrupt you; darkness will control you; and darkness will destroy you.

IN CLOSING

The god of this world has blinded many in our society who believe you are strange for not indulging in sin with them, and they may even persecute you when you stand by your convictions. Have you ever wondered why? The answer is simple: "The light shineth in darkness; and the darkness comprehended it not" (John 1:5 KJV). Don't be discouraged! When those in darkness respond to the God-given measure of faith and turn toward the path of righteousness, they too will see "the first gleam of dawn." They too will come to recognize, "In him [is] life; and the life [is] the light of men" (John 1:4 KJV).

Thank God, He came as a light shining in darkness. "For God, who commanded the light to shine out of darkness, hath shined in our hearts, to *give* the light of the knowledge of the glory of God in the face of Jesus Christ" (2 Corinthians 4:6 KJV). By turning toward Jesus, you choose the way of righteousness, which leads to an ever-brightening day. Some fear taking the first step toward the light. However, those who do will find the light "shining ever brighter till the full light of day."

LESSON 29

HOW TO HAVE
A HOLY LIFE

PROVERBS 4:20-27

20 My son, pay attention to what I say; turn your ear to my words. 21 Do not let them out of your sight, keep them within your heart; 22 for they are life to those who find them and health to one's whole body. 23 Above all else, guard your heart, for everything you do flows from it. 24 Keep your mouth free of perversity; keep corrupt talk far from your lips. 25 Let your eyes look straight ahead; fix your gaze directly before you. 26 Give careful thought to the paths for your feet and be steadfast in all your ways. 27 Do not turn to the right or the left; keep your foot from evil.

We know from Solomon's earlier writings that he took to heart his father's instructions. (See Proverbs 4:3–4.) And his father, David, had learned some of his lessons from the school of hard knocks. As with most fathers, Solomon's desire was that his sons would live upright and holy lives. We hear it in his voice:

> Pay attention to what I say; turn to my words. Do not let them out of your sight, keep them within your heart; for they are life to those who find them and health to one's whole body. (Proverbs 4:20–22)

THE WAY TO A HOLY LIFE

In his admonition, he addressed four areas: a clean heart, a cautious mouth, a controlled eye, and a careful foot.

A clean heart. To live a holy life, it is essential to have a clean heart. "Above all else, guard your heart, for everything you do flows from it" (Proverbs 4:23). The King James Version renders the same verse, "Keep thy heart with all diligence; for out of it are the issues of life." The heart symbolizes our hidden inner life. It is closely connected with our emotions, and it is the source of all our behaviors. It is the very center of our being. Since it is that part that can feel, it is that part that can love or reject love. A pure heart and clean hands are linked together. David asked the following questions, "Who shall ascend into the hill of the LORD? or who shall stand in his holy place?" (Psalm 24:3 KJV). He very quickly answered his own question, "He that hath clean hands, and a pure heart" (Psalm 24:4 KJV). The heart determines what we are and therefore what we do. Jesus reminded His listeners:

> The things that come out of a person's mouth come from the heart, and these defile them. For out of the heart come evil thoughts—murder, adultery, sexual immorality, theft, false testimony, slander. These are what defile a person. (Matthew 15:18–20)

> The heart determines what we are and therefore what we do.

What humans need most is a new heart, because "the heart *is* deceitful above all *things*, and desperately wicked" (Jeremiah 17:9 KJV). David prayed the only solution to a sinful heart: "Create in me a clean heart, O God; and renew a right spirit within me" (Psalm 51:10 KJV). Both David and Jeremiah operated under the Old Covenant. Under the New Covenant, the Lord moved the law from stone tablets to the tablets of our hearts: "This *shall be* the covenant that I will make with the house of Israel; After those days … I will put my law in their inward parts, and write it in their hearts" (Jeremiah 31:33 KJV).

A cautious mouth. Solomon admonished his son, "Keep your mouth free of perversity; keep corrupt talk far from your lips" (Proverbs 4:24). Evil speech is an indication of an evil heart. People can control their speech when they want to and when it is in their best interest. The example below, adapted from *Dealing with Everyday Problems* (Native Family Studies 1985, Book 5, pp. 10–11), illustrate that people are much more in control of their speech than they often are willing to admit:

Mary Controls Anger

Mary was at home with her three children. It was late in the afternoon on a rainy day. The children had been cooped up all day. It seemed as though everything had gone wrong, and she was tired.

The children began whining and screaming and finally got into a fight. Mary restrained her anger for a while, but finally erupted like a volcano. Angry words poured out, objects began to fly around the room, and children were diving under the table and hiding in closets.

Suddenly the phone rang. It was her dear friend, Sally. Mary's voice changed dramatically. Her conversation was restrained and quiet. It was very evident that Mary could control her anger when she really wanted to. She chose when to restrain her angry feelings and when to explode.

> People can control their speech when they want to and when it is in their best interest.

Solomon wrote, "Death and life *are* in the power of the tongue" (Proverbs 18:21 KJV). The following tale provides an excellent illustration of this proverb:

A group of frogs were traveling through the woods, and two of them fell into a deep pit. All the other frogs gathered around the pit. When they saw how deep the pit was, they told the two frogs they were as good as dead.

However, the two frogs ignored the comments and tried to jump up out of the pit with all of their might. The other frogs kept telling them to stop, that they were as good as dead.

Finally, one of the frogs took heed to what the other frogs were saying and gave up. He fell down and died. The other frog continued to jump as hard as he could.

Once again, the crowd of frogs yelled at him to stop the pain and just die. He jumped even harder and finally made it out. When he got out, the other frogs questioned, "Did you not hear us?"

The frog explained to them that he was deaf. He thought they were encouraging him the entire time.

There is power of life and death in the tongue. This story teaches two contrasting lessons: (1) An encouraging word to someone who is down can lift that person up and help them make it through the day. And (2) a discouraging word to someone who is down may be all that's necessary to destroy them. So be careful what you say. Speak life to those who cross your path; an encouraging word can have an amazing impact on the hearer.

> Speak life to those who cross your path; an encouraging word can have an amazing impact on the hearer.

A controlled eye. If we are to live a holy life, we must have our eyes under control. "Let your eyes look straight ahead, fix your gaze directly before you" (Proverbs 4:25). This is not intended to be a prohibition against greeting someone of the opposite sex you meet along the street. It is a cautionary statement to not allow your eyes to wander into areas that would lead to sin. The eye is a pathway to sin. A great many of the temptations we experience come through our eyes. To avoid looking at something appealing to the lust of the flesh requires considerable discipline. Satan's strategy in the garden was to get Eve to look:

> When the woman saw that the tree *was* good for food, and that it *was* pleasant to the eyes, and a tree to be desired to make *one* wise, she took of the fruit thereof, and did eat, and gave also unto her husband with her; and he did eat. (Genesis 3:6 KJV)

Once her gaze was fixed upon that which was forbidden, the desire increased. The longer she looked, the easier it was for her to cross that forbidden line. Soon she lost all sense of discretion. She forgot all about God's warning of certain judgment: "The day that thou eatest thereof thou shalt surely die" (Genesis 2:17 KJV). Once a covenant is broken, and once that invisible boundary is crossed, it is easier to do it again. And it becomes more difficult to keep the devil from knocking at your door.

> Once a covenant is broken, and once that invisible boundary is crossed, it is easier to do it again.

Job declared, "I made a covenant with my eyes not to look lustfully at a young woman" (Job 31:1). We should make a covenant between God and every part of our body. Jesus reminded us of the essentiality of doing so, because "whosoever looketh on a woman to lust after her hath committed adultery with her already in his heart" (Matthew 5:28 KJV). When considering this statement, a question often arises. Is it worse to commit the physical act of adultery than to commit adultery in your mind? Of course, it's worse to commit the act! Just consider the potential ramifications. However, a lustful look—the seed of sin—creates a slippery slope: "When lust hath conceived, it bringeth forth sin: and sin, when it is finished, bringeth forth death" (James 1:15 KJV).

Make a covenant; do not covet. Those two words sound alike, but they are quite different. The tenth commandment declares, "Thou shalt not covet thy neighbour's house, thou shalt not covet thy neighbour's wife, nor his manservant, nor his maidservant, nor his ox, nor his ass, nor any thing that is thy neighbour's" (Exodus 20:17 KJV). Many a man forgot the covenant with his wife and began to covet that which was not his, particularly after his wife gained a few pounds and lost her youthfulness. Many a woman forgot the covenant she made with her husband when another man paid attention to her and catered to her emotional needs. Take note of what your eyes and heart are focusing on at all times and reject any thought that violates your covenant with God and the spouse of your youth. (See Proverbs 2:16–17.)

A careful foot. Solomon admonished, "Give careful thought to the paths for your feet and be steadfast in all your ways. Do not turn to the right or the left; keep your foot from evil" (Proverbs 4:26–27). There are some places you should not go and some doorways you should never enter. Lot stands out as one whose feet carried him and his family into evil. "Lot dwelled in the cities of the plain, and pitched his tent toward Sodom" (Genesis 13:12 KJV). The direction Lot chose to walk and the place he chose to pitch his tent were indicative of what was in his heart. Before it was over, it would cost him his wife and everything he owned. Abraham, on the other hand, went a different direction and pitched his tent away from Sodom. "Abram removed *his* tent, and came and dwelt in the plain of Mamre, which *is* in Hebron, and built there an altar unto the LORD" (Genesis 13:18 KJV). The only legacy Lot left behind was two grandsons conceived by incest. Abraham, on the other hand, built a heritage in Hebron that extends to this very day. The LORD promised him, "All peoples on earth will be blessed through you" (Genesis 12:3).

> There are some places you should not go and some doorways you should never enter.

IN CLOSING

Once, when our children were young, we visited Universal Studios. The only thing I remember from that visit is the words of the guide, "Everything here is fake." Solomon wanted his son to avoid taking the treacherous trip to the land where everything is fake. He wanted his son to live a holy life, and he gave him instructions as to how to do it. He knew he had to do more than just tell him to be good; he had to instruct him:

> Attend to my words; incline thine ear unto my sayings. Let them not depart from thine eyes; keep them in the midst of thine heart. For they are life unto those that find them, and health to all their flesh. (Proverbs 4:20–22)

And then he proceeded to instruct him in four areas that would help him live a holy life: a clean heart, a cautious mouth, a controlled eye, and a careful foot. We, too, need to learn from Solomon's instructions to live a holy life. We must be proactive! We, too, must take steps to maintain a clean heart, to think before we speak, to exercise caution as to where we allow our eyes to roam, and we must take great care as to where our feet carry us. Further, we must follow Solomon's instructions and teach our children how to live a holy life.

LORIN BRADBURY, PH.D.

THE CALL OF THE WORLD

PROVERBS 5:1-6

¹ My son, pay attention to my wisdom, turn your ear to my words of insight, ² that you may maintain discretion and your lips may preserve knowledge. ³ For the lips of the adulterous woman drip honey, and her speech is smoother than oil; ⁴ but in the end she is bitter as gall, sharp as a double-edged sword. ⁵ Her feet go down to death; her steps lead straight to the grave. ⁶ She gives no thought to the way of life; her paths wander aimlessly, but she does not know it.

Throughout the first four chapters of the book of Proverbs, Solomon urged his sons to listen to his instruction and teaching. But as the fifth chapter opens, there is the feeling of desperation in his voice, "My son, pay attention to my wisdom" (Proverbs 5:1). Prior to this chapter, Solomon wrote about wisdom, but this is the first time he refers to his wisdom. He was concerned about the son he was speaking to. There is a sound of desperation in his voice. Solomon does not want his son going down the path toward the world.

THE GOD OF THIS WORLD

The scriptures repeatedly depict the world as a prostitute. Whenever Israel went away from the one true God and went after the things of the world, the LORD depicted her as prostituting herself to the world:

- And if the people of the community ignore those who offer their children to Molech and refuse to execute them, I myself will turn against them and their families and will cut them off from the community. This will happen to all who commit spiritual prostitution by worshiping Molech. (Leviticus 20:4–5 NLT)
- I will also turn against those who commit spiritual prostitution by putting their trust in mediums or in those who consult the spirits of the dead. I will cut them off from the community. (Leviticus 20:6 NLT)
- O people of Israel, do not rejoice as other nations do. For you have been unfaithful to your God, hiring yourselves out like prostitutes, worshiping other gods on every threshing floor. (Hosea 9:1 NLT)

The world can be very seductive. "For the lips of an adulteress woman drip honey, and her speech is smoother than oil" (Proverbs 5:3). It's important to remember that Satan, the god of this world, masquerades as an angel of light. (See 2 Corinthians 11:14.) The Bible does not say Satan is an angel of light; it says only that he masquerades as an angel of light. He is not an angel of light; he is a devil of darkness. In fact, Jesus said Satan "was a murderer from the beginning, not holding to the truth, for there is no truth in him. When he lies, he speaks his native language, for he is a liar and the father of lies" (John 8:44). In other words, Satan puts on a disguise to seduce the unsuspecting.

> The Bible does not say Satan is an angel of light; it says only that he masquerades as an angel of light.

LORIN BRADBURY, PH.D.

Modern-day examples of the god of this world masquerading as light are the advertisements and billboards seen along highways. How much booze would pictures of skid row sell? How many cigarettes would pictures of people dying of lung cancer sell? "The god of this world hath blinded the minds of them which believe not" (2 Corinthians 4:4 KJV).

People are not sinners because they lust; they lust because they are sinners. Satan takes advantage of the cravings and desires of the human nature. The apostle Paul wrote, "For we ourselves also were sometimes foolish, disobedient, deceived, serving divers lusts and pleasures, living in malice and envy, hateful, *and* hating one another" (Titus 3:3 KJV). "There is great affinity and alliance between the world and the flesh, and this world intrudes and encroaches upon the flesh, and thereby makes a party against God" (Henry, n.d., Vol. 6, p. 1069).

> People are not sinners because they lust; they lust because they are sinners.

SATAN'S PATHWAYS

There are pathways Satan follows to get to the hearts of people. John described these in his first epistle—"The lust of the flesh, and the lust of the eyes, and the pride of life" (1 John 2:16 KJV). These are the pathways Satan used to entice Eve and then Adam. She was encouraged to notice—to look and to taste—and Satan convinced her that God was holding out on her. He convinced her that if she would only partake, there was knowledge available to her, and she would be wise like God. She partook of that which was forbidden and gave a sample to her husband. The only knowledge they received that they didn't already have was the knowledge of good and evil—the knowledge of sin. And along with that came fear and guilt.

The heart cannot love both God and the world:

> The heart of man is narrow and cannot contain both
> loves. The world draws down the heart from God; and

so the more the love of the world prevails the more the
love of God dwindles and decays. ... This love or lust
is not appointed of God (he calls us from it), but it
intrudes itself from the world; the world is a usurper
of our affection. (Henry, Vol. 6, p. 1069)

Joshua understood that humans cannot love both God and
the world. He understood how important it was that Israel make
a choice when he declared, "Choose you this day whom ye will
serve ... but as for me and my house, we will serve the LORD" (Joshua
24:15 KJV). And Jesus reminded his followers, "No one can serve
two masters. ... You cannot serve God and be enslaved to money"
(Matthew 6:24 NLT).

MOMENTARY PLEASURE

There is pleasure in the world, but the pleasure is short-lived. (See
Hebrews 11:25.) The pleasure of sin never lasts as long as a guilty
conscience. I wonder how long David's sexual encounter with Bathsheba
lasted. Compare that with the anxiety of dealing with an unwanted
pregnancy. Consider the guilt of knowing you killed a man to cover
up your sin. Later David wrote, "For I acknowledge my transgressions:
and my sin *is* ever before me" (Psalm 51:3 KJV). I wonder how much
pleasure Achan really derived from those items dedicated to the LORD.
What was it like knowing he was guilty and waiting to see if Joshua
would find out? How long did Judas get to run his fingers through
those thirty pieces of silver?

> When Judas, who had betrayed him, realized that
> Jesus had been condemned to die, he was filled with
> remorse. So he took the thirty pieces of silver back to
> the leading priests and the elders. "I have sinned," he
> declared, "for I have betrayed an innocent man."
> "What do we care?" they retorted. "That's your
> problem."

Then Judas threw the silver coins down in the Temple and went out and hanged himself. (Matthew 27:3–5 NLT)

> The pleasure of sin never lasts as long as a guilty conscience.

How long does a high really last? When does the enslavement begin? Jonah's experience of running from the will of God provides a vivid description of the engulfing, enslaving process:

> The waters compassed me about, *even* to the soul: the depth closed me round about, the weeds were wrapped about my head. I went down to the bottoms of the mountains; the earth with her bars *was* about me for ever. (Jonah 2:5–6 KJV)

LEARNING TO SAY NO

Every saint of God must learn to say no to temptation, the pleasures of sin, and the call of the world. Paul's instruction to Titus says it well:

> For the grace of God has appeared that offers salvation to all people. It teaches us to say "No" to ungodliness and worldly passions, and to live self-controlled, upright and godly lives in this present age, while we wait for the blessed hope—the appearing of the glory our great God and Savior, Jesus Christ, who gave himself for us to redeem us from all wickedness and to purify for himself a people that are his very own, eager to do what is good. (Titus 2:11–14)

When Peter tempted Jesus not to go to the cross, Jesus responded, "Get behind me, Satan! You are a hindrance to me. For you are not setting your mind on the things of God, but on the things of man" (Matthew 16:23 ESV). We should respond to the enticements of this world and the pull of the flesh with the same blunt "Get behind me, Satan." Truly, Satan's enticements are nothing but a stumbling block to spiritual growth.

The night before the crucifixion, Jesus prayed with greater intensity than anyone has ever prayed. The scripture described the event, "And being in an agony he prayed more earnestly: and his sweat was as it were great drops of blood falling down to the ground" (Luke 22:44 KJV). His humanity struggled with thoughts of the weight of the sins of humankind, the agony of the cross, and dying. He wrestled and pleaded, "O my Father, if it be possible, let this cup pass from me: nevertheless not as I will, but as thou *wilt*" (Matthew 26:39 KJV). He won the battle; his flesh submitted to the Spirit. That is what must happen if we are to do the will of God. We must crucify the flesh and reject the call of the world.

> Samson was a he-man with a she-weakness. In spite of the fact that he was born of godly parents, set apart from his birth to be a Nazarite, and elevated to the enviable position of judge in Israel, he never conquered his tendency toward lust. On the contrary, it conquered him. (Swindoll 1985, p. 31)

When he crossed that undefined line and the Spirit of God left him, "he awoke out of his sleep, and said, I will go out as at other times before, and shake myself. And he [knew] not that the LORD was departed from him" (Judges 16:20 KJV). Solomon described Samson well. "The wicked man is doomed by his own sins; they are ropes that catch and hold him. He shall die because he will not listen to the truth; he has let himself be led away into incredible folly" (Proverbs 5:22–23 TLB).

PLEASURE FOREVER MORE

There is a pleasure that is greater than the pleasures the world has to offer. "In [His] presence *is* fulness of joy; at [His] right hand *there are* pleasures for evermore" (Psalm 16:11 KJV). There are many benefits associated with rejecting the call of the world and submitting to the will of God. First, there is a clean conscience. For example, Paul declared to the Sanhedrin, "Men *and* brethren, I have lived in all good conscience before God until this day" (Acts 23:1 KJV). And to the Corinthians he wrote, "We can say with confidence and a clear conscience that we have lived with a God-given holiness and sincerity in all our dealings" (2 Corinthians 1:12 NLT). Second, there is freedom from guilt. When Paul wrote the Corinthians, he listed a plethora of sins and followed with this statement, "That's what some of you were! But you have been washed and made holy, and you have received God's approval in the name of the Lord Jesus Christ and in the Spirit of our God" (1 Corinthians 6:11 GW). "That's what some of you were!" Past tense! "Old things are passed away; behold, all things are become new!" (2 Corinthians 5:17 KJV). Therefore, "Set your affection on things above, not on things on the earth" (Colossians 3:2 KJV).

> There are many benefits associated with rejecting the call of the world and doing the will of God.

IN CLOSING

Everyone will face the temptation described by Solomon. The world may be pretty to look at, and it may have a tremendous draw upon your flesh, "But in the end she is bitter as gall, sharp as a double-edged sword" (Proverbs 5:4). However, victory is available to every child of God, but it is essential to guard your thoughts and your eyes and to set your affection on things above. When temptations come, and they are guaranteed to come, it is essential to do as Paul instructed Titus—say no to all ungodliness and worldly passions. Don't be shy and don't mumble. Be emphatic, be clear, and don't get into a discussion with the devil. The answer is *no*, and that's final. Then turn your eyes upon Jesus. When you are focused on Him, you will not be focused on the things of the world.

LESSON 31

THE DANGER OF PLAYING TOO CLOSE TO THE WORLD

PROVERBS 5:7–14

7 Now then, my sons, listen to me; do not turn aside from what I say. 8 Keep to a path far from her, do not go near the door of her house, 9 lest you lose your honor to others and your dignity to one who is cruel, 10 lest strangers feast on your wealth and your toil enrich the house of another. 11 At the end of your life you will groan, when your flesh and body are spent. 12 You will say, "How I hated discipline! How my heart spurned correction! 13 I would not obey my teachers or listen to my instructors. 14 And I was soon in serious trouble in the assembly of God's people."

Once again, a heightened concern can be heard in Solomon's voice as he attempts to persuade his sons to avoid falling into the snare of the prostitute. There seems to be a tendency for humans to play as close to the edge of the cliff as possible without falling over. Preachers of the Gospel, through the centuries, have done their best to persuade their congregations not to play too close to the world. The quotes listed below could have been written in the last decade, but the first is from a sermon by Augustine more than 1,700 years ago, and Charles Spurgeon preached the second in 1861:

A good Christian has no wish to attend the public shows. In this very thing, that he bridles his desire of going to the theater, he cries out after Christ, cries out to be healed. Others run together thither, but perhaps they are heathens or Jews? Ah! indeed, if Christians went not to the theaters, there would be so few people there that they would go away for very shame. So then Christians run thither also, bearing the Holy Name only to their condemnation. Cry out then by abstaining from going, by repressing in thy heart this worldly concupiscence; hold on with a strong and persevering cry unto the ears of the Savior, that Jesus may stand still and heal thee. (Augustine in Wiersbe 1977, p. 12)

And then, convinced sinner, another question. You are under conviction of sin, and you have been lately ... you have been frequenting the dancing-room, or the theatre. Now these are amusements for worldlings; let them have them; I would not prevent them for a moment; let every man have his own amusement and his own joy. But what is this to you? What hast thou to do with it? Why you know you thought the place would fall down while you were sitting there. What business had you there? Suppose the devil had come in to take one of his own away and had taken you; he might have been forgiven for his mistake, for he found you on his grounds. You were trespassing, and therefore if the old Giant Grim had taken you away to Despair's castle, who could have blamed him? Were you not for the time in his own limits? Had he not therefore a right to do as he would with you? (Spurgeon 1976, p. 71)

> There seems to be a tendency for humans to play as close to the edge of the cliff as possible without falling over.

RIGHTEOUSNESS AND UNRIGHTEOUSNESS WILL NEVER MIX

The adulteress, as described by Solomon, typifies the world. He pleaded, "Keep to a path far from her, do not go near the door of her house" (Proverbs 5:8). Like oil and water, righteousness and unrighteousness do not mix. Some have questioned why the LORD gave laws to the Israelites such as: "Do not plant your field with two different kinds of seed. Do not wear clothing woven from two different kinds of thread" (Leviticus 19:19 NLT). Those laws, though they might seem irrelevant today, were to be a daily reminder that righteousness and unrighteousness will never mix.

Not only do some Christians live far too close to the edge of the cliff, they drag sin along with them, instead of purging sin from their lives. This is not new; Isaiah pleaded with Judah more than seven hundred years before Jesus walked upon the earth:

> Woe unto them that draw iniquity with cords of vanity, and sin as it were with a cart rope: ... Woe unto *them that are* wise in their own eyes, and prudent in their own sight! ... Therefore is the anger of the LORD kindled against his people, and he hath stretched forth his hand against them, and hath smitten them. (Isaiah 5:18, 21, 25 KJV)

Not only do some Christians live far too close to the edge of the cliff, they drag sin along with them, instead of purging sin from their lives.

THE DESTRUCTIVENESS OF AN AFFAIR

When you were born again of the water and the Spirit, you entered into a covenant similar to the marriage covenant. One of the most destructive effects of an affair is that it takes energy away from the legitimate relationship. Most affairs never reach the level of sexual activity, yet they still destroy relationships. Whenever you begin to cast your eyes upon that which takes away from your relationship with Christ; whenever you disregard godly principles; whenever you attempt to get as close to the world as possible without actually denying the Lord, you are entering into an affair with the world.

> Don't give your affections to the world. Do you not
> know that your bodies are members of Christ? Shall
> I then take the members of Christ and make them
> members of a prostitute? Never! Or do you not know
> that he who is joined to a prostitute becomes one body
> with her? For, as it is written, "The two will become
> one flesh." But he who is joined to the Lord becomes
> one spirit with him. (1 Corinthians 6:15–17 ESV)

SEEK THE LORD IN ALL CIRCUMSTANCES

Joshua had seen many things in his one hundred ten years. He well remembered the error of not asking the LORD for guidance before making a covenant with the Gibeonites. This stands out as one of the greatest examples of failing to seek the LORD before acting. The Gibeonites were one of the tribes the Israelites were to drive out and destroy. However, in order to save their lives, they pretended to be a people from a far-off country. As a result, "The Israelites sampled their provisions but did not inquire of the LORD. Then Joshua made a treaty of peace with them to let them live, and the leaders of the assembly ratified it by oath" (Joshua 9:14–15). As a result, many of their young people ended up dating and marrying Gibeonites (those outside of the church in the wilderness) because of his error in leadership.

How well Joshua remembered being defeated at Ai because Achan had an affair with the world. Instead of waiting on the LORD to provide him with the fruit of the land, he lusted after and took some of the spoils of Ai that were devoted to God. (See Joshua 7:1–26.) How many of our young adults are destroyed, or at the very least crippled, spiritually because they don't wait on God to provide them with a husband or wife of like precious faith? Instead they become infatuated with a substitute sent along by the deceiver.

> How many of our young adults are destroyed, or at the very least crippled, spiritually because they don't wait on God to provide them with a husband or wife of like precious faith?

Joshua went on to warn the Israelites of the danger of looking for a spouse outside the church of the living God:

> But if you turn away from [the LORD] and cling to the customs of the survivors of these nations remaining among you, and if you intermarry with them, then know for certain that the LORD your God will no longer drive them out of your land. Instead, they will be a snare and a trap to you, a whip for your backs and thorny brambles in your eyes, and you will vanish from this good land the LORD your God has given you. (Joshua 23:12–13 NLT)

IN CLOSING

Remember the words of Jesus, "No man can serve two masters: for either he will hate the one, and love the other; or else he will hold to the one, and despise the other" (Matthew 6:24 KJV). For the one who does not heed the words of our Lord, Solomon's words apply: "At the end of your life you will groan, when your flesh and body are spent" (Proverbs 5:11).

There is a cost for defying the principles of God. "The wages of sin *is* death" (Romans 6:23 KJV). It is a grievous fact that the man who instructed his sons to stay far from the path of the harlot failed to heed his own warnings:

> King Solomon loved many strange women, together with the daughter of Pharaoh, women of the Moabites, Ammonites, Edomites, Zidonians, *and* Hittites; Of the nations *concerning* which the LORD said unto the children of Israel, Ye shall not go in to them, neither shall they come in unto you: *for* surely they will turn away your heart after their gods: Solomon clave unto these in love. And he had seven hundred wives, princesses, and three hundred concubines: and his wives turned away his heart. For it came to pass, when Solomon was old, *that* his wives turned away his heart after other gods. (1 Kings 11:1–4 KJV)

Solomon slid down the slippery slope to the door of the harlot. Those many women he loved were probably never considered harlots, but they led him into spiritual adultery because they led him to worship other gods.

LESSON 32

THE JOY OF FIDELITY

PROVERBS 5:15-20

15 Drink water from your own cistern, running water from your own well. 16 Should your springs overflow in the streets, your streams of water in the public squares? 17 Let them be yours alone, never to be shared with strangers. 18 May your fountain be blessed, and may you rejoice in the wife of your youth. 19 A loving doe, a graceful deer—may her breasts satisfy you always, may you ever be intoxicated with her love. 20 Why, my son, be intoxicated by another man's wife? Why embrace the bosom of a wayward woman?

If the Victorian era was known for its prudishness, the last fifty years will go down in history for its debauchery. It will be known as a time of a failed moral experiment. Everywhere you look, sensuousness reigns. We are continually reminded that sexual satisfaction is the number one priority in our society. All you have to do is pick up a magazine, look at billboards, or walk down a checkout aisle in a grocery store.

Why else do perfumes have names like Taboo, My Sin, Skinny Dip, Ambush, or Any-Time? Everyone knows that if you use the toothpaste that gives your mouth "sex appeal" all the guys in the room will flock toward you and that every new car comes with a beautiful blond as standard equipment. Wear the right kind of aftershave that "all of my men use" and you will even smell masculine … You can even blow your nose and be the fairest of them all simply by purchasing a certain tissue. (Schmitt 1975, p. 49)

> If the Victorian era was known for its prudishness, the last fifty years will go down in history for its debauchery. It will be known as a time of a failed moral experiment.

SEXUAL INTIMACY—GOD'S IDEA

There is nothing any more wrong with sexual feelings than feelings of hunger and thirst. However, those feelings acted upon without guidelines have disastrous consequences. The Word of God gives us guidance for those sexual feelings. Sexual immorality is forbidden in both the Old and New Testaments. Because of the prevalence of sexual immorality, Paul wrote to the Corinthian church, "Do you not know that wrongdoers will not inherit the kingdom of God? Do not be deceived: Neither the sexually immoral … nor adulterers nor men who have sex with men … will inherit the kingdom of God" (1 Corinthians 6:9–10).

Abstaining from sexual activity until marriage is to be honored. And once married, the couple is bound to each other so long as they both shall live. (See 1 Corinthians 7:39.) A man or woman must forget about any other romantic relationships and concentrate on developing the most fulfilling relationship possible with his or her lawful spouse. The marriage covenant brings an end to all other potential romantic relationships. Consider the following vows:

> John, wilt thou have Mary to be thy wedded wife, to live together after God's ordinance in the holy estate of matrimony? Wilt thou love her, comfort her, honor, and keep her, in sickness and in health; and, forsaking all others, keep only unto her, so long as ye both shall live?

Mary, wilt thou have John to be thy wedded husband, to live together after God's ordinance, in the holy estate of matrimony? Wilt thou obey him, serve him, love, honor, and keep him, in sickness and in health; and, forsaking all others, keep thee only onto him, so long as ye both shall live?

Notice the commitment question: "Forsaking all others, wilt thou keep thee only onto him, so long as ye both shall live?" The question is not rhetorical, and it begs an answer—"I will." In that two-word answer is a covenant-commitment that is meant to last a lifetime. You cannot defy God's laws and win!

ENJOYING SEXUAL INTIMACY

God created man and woman to enjoy complete oneness of relationship spiritually, socially, and sexually. There is nothing sinful or dirty about a sexual relationship within the bounds of marriage. Paul wrote:

> The husband should fulfill his wife's sexual needs, and the wife should fulfill her husband's needs. The wife gives authority over her body to her husband, and the husband gives authority over his body to his wife. Do not deprive each other of sexual relations, unless you both agree to refrain from sexual intimacy for a limited time so you can give yourselves more completely to prayer. Afterward, you should come together again so that Satan won't be able to tempt you because of your lack of self-control. (1 Corinthians 7:3–5 NLT)

There is nothing sinful or dirty about a sexual relationship within the bounds of marriage.

"If sexual looseness has its dangers, sexual loyalty has its advantages" (Hubbard 1989, p. 92). When Paul wrote the Corinthian church, he made it clear that the physical relationship was for more than procreation; it was intended for pleasure. Commenting on Proverbs 5:15–20, Hubbard (1989) described Solomon: "Now, using his own words, not his pupil's, he moves into his air and variations on the joys of fidelity and sings them lustily and artfully in the major key" (p. 92). God expects there to be single-hearted passionate affection toward your spouse. "May you ever be intoxicated with her love" (Proverbs 5:19). Bickell paraphrased Proverbs 5:19 as "Let her always make thee quiver, Be ever ravished with her love" (cited in Toy 1999, p. 115). And Toy (1999) paraphrased it as "Let thy own wife be thy source of enjoyment, as refreshing as water to a thirsty man" (p. 112).

DISTINGUISHING BETWEEN LOVE AND LUST

Though sexual feelings are a part of the human experience, some sexual feelings must be suppressed. Not all warm feelings that rush through our bodies are love. Love and lust produce similar excitement. But lustful desires become fertile soil for the devil to plant his weeds of fornication and adultery. We must never forget how vulnerable human beings are to sexual temptations. James wrote, "The temptation to give in to evil comes from us and only us. We have no one to blame but the leering, seducing flare-up of our own lust" (James 1:14 MSG). We need to take to heart the wisdom in Daniel Segraves's (1990) writings: "If a man will forget about the other man's cistern and well and give up trying to sneak a drink from them, he will find his own cistern and well are fully satisfying" (p. 66).

> Not all warm feelings that rush through our bodies are love. Love and lust produce similar excitement.

Solomon wrote, "Drink water from your own cistern, running water from your own well" (Proverbs 5:15). A cistern and a well were prized possessions in a climate where rainfall was scarce and the technique of drilling deep wells was not yet developed. Drinking water from your own cistern is a poetic, euphemistic way of describing the sexual relationship. The writer of Hebrews wrote, "Honor marriage, and guard the sacredness of sexual intimacy between wife and husband. God draws a firm line against casual and illicit sex" (Hebrews 13:4 MSG).

DEVELOPING STANDARDS FOR PURITY

Every individual must establish principles to guide him or her in dealing with sexual feelings. Standards and boundaries must be well established before passion begins. "One teenager put it this way: 'Making out is like a toboggan slide. Once you get on it, you have to keep on going, and somewhere before the bottom, there is likely to be a crack-up'" (Schmitt 1975, p. 51).

> Charlie Shedd tells of a day when his daughter came home from school excited about what she had learned. They had been studying dinosaurs and there was this one character with a funny build. Up front he was all power—mammoth chest, muscular neck, big head. He had teeth that could crunch trees like celery. But along about the middle he began to run out of stuff. His hind quarters were weak; they were something of a drag. Still that wasn't all of him. He had a long tail which seemed like it would never end. And the weird thing was that his brain was in the tip of his tail.
>
> You can see at once that he would have kind of a problem. It took too long for his front to get the message from his tail. When he started to smash

things up, the hold orders came too late. By the time
he got stopped, he had messed up two counties. (cited
in Schmitt 1975, p. 51)

This story illustrates the problem of starting down the slippery
slope of the sexual slide. The hold orders come too late. Adults, not
just teenagers, need to live by principles well defined as preestablished
guidelines that prevent involvement in premarital sex or extramarital
relationships. Many affairs have developed "innocently" during choir
practice while the spouses were at home. Never joke about having an
affair; it can happen all too easily. And never tease your spouse about
having an affair; he or she might take your suggestion. Marriage is too
sacred to make jokes about.

> Never joke about having an affair; it can happen all too
> easily.

Chuck Swindoll (1985) wrote the following, and his warning
should be seriously considered:

No one is immune. You're not. I'm not. Lust is no
respecter of persons. Whether by savage assault or
subtle suggestion, the minds of a wide range of people
are vulnerable to its attack. Sharp professional men
and women, homemakers, students, carpenters,
artists, musicians, pilots, bankers, senators, plumbers,
promoters, and preachers as well. Its alluring voice
can infiltrate the most intelligent mind and cause
its victim to believe its lies and respond to its appeal.
And beware—it never gives up … it never runs out
of ideas. Bolt your front door and it'll rattle at the
bedroom window, crawl into the living room through
the TV screen, or wink at you out of a magazine in
the den.

How do you handle such an aggressive intruder? Try this: When lust suggests a rendezvous, send Jesus Christ as your representative. Have him inform your unwanted suitor that you want nothing to do with illicit desire … nothing. Have your Lord remind lust that since you and Christ have been united together, you are no longer a slave to sin. His death and resurrection freed you from sin's stranglehold and gave you a new Master. And before giving lust a firm shove away from your life, have Christ inform this intruder that the permanent peace and pleasure you are enjoying in your new home with Christ are so much greater than lust's temporary excitement that you don't need it around any longer to keep you happy. (p. 32)

IN CLOSING

Below is a list of ways to avoid succumbing to lustful temptations (adapted from Schmitt 1975, p. 51):

- Set your standards now, not when temptation arises.
- Be a coward for Christ: "Flee … youthful lusts: but follow righteousness, faith, charity, peace, with them that call on the Lord out of a pure heart" (2 Timothy 2:22 KJV).
- Let Jesus be your representative in dealing with lust.
- Keep a cool head.
- Read the Word of God: "My son, keep my words and store up my commands within you. Keep my commands and you will live; guard my teachings as the apple of your eye. … They will keep you from the adulteress woman, from the wayward woman with her seductive words" (Proverbs 7:1–2, 5).
- Practice prayer.

If you are married, draw water from your own well. The contrast between the harlot's honey that turns bitter and the wife's water that remains sweet is the point of the entire fifth chapter of Proverbs. "For the lips of an adulteress drip honey, and her speech is smoother than oil; but in the end she is bitter as gall, sharp as a double-edged sword" (Proverbs 5:3–4). Instead, "May your fountain be blessed, and may you rejoice in the wife of your youth. A loving doe, a graceful deer—may her breasts satisfy you always, may you ever be intoxicated with her love" (Proverbs 5:18–19).

LESSON 33

MOMENTARY ATHEISM

PROVERBS 5:21-23

²¹ For your ways are in full view of the Lᴏʀᴅ, and he examines all your paths. ²² The evil deeds of the wicked ensnare them; the cords of their sins hold him fast. ²³ For lack of discipline they will die, led astray by their own great folly.

The Word of God defines the atheist as a fool: "The fool hath said in his heart, *There is* no God" (Psalm 14:1 KJV). Webster (1999) defines atheism as "The belief that there is no God, or denial that God or gods exist" (p. 89). Spurgeon (1988) described the atheist emphatically:

> The Atheist is the fool pre-eminently, and a fool universally. He would not deny God if he were not a fool by nature, and having denied God it is no marvel that he becomes a fool in practice. Sin is always folly, and as it is the height of sin to attack the very existence of the Most High, so it is also the greatest imaginable folly. ... But as denying the existence of fire does not prevent its burning a man who is in it, so doubting the existence of God will not stop the Judge of all the earth from destroying the rebel who breaks his laws. (Vol. 1, Part 1, p. 160)

IN THE PRESENCE OF AN ALL-SEEING GOD

Yes, God Exists, and "The eyes of the LORD *are* in every place, beholding the evil and the good" (Proverbs 15:3 KJV). A traditional children's song describes this fact well:

> O be careful little hands what you do,
> O be careful little hands what you do.
> For the Father up above, he is looking down in love.
> So be careful little hands what you do.

This song is meant to teach children that no matter where they are, the Lord sees what they are doing. John Phillips (1995) remembers that thought from childhood:

> When I was a boy my parents hung a text on my bedroom wall. I cannot say that I always appreciated the plaque. It read, "Thou God seest me." It was supposed to convey a message of comfort as in Genesis 16:13. But the text conveyed a threat to me. The thought of that all-seeing eye spying on my youthful transgressions troubled my conscience. The text would haunt me even more today—looking back over things I have done that I ought not to have done and things I have not done that I ought to have done—if it were not for the fact that those things, some of which I confessed with bitter tears, are now under the blood. (p. 133)

BEHAVING AS IF GOD WERE BLIND

What if God were blind? Spurgeon (1988) speculated, "When the Master's eyes are put out, what will not the servants do?" (Vol. 1, Part 1, p. 161). If God were blind, what kind of a world would we live in?

The answer can be found in Noah's day when people lived as though God were blind.

> The Lord saw that the wickedness of man was great in the earth, and that every intention of the thoughts of his heart was only evil continually. And the Lord regretted that he had made man on the earth, and it grieved him to his heart. So the Lord said, "I will blot out man whom I have created from the face of the land, man and animals and creeping things and birds of the heavens, for I am sorry that I have made them." (Genesis 6:5–7 ESV)

WHAT IF GOD WERE BLIND?

Unfortunately, it wasn't only in Noah's day that people behaved as though God were blind. When Paul wrote to the church in Rome, he described the licentiousness of the culture in which the church was immersed. Men and women indulged in sinful behaviors, as though God were blind:

> They knew God but did not praise and thank him for being God. Instead, their thoughts were total nonsense, and their misguided minds were plunged into darkness. While claiming to be wise, they became fools. They exchanged the glory of the immortal God for statues that looked like mortal humans, birds, animals, and snakes.
>
> For this reason God allowed their lusts to control them. As a result, they dishonor their bodies by sexual perversion with each other. These people have exchanged God's truth for a lie. So they have become ungodly and serve what is created rather than the Creator, who is blessed forever. Amen!

For this reason God allowed their shameful passions to control them. Their women have exchanged natural sexual relations for unnatural ones. Likewise, their men have given up natural sexual relations with women and burn with lust for each other. Men commit indecent acts with men, so they experience among themselves the punishment they deserve for their perversion.

And because they thought it was worthless to acknowledge God, God allowed their own immoral minds to control them. So they do these indecent things. Their lives are filled with of all kinds of sexual sins, wickedness, and greed. They are mean. They are filled with envy, murder, quarreling, deceit, and viciousness. They are gossips, slanderers, haters of God, haughty, arrogant, and boastful. They think up new ways to be cruel. They don't obey their parents, don't have any sense, don't keep promises, and don't show love to their own families or mercy to others. Although they know God's judgment that those who do such things deserve to die, they not only do these things but also approve of others who do them. (Romans 1:21–32 GW)

Peter declared that those who live that way are nearsighted and blind. (See 2 Peter 1:9.) It's not God who cannot see; it's the one who rejects God who cannot see. Paul wrote that when humans lived in unbelief, a veil of blindness covered their eyes. However, when anyone turns to the Lord, that veil is removed. (See 2 Corinthians 3:16.)

> It's not God who cannot see; it's the one who rejects God who cannot see.

Paul bluntly described the past lives of many who were in the church in Corinth—"sexually immoral ... idolaters ... adulterers ...

those who engage in homosexual acts." (See 1 Corinthians 6:9.) But he emphasized, "And such were some of you: but ye are washed, but ye are sanctified, but ye are justified in the name of the Lord Jesus, and by the Spirit of our God" (1 Corinthians 6:11 KJV). Washed, sanctified, and justified—we would never consider returning to a state of unbelief! Or would we?

FORGETFULNESS OF GOD

We look at others and declare that we would never live like those heathens in the world. We think, *It's amazing God doesn't just send fire from heaven and turn them into crispy critters.* In fact, if He gave us the opportunity, we would do it for Him. However, every time we enter a state of rebellion against the holiness of our God, we have temporarily entered a state of atheism. Every time we attempt to put blinders over our Master's eyes, we are dangling ourselves over hell by a thread.

> Every time we attempt to put blinders over our Master's eyes, we are dangling ourselves over hell by a thread.

Bonhoeffer (1955) made the following observation concerning a Christian sinning: "At [that] moment God is quite unreal to us, he loses all reality, and only desire for the creature is real ... Satan does not fill us with hatred of God, but with forgetfulness of God" (Bonhoeffer 1955, p. 33). What he described is what I am calling momentary atheism. In other words, an eclipse occurs. King David experienced just such a moment.

> In the spring of the year, the time when kings go out to battle, David sent Joab, and his servants with him, and all Israel. And they ravaged the Ammonites and besieged Rabbah. But David remained at Jerusalem.
> It happened, late one afternoon, when David arose from his couch and was walking on the roof of the king's house, that he saw from the roof a woman

bathing; and the woman was very beautiful. And David sent and inquired about the woman. And one said, "Is not this Bathsheba, the daughter of Eliam, the wife of Uriah the Hittite?" So David sent messengers and took her, and she came to him, and he lay with her. (2 Samuel 11:1–4 ESV)

David became relaxed after God delivered him from his enemies. In idleness, he defied boundaries that previously had been established in his life. David saw the woman was beautiful. He lusted after her, and then he chose to use her as a prostitute. David defied his conscience when the servant reminded him that she was a married woman. He used her and sent her home. David entered a state of momentary atheism.

> David defied his conscience when the servant reminded him she was a married woman. He used her and sent her home. David entered a state of momentary atheism.

When David lived in God's sunlight, he made good decisions. For example, when given the opportunity to kill King Saul, integrity kept him from it. "And David said to Abishai, Destroy him not: for who can stretch forth his hand against the LORD's anointed, and be guiltless?" (1 Samuel 26:9 KJV). At that moment, David was fully aware of the eyes of the LORD. His boundaries were well fixed.

One is left wondering why David could maintain faith in God when under severe trial but break faith with God when life became much easier. Paul gives us some insight into that question. The Lord explained to Paul that affliction worked to his advantage: "Lest I should be exalted above measure through the abundance of the revelations, there was given to me a thorn in the flesh, the messenger of Satan to buffet me, lest I should be exalted above measure" (2 Corinthians 12:7 KJV). While David lived under the constant threat of death, he had to rely on the LORD, and his eyes were very aware of the presence of the LORD. However, in his relaxed stated, he became spiritually drowsy.

The path of evil deeds does not have to be traveled. David knew the prayer to pray: "Examine me, O Lord, and try me; Test my mind and my heart" (Psalm 26:2 NASB). He failed to pray it. And Solomon described the progression of that failure: "The evil deeds … ensnare them; the cords of their sins hold them fast. For lack of discipline they will die, led astray by their own great folly" (Proverbs 5:22–23). As a result of momentary atheism, David's momentary pleasure became slavery. No one would choose to become a slave. However, every time you take the journey down the path from light into darkness, you are allowing the cords of slavery to wrap around you.

> As a result of momentary atheism, David's momentary pleasure became slavery.

IN CLOSING

The idea of being an atheist, even for a moment, is repulsive to most of us. It's much easier to think of our sin as a mistake, a problem, or even a momentary lapse in our Christian walk. But to think of sin and rebellion against a holy God as atheism should make us want to take the blinders off of God: "Search me, O God, and know my heart: try me, and know my thoughts: And see if *there be any* wicked way in me, and lead me in the way everlasting" (Psalm 139:23–24 KJV).

LESSON 34

FREE YOURSELF

PROVERBS 6:1-5

¹ My son, if you have put up security for your neighbor, if you have shaken hands in pledge for a stranger, ² you have been trapped by what you said, ensnared by the words of your mouth. ³ So do this, my son, to free yourself, since you have fallen into your neighbor's hands: Go—to the point of exhaustion— and give your neighbor no rest! ⁴ Allow no sleep to your eyes, no slumber to your eyelids. ⁵ Free yourself, like a gazelle from the hand of the hunter, like a bird from the snare of the fowler.

At first glance, this passage would seem to be no more than a warning against providing security for another. But a closer look finds that not only should you not get entangled financially by putting up security for someone, you should not become weighted down with indebtedness of any kind. There is almost a frantic tone to this command. "Free yourself, like a gazelle from the hand of the hunter, like a bird from the snare of the fowler" (Proverbs 6:5). It is a must! How many men and women are kept from doing the work of God because they have bound themselves through indebtedness?

> How many men and women are kept from doing the work of God because they have bound themselves through indebtedness?

ISSUES RELATED TO INDEBTEDNESS

Desire for the things we can live without. Sadly, there are those who have been delivered from drugs, alcohol, and promiscuity who turn around and allow the flesh to bind them with indebtedness. Debt is a symptom of greater issues. The first of these is lust, or desire for things that we can live without.

> It has been my observation that whatever a person hungers for, Satan will appear to offer it in exchange for a spiritual compromise. In my case, a new automobile was the perfect enticement to unleash my greed. But if illicit sex is your desire, it will eventually be made available. Don't be surprised when a willing partner beckons you. If your passion is for fame or power, that object of lust will be promised (even if never delivered). Remember that Jesus was offered bread following His forty-day fast in the wilderness. He was promised power and glory after He had been contemplating His upcoming road to the cross. My point is that Satan uses our keenest appetites to destroy us. (Dobson 1980, pp. 143–144)

Sadly, there are those who have been delivered from drugs, alcohol, and promiscuity who turn around and allow the flesh to bind them with indebtedness.

> Desire is like a river. As long as it flows within the banks of God's will—be the current strong or weak—all is well. But when it flows over those boundaries and seeks other channels, then disaster lurks in the rampage. (James Dobson Sr. in Dobson 1980, p. 147)

A consumptive lifestyle. A second symptom is a consumptive lifestyle. There are two ways for us to acquire and accumulate things:

income and debt. Income is the legitimate way to acquire things. "Debt enables men to pretend to be somebody else" (Morley 1992, p. 146). Solomon wrote that it's "better to be a nobody and yet have a servant than pretend to be somebody and have no food" (Proverbs 12:9). Jesus provided a stern warning, "Take heed, and beware of covetousness: for a man's life consisteth not in the abundance of the things which he possesseth" (Luke 12:15 KJV).

The love of money. Another cause of debt is the love of money. "Those who love money will never have enough" (Ecclesiastes 5:10 NLT). Patrick Morley (1992) described the power of money to seduce and control:

> Money is intoxicating. It is an opiate that addicts as easily and as completely as the iron grip of alcohol or narcotics. Its power to change us is close to that of Jesus Christ. Money possesses the power to rule our lives, not for good and forever, as Christ; but to lure us, like a moth, too close to the flame until, finally, our wings are set ablaze.
>
> Money enslaves men—it will work you till you die. And, after it has conquered your poor soul, its haunting laughter can be heard howling through the chambers of hell. And then it seeks out another hapless, unsuspecting victim—an ambitious fellow who wants just a little bigger slice of the good life. (pp. 130–131)

Spiritually, this can be a person's undoing. Jesus told a parable of four types of soil. He described one type of soil as full of thorns and thistles. The one who received the seed that fell among the thorns "is the one who hears the word, but the worries of this age and the seduction of wealth choke the word, and it becomes unfruitful" (Matthew 13:22 HCSB). Though the seed had a good start, the thorns and thistles outgrew the seedling, causing it to die. This is what happens when Christians allow their addiction to acquisition of wealth to draw them away from the better things that come through delayed gratification.

"Howard Dayton, financial author and founder of Crown Ministries, a financial training ministry, has counted about five hundred verses in the bible on prayer but over 2,350 verses on how to handle money and possessions" (Morley 1992, p. 13). Jesus summed up the problem with money: "No man can serve two masters: for either he will hate the one, and love the other; or else he will hold to the one, and despise the other. Ye cannot serve God and [money]" (Matthew 6:24 KJV). It is not a question of advisability; "You should not serve both God and Money." It is not a question of accountability; "You must not serve both God and Money." It is a matter of impossibility; "You cannot serve both God and Money." It is simply a choice; we each serve one and only one master.

VIEWPOINTS ON MONEY

Poverty theology. There is a viewpoint within Christianity called poverty theology. This viewpoint disdains material possessions. Adherents to this viewpoint strongly promote helping the poor but have very few possessions to contribute to the poor. They believe they have a scriptural mandate to give to the poor. They base their belief on the story of the rich young ruler: "Sell all that thou hast, and distribute unto the poor, and thou shalt have treasure in heaven: and come, follow me" (Luke 18:22 KJV).

Prosperity theology. In contrast to poverty theology is prosperity theology. Disciples of prosperity theology believe if you don't have, it's because you failed to ask. If you had enough faith, financial blessing would be yours. Like poverty theology, proponents of prosperity theology base their belief on the teachings of Jesus: "Ask, and it shall be given you; seek, and ye shall find; knock, and it shall be opened unto you: For every one that asketh receiveth; and he that seeketh findeth; and to him that knocketh it shall be opened" (Matthew 7:7–8 KJV).

Stewardship theology. Both of the above theologies fail to consider the totality of Jesus's teachings. A more complete view would be what is called stewardship theology. Stewards believe God owns and controls everything. Possessions are a privilege and not a right; stewards give up their rights. Possessions are a trust given in varying proportions, depending upon God-given abilities and an individual's faithfulness and obedience to biblical principles: "Moreover it is required in stewards, that a man be found faithful" (1 Corinthians 4:2 KJV).

> Stewardship theology: God owns and controls everything. Possessions are a privilege and not a right. Possessions are a trust given in varying proportions, depending upon God-given abilities and an individual's faithfulness and obedience to biblical principles.

When Ronald Reagan became president, he led the United States into an austerity program. Inflation was out of control, and interest rates were high. As president, he rallied support for belt tightening that broke the back of inflation. Every Christian must develop an austerity program. If you do, "God shall supply all your need according to his riches in glory by Christ Jesus" (Philippians 4:19 KJV). Since God has promised to meet all of our needs, as determined by Him and not us, then we can conclude that being out of control with our finances is a symptom of serving money instead of God. Therefore, it is essential that Christians recognize the danger signs of serving money instead of God. Some of these danger signs (adapted from Yonts 1980, p. 2) are noted below:

- charging daily expenditures due to lack of funds
- being forced to delay paying bills
- borrowing money to pay taxes and bills
- being unaware of how much you presently owe your creditors
- receiving past-due notices from creditors
- paying current bills with savings, or not having any savings
- refinancing old loans with new consolidation loans
- relying on a second income to pay regular bills
- being unable to accumulate a savings—even a small amount
- finding it difficult to give God His tenth

To make your way back to safety, it is important that you face your situation and honestly admit how far you are in debt. Make a complete list of all your debts; do not leave anything out. Make yourself accountable to someone else (an accountability partner). Recognize that in most cases, indebtedness is sin. "Confess *your* faults one to another, and pray one for another, that ye may be healed" (James 5:16 KJV). Meet with your accountability partner on a regularly appointed schedule.

To make your way back to safety, it is important that you face your situation and honestly admit how far you are in debt.

IN CLOSING

Like losing weight, freeing oneself from indebtedness requires a lifestyle change. It is not the will of God for you to live in financial bondage. It is His will for you to live with a clear conscience, without tension, and with the knowledge that God is in control of your life. Adjust your standard of living to your income level. If you are in debt, you will now have to adjust your standard of living below your income level. Do not yield to financial peer pressure. Do not be ashamed that you cannot afford something. Resist impulsive buying—even bargains—when you don't need them or you don't have the cash to buy them.

"If we really want to know what is important to us, let's get out our calendars and our checkbooks—let's look at how we spend our time and our money—then we will know what's really important to us" (Morley 1992, p. 132). James Dobson (1975) wrote the following:

> I have concluded that the accumulation of wealth, even if I could achieve it, is an insufficient reason for living. When I reach the end of my days, a moment or two from now, I must look backward on something more meaningful than the pursuit of houses and land

and machines and stocks and bonds. Nor is fame of any lasting benefit. I will consider my earthly existence to have been wasted unless I can recall a loving family, a consistent investment in the lives of people, and an earnest attempt to serve the lives of people, and an earnest attempt to serve the God who made me. Nothing else makes much sense. (p. 108)

It's unfortunate when there is little difference between the behaviors of Christians and non-Christians. Patrick Morley (1992) observed: "We have become a society of pretenders, bent on portraying an image of financial success whether or not there is any substance to it. And there is little marginal difference between the way Christians and non-Christians handle their money in our secularized society" (pp. 132–133).

> It's unfortunate when there is little difference between the behaviors of Christians and non-Christians.

But we must never forget, "The rich ruleth over the poor, and the borrower *is* servant to the lender" (Proverbs 22:7 KJV). Therefore, "Allow no sleep to your eyes, no slumber to your eyelids. Free yourself, like a gazelle from the hand of the hunter, like a bird from the snare of the fowler" (Proverbs 6:4–5).

LESSON 35

THERE'S TREASURE IN THAT VINEYARD

PROVERBS 6:6-11

⁶Go to the ant, you sluggard; consider its ways and be wise! ⁷It has no commander, no overseer or ruler, ⁸yet it stores its provisions in summer and gathers its food at harvest.

⁹How long will you lie there, you sluggard? When will you get up from your sleep? ¹⁰A little sleep, a little slumber, a little folding of the hands to rest—¹¹and poverty will come on you like a thief and scarcity like an armed man.

A close friend of mine made the following observation: "If a man will not work, he will probably never make a Christian." Having considered those words for many years and having observed people in general, I have concluded his words are true.

> If a man will not work, he will probably never make a Christian.

LOOK TO THE ANT

The wise man Solomon, endowed by God with an ingrained habit of careful observation and a lively curiosity, apparently had often watched ants at work. It appears he admired their efficiency. Phillips (1995) described Solomon's observation of an ant colony:

> He had seen the busy ant scouts ranging far and wide to look for sources of food. He had seen the ant soldiers quickly taking on intruders. He had seen the panic when an anthill was disturbed and the little creatures ran to and fro; the concern was to get the eggs away from the danger zone and the activity swiftly settled down to organized efficiency. Almost miraculously the damage was repaired and the ants resumed the ordinary business of life—seeking out and storing up food. (p. 139)

Solomon, being the wise man he was, instructs us, particularly if we have a tendency toward laziness, to go to the ant hill and observe it for a while, ponder the activity, and learn a lesson for life from the ant. It appears the ant doesn't require an overseer to specify every task that needs to be done. The ant sees the need and completes the task necessary to meet the need. Solomon points out how the ant gathers the necessary food in summer to meet the needs of a long, cold winter.

The apostle Paul, like Solomon, saw virtue in work as a means of providing for one's basic needs. When he wrote the Thessalonians, he was emphatic that if they did not work, they should not eat. (See 2 Thessalonians 3:10.) Neither Solomon nor Paul were advocates of welfare or a guaranteed basic income whether you work or not. God intended work to be the means by which men and women obtain their daily provisions.

> God intended work to be the be means by which men and women obtain their daily provisions.

Considering those amazing little creatures, Horton (1903) wrote, "The vast and symmetrical mounds, which they rear as habitations and barns, are, relative to the size of the builders, three or four times larger than the pyramids" (p. 83). For a moment, let's look in on the ant's world:

> The ant colony is centered around the queen. The queen is bigger than her subjects, but she is really simply an egg-laying machine. Her function is to provide millions of eggs that the workers take and cultivate as needed. The workers tell the queen what kind of ants are needed for the continuing well-being of the colony. Thus, keeping the colony in balance is a joint effort of the workers and the queen. The workers continually attend to the queen and she responds to the stimuli she receives. This joint enterprise ensures that there will always be the proper proportion of workers, soldiers, pupae, and future queens in the colony. (Phillips 1995, p. 138)

AN EXAMPLE OF INDUSTRY

Ants are an example of industry. They do not need slave drivers to make sure that they get up in the morning and fulfill their appointed tasks. Ants work without fail. They don't seem to be affected by the weather or how they feel on a particular day. How much more would be accomplished if we would take a lesson from the ant? "Go to the ant, you sluggard; consider its ways and be wise!" (Proverbs 6:6). The ant prepares for its future. "It stores its provisions in summer and gathers its food at harvest" (Proverbs 6:8). The ant depicts the individual with ambition, the one who works to provide for his family. On the other hand, "Sluggards do not plow in season; so at harvest time they look but find nothing" (Proverbs 20:4). These are the same individuals who complains that other people get all the breaks—that life is unfair. The truth of the matter is they lack ambition.

> Ants do not need slave drivers to make sure that they get up in the morning and fulfill their appointed tasks.

Solomon wrote, "The desires of the diligent are fully satisfied" (Proverbs 13:4). The diligent are fully satisfied because they have put in a good day's labor and eat the fruit of it. They provide for their families and experience self-esteem. In the final chapter of Proverbs, the writer describes the "wife of noble character." She fits the description of an ant:

> Her price is far above rubies. ... She seeketh wool, and flax, and worketh willingly with her hands. She is like the merchants' ships; she bringeth her food from afar. She riseth also while it is yet night, and giveth meat to her household, and a portion to her maidens. She considereth a field, and buyeth it: with the fruit of her hands she planteth a vineyard. She girdeth her loins with strength, and strengtheneth her arms. (Proverbs 31:10, 13–17 KJV)

At the end of her day, she is fully satisfied. She put in a good day's work, and she experienced self-esteem.

> The diligent are fully satisfied because they have put in a good day's labor and eat the fruit of it.

THE DIGNITY OF WORK

Hughes (1991) observed, "The way we work will reveal how much we have allowed the image of God to develop in us" (p. 149). God being a worker Himself blesses all legitimate work with dignity. Throughout the creation process, we see God admiring His work: "God saw that it was good" (Genesis 1:10, 12, 18, 25 KJV). Work—a job well done—is the source of all true self-esteem. Trying to obtain self-esteem from what others say or think of you might better be called other-esteem, because self-esteem comes from within when you recognize you have done a task well, not by what others say about you. When you have worked hard and completed a task that needed to be done, you too can look upon that work, admire the finished product, and experience a sense of self-esteem.

> Trying to obtain self-esteem from what others say or think of you might better be called other-esteem, because self-esteem comes from within when you recognize you have done a task well, not by what others say about you.

Some look upon work as drudgery, seeing it only as a result of the curse. But work existed before the curse. "The LORD God took the man and put him in the garden of Eden to work it and keep it" (Genesis 2:15 ESV). It's true that work appears to have been made less pleasant by the curse, but work existed before the curse. Being created in God's image, humans are to be workers. That's why the apostle Paul could even instruct slaves in their work: "Slaves, obey your earthly masters with deep respect and fear. Serve them sincerely as you would serve Christ. Try to please them all the time, not just when they are watching you" (Ephesians 6:5–6 NLT).

Work is honorable, regardless of your position in life. All work should be viewed as God's work. Regardless of the age of the worker, the work belongs to God, and it must be offered unto Him. It's an opportunity to be able to teach your children that when they pick up the toys and put them where they belong, Jesus is pleased. At that stage in their lives, that is their work. I believe God is pleased when parents teach their children how to work. And instead of trying to build self-esteem in your children by telling them how wonderful they are, let them experience self-esteem by a job well done.

Consider the following scripture:

Whatever you do, work at it with all your heart, as working for the Lord, not for human masters, since you know that you will receive an inheritance from the Lord as a reward. It is the Lord Christ you are serving. (Colossians 3:23–24)

Everything we do must be done unto the Lord. Understanding this will change our whole outlook on work. Elisabeth Elliot (July 11, 2001) described how we ought to view work: "The offering of my consecrated will and my physical strength, that's what work ought to be." She went on to state the following:

Remember in whatever stage you are in, whatever kind of work that God has given you, that you are serving the Lord Christ. Think about that! As I wash dishes I am serving the Lord Christ. As I am cleaning the bathroom I am serving the Lord Christ. As I am writing a book I am serving the Lord Christ. It's work. It's hard work and it's repetitive" (Elliot July 11, 2001).

> Everything we do must be done unto the Lord.

THE FRUIT OF LABOR

Aesop provides us with a bit of wisdom concerning work:

A farmer, being at death's door, and desiring to impart to his sons a secret of much moment, called them round him and said, 'My sons, I am shortly about to die. I would have you know, therefore, that in my vineyard there lies a hidden treasure. Dig, and you will find it.' As soon as their father was dead, the sons took spade and fork and turned up the soil of the vineyard over and over again, in their search for the treasure which they supposed to lie buried there. They found none, however: but the vines, after so thorough a digging, produced a crop such as had never before been seen. (cited in Bennett 1993, p. 370)

The fruit of the vineyard was in their work.

THE CONSEQUENCE OF LAZINESS

Just as work is honorable, the Bible describes the consequence of laziness. "Laziness leads to a sagging roof; idleness leads to a leaky house" (Ecclesiastes 10:18 NLT). Lazy people will never please the one who is counting on them to do the work. "As vinegar to the teeth, and as smoke to the eyes, so *is* the sluggard to them that send him" (Proverbs 10:26 KJV). In reality, the sluggard is a thief of another person's time. Unfortunately, there appears to be a diminishing of the work ethic in our day. According to a survey in 1991, only twenty-five percent of employees reported giving their best effort on their jobs (Patterson & Kim 1991). Workers reported wasting about 20 percent of their working time, thus reducing their productivity to a four-day workweek. How shameful for a Christian to adopt the way of the sluggard! It is the role of the Christian to present the Bible to the world by giving a good day's work for a day's pay.

> The sluggard is a thief of another person's time.

IN CLOSING

As Christians, we must return to the teachings of the Word of God concerning work, regardless of what others do. What we need is a work ethic shaped by God's Word and religiously lived out in the workplace and the church. The reason this is so important is that most of us spend eight to ten of our sixteen waking hours at work five or six days a week. So how we work not only reveals who we are, but it determines what we are. Anyone should be able to show up on time and give a day's work for a day's pay. The apostle Paul laid down a rule in every church: "If anyone is not willing to work, let him not eat" (2 Thessalonians 3:10 ESV).

> How long will you lie there, you sluggard? When will you get up from your sleep? A little sleep, a little slumber, a little folding of the hands to rest—and poverty will come on you like a thief and scarcity like an armed man. (Proverbs 6:9–11)

As Christians, we must return to the teachings of the Word of God concerning work, regardless of what others do.

You have the same opportunity as your neighbor. Take a lesson from the ant; arise and start working. There's treasure in that vineyard.

LESSON 36

THE TROUBLEMAKER

PROVERBS 6:12-15

¹² A troublemaker and villain, who goes about with a corrupt mouth, ¹³ who winks with his eye, signals with his feet and motions with his fingers, ¹⁴ who plots evil with deceit in his heart—he always stirs up conflict. ¹⁵ Therefore disaster will overtake him in an instant; he will suddenly be destroyed—without remedy.

There are two reasons for this proverb. The first is to make us aware of the troublemaker, and the second is to make us aware of the troublemaker's end. The word translated *troublemaker* literally means *a man of Belial* or *a worthless person*. And the word translated *villain* means *injurious*. It is derived from a word meaning *the breaking up of all that is good*. This kind of person sounds an awful lot like the devil because he is under the influence of the devil. Jesus described the devil as a thief: "The thief cometh not, but for to steal, and to kill, and to destroy" (John 10:10 KJV). Deceitfulness and discord are the troublemaker's daily delight. For purpose of this lesson, *troublemaker and villain* will be referred to simply as *the troublemaker*. Solomon was making us aware that we are likely to have contact with those that fit the description of a troublemaker on a regular basis. There will be people we are forced to interact with that seemingly are under the sway of the devil.

A HEART CONDITION

Troublemakers are not concerned that what they say and do destroys lives. In some cases, they say little, but their body language speaks volumes. He or she "winks with his eye, signals with his feet and motions with his fingers" (Proverbs 6:13). Horton (1903) well described this kind of person:

> It is this kind of man that is the pest of commerce. He introduces dishonest practices into every business that he touches ... When he has been in business for a little while the whole concern becomes tainted, there is a slime over everything; the very atmosphere is fetid.
>
> It is this kind of man that is the bane of every social circle. In his presence, all simplicity and innocence, all charity and forbearance and compassion, seem to wither away. If you are true and straightforward he manages to make you ridiculous; under his evil spell you seem a simpleton. All genial laughter he turns into sardonic smiles and sneers; and kindly expressions he transforms into empty compliments which are not devoid of a hidden venom. He is often very witty, but his wit clings like an eating acid to everything that is good and pure; his tongue will lodge a germ of putrescence in everything which it touches.
>
> It is this kind of man that is the leaven of hypocrisy and malice in the Christian Church ... He sets people against the minister and stirs up the minister to suspect his people ... He is never better pleased than when he can pose as the champion of orthodoxy. (pp. 86–87)

The troublemaker has a heart condition, and the diagnosis is a deceptive heart. (See Proverbs 6:14.) Jesus stated, "An evil man out of the evil treasure of his heart bringeth forth that which is evil: for of the abundance of the heart his mouth speaketh" (Luke 6:45 KJV). Because of the deceitfulness of the heart, troublemakers have little insight into their behaviors.

> The troublemaker has a heart condition, and the diagnosis is a deceptive heart.

THE TROUBLEMAKER'S MANY DEVICES

We must be aware of the devices used by troublemakers so that they "might not outwit us" (2 Corinthians 2:11). Their devices fall into two categories: frontal assault and subtle infiltration. Since a frontal assault is obvious, it will not be addressed here. Instead, the focus will be on raising awareness of the attempts by troublemakers to infiltrate the life of a Christian. Their devices take many forms, ranging from deceit to compromise to distortion of truth to spiritual blindness. And you can rest assured that they will use one of their favorite tools—dissension.

Deceit. We must remain alert to the troublemaker's use of deceit. "See then that ye walk circumspectly" (Ephesians 5:15 KJV). A good example of deceit in the Old Testament is the story of the Gibeonites. The Gibeonites were never a military threat to Israel, but once Israel opened herself to their deception, they remained a thorn in her side forever. The irony of that story was the ease with which the Gibeonites deceived God's people. They simply told a tall tale that they had come from a far country, and "the Israelites sampled their provisions but did not inquire of the Lord" (Joshua 9:14). A short conversation with the Lord would have saved Israel years of suffering. Christians must seek God in all circumstances. Paul urged the Ephesian church, and it has equal application for the church today, "Pray in the Spirit in every situation. Use every kind of prayer and request there is. For the same reason be alert. Use every kind of effort and make every kind of request for all of God's people" (Ephesians 6:18 GW).

Christians must avoid the temptation to get what they want through deception. "Be not deceived; God is not mocked: for whatsoever a man soweth, that shall he also reap" (Galatians 6:7 KJV). Sowing deceit will result in a harvest of deceit. We see that in the life of Jacob. He deceived his brother, Esau, and the law of harvest resulted in more than twenty years of reaping deception. (See Genesis 31.)

Compromise. You don't have to preach against truth for compromise to occur. All you have to do is stop preaching the truth. You don't have to preach against standards of holiness for standards of holiness to drop. All you have to do is stop teaching standards of holiness. Troublemakers are calculating, and they are cognizant of the fact that a little untruth goes a long way. Jesus warned, "Beware of false prophets [troublemakers], which come to you in sheep's clothing, but inwardly they are ravening wolves" (Matthew 7:15 KJV). The troublemaker knows that a little compromise will lower the standards of the entire group. This is not new. Paul warned the Corinthians "that a little yeast leavens the whole lump" (1 Corinthians 5:6 KJV). The troublemaker is an expert in the use of this method. Their idea is to mix evil with good, thus making the whole evil. The LORD was emphatic, "Woe unto them that call evil good, and good evil; that put darkness for light, and light for darkness; that put bitter for sweet, and sweet for bitter!" (Isaiah 5:20 KJV).

> Troublemakers are calculating, and they are cognizant of the fact that a little untruth goes a long way.

Troublemakers work just as effectively today as in the good old days. Jude blew the whistle on them when he wrote his letter:

> For certain individuals whose condemnation was written about long ago have secretly slipped in among you. They are godless people, who pervert the grace of our God into a license for immorality and deny Jesus Christ our only Sovereign and Lord. (Jude 1:4)

Distortion of truth. If compromise doesn't work, troublemakers will twist the scriptures. They have no internal inhibition against using outrageous lies or distortion of the truth to accomplish their work. The Jews of Jesus's day were not beyond distorting and denying the truth to maintain power and control, and Jesus confronted them to their faces:

> You belong to your father, the devil, and you want to carry out your father's desire. He was a murderer from the beginning, not holding to the truth, for there is no truth in him. When he lies, he speaks his native language, for he is a liar and the father of lies. (John 8:44)

Since troublemakers are under the direct influence of the devil, they feel no obligation to tell the truth. In fact, you can be certain that anything spoken under the influence of the unholy spirit is either an outright lie or a distortion of truth.

> The troublemaker has no internal inhibition against using outrageous lies or distortion of the truth to accomplish their work.

Spiritual blindness. If none of the above tactics work effectively, then there is always blindness. Since blindness is the state of the unconverted, it is Satan's goal to keep people in the dark: "The god of this world hath blinded the minds of them which believe not, lest the light of the glorious gospel of Christ, who is the image of God, should shine unto them" (2 Corinthians 4:4 KJV). Troublemakers lose influence when someone awakens spiritually, so they will do all they can to keep people in the dark. But an even more pitiful condition is the blindness of those who once were enlightened. The troublemaker takes delight in leading people away from the light. An example was the church in Laodicea. Someone had led the church in Laodicea away from the light, and Jesus was attempting to get the people to recognize their blinded condition.

Like physical blindness, spiritual blindness can come on slowly—so slowly that it is hard to notice the world around you growing dark. A friend of mine told of how cataracts had dimmed his vision. He is an evangelist, and he began to wonder why pastors kept their churches so dark. Only after removal of the cataracts did he realize it wasn't the churches that were dark; it was his own blindness. Jesus confronted the members of the church at Laodicea: "For you claim, 'I'm rich and getting richer—I don't need a thing.' Yet you are clueless that you're miserable, poor, blind, barren, and naked!" (Revelation 3:17 TPT). When that occurs, there is only one solution—repentance. (See Revelation 3:19–20.) Repentance is like cataract surgery—suddenly everything is brighter; suddenly you can see!

> Like physical blindness, spiritual blindness can come on slowly—so slowly that it is hard to notice the world around you growing dark.

I am concerned that there is a dimming or a loss of spiritual eyesight in our day. Paul Mooney (2016) wrote the following:

> There is, in my view, a growing carelessness in the way we deal with the world and its influences. It's also clear we are weakening our traditional stance against worldly entertainment and, shall we say, worldliness in general. But what is more troubling is the growing cavalier attitude toward immorality, at times coupled with a kind of protectionism—an unwillingness to address the problem. Sin is no longer called sin, the definitions are muddled, unrighteousness is left unaddressed, unchallenged until at some point the apathy turns into defense of the very thing we were supposed to war against. I pray that we will not turn a blind eye to sin. I pray that we will not allow ourselves to become comfortable with the world, afraid to confront unrighteousness, ungodly lifestyles. (p. 2)

Have we become so strong that we can now sit in front of a computer and watch the same Hollywood production our elders condemned when shown on television? Do you find yourself defending as okay the very thing that was condemned by the last generation as sin? Are you really spiritually stronger, or have your spiritual eyes become dim? Have you noticed that you are no longer wearing your spiritual armor, that it's stacked off in the corner of your living room, while you sit in front of a blue screen joining the world in its entertainment and games? Why is it you no longer feel any conviction? Could it be spiritual blindness?

Have we become so strong that we can now sit in front of a computer and watch the same Hollywood production our elders condemned when shown on television? Do you find yourself defending as okay the very thing that was condemned by the last generation as sin? Are you really spiritually stronger, or have your spiritual eyes become dim?

Dissension. The troublemaker not only plots evil in a calculated manner, "he always stirs up conflict" (Proverbs 6:14). In Galatians 5:19, the apostle Paul listed the sins that he called "works of the flesh" or "works of the sinful nature" and tells us very pointedly, "They which do such things shall not inherit the kingdom of God" (Galatians 5:21 KJV). That list includes behaviors like sexual immorality, drunkenness, and orgies—behaviors that are generally accepted as sins. But in that list, there also is a sin that we seldom think will prevent us from inheriting the kingdom of God—dissension. Our Lord takes this sin so seriously that the apostle Paul uses three different expressions of the same idea to describe it—discord, dissensions, and factions. There are not enough words to express what serious consequences dissension creates in families and churches. What have you done to prevent the troublemaker from stirring up quarrels and divisions? Jesus said, "Blessed *are* the peacemakers: for they shall be called the children of God" (Matthew 5:9 KJV). One day, He will ask us whether we have worked to maintain peace, or whether we have yielded to the spirit of the troublemaker.

TURNING THE TABLE ON
THE TROUBLEMAKER

Solomon concluded that we need not fear the troublemaker because "disaster will overtake him in an instant; he will suddenly be destroyed—without remedy" (Proverbs 6:15). So, don't follow them; their fate is sealed.

The book of Esther provides the best example in the Bible of God rescuing His own and turning the table on the troublemaker. Mordecai and his cousin Esther were captives in a foreign land. As worshipers of Jehovah, they would not bow to a man or anything other than their God. This stirred up the wrath of a troublemaker by the name of Haman. Standing strong for truth always infuriates the enemy.

> When Haman saw that Mordecai would not kneel down or pay him honor, he was enraged. Yet having learned who Mordecai's people were, he scorned the idea of killing only Mordecai. Instead Haman looked for a way to destroy all Mordecai's people, the Jews, throughout the whole kingdom of Xerxes. (Esther 3:5–6)

> Standing strong for truth always infuriates the enemy.

When Mordecai would not bow, Haman informed King Xerxes that the Jews who had been dispersed to his nation were a people who would not keep the laws of any nation but their own. In going to the king, the troublemaker had one intent: "Let it be written that they may be destroyed" (Esther 3:9 KJV).

It may have looked like the righteous were headed for extinction, but the Lord was about to turn the tables. The situation called for the use of spiritual weapons. Fasting and prayer were employed. Coming against Haman was no different than David coming against Goliath, because the LORD saves "not with sword and spear: for the battle is the LORD's" (1 Samuel 17:47 KJV). Esther called for every Jew in the city of Shushan to join her and her maidens in three days of fasting and prayer. The risk of going into the presence of the king uninvited was death. Regardless of the risk, Esther had to do her part if the Jews were to be saved. Before entering the king's chamber, she fully committed herself to do the work of God—"If I perish, I perish" (Esther 4:16 KJV).

There is a time to pray, and there is a time to step out by faith. Esther donned her royal robes and stood in the inner court of the palace, waiting for a signal from the king. "When he saw Queen Esther standing in the court, he was pleased with her and held out to her the gold scepter that was in his hand. So Esther approached and touched the tip of the scepter" (Esther 5:2). He accepted her! The Lord had intervened!

> There is a time to pray, and there is a time to step out by faith.

The plot thickened, and the Lord decided to have a little fun with the troublemaker. "That night the king could not sleep. So he told [a servant] to bring the official daily records, and they were read to the king" (Esther 6:1 GW). In reading the chronicles, the king found that nothing had been done to reward Mordecai for saving him from a plot to overthrow his kingdom, so he decided to honor Mordecai for his faithful service. The Lord was turning the table. The king asked Haman for advice concerning what he should do for someone he wanted to honor. Haman, being blinded by pride, believed the king was referring to him. He responded as follows:

> For the man whom the king delighteth to honour, Let the royal apparel be brought which the king useth to wear, and the horse that the king rideth upon, and the crown royal which is set upon his head: And let this apparel and horse be delivered to the hand of one of the king's most noble princes, that they may array the man withal whom the king delighteth to honour,

and bring him on horseback through the street of the city, and proclaim before him, Thus shall it be done to the man whom the king delighteth to honour! (Esther 6:7–9 KJV)

The king was pleased with Haman's suggestions: "'Excellent!' the king said to Haman. 'Quick! Take the robes and my horse, and do just as you have said for Mordecai the Jew, who sits at the gate of the palace. Leave out nothing you have suggested'" (Esther 6:10 NLT). Humiliated, Haman got the apparel and the horse and did for Mordecai just as he had suggested.

Haman—the troublemaker—did not recognize the workings of the Almighty God. Therefore, disaster overtook him, and he was suddenly destroyed. When God is ready to perform a miracle, it seems He chooses the most unlikely method. The king discovered the wicked plot of the troublemaker. "So they hanged Haman on the gallows that he had prepared for Mordecai" (Esther 7:10 KJV). In turn, King Xerxes gave the house of Haman to Esther. And to Mordecai he took the ring that he had taken from Haman, and he gave it to Mordecai. And Esther appointed Mordecai over the house of Haman.

IN CLOSING

Some of the greatest victories in life are the result of situations over which you have little control. Seldom do we look back at happy, prosperous, and normal days as life-changing moments. Instead, events that have brought the most stress, pain, or loss are frequently the defining moments that demonstrate the working of God in our lives. We learn to trust in God in times of our greatest weakness. When we are faced with our own deficiencies, we learn to trust His sufficiency. In our moments of greatest potential loss, we learn to trust God to come to our rescue. The darkest valley experiences often produce the greatest victories in life.

As long as this life continues, the troublemaker will not be far away with their tool chest of deceit, compromise, distortion of truth, spiritual blindness, and dissension. Daily there are spiritual attacks against your soul. The Christian life is a battleground, not a playground. It is God's will that every single individual in this spiritual battle be victorious. So it is essential to recognize the significance of these spiritual conflicts. Jesus purchased the ability for His people to be overcomers.

> The Christian life is a battleground, not a playground.

Instead of succumbing to the subtle attacks of the troublemaker, or running in fear, it is essential that you go directly to the throne for help, and you never have to fear whether He will put forth the golden scepter. It is the King of kings who is able to turn the table and bring victory to every child of God. In doing so, you will be able to look back and declare, "My help comes from the LORD, the Maker of heaven and earth. He will not let your foot slip—he who watches over you will not slumber" (Psalm 121: 2–4).

LESSON 37

THE BIG SEVEN

PROVERBS 6:16-19

16 There are six things the LORD hates, seven that are detestable to him: 17 haughty eyes, a lying tongue, hands that shed innocent blood, 18 a heart that devises wicked schemes, feet that are quick to rush into evil, 19 a false witness who pours out lies and a person who stirs up conflict in the community.

In reading the scriptures, it becomes quite evident that there are things the LORD loves, and there are things the LORD hates. The seven things listed above all stand in stark contrast to the characteristics of a Christian.

THINGS THE LORD HATES

Haughty eyes. John Phillips (1995) wrote, "Pride is the father of all sin" (p. 145). The Word of God declares, "Pride *goeth* before destruction, and an haughty spirit before a fall" (Proverbs 16:18 KJV). And Isaiah described the fall of the king of Babylon when he attempted to exalt himself even above the Most High God:

> How art thou fallen from heaven, O Lucifer, son of
> the morning! *how* art thou cut down to the ground,
> which didst weaken the nations! For thou hast said in

thine heart, I will ascend into heaven, I will exalt my throne above the stars of God: I will sit also upon the mount of the congregation, in the sides of the north: I will ascend above the heights of the clouds; I will be like the most High. Yet thou shalt be brought down to hell, to the sides of the pit. (Isaiah 14:12–15 KJV)

Though that prophecy was to the king of Babylon, it referenced the fall of Lucifer from a much earlier time. Regardless of how secure you may believe you are, a haughty spirit guarantees a great fall.

> Regardless of how secure you may believe you are, a haughty spirit guarantees a great fall.

A lying tongue. The LORD hates a lying tongue. Wickedness in the heart makes it as easy to lie as to tell the truth. Satan is the father of all lies. Jesus made that very clear: "He was a murderer from the beginning, not holding to the truth, for there is no truth in him. When he lies, he speaks his native language, for he is a liar and the father of lies" (John 8:44). Therefore, we must never forget, "He is the author of all untruth, the ultimate source of all religious, philosophical, scientific, social, economic, and political error" (Phillips 1995, p. 146).

Hands that shed innocent blood. The LORD hates hands that shed innocent blood— "You shall not murder" (Exodus 20:13). Little did Eve realize when she listened to the serpent's lies that her firstborn son would grow up to become a murderer. Since that time, rivers of blood have flowed. There have been gruesome murders committed out of malice, spite, envy, and greed. Through the centuries, blood has been shed as a result of persecution, repression, rebellion, and slaughter. And it grieves the heart of the LORD. The LORD detests hands that shed innocent blood.

A heart that devises wicked schemes. Adam lived 930 years, long enough to see the wicked effects of sin. Seven hundred years after the death of Adam, the LORD declared, "Every imagination of the thoughts of [man's] heart *was* only evil continually" (Genesis 6:5 KJV).

During the reign of the wicked king Ahab, his evil wife, Jezebel, declared to her pouting husband that she would get him the vineyard he wanted. To do so, she devised a wicked scheme to kill the owner, Naboth:

> She wrote letters in Ahab's name, and sealed *them* with his seal, and sent the letters unto the elders and to the nobles that *were* in his city, dwelling with Naboth. And she wrote in the letters, saying, Proclaim a fast, and set Naboth on high among the people: And set two men, sons of Belial, before him, to bear witness against him, saying, Thou didst blaspheme God and the king. And *then* carry him out, and stone him, that he may die. (1 Kings 21:8–10 KJV)

By implementing her wicked scheme, evil men murdered righteous Naboth. Isaiah could very well have been describing Jezebel when he wrote, "Scoundrels use wicked methods, they make up evil schemes to destroy the poor with lies, even when the plea of the needy is just" (Isaiah 32:7). The LORD hates a heart that devises wicked schemes.

Feet that are quick to rush into evil. The apostle Paul warned Timothy of those who had become gossips and busybodies. (See 1 Timothy 5:13.) David described individuals who are quick to rush into evil as those "who speak cordially with their neighbors but harbor malice in their hearts" (Psalm 28:3). Solomon stated that God's favor is with the person who earnestly desires to know and to do what is good, "but evil comes to one who searches for it" (Proverbs 11:27). Busybodies are always on the cutting edge of the latest morsels of evil information. They are possessed with the sin of talebearing. If it's evil and sensational, they will be right there, notepad in hand, to carry that juicy morsel to the first ear willing to receive it. To the talebearer and the willing listener, a bit of sensational gossip is arousing, but to the LORD, it is detestable.

> Busybodies are always on the cutting edge of the latest morsels of evil information.

A false witness. In this context, *a false witness* seems to reference malicious intent, rather than personal gain. For example, a story is told of a young sailor who hated his captain and wrote in the logbook, "The captain was sober today." The truth was the captain never drank alcohol. Another example was the Sanhedrin's attempt to find someone to testify against our Lord. "The chief priests and the whole Sanhedrin were looking for false evidence against Jesus so that they could put him to death. But they did not find any, though many false witnesses came forward. Finally two came forward" (Matthew 26:59–60). The wretched men who ran that religious system were simply pawns in the hands of Satan bearing false witness against our Lord. And the LORD hates a false witness.

A man who stirs up dissension. One commentator described this kind of person as "a deliberate meddler" (Phillips 1995, p. 148). Satan, a deliberate meddler, has lost no sleep to increase the divorce rate in recent years by pitting husbands against wives and wives against husbands. Authority within the family has been eroded as the meddler has encouraged rebellion within the hearts of children and confusion as to the role of parents in correcting and disciplining children. Working busily, the meddler has turned whole communities against the police, and encouraged law enforcement officers to abuse their authority, resulting in members of those communities questioning police officers' motives. By yielding to Satan, men and women are woven into the fabric of confusion and chaos, becoming pawns stirring up dissension. Our proverb teaches that this kind of behavior is detestable (an abomination KJV) to the LORD.

> By yielding to Satan, men and women are woven into the fabric of confusion and chaos, becoming pawns stirring up dissension.

THINGS THE LORD LOVES

Now that we have examined the things the LORD hates, let's consider some things our LORD loves.

A humble attitude. A humble attitude is a prerequisite to entering the kingdom of God. The doorway into the kingdom is very low. "Blessed *are* the poor in spirit: for theirs is the kingdom of heaven" (Matthew 5:3 KJV). While the other beatitudes are manifestations of fullness, "poor in spirit" speaks of emptying. It's been said, "You cannot be filled until you are empty." The Greek word translated *poor* means *beggarly poor*, and in the context of the Sermon on the Mount, it references the view people have toward themselves: "Blessed are those who recognize they are spiritually helpless" (Matthew 5:3 GW).

Consider the LORD's own words: "These are the ones I look on with favor: those who are humble and contrite in spirit, and who tremble at my word" (Isaiah 66:2). And James wrote, "Humble yourselves in the sight of the Lord, and he shall lift you up" (James 4:10 KJV).

John the Baptist knew his purpose for existence, and when Jesus's ministry began to flourish, he recognized he was not in competition with our Lord. John proclaimed, "He must increase, but I *must* decrease" (John 3:30 KJV). There is a principle in this statement from which everyone can benefit: as John decreased in his own sight, he increased in the eyes of our Lord. Though John was not present to hear the compliment, Jesus honored him by saying, "Among those that are born of women there is not a greater prophet than John the Baptist" (Luke 7:28 KJV). The proud fear to let go, but the humble know the more they lose of themselves, the more they gain of the Lord.

> The proud fear to let go, but the humble know the more they lose of themselves, the more they gain of the Lord.

An honest tongue. When Paul wrote the Corinthians, he stressed the importance of an honest tongue. "We have renounced secret and shameful ways; we do not use deception, nor do we distort the word of God" (2 Corinthians 4:2). To be honest is more than what a person says or does; honesty includes the total person—thought patterns, outlook on others, how one goes about solving problems and reaching decisions, and how a person feels about oneself. Jesus stated, "A good man out of the good treasure of his heart bringeth forth that which is good ... for of the abundance of the heart his mouth speaketh" (Luke 6:45 KJV). Honesty adds dignity and honor to any life. It is listed among such virtues as noble, right, pure, lovely, and admirable. (See Philippians 4:8.)

Holy hands. Look to the hands of Jesus as an example of holy hands. His hands blessed the little children, gave sight to the blind, touched and healed lepers, and fed the hungry multitude. And from those hands dripped blood that provided atonement for our sins. Paul stressed to Timothy that the men in the church should be lifting up holy hands in prayer—not hurtful hands in anger: "I want men everywhere to pray lifting up holy hands without anger or disputing" (1 Timothy 2:8).

A pure heart. Jesus stated simply but emphatically, "Blessed *are* the pure in heart: for they shall see God" (Matthew 5:8 KJV). The Greek word translated *pure* in that verse means *cleansed from filth or iniquity.* Our English word *catharsis* is derived from the same Greek word. In other words, "Blessed are those who maintain 'a clean heart'; they will see God." The English word *pure* means *to have nothing added to it.* Our eyes must be focused on righteousness, and our hearts must remain pure. "No man can serve two masters" (Matthew 6:24 KJV). We must not allow anything to distract from our focus on Jesus.

Cautious feet. In contrast to feet that are quick to rush into mischief, Jesus's feet always took him to where He could help and heal. He was never in a hurry, yet He was always on time. A good example of this is when Lazarus was sick and died:

> Then when Mary was come where Jesus was, and saw him, she fell down at his feet, saying unto him, Lord, if thou hadst been here, my brother had not died.
>
> When Jesus therefore saw her weeping, and the Jews also weeping which came with her, he groaned in the spirit, and was troubled, And said, Where have ye laid him?
>
> Then they took away the stone *from the place* where the dead was laid. And Jesus lifted up *his* eyes, and said, Father, I thank thee that thou hast heard me.

And I knew that thou hearest me always: but because of the people which stand by I said it, that they may believe that thou hast sent me. And when he thus had spoken, he cried with a loud voice, Lazarus, come forth. And he that was dead came forth, bound hand and foot with graveclothes: and his face was bound about with a napkin. Jesus saith unto them, Loose him, and let him go. (John 11:32–33, 41–44 KJV)

> Jesus was never in a hurry, yet He was always on time.

An honest witness. There's no need to sugarcoat the Word of God. There's no need to take the stealth bomber approach and fly under the radar, avoiding revealing your identity. The first-generation converts to Christ did not try to hide who they were: "The disciples were called Christians first in Antioch" (Acts 11:26 KJV). Why? Because there was enough Christ in them to cause others to see them as Christians (followers of Christ). The Lord desires and loves an honest witness. Even when it meant certain arrest and eventual death, Jesus remained an honest witness:

> Jesus therefore, knowing all things that should come upon him, went forth, and said unto them, Whom seek ye? They answered him, Jesus of Nazareth. Jesus saith unto them, I am *he.* And Judas also, which betrayed him, stood with them. As soon then as he had said unto them, I am *he,* they went backward, and fell to the ground. Then asked he them again, Whom seek ye? And they said, Jesus of Nazareth. Jesus answered, I have told you that I am *he.* (John 18:4–8 KJV)

> There's no need to take the stealth bomber approach and fly under the radar, avoiding revealing your identity.

Peacemaking. Satan, the meddler, turned Cain against Abel, Ishmael against Isaac, Esau against Jacob, and the sons of Jacob against Joseph. Jesus, on the other hand, was a peacemaker. He became a healer of broken homes, the reconciler to those estranged from one another, and the Prince of Peace. Paul instructed us through the letter to the church in Rome, "Live peaceably with all men" (Romans 12:18 KJV). And Jesus stated, "Blessed *are* the peacemakers: for they shall be called the children of God" (Matthew 5:9 KJV).

IN CLOSING

The writer of Proverbs listed seven behaviors the LORD hates—things that are detestable to Him. And if he hates them and they are detestable to Him, we too should abhor those characteristics and put them out of our lives. In addition to putting those things God hates out of our lives, we must also love what God loves and manifest those characteristics. As noted above, every Christian should aspire to be filled with virtues that are pleasing to our Lord. Every Christian should strive to possess a humble attitude, an honest tongue, holy hands, a pure heart, and cautious feet. Further, every Christian should strive to become an honest witness and a peacemaker. It's time for a new set of clothes; put off the things the Lord hates; clothe yourself with the things He loves. (See Colossians 3:12.)

LESSON 38

FATHER'S COMMANDS; MOTHER'S TEACHINGS

PROVERBS 6:20-29

²⁰ My son, keep your father's commands and do not forsake your mother's teaching. ²¹ Bind them always on your heart; fasten them around your neck. ²² When you walk, they will guide you; when you sleep, they will watch over you; when you awake, they will speak to you. ²³ For this command is a lamp, this teaching is a light, and correction and instruction are the way to life, ²⁴ keeping you from your neighbor's wife, from the smooth talk of a wayward woman.

²⁵ Do not lust in your heart after her beauty or let her captivate you with her eyes.

²⁶ For a prostitute can be had for a loaf of bread, but another man's wife preys upon your very life. ²⁷ Can a man scoop fire into his lap without his clothes being burned? ²⁸ Can a man walk on hot coals without his feet being scorched? ²⁹ So is he who sleeps with another man's wife; no one who touches her will go unpunished.

The scriptures are clear that God, as Creator, is the Father of the human family. (See Malachi 2:10.) There is something inherent in being the Creator that allows for the establishment of rules. People repeatedly have gotten into trouble when they did not recognize the Creator's right to govern. We must not allow our arrogance to destroy us. For example,

"Can the ax boast greater power than the person who uses it? Is the saw greater than the person who saws? Can a rod strike unless a hand moves it? Can a wooden cane walk by itself?" (Isaiah 10:15 NLT). In other words, is it really possible for the tail to wag the dog? Considering any one of these questions is almost humorous.

> People repeatedly have gotten into trouble when they did not recognize the Creator's right to govern.

What is it within the human nature that challenges the Creator's right to set the rules and expect the creation to live by them? When Paul wrote to the church in Rome, he asked the following:

> Shall what is formed say to him who formed it, "Why did you make me like this?" Does not the potter have the right to make out of the same lump of clay some pottery for special purposes and some for common use? (Romans 9:20–21)

FATHER'S RIGHT TO GOVERN

Our heavenly Father has the supreme right to govern, and His words are certain! David declared, "All your words are true; all your righteous laws are eternal" (Psalm 119:160). "For ever, O LORD, thy word is settled in heaven" (Psalm 119:89 KJV). In studying the scriptures, one cannot but see the certainty of our Father's words. Six thousand years beyond the creation of humankind, we are able to point to numerous prophecies and the fulfillment of those prophecies. One good example is the words penned by Joel: "And it shall come to pass afterward, *that* I will pour out my spirit upon all flesh" (Joel 2:28 KJV). Eight hundred years later, Peter returns to those words in explaining the outpouring of God's Spirit on the Day of Pentecost: "This is that which was spoken by the prophet Joel" (Acts 2:16 KJV). From this prophetic utterance, Peter preached the first sermon in the New Testament church. At the end of that sermon, hungry, desperate souls asked Peter and the others present what they must do to remedy their situation. In response, "Peter said unto them, Repent, and be baptized every one of you in the name of Jesus Christ for the remission of sins, and ye shall receive the gift of the Holy Ghost" (Acts 2:38 KJV). Two thousand years after those words were spoken, I obeyed, and my sins were remitted (forgiven) through repentance and baptism. I believed the certainty of Father's promise, and I was filled with the Holy Spirit.

Father's commands are for our benefit. "When you walk, they will guide you; when you sleep, they will watch over you; when you awake, they will speak to you" (Proverbs 6:22). David asked the following question: "How can a young man keep his way pure?" (Psalm 119:9 ESV). And he immediately concluded, "By living according to your word" (Psalm 119:9). In fact, God's Word "is a lamp unto my feet and a light unto my path" (Psalm 119:105 KJV).

The purpose of Father's commands was for the explicit purpose of keeping the young man from the immoral woman:

> My son, obey your father's commands, and don't neglect your mother's instruction. Keep their words always in your heart. Tie them around your neck. When you walk, their counsel will lead you. When you sleep, they will protect you. When you wake up, they will advise you. For their command is a lamp and their instruction a light; their corrective discipline is the way to life. It will keep you from the immoral woman, from the smooth tongue of a promiscuous woman. ... He who embraces her will not go unpunished. (Proverbs 6:20–24, 29 NLT)

The purpose of Father's commands was for the explicit purpose of keeping the young man from the immoral woman.

MOTHER AFFIRMS FATHER'S AUTHORITY

But just as God is our Father, the church is our mother. In writing to the Galatians, Paul described the church as a spiritual Jerusalem, "and she is our mother" (Galatians 4:26 ESV). Just as the Lord defined the role of a father, He clearly defined the role of the mother.

The first expectation of mother's role is submission to father. Though submission seems to be a marginalized and even scorned word in our contemporary society, it is biblical. It was not man that came up with this concept; it was God Himself. Thus, we get the term *divine order*. He stated to the woman, "Thy desire *shall be* to thy husband, and he shall rule over thee" (Genesis 3:16 KJV). And when Paul wrote to the Ephesians, he described divine order as a way of life for the Christian:

> Wives, submit yourselves unto your own husbands, as unto the Lord. For the husband is the head of the wife, even as Christ is the head of the church. ... Therefore as the church is subject unto Christ, so *let* the wives be to their own husbands in every thing. (Ephesians 5:22–24 KJV)

In essence, fathers and mothers are only reflecting a picture of what God intended between our heavenly Father and mother—Jesus Christ and the church. (See Ephesians 5:32.)

> Fathers and mothers are only reflecting a picture of what God intended between our heavenly Father and mother—Jesus Christ and the church.

As head of the human family, it is Father who establishes order and sets the rules, and it is the mother who teaches and enforces the rules and expectations of Father. When the mother fulfills her role, she teaches Father's commands to her children. "My son, keep your father's commands and do not forsake your mother's teaching" (Proverbs 6:20). When Father says, "If any man defile the temple of God, him shall God destroy; for the temple of God is holy, which *temple* ye are" (1 Corinthians 3:17 KJV), the mother says, "Son, tobacco, alcohol, drugs, and overeating are destructive to your body." When Father says, "Thou shalt not kill" (Exodus 20:13 KJV), the mother says, "That includes the unborn." When Father says, "Thou shalt not commit adultery" (Exodus 20:14 KJV), the mother says, "That means you must abstain from sexual relations until you are married, not just until you decide you like one another, commit to one another, or get engaged." When Father says, "Set no wicked thing before [your] eyes" (Psalm 101:3 KJV), the mother says, "Son, be very careful of what you read, look at, and listen to. Let the Spirit convict you. In this area, it's better to be too cautious than too brave." When Father says, "Neither the sexually immoral nor idolaters nor adulterers nor men who have sex with men nor thieves nor the greedy nor drunkards nor slanderers nor swindlers will inherit the kingdom of God" (1 Corinthians 6:9–10), the mother says, "He means exactly what he says!" Further, the mother says, "That command applies equally to women who have sex with women. Neither shall they inherit the Kingdom of God." When Father says, "The woman shall not wear that which pertaineth unto a man, neither shall a man put on a woman's garment: for all that do so are abomination unto the LORD thy God" (Deuteronomy 22:5 KJV), the mother says, "'Abomination unto the LORD' means it's still in effect today—not just during church attendance, but in your daily life outside of church as well—not just for adults, but for children too." She explains, "It is imperative that our gender be declared by what we wear. Man must not wear anything that looks like a dress, and women must not wear anything that looks like pants."

> As head of the human family, it is Father who establishes order and sets the rules, and it is the mother who teaches and enforces the rules and expectations of Father.

Mother's teachings were never meant to be burdensome, only to protect.

True Mother's Love

How frail, how weak that mother's love that cannot say, "no."

How selfish, how pitiful the Mother's love that cannot let go;

How menacing, how alarming the Mother's love that knows not how to step aside,

But chokes and smothers and kills every fiber of her child's pride.

How perceptive, how deep the love which balances "yes" and "no,"

How blessed the child whose Mother knows when to hold on and when to let go.

How patient the Mother who stands guard,

How courageous the Mother who walks away, no matter how hard,

How wise the Mother who does not ALL the giving,

For true Mother's love teaches her child the precepts of living.

True Mother's love says, "Yes, I'll work, cook, wash, fight, pray and even die for you, I'll play, cry, walk the floor and grow with you."

But, "No, I will not lie, cheat, or compromise for you,

For to do so would weaken both of us."

True Mother's love holds

... your hand when the dream was frightening.

... you up when fear of the crowd weakens your knees,

... the reins when you would follow the wrong crowd.

But it lets go

... when you must take those first steps,

... when the wings of youth must be tried,

... when 'I do' binds you to another.

"True Mother's love stands guard

... over the sick bed when others sleep,

... over the report cards when you could care less,

... over the neighborhood playground when bullies threaten.

But steps aside

... when you are receiving merited punishment,

... when you must work to prove your worth,

... when sympathy would only probe the wound.

True Mother's love gives

... minutes of wise counseling (that's all you've time for),

... hours of listening (that's what you need so badly),

... days of watching—watching you crawl, walk, run, fly,

... years of waiting, waiting for the seed of her love to bear fruit in you.

And demands

... courtesy to prepare you for meeting others,

... respect to humble you for obeying others,

... thoughtfulness to teach you to live with others.

(Author unknown, cited in Brown 1977, 1–2)

Mother's teachings were never meant to be burdensome, only to protect.

FATHER'S COMMANDS; MOTHER'S TEACHING—PROTECTION FROM THE WORLD

By extension, the seductiveness of the immoral woman typifies the seductiveness of this world. John instructed us:

> Love not the world, neither the things *that are* in the world. If any man love the world, the love of the Father is not in him. For all that *is* in the world, the lust of the flesh, and the lust of the eyes, and the pride of life, is not of the Father, but is of the world. (1 John 2:15–16 KJV)

It's important to remember that you must always remain on guard against the wiles of the devil. That immoral woman is always walking the street, attempting to entice you and lead you to destruction. The immoral woman came to Adam and Eve in the form of a serpent and changed only one word of the original command of Father. Many Christian singers thought they could cross over from singing gospel music to singing the songs of the world, only to discover that it was nearly impossible to find their way back. "For the lips of an adulteress drip honey, and her speech is smoother than oil; but in the end she is bitter as gall, sharp as a double-edged sword" (Proverbs 5:3–4). To avoid crossing over, to avoid being seduced, "Be sober, be vigilant; because your adversary the devil, as a roaring lion, walketh about, seeking whom he may devour" (1 Peter 5:8 KJV).

> Many Christian singers thought they could cross over from singing gospel music to singing the songs of the world, only to discover that it was nearly impossible to find their way back.

It was our heavenly Father who established the human family, including divine order. And as long as mother teaches Father's commands, Father will stand behind her. Anyone who says, "I don't need Mother; I go directly to Father," is in error. Hughes (1991) described such erroneous thinking:

> The natural inclination is to think that one needs only an individual relationship with Christ and needs no other authority. Such thinking produces Christian Lone Rangers who demonstrate their authenticity by riding not to church, but out to the badlands, reference Bible in hand, to do battle single-handedly with the outlaw world. (p. 160)

These are the same individuals who often commit sin and bring reproach upon the church and believe they are accountable to no one but God. Just as our heavenly Father established the human family, He established the church. As with our earthly family, it is the role of mother (the church) to teach Father's (our heavenly Father's) commands. And it is the role of God's children to follow the mother's teachings.

IN CLOSING

Obedience has always been Father's expectation. When Abraham heard Father's voice, he obeyed by leaving the Ur of Chaldea; he had no idea where he was going. "By faith Abraham, when he was called, obeyed by going out ... not knowing where he was going" (Hebrews 11:8 KJV). That's what this thing called the Christian life is all about—going ... yet not knowing. It's one thing to respond when you hear Father's commands directly, but what about when it comes from the mother? As followers of our Lord, we believe He leads us in a specific direction. However, it is very rare that you will hear directly from Father. Most often, Father's commands will come through the mother (the church), and her voice will be that of your pastor. Whether in spiritual warfare or in your service to God, you must be submitted to the Spirit of God and to spiritual leadership. It's essential for the church to acknowledge and submit to pastoral authority.

> Most often, Father's commands will come through the mother (the church), and her voice will be that of your pastor.

Everyone needs a shepherd—a pastor. The pastor needs to become an authority figure, an instructor, a role model, and a servant in your life. To become truly wise, you must acknowledge spiritual authority. The apostle Paul emphasized this truth to the Corinthian church. "If anybody thinks they are a prophet or otherwise gifted by the Spirit, let them acknowledge that what I am writing to you is the Lord's command" (1 Corinthians 14:37). If you really want to be wise, you must recognize the importance of the role of the pastor in your life. And if you really are spiritual, you will recognize that Father's commands come through the mother's teachings.

LESSON 39

THOU SHAT NOT COMMIT ADULTERY

PROVERBS 6:30–35

³⁰ *People do not despise a thief if he steals to satisfy his hunger when he is starving.* ³¹ *Yet if he is caught, he must pay sevenfold, though it costs him all the wealth of his house.* ³² *But a man who commits adultery has no sense; whoever does so destroys himself.* ³³ *Blows and disgrace are his lot, and his shame will never be wiped away.*

³⁴ *For jealousy arouses a husband's fury, and he will show no mercy when he takes revenge.* ³⁵ *He will not accept any compensation; he will refuse the bribe, however great it is.*

Solomon compared the consequences of breaking the seventh commandment with breaking the eighth commandment. He tells us there is more tolerance for a man who steals another man's wealth than one who steals another man's wife. Restitution can be made for stealing a man's wealth, but what restitution can be made for seducing a man's wife? The price of adultery is enormously high. Solomon wrote in a matter-of-fact manner: "The husband will show no mercy when he takes revenge. No amount of money will change his mind. The largest bribe will not satisfy him" (Proverbs 6:34–35 GW). Right or wrong, Solomon indicates this is a potential reaction when a man has been robbed of his wife.

> Restitution can be made for stealing a man's wealth, but what restitution can be made for seducing a man's wife?

THE IMPACT OF ADULTERY

Human beings are sexual beings because God made them that way. He designed man and woman to experience sexual desire and sexual pleasure. However, human sexuality has been corrupted by sin. God's plan is for the sexual relationship to be between a husband and his wife only. Any sexual expression outside the confines of the marital relationship is a sin against God, and many times it violates the dignity and purity of another person. God hates sexual immorality, and He punishes those who are guilty of it. Violation of the seventh commandment is far-reaching, and it impacts not only one's spouse but also every area of the family and society. Adultery is a very destructive sin!

Impact on the marriage. God's prohibition against adultery is not to ruin someone's fun; it is to protect marriage, the foundation of society. The great patriarch Job gave a speech affirming his moral character:

> If my heart has been seduced by a woman, or if I have lusted for my neighbor's wife, then let my wife serve another man; let other men sleep with her. For lust is a shameful sin, a crime that should be punished. (Job 31:9–11 NLT)

In this context, "a heart deceived by a woman" is nothing less than adultery, and Job declares that is "a crime that should be punished." And under the law, it was a crime punishable by death: "If a man commits adultery with another man's wife—with the wife of his neighbor—both the adulterer and the adulteress must be put to death" (Leviticus 20:10).

> God's prohibition against adultery is not to ruin someone's fun; it is to protect marriage, the foundation of society.

The question arises: "Why would God consider adultery such a terrible crime?" It is so terrible because it shatters the covenant made before both God and other people, making the adulterer a liar. It destroys the centerpiece of the marriage covenant and the marriage relationship—trust! Ross Perot, when asked by the news media about his company's policy of firing executives who cheated on their wives, said, "If your wife can't trust you, why should I?" (Lavin 1992). Once that trust has been violated, it is very difficult to restore to its original form.

Impact on the spouse. Adultery does incredible damage to one's spouse. When a man and woman marry, they become one flesh. These are not the words of humans or words found in a minister's service book, but the Words of God. The Lord Himself declared: "Therefore shall a man leave his father and his mother, and shall cleave unto his wife: and they shall be one flesh" (Genesis 2:24 KJV). When a husband or wife steps outside the marriage relationship and unites with another in adultery, he or she has broken the marriage covenant. Violation of the seventh commandment permeated the culture of Corinth in Paul's day, and as with any culture, the zeitgeist of the world followed people into the church. Paul minced no words in addressing the leadership of the church: "Do you not know that he who unites himself with a prostitute is one with her in body? For it is said, 'The two will become one flesh'" (1 Corinthians 6:16). Adultery says to the innocent spouse, "You weren't good enough for me." It brings a crushing blow to the self-esteem of the innocent and often unsuspecting partner. Violation of the marriage covenant by adultery destroys future trust if the marriage survives, and future trust if the innocent spouse remarries.

> Violation of the marriage covenant by adultery destroys future trust if the marriage survives, and future trust if the innocent spouse remarries.

Every couple should strive to adultery-proof their marriage. Each partner in the marriage relationship should remain infatuated with the other. Perhaps that is why Paul was as plainspoken as he was to the believers in the church in Corinth: "The husband should fulfill his wife's sexual needs, and the wife should fulfill her husband's needs. The wife gives authority over her body to her husband, and the husband gives authority over his body to his wife" (1 Corinthians 7:3–4 NLT). Further, he recommended the following:

> Do not deprive each other of sexual relations, unless you both agree to refrain from sexual intimacy for a limited time so you can give yourselves more completely to prayer. Afterward, you should come together again so that Satan won't be able to tempt you because of your lack of self-control. (1 Corinthians 7:5 NLT)

Impact on the children. One's spiritual influence is compromised when adultery has been committed. Sexual immorality has a way of filtering down to the children. Children lose respect for a parent that shames the family by illicit and indecent behaviors. David's leadership in Israel never regained its previous glory after he committed adultery, and it had a tremendously negative impact on his children. David's son, Amnon, raped his daughter, Tamar. Because David did not address Amnon's behavior (possibly because of his own guilt), his son, Absalom (Tamar's full brother), took the matter into his own hand and killed Amnon (his half brother). Later, those who rebelled against David "set up a tent on the palace roof where everyone could see it, and Absalom went in and had sex with his father's concubines" (2 Samuel 16:22 NLT).

> Children lose respect for a parent that shames the family by illicit and indecent behaviors.

Impact on the adulterer. Adultery changes the adulterer. Once the boundary of moral purity has been crossed and the covenant has been broken, it becomes easier to do it again. You can rest assured the enemy will continue to tempt in that area.

Many people are guilty of adultery even though they have never had sexual relations with anyone other than their spouse. In fact, most affairs never reach the level of sexual contact. Jesus let us know that adultery is as much a matter of the heart and the mind as it is of the flesh: "I tell you that anyone who looks at a woman lustfully has already committed adultery with her in his heart" (Matthew 5:28). Though it may not have the same consequences as sexual contact, pornography and sexual fantasies are adultery of the heart, and they make a person just as guilty before God as physical adultery.

There is a high price to pay for violating sexual boundaries. "Don't lust for her beauty. Don't let her coy glances seduce you. For a prostitute will bring you to poverty, but sleeping with another man's wife will cost you your life" (Proverbs 6:25–26 NLT). Committing adultery has cost many their usefulness to the kingdom of God by destroying their testimonies. Nathan's words to David still ring true: "By this deed thou hast given great occasion to the enemies of the LORD to blaspheme" (2 Samuel 12:14 KJV).

> Committing adultery has cost many their usefulness to the kingdom of God by destroying their testimonies.

Impact on the church. Immorality in the life of a church member can tarnish the entire work of God. "If one part suffers, every part suffers with it" (1 Corinthians 12:26). The apostle Paul was very concerned about the extent to which sexual immorality had permeated the church in Corinth: "I can hardly believe the report about the sexual immorality going on among you—something that even pagans don't do. I am told that a man in your church is living in sin with his stepmother" (1 Corinthians 5:1 NLT).

Though sexual immorality often occurs privately and secretly, sexual immorality is not a private matter. "A little yeast leavens the whole batch of dough" (1 Corinthians 5:6). It tarnishes the name of the church, and it destroys the church's ministry to the community. When a Christian commits adultery, the cause of Christ is hindered, and the name of Jesus is tarnished. Our duty to God, to our spouses, to our church, and to all is to remain sexually pure. We are to avoid any activity that may fuel sexual passion and lead to adultery. God's desire is that this type of behavior never be found among His people. And He made that point clear, "Among you there must not be even a hint of sexual immorality" (Ephesians 5:3).

> Though sexual immorality often occurs privately and secretly, sexual immorality is not a private matter.

Impact on society. Adultery is such a sin against society that G. Campbell Morgan (2015) wrote this:

> The adulterer is the enemy of the state ... It is an act of treason to the state to allow such persons to go free. ... The greatness of a people depends upon the purity and strength of the people, and in every nation where the marriage relation is violated with impunity the virus of death is surely and certainly at work. (p. 37)

The enemy of society! That's terribly strong language. Can adultery and sexual immorality really be the enemy of the state? Historical research lends support to G. Campbell Morgan's statement. English anthropologist J.D. Unwin extensively studied eighty-six societies through five thousand years of history. After his death in 1936, the results of his research were published under the title *Hopousia: The Sexual and Economic Foundations of a New Society.*

Unwin studied cultures and empires from the standpoint of their sexual behavior. In particular, he was interested in their prenuptial and postnuptial sexual behavior. He noticed a correlation between sexual immorality and what he termed a nation's "expansive energy." Expansive energy can be defined as the capability to remain productive and maintain a position of influence and leadership among other nations. In other words, when the monogamous marriage relationship lost predominance in a society, that society lost influence in the world. Unwin (1940) wrote, "expansive energy has never been displayed by a society that inherited a modified monogamy or a form of polygamy" (p. 82).

> Anthropologist J. D. Unwin researched and found that when the monogamous marriage relationship lost predominance in a society, that society lost influence in the world.

Impact on your relationship with God. Of all the reasons for not committing adultery, Joseph said it best: "How then could I do great wickedness, and sin against God?" (Genesis 39:9 KJV). If you are a Christian, you will want to please the Lord. And this should be your greatest reason for sexual purity, but often it is the very last consideration. Since God is commanding everyone not to commit adultery, what this now means is that if you do it, you have committed transgression directly against Him. So not only are you hurting yourself, your spouse, and your own children with this kind of unfaithfulness, but you are also hurting, grieving, and sinning against God Almighty.

By not being willing to stay true, loyal, and faithful to your spouse, God suffers. Recognize that when you look your spouse in the eyes, you are looking into the eyes of God. Can you do so with a clean conscience and a pure heart? There is a principle of God that applies here, "When you did it to one of the least of these my brothers and sisters, you were doing it to me" (Matthew 25:40 NLT).

AVOIDING THE SNARE OF ADULTERY

What can you do to avoid the trap of adultery? There are steps that must be taken that will safeguard your life against this horrible sin.

Walk in the Spirit. "Walk in the Spirit, and ye shall not fulfil the lust of the flesh" (Galatians 5:16 KJV). Be aware of God's abiding presence. If you truly walk in the Spirit, you will have the conviction necessary to withstand any temptation that arises.

Avoid suggestive activities. Never allow your eyes to behold things that will cause you to stumble. Eugene Peterson paraphrases well the writing of King David: "I refuse to take a second look at corrupting people and degrading things. I reject made-in-Canaan gods, stay clear of contamination" (Psalm 101:3, MSG). Keep your life clean!

Do not flirt—except with your spouse. Stay far away from the person who sends a flirty message. Watch out for any friendship that arouses intimate and sexual feelings. Never ever become too intimate with someone who is not your spouse! No one simply wakes up one day and says, "I think I'll go out and commit adultery today." It is always the result of previous inappropriate intimate contact. If you stay away from those little things, the big one will never happen to you.

Count the cost. Take a moment to consider the incredible damage adultery would do to your spouse, your children, your Lord, and your own life. Consider the shame, embarrassment, loss of integrity, and loss of self-esteem. No momentary sexual excitement, however great, is worth what you will lose!

Desire only the spouse God gave you. Solomon described the desire each man should have for his wife in beautiful, poetic language:

> Drink water from your own cistern, running water from your own well. ... May her breasts satisfy you always, may you ever be intoxicated with her love. Why be captivated, my son, by an adulteress? ... Why embrace the bosom of another man's wife. (Proverbs 5:15, 19–20)

IN CLOSING

Paul wrote, "Flee fornication" (1 Corinthians 6:18 KJV). Albert Barnes (1872) leaves us with a summary comment on those two words:

There is force and emphasis in the word "flee." Man should escape from it; he should not stay to reason about it; he should not wait to debate the matter; he should not even pause long enough to contend with his propensities, and to try the strength of his virtue. There are some sins which a man can resist; some about which he can reason without danger of pollution. But this is a sin where a man is safe only when he flies; free from pollution only when he refuses to entertain a thought of it; secure when he seeks a victory by flight, and a conquest by retreat. Let a man turn away from it without reflection on it, and he is safe. Let him pause even to think about it, and he may be ruined. "The very passage of an impure thought through the mind leaves pollution behind it." An argument on the subject often leaves pollution; a description ruins; even the presentation of motives against it may often fix the mind with dangerous inclination on the crime. There is no way of avoiding the pollution but in the manner prescribed by Paul; there is no man safe who will not follow his direction. How many a young man would be saved from disgrace, remorse, disease, curses, tears, and hell, could these two words be made to blaze before him like the writing before the astonished eyes of Belshazzar (Daniel 5), and could they terrify him from even the momentary contemplation of the crime. (p. 111)

Flee fornication! "Run from sexual sin!" (1 Corinthians 6:18 NLT).

LESSON 40

MY SISTER AND DEAR FRIEND

PROVERBS 7:1-5

¹ My son, keep my words and store up my commands within you. ² Keep my commands and you will live; guard my teachings as the apple of your eye. ³ Bind them on your fingers; write them on the tablet of your heart. ⁴ Say to wisdom, "You are my sister," and call insight, "You are my relative." ⁵ They will keep you from the adulteress woman, from the wayward woman with her seductive words.

Solomon's command to his son in this text has a sense of urgency. Again, the Word of God is exalted. He wants his son to know that when God's commandments are obeyed, life is enhanced. To love the Word is to love the Lord. God's Word should guide the intent of our hearts and the actions that follow. Personified, wisdom from God is compared to a sister, and understanding is depicted as a kinsman or a relative. It's like your big sister taking you to school on that very first day of school and instructing you so you will know what you should and shouldn't do. Her intention is good; she wants to keep you from embarrassment and harm. "Keep my commands and you will live" (Proverbs 7:2).

Sister will help you establish priorities—"But seek ye first the kingdom of God, and his righteousness; and all these things shall be added unto you" (Matthew 6:33 KJV). With sister close by, finding the will of God for your life is not difficult. Interestingly, the best and easiest way to find the will of God is to seek Him first; give Him your entire being. Paul gave us a simple formula:

> I beseech you therefore, brethren, by the mercies of God, that ye present your bodies a living sacrifice, holy, acceptable unto God, *which* is your reasonable service. And be not conformed to this world: but be ye transformed by the renewing of your mind, that ye may prove what *is* that good, and acceptable, and perfect, will of God. (Romans 12:1–2 KJV)

The Word of God not only keeps you from harm, but when followed, it leads to a very full and satisfied life. Many suffer a harvest of disobedience, but the LORD invites His people to enjoy the fruit of surrender to His will:

> Listen carefully to me: Eat what is good, and enjoy the best foods. Open your ears, and come to me! Listen so that you may live! I will make an everlasting promise to you—the blessings I promised to David. (Isaiah 55:2–3 GW)

THE RISK OF BLESSINGS

Whatever you do, it must not distract you from doing the will of God. If there are unnecessary things that take you away from the house of God, or keep you from praying, or keep you from devotion to God, those things have become idols. Moses warned the people of Israel of the risks associated with the blessings of God. And those warnings are still applicable:

> When thou hast eaten and art full, then thou shalt bless the LORD thy God for the good land which he hath given thee. Beware that thou forget not the LORD thy God, in not keeping his commandments, and his judgments, and his statutes, which I command thee this day: Lest *when* thou hast eaten and art full, and hast built goodly houses, and dwelt *therein*; And *when* thy herds and thy flocks multiply, and thy silver and thy gold is multiplied, and all that thou hast is multiplied; Then thine heart be lifted up, and thou forget the LORD thy God, which brought thee forth out of the land of Egypt, from the house of bondage. (Deuteronomy 8:10–14 KJV)

Those blessed are exposed to an additional spiritual risk—a false sense of security. In fact, Paul exhorted Timothy, "Command those who are rich in this present world not … to put their hope in wealth" (1 Timothy 6:17). The proper object of our trust is not a thing but a being; it is not wealth but God. "Put [your] hope in God, who richly provides us with everything for our enjoyment" (1 Timothy 6:17).

> Thus saith the LORD, Let not the wise *man* glory in his wisdom, neither let the mighty *man* glory in his might, let not the rich *man* glory in his riches: But let him that glorieth glory in this, that he understandeth and knoweth me, that I *am* the LORD which exercise

lovingkindness, judgment, and righteousness, in the earth: for in these *things* I delight, saith the Lord. (Jeremiah 9:23–24 KJV)

> Those blessed are exposed to an additional spiritual risk—a false sense of security.

THE APPLE OF YOUR EYE

Solomon encouraged his son, "Keep my commands and you will live; guard my teachings as the apple of your eye" (Proverbs 7:2). We all know the value of sight. Most of us have experienced having some foreign object in an eye. The intense pain demands our attention. At that moment, everything else is less important than caring for the affected eye. We will do whatever it takes to remove that object and eliminate the pain. "Morally speaking, the slightest impurity presented to our eyes should cause intense awareness that something is wrong and that God's Word is demanding attention" (Phillips 1995, p. 167). Charles Bridges (1846/1968) wrote the following:

> Maintain a jealous regard for the law. What care is necessary to keep the apple of the eye—that most tender part of the most tender member! With the same care preserve the integrity of the law. Let every part of it have its full weight. To explain it away, or to lower its requirements, breaks down the barrier, and gives an easy entrance to temptation. The sensual sinner is often a covert infidel. (pp. 67–68)

Sister will keep you from the way of the world. She says,

> Turn your eyes upon Jesus.
> Look full in his wonderful face.
> And the things of this life

will grow strangely dim
In the light of his glory and grace.
(Helen H. Lemmel in *Sing unto the Lord* 1978, p. 335)

SCRIPTURE BOXES IN YOUR HEART

Sister will be ever present in the words, commands, and teachings of God. Solomon taught his son, "Bind them on your fingers" (Proverbs 7:3). I am convinced that it never was God's intent for His people to run around with little scripture boxes taped to their fingers. His intent was for His Word to be so close to your heart that the very moment your hands begin to move in the direction of touching that which they shouldn't, sister says, "Stop! Don't touch!" Phillips (1995) stated, "Once a person gets God's Word into his heart—not just into his head—God's Word will slay each temptation the moment it comes to mind. When we love God's Word, it monitors everything else" (p. 167).

> God's intent was for His Word to be so close to your heart that the very moment your hands begin to move in the direction of touching that which they shouldn't, sister says, "Stop! Don't touch!"

IN CLOSING

In our text, the world is presented as an adulteress, but if you listen to "sister," you won't even be out on the street to be lured by the adulteress. Sister reminds you of who you are, your great heritage, and the purpose of your existence upon this earth: "You are a chosen people, a royal priesthood, a holy nation, God's special possession, that you may declare the praises of him who called you out of darkness into his wonderful light" (1 Peter 2:9). The glitter of the world has nothing to offer compared with the glory of the kingdom of God. Listen to sister, and you will find "the right woman will keep a man from the wrong woman" (Segraves 1990, p. 79).

> "It is [Wisdom's] embrace that throws the harlot's beauty into the shade. Man must have his object of delight. If wisdom is not loved, lust will be indulged. The Bible therefore—not merely read, but the cherished object of familiar intercourse—proves a sacred exorcist to expel the power of evil" (Bridges 1846/1968, p. 68).

And Phillips (1995) stated, "The roots of holiness lie much deeper than the obedience of the mind. God's Word must be dear to our hearts and we must abide by its wisdom if we are to resist the temptations of Satan" (p. 168).

LESSON 41

THE HEARTBEAT OF OUR LORD

PROVERBS 7:6–9

⁶At the window of my house I looked down through the lattice. ⁷I saw among the simple, I noticed among the young men, a youth who had no sense. ⁸He was going down the street near her corner, walking along in the direction of her house ⁹ at twilight, as the day was fading, as the dark of night set in.

In these verses, we see a picture of the heartbeat of our Lord: "For the Son of man is come to seek and to save that which was lost" (Luke 19:10 KJV). The Lord will do everything possible to prevent you from sinning, except make the choice for you. He will nudge you privately to encourage you to repent, but if necessary, He will shame you openly. One thing to remember, He will never shame anyone for the sheer pleasure of doing so. All His actions are motivated by love:

> For God so loved the world, that he gave his only begotten Son, that whosoever believeth in him should not perish, but have everlasting life. For God sent not his Son into the world to condemn the world; but that the world through him might be saved. (John 3:16–17 KJV)

PEERING THROUGH THE LATTICE

Reading our text, one gets the feeling that God is watching someone from a distance, as though peering through partially closed window blinds. It's evident the one being watched is going the wrong direction, moving from light into darkness, moving from a place of safety to a place of death, walking down the path with every intention to engage in sin. Grief grips the heart of the one peering through the window: "At the window of my house I looked down through the lattice" (Proverbs 7:6). You can almost hear the cries of the one watching: "Stop! Don't go any farther! Turn around! You're heading into a trap! There's death in that house!"

This was not just the peeping of a people watcher, but it was an emotional gaze of someone who really cared. "From heaven the LORD looks down and sees all mankind; from his dwelling place he watches all who live on earth—he who forms the hearts of all, who considers everything they do ... to deliver them from death" (Psalm 33:13–15, 19). Though He may be watching from a distance, He is also a God up close. "The eyes of the LORD *are* in every place, beholding the evil and the good" (Proverbs 15:3 KJV). There was alarm in the heart of the onlooker as to the direction the young man was going. I do not detect anger or hatred. Rather, I sense deep concern and compassion.

This was not just the peeping of a people watcher, but it was an emotional gaze of someone who really cared.

WALKING INTO DARKNESS

It was growing dark. "I saw among the simple, I noticed among the young men, a youth who had no sense. He was going down the street near her corner, walking along in the direction of her house" (Proverbs 7:7–8). The sun was going down on the life of this young man—not because the sun was moving away from him but because he was moving away from the sun. Any time your back is toward the sun, you are walking into darkness. Any time you turn your back on the Word of the Lord, you are walking into darkness.

> Any time you turn your back on the Word of the Lord, you are walking into darkness.

David prayed to the LORD, "Thy word *is* a lamp unto my feet, and a light unto my path" (Psalm 119:105 KJV). Any time you develop an allegiance with the world, you are walking into darkness. "Lot dwelled in the cities of the plain, and pitched his tent toward Sodom" (Genesis 13:12 KJV). When Lot left the rocky hillside of Canaan, the sun was to his back, and he was walking into darkness. The farther he went, the darker it got until he "vexed *his* righteous soul from day to day with *their* unlawful deeds" (2 Peter 2:8 KJV).

Toward the end of his life, Joshua warned the nation of Israel of the danger of turning her back on the sun and walking into darkness:

> But if you turn away and ally yourselves with the survivors of these nations that remain among you and if you intermarry with them and associate with them, then you may be sure that the LORD your God will no longer drive out these nations before you. Instead, they will become snares and traps for you, whips on your backs and thorns in your eyes, until you perish from this good land, which the LORD your God has given you. (Joshua 23:12–13)

In the New Testament, Paul pleaded with the Corinthian believers, "Be ye not unequally yoked together with unbelievers: for what fellowship hath righteousness with unrighteousness? and what communion hath light with darkness?" (2 Corinthians 6:14 KJV). If you ally yourself with sinners, you will be impacted by their sin. King Jehoshaphat, king of Judah, allied himself with wicked King Ahab, and the alliance nearly cost him his life. First, Jehoshaphat approved of the marriage of his son, Jehoram, to Ahab's daughter, Athaliah. Now that they were family, he went down to Israel to hang out with Ahab, and Ahab convinced him to go to war against Aram. Even though the prophet Micaiah warned of the outcome of the battle, he followed the lead of Ahab. Ahab was killed in the battle, and only the hand of the LORD prevented Jehoshaphat from being killed. (See 2 Chronicles 18.) You cannot play with fire without eventually getting burned. When Jehoshaphat allied his family to Ahab's family through marriage, the sun was at his back, and he was walking into darkness. Any time you turn your back on the light, you are walking into darkness.

WHEN AN ECLIPSE OCCURS IN THE LIFE OF A BELIEVER

King David is one who experienced an eclipse in his life, and the light went out in his life. You may run, but you can't hide from the presence of God, nor can you run so far that you diminish the heartbeat of God. It may take the Lord a year, or maybe even ten years, but rest assured, He will come knocking on your door. He knows exactly where you live. Yes, David sinned. And Yes, David walked out of the light into darkness. But the heartbeat of the LORD sought him out and knocked on his door in the voice of the prophet Nathan.

> You may run, but you can't hide from the presence of God, nor can you run so far that you diminish the heartbeat of God.

Having walked down that road into darkness and made his way back to safety, David wanted everyone to know you can run, but you cannot hide; you can attempt to pull the cloak of darkness over your sin, but light dispels darkness:

> Where shall I go from your Spirit? Or where shall I flee from your presence? If I ascend to heaven, you are there! If I make my bed in Sheol, you are there! If I take the wings of the morning and dwell in the uttermost parts of the sea, even there your hand shall lead me, and your right hand shall hold me. If I say, 'Surely the darkness shall cover me, and the light about me be night,' even the darkness is not dark to you; the night is bright as the day, for darkness is as light with you. (Psalm 139:7–12 ESV)

LIMITATIONS OF AN UNLIMITED GOD

The Lord remembers what He rescued you from. He remembers the times you said you would never do it again and how free you felt at that moment. Don't pitch your tent in the direction of the world! "Remember Lot's wife" (Luke 17:32 KJV). "Ye are all the children of light, and the children of the day: we are not of the night, nor of darkness" (1 Thessalonians 5:5 KJV). Whenever you are walking in the wrong direction, there's pain in God's heart and a lump in His throat. The LORD has no desire that anyone be lost: "*As* I live, saith the LORD GOD, I have no pleasure in the death of the wicked" (Ezekiel 33:11 KJV). And Peter reminded us, "The Lord ... is longsuffering to us-ward, not willing that any should perish, but that all should come to repentance" (2 Peter 3:9 KJV).

> Whenever you are walking in the wrong direction, there's pain in God's heart and a lump in His throat.

As the Lord looks on, peering through the lattice, isn't there something He can do? Is He omnipotent or helpless? Can't He stop the one walking away from light and heading into darkness? He declared, "I *am* the LORD, the God of all flesh: is there any thing too hard for me?" (Jeremiah 32:27 KJV). Some have discounted God for this very reason. "If God is a God of love, why is there so much pain and suffering in this world?" "If God didn't want humans to sin, why did He create the Tree of Knowledge of Good and Evil?" Those are difficult questions, but the answer is really quite simple: God is limited by humankind's will.

God speaks to your heart, and you shrug it off. He brings dreams to you while you sleep; you know He's speaking to you. Your spirit longs for sunshine, but your flesh wants darkness. He sends a saint of God into your life—just at the moment it's evident you are going the wrong direction. You know you are going the wrong direction; the saint of God knows you're going the wrong direction. Sheepishly you look into the eyes of that saint of God; compassionately the saint of God looks back. Only superficial words are exchanged. What more is there to say? You know you are going the wrong direction; your shadow is cast out front, and your back is to the sun. Scriptures begin to ring in your ears: Adam, "Where *art* thou?" (Genesis 3:9 KJV). Cain, "Why are you angry, and why has your face fallen?" (Genesis 4:6 ESV). Cain, "Where *is* Abel thy brother?" (Genesis 4:9 KJV). You go to church, and the preacher preaches; you know God is speaking. You sit in your chair. You're torn; your spirit is longing to go to the altar, but your flesh is pulling the other direction. "God, make me do what I'm supposed to do!" But God is limited by *your* will.

> "God, make me do what I'm supposed to do!" God is limited by your will.

IN CLOSING

Looking through the lattice of the windows of heaven, the Lord sees every move we make. He knows the direction we take, and He longs for His children to walk in the light. His heartbeat is to guide His children to a better life on this earth and an eternal home in the future. Whenever a child of His turns his or her back on the sun and begins the process of walking into darkness, there is grief in the heart of our Lord. John said it well: "But if we walk in the light, as he is in the light, we have fellowship one with another, and the blood of Jesus Christ his Son cleanseth us from all sin" (1 John 1:7 KJV).

> Whenever a child of His turns his or her back on the sun and begins the process of walking into darkness, there is grief in the heart of our Lord.

Most of your success in both the natural and the spiritual realms is based upon the small decisions you make each and every day. This is because you alone control where you will go, what you will do, your choice of friends, your prayer life, your attendance at church, and other factors. And if you will make the right decisions, they will take you closer and closer to God.

LESSON 42

THE DEVIL WITHIN AND THE DEVIL WITHOUT

PROVERBS 7:10-23

¹⁰ Then out came a woman to meet him, dressed like a prostitute and with crafty intent. ¹¹ (She is unruly and defiant, her feet never stay at home; ¹² now in the street, now in the squares, at every corner she lurks.) ¹³ She took hold of him and kissed him and with a brazen face she said: ¹⁴ "Today I fulfilled my vows, and I have food from my fellowship offering at home. ¹⁵ So I came out to meet you; I looked for you and have found you! ¹⁶ I have covered my bed with colored linens from Egypt. ¹⁷ I have perfumed my bed with myrrh, aloes and cinnamon. ¹⁸ Come, let's drink deep of love till morning; let's enjoy ourselves with love! ¹⁹ My husband is not at home; he has gone on a long journey. ²⁰ He took his purse filled with money and will not be home till full moon."

²¹ With persuasive words she led him astray; she seduced him with her smooth talk. ²² All at once he followed her like an ox going to the slaughter, like a deer stepping into a noose ²³ till an arrow pierces his liver, like a bird darting into a snare, little knowing it will cost him his life.

The metaphor of the harlot in our text provides us with an excellent illustration of the enemy, Satan, in action. But not every temptation is as blatant as the picture given in this text. Satan has the ability to transform himself into very attractive forms for the purpose of deception. In Paul's day, Satan even used those who were upstanding religious leaders. Paul warned, "For such men are false apostles, deceitful workmen, disguising themselves as apostles of Christ. And no wonder, for even Satan disguises himself as an angel of light" (2 Corinthians 11:13–14 ESV). Likewise, John wrote his readers with the express intent of raising their awareness of the subtle nature of the evil spirits in this world. "Beloved, believe not every spirit, but try the spirits whether they are of God: because many false prophets are gone out into the world" (1 John 4:1 KJV). Don't ever expect Satan to show up in a red suit with horns and a pitchfork. It is through good, solid biblical teaching that we learn to distinguish between good and evil. The church needs a balanced diet of nutritious food (solid food) that comes through teaching. The writer of Hebrews made it clear, "Solid food is for the mature, for those who have their powers of discernment trained by constant practice to distinguish good from evil" (Hebrews 5:14 ESV).

> Don't ever expect Satan to show up in a red suit with horns and a pitchfork.

When Paul wrote his first letter to the Corinthian church, they were in the snare of the evil one:

> I also received a report of scandalous sex within your church family, a kind that wouldn't be tolerated even outside the church: One of your men is sleeping with his stepmother. And you're so above it all that it doesn't even faze you! Shouldn't this break your hearts? Shouldn't it bring you to your knees in tears? Shouldn't this person and his conduct be confronted and dealt with? (1 Corinthians 5:1–2 MSG)

Fortunately, by repenting, they were able to free themselves from her deceptive allurements. And by the time he wrote his second letter to the Corinthian church, Paul expressed great confidence that the members of that congregation had come to recognize the schemes of the devil. He commended them by stating, "For we are not ignorant of his devices" (2 Corinthians 2:11 KJV).

SIMILARITIES BETWEEN THE HOLY SPIRIT AND THE UNHOLY SPIRIT

The concern expressed by both Paul and John leads to one conclusion: there are similarities between the operation of the Holy Spirit and the operation of the devil. Though Satan is not the opposite of God, having been created rather than self-existent, both God and Satan operate in the spirit realm. Both deal directly with humans. Both want the same thing from humans—worship and praise. Both have access to ministering angelic beings. Both give humans personal attention. Both are ready to exercise whatever dominion humans permit. And both can produce signs, wonders, and miracles, though God will always be greater. For example, the rod of Aaron was greater than the rods of the Egyptian magicians:

> Aaron cast down his rod before Pharaoh, and before his servants, and it became a serpent. Then Pharaoh also called the wise men and the sorcerers: now the magicians of Egypt, they also did in like manner with their enchantments. For they cast down every man his rod, and they became serpents: but Aaron's rod swallowed up their rods. (Exodus 7:10–12 KJV)

> There are similarities between the operation of the Holy Spirit and the operation of the devil.

The production of signs, wonders, and miracles is enticing to humans and ensnares many who are not grounded in the Word. Like the evil spirits working through the magicians, producing signs and wonders, miracles will be among the repertoire of tricks of the antichrist in the end-time:

> Whose coming is after the working of Satan with all power and signs and lying wonders, And with all deceivableness of unrighteousness in them that perish; because they received not the love of the truth, that they might be saved. (2 Thessalonians 2:9–10 KJV)

John saw the end of time, and he described a beast coming out of the earth that looked like a lamb but spoke like a dragon. This presents a picture of the deceptiveness of Satan. "He doeth great wonders, so that he maketh fire come down from heaven on the earth in the sight of men" (Revelation 13:13 KJV). With great subtlety, he utilizes everything available to him in the world to entice humans through the carnal desires of human nature, the lusting of eyes, and plain old pride. (See 1 John 2:16.) That is why John warned his readers to "try the spirits" to see if they are of God or not. Satan is the great imitator.

> The first thing to remember in identifying the enemy is that with great subtlety he utilizes everything available to him in the world to entice humans through the carnal desires of human nature, the lusting of eyes, and plain old pride.

THE DEVIL WITHIN

Adam and Eve's failure to resist sin stands in stark contrast to how humans should deal with both sin and Satan. Jesus's response to Satan's enticement is the antithesis of Adam and Eve's response:

> And when the tempter came to him, he said, If thou be the Son of God, command that these stones be made bread. But he answered and said, It is written, Man shall not live by bread alone, but by every word that

proceedeth out of the mouth of God. Then the devil taketh him up into the holy city, and setteth him on a pinnacle of the temple, And saith unto him, If thou be the Son of God, cast thyself down: for it is written, He shall give his angels charge concerning thee: and in their hands they shall bear thee up, lest at any time thou dash thy foot against a stone. Jesus said unto him, It is written again, Thou shalt not tempt the Lord thy God. Again, the devil taketh him up into an exceeding high mountain, and sheweth him all the kingdoms of the world, and the glory of them; And saith unto him, All these things will I give thee, if thou wilt fall down and worship me. Then saith Jesus unto him, Get thee hence, Satan: for it is written, Thou shalt worship the Lord thy God, and him only shalt thou serve. Then the devil leaveth him, and, behold, angels came and ministered unto him. (Matthew 4:3–11 KJV)

Notice, Jesus spent no time considering Satan's offer. He used the sword of the Spirit—the Word of God—on him. When he persisted, Jesus simply told him to take a hike: "Get they hence!"

Notice, Jesus spent no time considering Satan's offer.

Peter cautioned his readers, "Your adversary the devil, as a roaring lion, walketh about, seeking whom he may devour" (1 Peter 5:8 KJV). And if you are going to successfully walk with God, you must recognize the influence of the devil within and upon you. This is not to suggest that most people are walking around demon possessed. But the human nature is so susceptible to the suggestions of the devil that we can speak of those carnal weaknesses as the devil within.

Let no man say when he is tempted, I am tempted of God: for God cannot be tempted with evil, neither tempteth he any man: But every man is tempted, when he is drawn away of his own lust, and enticed. Then when lust hath conceived, it bringeth forth sin: and sin, when it is finished, bringeth forth death. (James 1:13–15 KJV)

Notice that humans are tempted by their own evil desires. It is the devil within that leads to temptation by the devil without. So, if the devil within were crucified, the devil without would lose influence.

> It is the devil within that leads to temptation by the devil without.

Unfortunately, many fail to crucify the devil within. People with great potential have succumbed to the cravings of the sinful nature, often cutting short their lives and brilliant careers.

His was a routine admission to busy Bellevue Hospital. A charity case, one among hundreds. A bum from the Bowery with a slashed throat. The Bowery ... last stop before the morgue. Synonym of filth, loneliness, cheap booze, drugs, and disease. ... The Bowery became the dead-end street of an incredible life. But all that was over. A twenty-five-cent-a-night flophouse had rooms you hear about, but never want to see ... full of stinking humanity too miserable to describe. He was one among many. Like all the rest, he now lived only to drink. His health was gone and he was starving. On that icy January morning before the sun had crept over New York's skyline, a shell of a man who looked twice his age staggered to the wash basin and fell. The basin toppled and shattered.

He was found lying in a heap, naked and bleeding from a deep gash in his throat. His forehead was badly bruised and he was semiconscious. A doctor was called, no one special—remember, this was the Bowery. He used black sewing thread somebody found to suture the wound. That would do. All the while the bum begged for a drink. A buddy shared the bottom of a rum bottle to calm his nerves.

He was dumped in a paddy wagon and dropped off at Bellevue Hospital, where he would languish, unable to eat for three days … and die. Still unknown.

… When they scraped together his belongings, they found a raged, dirty coat with thirty-eight cents in one pocket and a scrap of paper in the other. All his earthly goods. Enough coins for another night at the Bowery and five words, 'Dear friends and gentle hearts.'

Why in the world would a forgotten drunk carry around a line of lyrics? Maybe he still believed he had it in him. Maybe that derelict with the body of a bum still had the heart of a genius. For once upon a time long before his tragic death at age thirty-eight, he had written songs that literally the whole world sung, like:

"Camptown Races,"
"Oh! Susanna!"
"Beautiful Dreamer"
"Jeanie with the Light Brown Hair"
"Old Folks at Home"
"My Old Kentucky Home." (Swindoll 1985, pp. 36–37)

Stephen Foster—dead at thirty-eight. What happened to a man who wrote hymns like "Give Us This Day Our Daily Bread" and "The Pure, the Bright, the Beautiful?" He failed to conquer—to crucify—the devil within.

> He failed to conquer—to crucify—the devil within.

GOING WHERE YOU SHOULDN'T GO

"He was going down the street near her corner, walking along in the direction of her house" (Proverbs 7:8). When we walk on Satan's turf, should we be surprised if he suddenly snatches us away? The metaphor of the prostitute so well depicts humankind in relation to the world.

> If ... he thought he could lead her on, flirt a little, and then run on home for supper and boast to his friends the next day of his 'little bit of fun,' he had grossly miscalculated. He had underestimated her expertise and overcalculated his own powers of resistance. His miscalculations are typical mistakes of those who deliberately walk in temptation's path.
>
> ... Like any boy becoming a man, this foolish youth had strong drives and desires and found it hard to say no. Also he liked to be thought of as a man of the world. He wanted to be considered sophisticated and suave. He wanted to save face at all costs, so he was vulnerable. (Phillips 1995, p. 172–173)

Paul, a single man, knew the importance of not dallying on Satan's turf. To the Corinthians, he urged, "Flee fornication" (1 Corinthians 6:18 KJV). And when he wrote to Timothy, he encouraged him to "Flee also youthful lusts: but follow righteousness, faith, charity, peace, with them that call on the Lord out of a pure heart" (2 Timothy 2:22 KJV). Pride made the young man vulnerable.

> If he had simply shoved her off and taken to his heels, ignoring her mocking laughter, he could have escaped. But he didn't. He rather liked that kiss. It held the tantalizing promise of something more. He dallied and was lost. Her coils tightened around him. (Phillips 1995, p. 173)

MUST CRUCIFY THE FLESH

It is impossible to love the world and love our heavenly Father at the same time. "Love not the world, neither the things *that are* in the world. If any man love the world, the love of the Father is not in him" (1 John 2:15 KJV). Paul warned:

> Letting your sinful nature control your mind leads to death. But letting the Spirit control your mind leads to life and peace. For the sinful nature is always hostile to God. It never did obey God's laws, and it never will. (Romans 8:6–7 NLT)

It will not submit; therefore, it must be crucified. "For if you live according to the flesh you will die, but if by the Spirit you put to death the deeds of the body, you will live" (Romans 8:13 ESV). That is the *only* solution: "Put to death, therefore, whatever belongs to your earthly nature: sexual immorality, impurity, lust, evil desires and greed, which is idolatry" (Colossians 3:5).

SUBMIT TO GOD

James gave us some simple steps. "Submit yourselves therefore to God. Resist the devil, and he will flee from you" (James 4:7 KJV). The people of God have a tendency to speak of the second step—resisting the devil—while leaping over the first step, submitting to God. Submission to God is the key to spiritual success.

When I went to Hoonah, Alaska, to pastor, I met a white-haired gentleman in his seventies. I used to visit him at his sister's house. His room smelled of human filth. On occasion, I would put his clothes in a plastic bag, my wife would wash them, and then I would return them to him, hoping to get him to church when he sobered up.

He had been baptized and rebaptized by nearly every pastor that came to town, hoping it would finally take. When he approached me, I refused to baptize him again but instead pointed him in the direction of the altar. He had been baptized in Jesus's name, so there was no need to do it again. What he needed was to crucify the devil within, resist the devil from without, and flee from the tree in the midst.

> Crucify the devil within, resist the devil from without, and flee from the tree in the midst.

One night, while a guest minister was preaching, he hobbled to the altar, and God filled him with the Holy Ghost. Something else happened: once and for all, he crucified the flesh and went on to live a victorious life, serving the Lord until his death at more than eighty years of age.

IN CLOSING

That's a wonderful testimony, but think of the years of suffering, simply because he kept yielding to the flesh. I can only imagine the days of struggle, guilt, shame, and feelings of failure. It did not have to be. That's why it is essential we come to know the enemy and deal with him God's way: put to death the devil within by genuine repentance. "For if ye live after the flesh, ye shall die: but if ye through the Spirit do mortify the deeds of the body, ye shall live" (Romans 8:13 KJV). Then be filled with the Spirit of God and submit to the Spirit's guidance, "For as many as are led by the Spirit of God, they are the sons of God" (Romans 8:14 KJV).

LESSON 43

HIGHWAY TO THE GRAVE

PROVERBS 7:24-27

²⁴ Now then, my sons, listen to me; pay attention to what I say. ²⁵ Do not let your heart turn to her ways or stray into her paths. ²⁶ Many are the victims she has brought down; her slain are a mighty throng. ²⁷ Her house is a highway to the grave, leading down to the chambers of death.

Serving the Lord is a choice. Joshua famously declared: "If it seem evil unto you to serve the LORD, choose you this day whom ye will serve; … but as for me and my house, we will serve the LORD" (Joshua 24:15 KJV). Unfortunately, many will make a wrong choice and choose the highway to the grave. They are focused only on momentary pleasure, hoping the "chambers of death" are not true. But Jesus warned His listeners, "wide is the gate, and broad *is* the way, that leadeth to destruction, and many there be which go in thereat" (Matthew 7:13 KJV).

PEOPLE WHO WILL BE IN HELL

The Bible speaks of various kinds of people who will be in hell: the impostors (tares), the unregenerate (those without the wedding garment), and backsliders. Then there is the frequently cited list of sins that will keep one out of the kingdom of God: "Sexual immorality, impurity, lustful pleasures, idolatry, sorcery, hostility, quarreling, jealousy, outbursts of anger, selfish ambition, dissension, division, envy, drunkenness, wild parties, and other sins like these" (Galatians 5:19–21 NLT). But the scriptures describe another kind of individual who will spend eternity in hell—those who do not possess a love for truth:

> They perish because they refused to love the truth and so be saved. For this reason God sends them a powerful delusion so that they will believe the lie and so that all will be condemned who have not believed the truth but have delighted in wickedness. (2 Thessalonians 2:10–12)

THE TIMID PULPIT

When the pulpit goes silent and does not preach against sin, or when the pulpit goes silent and does not define sin, sin becomes a way of life in society. Because of timid and sometimes silent pulpits, our society has experienced a gradual acceptance of immorality that would have been deplorable sixty years ago. Unless there is a continual flow of a message that condemns sin and promotes righteousness from the pulpit to the congregation and out to society, there will be a decline of godliness at all levels. Consider the following research, cited in a Bible college periodical:

> It's not only the world that no longer believes in right and wrong—acceptance of absolute truth is fast disappearing in the church, also. Almost as many Christians are likely to base their moral decisions on what they feel rather than the Word of God, according to a new survey.
>
> Leading Christian researcher George Barna has warned of a growing crisis if churches fail to address this drift. "When a majority of Christian adults, as well as 3 out of 4 born again teens, proudly cast their vote for moral relativism, the Church is in trouble," he said.

Recent research revealed that among all adults, only 22 percent believed in moral absolutes, while 64 percent thought truth was always relative to the person and their situations. Among those identified as being "born again," just 32 percent believed in moral absolutes.

The picture was even gloomier among teenagers. Eighty-three percent of all teens thought moral truth depended on the circumstances, with just 6 percent believing in absolute truth. Only 9 percent of teens identified as being born again accepted the idea of absolute truth, compared with 4 percent of other teens.

"Christian parents, educators and church leaders must make the loss of truth a matter of priority," he said. "The virtual disappearance of this cornerstone of the Christian faith—that is, God has communicated a series of moral principles in the Bible that are meant to be the basis of our thoughts and actions, regardless of our preferences, feeling or situations—is probably the best indicator of the waning strength of the Christian church in America today."

Only 13 percent of those interviewed and 26 percent of those born again, based their ethical/moral decision-making on the Bible. The most common decision-making method: "whatever feels right." (Massengale 2002, p. 9)

Familiarity with sin diminishes the awfulness of sin. "Wherefore let him that thinketh he standeth take heed lest he fall" (1 Corinthians 10:12 KJV).

> When the pulpit goes silent and does not preach against sin, or when the pulpit goes silent and does not define sin, sin becomes a way of life in society.

SATAN IS NEVER FAR AWAY

Regardless of how many miracles you have seen or how many times the Lord has visited you, you must always be on guard. No matter how secure your surroundings, temptation is always lurking nearby. For example, while Jesus was fasting in the desert, temptation came strolling by. If Jesus had chosen to sin, He would not have had to leave the desert to do so. Peter reminded us, "Be alert and of sober mind. Your enemy the devil prowls around like a roaring lion looking for someone to devour" (1 Peter 5:8). It's important to remember that the end of a temptation is not the end of temptation. Jesus was tempted by everything that you and I will ever be tempted by, but at the end of those forty days, "When the devil had finished all this tempting, he left him until an opportune time" (Luke 4:13). Rest assured, Satan will be back—looking for that weak moment, an opportune time.

> It's important to remember that the end of a temptation is not the end of temptation.

A SOLUTION TO THE SIN PROBLEM

There is a solution to the sin problem—developing a genuine love for our Lord Jesus. A love for Christ is the counteracting principle to a love for the things in this world: "Set your affection on things above, not on things on the earth" (Colossians 3:2 KJV).

John's words serve as a warning, "Love not the world, neither the things *that are* in the world. If any man love the world, the love of the Father is not in him" (1 John 2:15 KJV).

> If impure love solicits, remember the holy love of thy Saviour to thee, proved by his most shameful death. Think of him, as looking into thy heart boiling over with corruption, showing thee his wounds, and

exciting thee to a reciprocal love of himself. (Geier quoted in Bridges 1846/1968, p. 71)

When human nature raises its ugly head, we are told, "Put to death, therefore, whatever belongs to your earthly nature" (Colossians 3:5). Don't hang around wondering if you should consider sin. Flee!

> Don't hang around wondering if you should consider sin.

Jesus told the story of a rich man and Lazarus. The rich man chose the highway to the grave.

> And in hell he lift up his eyes, being in torments, and seeth Abraham afar off, and Lazarus in his bosom. And he cried and said, Father Abraham, have mercy on me, and send Lazarus, that he may dip the tip of his finger in water, and cool my tongue; for I am tormented in this flame. But Abraham said, Son, remember that thou in thy lifetime receivedst thy good things, and likewise Lazarus evil things: but now he is comforted, and thou art tormented. And beside all this, between us and you there is a great gulf fixed: so that they which would pass from hence to you cannot; neither can they pass to us, that would come from thence. (Luke 16:23–26 KJV)

That message was not for the unregenerate, but it was for church members.

THE HIGHWAY OF HOLINESS

In contrast to the highway to the grave, the scriptures describe another highway—the highway of holiness. Isaiah saw the coming of Christ and the age of grace. He declared, "A great road will go through that once deserted land. It will be named the Highway of Holiness. Evil-minded people will never travel on it. It will be only for those who walk in God's ways; fools will never walk there" (Isaiah 35:8 NLT).

The highway of holiness is not an option because the very nature of God is holiness. The devil would like to see the church abandon this biblical truth and return to the highway to the grave, but God has called us from that path and set us on the highway of holiness.

Being a Christian assumes holiness. That is why believers in the early church were called Christians. (See Acts 11:26.) There was enough of Christ in them for people to notice. "Therefore if any man *be* in Christ, *he is* a new creature: old things are passed away; behold, all things are become new (2 Corinthians 5:17 KJV).

Although holiness is often associated with outward appearance and behavior, outward appearance and behavior are not holiness. Holiness is not something you put on, and it's not an experience. If holiness could have been put on, the Pharisees would have received an endorsement from Jesus. If we measure our holiness only by outward standards and do not seek to fill our inward being with God's nature, we miss the purpose of the New Testament and the power of the new birth. Only as we partake of his nature can we truly possess holiness. Holiness is a work of the spirit of God.

> If we measure our holiness only by outward standards and do not seek to fill our inward being with God's nature, we miss the purpose of the New Testament and the power of the new birth.

To travel the highway of holiness demands separation. "For you are a people holy to the LORD your God" (Deuteronomy 7:6). Holiness requires being separated from sin and dedicated unto God. The Greek word for church, *ekklesia*, literally means the *called-out ones*. Those who travel the highway of holiness are called out, separated, and elevated for a purpose: "You are a chosen people. You are royal priests, a holy nation, God's very own possession. As a result, you can show others the goodness of God, for he called you out of the darkness into his wonderful light" (1 Peter 2:9–10 NLT).

To lower your standard or to live a life of hypocrisy not only disappoints God but may disappoint the ones you least expect.

> Although the Partons were very poor, they were a secure and loving family. "My daddy is what you call dyed-in-the-wool country," dolly says fondly. "He didn't believe women should cut their hair or wear trousers ... Not that he was mean, just strict. He didn't like me to wear makeup, so I put Mercurochrome on my lips instead. He was sad as his children grew up and went away."
>
> "When I was a little girl, going to the movies was considered sinful in our neck of the woods," she continues. "But when a movie called Thunder Road—a true Tennessee story that was filmed right near us and starred Robert Mitchum—came to town, Daddy said we could go. I was tickled to death, of course, but it also made me feel sad to be there. I didn't enjoy the movie. Up until that night Mama and Daddy were my heroes and it seemed as though they'd broken their own rule. Even though that meant I got to see the movie, I wished they hadn't" (Maynard 1977, p. 56).

IN CLOSING

If you recognize that you are on the highway to the grave—a highway leading to an eternity in hell—pull over, turn around, and find the highway of holiness. Once on that straight and narrow road, don't veer from it. Follow it all the way to the celestial city.

If Solomon could be brought back from hell, I believe he would declare the same message he declared at the end of his life: "Hear the conclusion of the whole matter: Fear God, and keep his commandments: for this *is* the whole *duty* of man" (Ecclesiastes 12:13 KJV).

LESSON 44

NO COMPARISON

PROVERBS 8:1-11

¹ Does not wisdom call out? Does not understanding raise her voice? ² At the heights along the way, where the paths meet, she takes her stand; ³ beside the gate leading into the city, at the entrance, she cries aloud: ⁴ "To you, O people, I call out; I raise my voice to all mankind. ⁵ You who are simple, gain prudence; you who are foolish, set your hearts on it. ⁶ Listen, for I have trustworthy things to say; I open my lips to speak what is right. ⁷ My mouth speaks what is true, for my lips detest wickedness. ⁸ All the words of my mouth are just; none of them is crooked or perverse. ⁹ To the discerning all of them are right; they are upright to those who have found knowledge. ¹⁰ Choose my instruction instead of silver, knowledge rather than choice gold, ¹¹ for wisdom is more precious than rubies, and nothing you desire can compare with her.

Every human being who has ever lived has been filled with desires, many of which could never be fulfilled in a lifetime. But nothing you could desire, no matter how magnificent, could ever compare with the wisdom that comes from God. It is beyond comparison with anything else. In the previous chapter of the book of Proverbs, we learned of the adulteress going out into the streets seducing a young man who gave into his desires. This chapter begins with another woman—Wisdom— publicly inviting all who will hear to partake of her virtues. But whereas the adulteress's ways were secretive and deceptive and accomplished in the dark, Wisdom is characterized by righteousness and truth. Nothing she does is hidden; nothing is shameful; her appearance is in broad daylight at the crossroad where everyone can see. Those coming to her are walking into light, rather than into darkness. Nothing can compare with what Wisdom has to offer.

READILY AVAILABLE

Some would have you believe wisdom is mystical and mysterious—hard to find and hard to discern. But nothing could be further from the truth. As we learn from the text above, Wisdom is readily available to all. Like the town crier, she raises her voice and calls out to all who will listen. To be even more available, she takes her stand at the crossroads of the city, calling out to all humanity, pleading and warning that it is not necessary to have to learn the hard way. Wisdom is not hiding from people in any way; she is not shut up in a vault with only a few having a key to her treasures; instead, Wisdom makes herself readily available.

> Wisdom is not hiding from people; she is not shut up in a vault with only a few having a key to her treasures; instead, Wisdom makes herself readily available.

Vance Havner once said, "If you lack knowledge, go to school. If you lack wisdom, get on your knees!" (Hester 1986, p. 243). And many years before Vance Havner spoke those words, James wrote, "If any of you lack wisdom, let him ask of God, that giveth to all *men* liberally" (James 1:5 KJV). Wisdom invites all humankind. Specifically, she calls to the simple and the foolish—those with the greatest need of her. Therefore, assuredly, we can ask God for wisdom, and He will give it. Only one criterion is required for receiving that wisdom; the one seeking must put their faith in God and not doubt. (See James 1:6.)

Wisdom comes from the Word of God, and the value of God's words is immeasurable. His words "are divine and heavenly things, so excellent that, in comparison with them, all other learning is but children's play" (Matthew Henry, n.d., Vol. 3, p. 832). All God's precepts are right.

One of the great things about the promises of the Lord is that even the simple can be made wise and the foolish can gain understanding. The first steps toward obtaining wisdom can be accomplished even by a child, and those steps are simply to acknowledge and reverence the LORD: "Fear of the LORD is the foundation of true wisdom. All who obey his commandments will grow in wisdom" (Psalm 111:10 NLT).

> The first steps toward obtaining wisdom can be accomplished even by a child, and those steps are simply to acknowledge and reverence the Lord.

It's important to note that both the adulteress and Wisdom appeal to the same crowd. But the adulteress appeals to the desires of the human nature, leading the simple and the foolish down the highway to the grave. Not so with Wisdom; she leads the simple to gain prudence and the foolish to gain understanding, therefore becoming wise.

THE ROLE OF THE PREACHER

If we are sensitive to the Spirit of God, everywhere we turn, we will see and hear Wisdom declaring the great works of God. For example, "The heavens proclaim the glory of God. The skies display his craftsmanship" (Psalm 19:1 NLT). Highly visible, her voice cries out to turn the sinner from their sinful ways, to guide the simple down the path of righteousness, and to steer the foolish away from the works of darkness. Though wisdom cries from the heavens to proclaim the glory of God, Wisdom most frequently cries out through the voices of God's messengers—preachers of the Gospel. It is the preacher's duty to declare it: "Cry aloud, spare not, lift up thy voice like a trumpet" (Isaiah 58:1 KJV). Therefore, there is no need for the preacher to attempt to sugarcoat the Word to make it more palatable. Matthew Henry (n.d.)

wrote, "The Adulterous woman spoke in secret, ... but Wisdom speaks openly; truth seeks no corners, but gladly appeals to the light" (Vol. 3, p. 832). That being said, there is no value or benefit in a preacher who has to check the direction of the wind before speaking. Truth is truth; culture does not change it. It is not something that can be altered by a church board or the vote of the people.

> There is no need for the preacher to attempt to sugarcoat the Word to make it more palatable.

When sin becomes accepted as the norm among church leaders, the church is in trouble. Isaiah described the state of the church in Israel—the northern kingdom—also referred to as Ephraim, at a time prior to its destruction by the Assyrians:

> Priests and prophets stagger from beer and are befuddled with wine; they reel from beer, they stagger when seeing visions, they stumble when rendering decisions. All the tables are covered with vomit and there is not a spot without filth. (Isaiah 28:7–8)

Their response to the prophet's message was much like that of rebellious children. When the prophet tried to speak, they held their hands over their ears and made unintelligible sounds, so as to drown out the voice of the prophet— "Da, da, da, da, blah, blah, blah, blah" (Isaiah 28:10 MSG). By ignoring the voice of the prophet, their fate was sealed. They would be captured, and their land of rest and repose the LORD had purchased for them would be plundered, and the people would be led away as slaves— "broken, and snared, and taken" (Isaiah 28:13 KJV) into a foreign land. This was the result of church leaders not speaking against sin, accepting sin as the norm, and becoming involved in sin themselves.

In our day, we see church organizations blatantly ignoring God and His Word. One example is accepting the atheistic concept of evolution as true. Though accepting evolution as true is not a sin of commission; it is still sin; it is a sin of omission. It is a failure on the part of ministry not to affirm all of God's Word. When you remove Genesis, chapter 2 from the Bible, you have to remove segments of almost every other book of the Bible. In the 1950 encyclical, *Humani Generis*, Pope Pius XII confirmed that there is no intrinsic conflict between Christianity and the theory of evolution. Today, the Catholic Church supports theistic evolution, also known as evolutionary creation, although their membership is free not to believe in any part of evolutionary theory if they so desire. This sounds very much like another terrible time in Israel's history—a time in which "every man did *that which was* right in his own eyes" (Judges 21:25 KJV).

Imagine the chaos that would reign if everyone was free to support or reject whichever doctrine was right in his own eyes. With chaos reigning in the Corinthian church, Paul posed a question that rings true yet today, "If the bugler doesn't sound a clear call, how will the soldiers know they are being called to battle?" (1 Corinthians 14:8 NLT). Many church denominational leaders fail to declare that the greatness of God and the wisdom of God are beyond comparison by adopting a viewpoint that was intended to undermine the Creator. By failing to cry out against untruth, they sin by omission.

> Many church denominational leaders fail to declare that the greatness of God and the wisdom of God are beyond comparison by adopting a viewpoint that was intended to undermine the Creator.

Then there are sins of commission that have become accepted as the norm among many clergy and congregants alike. For example, in 2003, Gene Robinson became the first noncelibate, openly homosexual priest in documented Christian history to be ordained as a bishop. By allowing this, his church organization became an accomplice in the sin of commission along with Bishop Robinson. Fortunately, not all members of that denomination were willing participants and fled, either to form a new organization or to find other more conservative denominations.

But it is clear that Bishop Robinson and the US Episcopal Church forgot the warnings of the apostle Paul: "For the wrath of God is revealed from heaven against all ungodliness and unrighteousness of men, who hold the truth in unrighteousness" (Romans 1:18 KJV). They failed to heed the warnings of Wisdom, though she conspicuously stood at the crossroads of the city and cried out. Had they adhered to the Word of God, they would have heard her stern warnings so many years before:

> That is why God abandoned them to their shameful desires. Even the women turned against the natural way to have sex and instead indulged in sex with each other. And the men, instead of having normal sexual relations with women, burned with lust for each other. Men did shameful things with other men, and as a result of this sin, they suffered within themselves the penalty they deserved. (Romans 1:26–27 NLT)

Several years ago, I was in a meeting with various denominational leaders from our community when one stated that he was no longer able to preach against fornication because so many of his church members were living together unmarried. My first thought was, *What a mission field!* Here was a group of people already going to church who may not even have known they were living in sin. If he had only begun to teach them the truth, it is likely many of them would have repented, or as it is rendered in the Geneva Bible, "amended their ways." I am certain that Wisdom would have taken the opportunity to declare the truth.

THE OPPORTUNITY TO CHOOSE

The opportunity to choose right from wrong is openly set before humankind. The Lord has never forced himself on anyone. Conviction can be so heavy as to cause one to fall to the ground (see Acts 9:1–6), but the Lord never forces Himself on anyone. Everyone is free to make a choice. And that was Joshua's message to the Israelites near the end of his life— "Choose you this day whom ye will serve" (Joshua 24:15 KJV). But since it is a choice, not everyone responds in the affirmative. In fact, Paul spoke of a day when the people's choice would be to refuse Him who speaks:

> For the time will come when people will not put up with sound doctrine. Instead, to suit their own desires, they will gather around them a great number of teachers to say what their itching ears want to hear. They will turn their ears away from the truth and turn aside to myths. (2 Timothy 4:3–4)

> Conviction can be so heavy as to cause one to fall to the ground (see Acts 9:1-6), but the Lord never forces Himself on anyone.

But we must do more than hear Wisdom when she cries out at the crossroads; we must put her words into practice.

IN CLOSING

The value of godly wisdom is beyond comparison. We cannot live life to the fullest if we ignore wisdom that comes from the mind behind all creation. Wisdom of the elders and wisdom that comes from academic instruction is helpful in navigating this life, but these sources of wisdom cannot compare with the wisdom that comes from the Spirit of God. What we really need is the Spirit of God actively working in our lives. And the scriptures state, *"For it is not from man that we draw our life but from God as we are being joined to Jesus, the Anointed One. And now he is our God-given wisdom"* (1 Corinthians 1:30 TPT). As noted earlier, "If you lack knowledge, go to school. If you lack wisdom, get on your knees!" (Hester 1985, p. 243). That's exactly what the apostles did, and the Jewish rulers took note: "Now when they saw the boldness of Peter and John, and perceived that they were unlearned and ignorant men, they marvelled; and they took knowledge of them, that they had been with Jesus" (Acts 4:13 KJV).

> Wisdom of the elders and wisdom that comes from academic instruction is helpful in navigating this life, but these sources of wisdom cannot compare with the wisdom that comes from the Spirit of God.

Given its value, how do you live by God's wisdom? By prayerfully allowing the Spirit of God to reveal the wisdom of God through His Word. You cannot ignore His Word and be wise. So, if you are going to walk in wisdom, you must immerse yourself in His Word until it becomes assimilated into the fabric of your character. Then, that wisdom will guide you in all your living and decision making. Your responses and your actions will be the result of wisdom woven into the fabric of your transformed nature.

LESSON 45

WISDOM REVEALS HERSELF

PROVERBS 8:12-21

¹² I, wisdom, dwell together with prudence; I possess knowledge and discretion. ¹³ To fear the Lᴏʀᴅ is to hate evil; I hate pride and arrogance, evil behavior and perverse speech. ¹⁴ Counsel and sound judgment are mine; I have insight, I have power. ¹⁵ By me kings reign and rulers issue decrees that are just; ¹⁶ by me princes govern, and nobles—all who rule on earth. ¹⁷ I love those who love me, and those who seek me find me. ¹⁸ With me are riches and honor, enduring wealth and prosperity. ¹⁹ My fruit is better than fine gold; what I yield surpasses choice silver. ²⁰ I walk in the way of righteousness, along the paths of justice, ²¹ bestowing a rich inheritance on those who love me and making their treasuries full.

Many years before Solomon, Job asked the question, "Where then does wisdom come from? Where does understanding dwell?" (Job 28:20). His conclusion was that only God knows. Only God knows because He is the source of wisdom.

The above verses give the sense of a summary concerning wisdom. One might say that Wisdom, personified as a lady, chooses to reveal herself. In those ten verses, the pronouns I, mine, me, and my are used sixteen times. The frequency of use of those personal pronouns makes

Wisdom the focus of Solomon's writings, rather than her rewards. Yes, there are rewards for seeking Wisdom, but the focus must always be on Wisdom and not on the rewards. Her rewards will follow!

> There are rewards for seeking Wisdom, but the focus must always be on Wisdom and not on the rewards. Her rewards will follow!

DWELLING TOGETHER WITH PRUDENCE

In these verses, Wisdom informs us that she dwells together with Prudence. Prudence is the quality of being prudent, which is defined as "(1) capable of exercising sound judgment in practical matters, especially as concerns one's own interests (2) cautious or discreet in conduct; circumspect; not rash (3) managing carefully" (Webster 1999, p. 1156). It might also be defined as good common sense—possessing the ability to foresee the snares of life, avoiding obstacles and pitfalls. Regardless of the presence of Wisdom, it's up to the individual to exercise prudence. When Christians act foolishly, the cause of Christ is harmed. It's imperative that we seek the LORD for wisdom and act with prudence.

For example, Wisdom warns, "See then that ye walk circumspectly, not as fools, but as wise, Redeeming the time, because the days are evil" (Ephesians 5:15–16 KJV). In response, Prudence gets up early and prays. Wisdom instructs, "Live such good lives among the pagans that, though they accuse you of doing wrong, they may see your good deeds and glorify God on the day he visits us" (1 Peter 2:12). In response, knowing the weakness of the flesh, Prudence sets boundaries for self. In fact, Prudence avoids even the appearance of evil. (See 1 Thessalonians 5:22.) Again, because Wisdom strongly urges, "Not forsaking the assembling of ourselves together" (Hebrews 10:25 KJV), Prudence is careful to attend church even when it means missing other activities.

Yes, we are called upon to exercise prudence by avoiding all appearance of evil, but we also are called upon to exercise prudence by being soldiers. And as such, there will be times that it will be necessary to take a stand and fight for godliness. There will be times we must stand contrary to the prevailing worldview. Remember, to depart from evil is not the same as hating evil. It is possible to depart from evil but still have evil desires in our hearts. When our flesh cries out after evil, we must carry it to an altar as a living sacrifice, making certain, through prayer and fasting, that the desire dies and remains dead.

When the world comes in like a flood, demanding its ungodly philosophies be accepted, the church must not hang her head as impotent but must exercise prudence. Jesus declared, "I will build my church; and the gates of hell shall not prevail against it" (Matthew 16:18 KJV). "The gates of hell shall not prevail against the church" should not be perceived as a picture of the church in a defensive posture, helplessly pinned in a corner. Instead, Jesus was describing a church on the offensive, challenging the enemy and defining culture, not being defined by culture.

> When the world comes in like a flood, demanding its ungodly philosophies be accepted, the church must not hang her head as impotent but must exercise prudence.

Unfortunately, the church has taken a back seat to secular institutions, such as the school, in defining culture. Why should the church be impacted by Wednesday-evening school activities? If the church becomes what Jesus intended it to become, it will be the school checking the church schedule so as to not conflict with church activities.

Why should church organizations be appointing committees to examine whether or not to ordain homosexuals? Did Wisdom not already declare that those who "practice homosexuality" (1 Corinthians 6:9 NLT) "will not inherit the Kingdom of God" (1 Corinthians 6:9 NLT)? It is the church's job to be out front defining culture so that homosexuality is defined as a sinful behavior that is to be repented of, rather than considered an alternate lifestyle. Prudence takes action to not just defend but promote marriage as a monogamous relationship between a male and a female.

The church has spent the past fifty years in a defensive position fighting abortion rights, but had the church exercised prudence and taken an offensive position a century ago, the church would have defined culture in such a way that abortion would never have made its way to the Supreme Court, and it never would have become a birth control method.

Further, there is no need for the church to take a defensive posture in defining gender identity. Wisdom declares that in the beginning, "God created man in his *own* image, in the image of God created he him; male and female created he them" (Genesis 1:27 KJV). There was no third person created with a third gender identity. And Adam and Eve didn't draw straws to determine who was male and who was female; it was defined by God at the moment of creation. Beginning with the first child born to Adam and Eve through God's reproductive process, gender has been determined by God at the time of conception. When the church takes its proper position in a culture, Prudence clearly demonstrates maleness and femaleness even in outward appearance of dress and hair.

> Adam and Eve didn't draw straws to determine who was male and who was female; it was defined by God at the moment of creation.

KNOWLEDGE AND DISCRETION

Not only does Wisdom dwell together with Prudence, she possesses both knowledge and discretion. Knowledge here refers to revelatory knowledge. In particular, this refers to knowledge concerning the things of God. Our Lord never intended for us to grope in darkness. A. W. Tozer (2017) made the following comment, "If we co-operate with Him in loving obedience God will manifest Himself to us, and that manifestation will be the difference between a nominal Christian life and a life radiant with the light of His face" (p. 42).

Just as Moses's face shone after encountering the presence of God, so also should our lives shine once we have encountered the presence of God. God is continually attempting to reveal Himself to us and through us. Knowledge of God is revealed to us both through His Word and by His Spirit. Therefore, Wisdom unfolds God's truths to those who desire to know Him better. David sang, "The unfolding of your words gives light; it gives understanding" (Psalm 119:130). Under the New Covenant, the "deep things of God" are revealed to us by the Holy Spirit:

> As it is written, Eye hath not seen, nor ear heard, neither have entered into the heart of man, the things which God hath prepared for them that love him. But God hath revealed *them* unto us by his Spirit. (1 Corinthians 2:9–10 KJV)

So often, people quote verse 9, "Eye hath not seen, nor ear heard, neither have entered into the heart of man, the things which God hath prepared for them that love him," as though we are still floundering in darkness, but nothing could be further from the truth. We are no longer living under the Old Testament; we are living on this side of the Day of Pentecost, and God has revealed to us by His Spirit things that in the past the eye had not seen, nor had the ear heard. Knowledge into the mystery of Christ "was not made known to people in other generations as it has now been revealed by the Spirit to God's holy apostles and prophets" (Ephesians 3:5).

We need the power of the Spirit working within us to open our eyes. Paul's desire and prayer for the Ephesians was that the eyes of their hearts might be enlightened that they would be able to more clearly understand the things of God:

> I keep asking that the God of our Lord Jesus Christ, the glorious Father, may give you the Spirit of wisdom and revelation, so that you may know him better. I pray that the eyes of your heart may be enlightened in order that you may know the hope to which he has called you, the riches of his glorious inheritance in

holy people, and his incomparably great power for us
who believe. (Ephesians 1:17–19)

In addition to knowledge, Wisdom possesses discretion. Discretion
is the ability to keep your mind focused on making sound decisions,
giving serious attention and thought to what is going on around you.
Discretion will allow you to recognize and avoid the wrong attitudes
that create hurtful words and actions that might denigrate others or
bring much pain and embarrassment to others and self. A friend of
mine used to say, "Keep your words sweet, kind, and wonderful, for
tomorrow you may have to eat them." It's much easier to eat those words
if they are sweet, kind, and wonderful. That's why Solomon could
write, "Discretion will protect you" (Proverbs 2:11). The translators
of God's Word (GW) translation rendered the word *discretion* as
foresight. "Foresight will protect you." Often those who lack discretion
or foresight have the mentality of *tell it like it is*, which can result in
pain, suffering, and even destruction of others.

> Keep your words sweet, kind, and wonderful, for tomorrow
> you may have to eat them.

THE INFLUENCE OF WISDOM

Wisdom informs us that sound judgment and insight are hers. (See
Proverbs 8:14.) She will guide you in the ways of God, according to
His Word. Wisdom is essential for one to rule and govern efficiently
and properly. "By me kings reign, and rulers decree what is just; by me
princes rule, and nobles, all who govern justly" (Proverbs 8:15–16 ESV).
Wisdom provides the insight necessary to know what to do, but it's up
to you to make those tough decisions and do what needs to be done.

Moses stands out as one of the greatest leaders of all time. While
he was on the mountain receiving the law, Aaron caved into the will of
the people and made them a golden calf as an object of worship. Two

acts of leadership stand out: First, when the LORD threatened to destroy the entire nation of Israel and start over with Moses and his family, he became their intercessor, pleading for their lives. Moses demonstrated the heart of a shepherd, and the LORD was pleased. Second, after the LORD relented and did not destroy the whole nation, Moses took action against the rebellious element among them:

> "Put your sword on your side each of you, and go to and fro from gate to gate throughout the camp, and each of you kill his brother and his companion and his neighbor." And the sons of Levi did according to the word of Moses. And that day about three thousand men of the people fell. (Exodus 32:27–28 ESV)

That sounds harsh, but sinning had to stop, and no favoritism was to be shown to a relative or friend. All who had not repented and turned back to the LORD were to be destroyed. Moses demonstrated great leadership by taking action necessary to sanctify the people. There is a reason for church discipline, and church leaders who are afraid to take action against sin do not do the offender or the people under his leadership a favor.

> There is a reason for church discipline, and church leaders who are afraid to take action against sin do not do the offender a favor.

Many a corporate leader wished they had the wisdom of Solomon. Many a supervisor has desired to have the ability to lead effectively. Many a husband longed for answers to meet the needs of his wife. Many parents have wept over their children, not knowing what to do. However, wisdom is not elusive; wisdom is readily accessible. And God is ready to dispense insight to the one who will ask Him. All one has to do is ask God. (See James 1:5.)

Those who possess wisdom will make decisions and pass judgment based on the Word of God. Solomon knew firsthand the influence of wisdom on his life. The greatness of a nation depends on civil rulers utilizing wisdom to enact and enforce justice. "A ruler who lacks understanding is a cruel oppressor" (Proverbs 28:16 ESV). A king without wisdom is a cruel oppressor. Many kings have reigned without wisdom, but they were not good kings; many princes have decreed laws, but they were not good or righteous laws. Good kings are good kings only when they rule with the wisdom that comes from God.

> Those who possess wisdom will make decisions and pass judgment based on the Word of God.

WISDOM'S WARRANTY

The time period in which the United States of America was founded was known as the Enlightenment. Many of the philosophers of that day regarded God as a watchmaker, or a distant Creator who wound up the universe, set it in motion, and then stepped away; it was pointless to pray to such a God who surely wasn't listening. Wisdom revealed by God was discredited in favor of humankind's wisdom. So they could not conceive of a God who would remain intimately involved with His creation. However, nothing could be further from the truth. The God of the Bible is interested in and intimately involved in the lives of His people. He desires communion, relationship, and companionship.

Wisdom is a committed and faithful partner to those who choose to seek her. When you make a commitment to her, she makes a commitment to you. Wisdom loves those who love her and seek her, and she is not ashamed or unwilling to return the affection. You will receive the full and faithful benefit of her devotion. She will not abandon you along the way. Wisdom promises, "I walk in the way of righteousness, along the paths of justice, bestowing wealth on those who love me and making their treasuries full" (Proverbs 8:20–21). She is loyal to the ways of righteousness and always leads her admirers toward the Lord.

> Wisdom loves those who love her and seek her, and she is not ashamed or unwilling to return the affection.

Wisdom is not stingy or selfish with her wealth, gladly sharing her abundance with those who desire her. Those who seek her riches are promised to receive a full measure of them. "With me are riches and honor, enduring wealth and prosperity. My fruit is better than fine gold; what I yield surpasses choice silver" (Proverbs 8:18–19). Wisdom has traits that will endure, traits of value that can be passed on to future generations. Her blessings lead her followers in the ways of righteousness. You may not have much in the way of riches and treasures from this world, but the blessings of Wisdom are eternal. Jesus gave the following advice:

> Lay not up for yourselves treasures upon earth, where moth and rust doth corrupt, and where thieves break through and steal: But lay up for yourselves treasures in heaven, where neither moth nor rust doth corrupt, and where thieves do not break through nor steal. (Matthew 6:19–20 KJV)

It would be untrue to say that only those who seek wisdom will be blessed in this life. However, when they come to the end of this life's road, they will have to abandon all of their material possessions there; they cannot take them with them.

IN CLOSING

Wisdom and prudence are twin sisters. Prudence brings wisdom down to earth; it allows wisdom to walk in shoe leather. When prudence is exercised, some of the benefits of wisdom include prosperity and success. We see this modeled in the life of King Uzziah as long as he sought the LORD:

He did *that which was* right in the sight of the LORD, according to all that his father Amaziah did. And he sought God in the days of Zechariah, who had understanding in the visions of God: and as long as he sought the LORD, God made him to prosper. (2 Chronicles 26:4–5 KJV)

> Prudence brings wisdom down to earth; it allows wisdom to walk in shoe leather.

It's one thing to know what to do or to have the wisdom to know what to do; it's another to put it into practice. "Therefore to him that knoweth to do good, and doeth *it* not, to him it is sin" (James 4:17 KJV). As long as King Uzziah exercised prudence, God gave him success. Riches and honor were his, but when he failed to follow the LORD, he failed to exercise prudence and success slipped through his fingers. It is essential that you not only seek wisdom but that you exercise prudence by doing what you know to do.

LESSON 46

THE PREEMINENCE OF WISDOM

PROVERBS 8:22-31

22 "The LORD brought me forth as the first of his works, before his deeds of old; 23 I was formed long ago, at the very beginning, when the world came to be. 24 When there were no watery depths, I was given birth, when there were no springs overflowing with water; 25 before the mountains were settled in place, before the hills, I was given birth, 26 before he made the world or its fields or any of the dust of the earth. 27 I was there when he set the heavens in place, when he marked out the horizon on the face of the deep, 28 when he established the clouds above and fixed securely the fountains of the deep, 29 when he gave the sea its boundary so the waters would not overstep his command, and when he marked out the foundations of the earth. 30 Then I was constantly at his side. I was filled with delight day after day, rejoicing always in his presence, 31 rejoicing in his whole world and delighting in mankind.

Who or what is the above verses talking about? Is Wisdom, as referenced here, describing God the Son who was created first and then worked alongside the Father throughout the rest of creation? Or is Wisdom a personification of a characteristic of God? The original intent of Solomon has been taken out of context and misused in various ways throughout the history of the church, even up to today.

In the 4th century C.E., this passage was used both to support and to refute the Arians' claims. Assuming first that Christ could be equated with "the wisdom of God" (1 Corinthians 1:24), the Arians argued that the Son, like Wisdom, was created. And to be a creature, whether the first or the most prominent of creatures, is to be subordinate to the Creator. But those who formulated the Nicene declaration that the Son was "begotten, not made" were inclined to translate "qanani" in Proverbs 8:22 as "begot me" in order to argue that God and Christ were "consubstantial" (of the same essence and status). (Farmer 1991, p. 54)

For those who insist the verses in our text are in some mysterious way speaking of a Trinity express confusion in their own writings. Phillips (1995) commented on those verses:

The whole passage now before us is one of great majesty and mystery as wisdom and various members of the godhead are introduced in such a way that we cannot always be sure which is which. Obviously at times the passage is speaking of wisdom, but is equally obvious that at times the passage is speaking of Christ. It is not easy, however, to draw a hard and fast line and say, "Here the passage is speaking of wisdom (personified) and here the passage is speaking of the Son." (p. 197)

As a result of these early controversies and errors, most recent English translations have reflected the concept that Wisdom referred to in this passage is God the Son, who aided God the Father in the creation process. Both the Arians and the Trinitarians erred in that they had a picture of persons in mind. Daniel Segraves (1990) provides us with an alternative: "Wisdom is an attribute of God, and as such it was with Him from the very beginning, even before the dawn of creation" (p. 89). Therefore, if we begin with understanding that Wisdom is an attribute of the Almighty God and that it was by that attribute God created the world, these verses all flow together, and there is no confusion or controversy.

If we begin with understanding that Wisdom is an attribute of the Almighty God and that it was by that attribute God created the world, these verses all flow together, and there is no confusion or controversy.

THE ORIGIN OF WISDOM

Like the prophets who told their listeners how they were called into the ministry of the LORD, Wisdom tells her listeners about her origin. "In effect [Wisdom] says, 'I trace my beginnings and my authority back to the LORD" (Farmer, 1991, p. 52). "I was formed long ago, at the very beginning, when the world come to be." (Proverbs 8:23). The word translated *formed* in the NIV was translated *set up* in the KJV, but neither clearly reflect the meaning of the word. The Hebrew word (*nacak, naw-sak'*) means to pour out, especially a libation, or drink offering (Strong 1990, #5258, p. 79). Paul used this idea when he spoke of his final sacrifice for the cause of Christ. "For I am already being poured out as a drink offering, and the time of my departure has come" (2 Timothy 4:6 ESV). I believe I would be theologically correct to make the assertion that Wisdom in this context could be heard to declare, "You can trust my principles because I Am. I was there when the world and all that is in it were created; I Am that designer, that creative force within that which is called God."

WISDOM IN CREATION

God's wisdom was made available or distributed, and it can be seen in all of creation. It can be seen in everything God made. "God made the beast of the earth after his kind, and cattle after their kind, and every thing that creepeth upon the earth after his kind: and God saw that *it was* good" (Genesis 1:25 KJV). After the final act, he stepped back again and made a complimentary exclamation, "It is very good"—perfect! (See Genesis 1:31.) Consider just how perfect this creation really is. The elements in the atmosphere were created perfect to sustain life, and living things were created perfect for that atmosphere. The earth provides all that is necessary to sustain life.

Wisdom declared, "Then I was constantly at his side. I was filled with delight day after day, rejoicing always in his presence, rejoicing in his whole world and delighting in mankind" (Proverbs 8:30–31). In other words, the creative force in the mind of God—that characteristic of God that longs to pour out blessings, delights in, takes pleasure in, and finds shear enjoyment in blessing His creationb—is none other than Wisdom. With great wisdom, God supplies our daily food, and He gives us health and strength. All the material blessings of life flow from His bountiful creative supply. When we sit at the table, we should bow our heads in thanksgiving because every morsel of food we eat has been provided by His goodness. It is His delight to give it. When we arise each morning and dress to go to work, we should bow our knees and raise our hands in thanksgiving, for it is the Lord who has given us employment. He daily provides us with health and strength to go to our jobs and work faithfully throughout the day. "Count your many blessings, name them one by one" (Johnson Oatman Jr. in *Sing unto the Lord*, p. 23).

> The creative force in the mind of God—that characteristic of God that longs to pour out blessings, delights in, takes pleasure in, and finds shear enjoyment in blessing His creation—is none other than Wisdom.

THE BLESSINGS OF WISDOM

In His infinite wisdom, God has blessed us with mercy, forgiveness, kindness, generosity, and love. The psalmist stated the following:

Thou preparest a table before me in the presence of mine enemies: thou anointest my head with oil; my cup runneth over. Surely goodness and mercy shall follow me all the days of my life: and I will dwell in the house of the LORD for ever. (Psalm 23:5–6 KJV)

And James wrote, "Every good and perfect gift is from above, coming down from the Father of the heavenly lights, who does not change like shifting shadows" (James 1:17).

What is the greatest gift of all that the wisdom of God poured out upon humankind? It is not necessarily hidden but often overlooked in a verse so often quoted concerning prayer:

I say unto you, Ask, and it shall be given you; seek, and ye shall find; knock, and it shall be opened unto you. For every one that asketh receiveth; and he that seeketh findeth; and to him that knocketh it shall be opened. If a son shall ask bread of any of you that is a father, will he give him a stone? or if he ask a fish, will he for a fish give him a serpent? Or if he shall ask an egg, will he offer him a scorpion? If ye then, being evil, know how to give good gifts unto your children: how much more shall *your* heavenly Father give the Holy Spirit to them that ask him? (Luke 11:9–13 KJV)

The greatest gift of all—the earnest of our inheritance, the gift of the Holy Spirit—is now available to all who will ask, seek, and knock.

> The greatest gift of all—the earnest of our inheritance, the gift of the Holy Spirit—is now available to all who will ask, seek, and knock.

David asked a question that we all should ask, "When I consider thy heavens, the work of thy fingers, the moon and the stars, which thou hast ordained; What is man, that thou art mindful of him?" (Psalm 8:3–4 KJV). According to Screwtape in *Screwtape Letters*, it is a source of astonishment and outrage to the demon world that God delights in the "disgusting human vermin" (Lewis 1961, p. 17). "The only explanation for God's infinite love, compassion, and grace for the poor lost sinners of Adam's ruined race lies in His character. He loves us because He loves us" (Phillips 1995, p. 210). Though Satan will do anything to tempt you and entice you away from the Creator, his opinion of you is simply "disgusting human vermin." God, on the other hand, delights in His children:

> For thou *art* an holy people unto the LORD thy God: the LORD thy God hath chosen thee to be a special people unto himself, above all people that are upon the face of the earth. The LORD did not set his love upon you, nor choose you, because ye were more in number than any people; for ye *were* the fewest of all people: But because the LORD loved you. (Deuteronomy 7:6–8 KJV)

IN CLOSING

Since the Lord loves you and delights in you, why don't you come and play before Him? He loves to watch His kids play before Him with all their might. "When the Spirit of the Lord moves upon my heart, I will dance like David danced" (Duvall, 1989). And when you do, Wisdom steps back, claps her hands in time with your dance, and says, "It is good! It is very good! Perfect!"

LESSON 47

WISDOM'S BLESSINGS

PROVERBS 8:32-36

³² Now then, my children, listen to me; blessed are those who keep my ways. ³³ Listen to my instruction and be wise; do not disregard it. ³⁴ Blessed are those who listen to me, watching daily at my doors, waiting at my doorway. ³⁵ For those who find me find life and receives favor from the LORD. ³⁶ But whoever fails to find me harm themselves; all who hate me love death."

As learned in previous lessons, Wisdom is inseparable from God. Wisdom is a characteristic of God and something to be sought after at all cost and cherished when found. Since Jesus is God manifest in the flesh (1 Timothy 3:16), Jesus no doubt is Wisdom personified.

> Wisdom is a characteristic of God and something to be sought after at all cost and cherished when found.

We are informed in the above paragraph (Proverbs 8:32–36) that all who will listen to Wisdom and keep her ways will be blessed. Two commands stand out in verses 33 and 34 respectively—"Listen to my instructions," and "Be watching and waiting." By doing so, you will receive favor from the LORD.

RECEIVING FAVOR FROM THE LORD

"Listen to my instruction and be wise; do not ignore it" (Proverbs 8:33). Being willing to listen to instruction and apply what is learned is a characteristic of the wise. But whoever ignores or resists instruction is a fool and will suffer the consequences of foolishness. At the conclusion of His Sermon on the Mount, Jesus stated, "Therefore whosoever heareth these sayings of mine, and doeth them, I will liken him unto a wise man, which built his house upon a rock" (Matthew 7:24 KJV). When the floods and storms of life came, this man stood strong, while those who had not built their lives upon His teachings were destroyed. This principle has not changed. Whether it be finding a spouse, building a marriage, or raising children, you will never go wrong by listening to the wisdom of the Word of God and applying it. Before going into debt, making a career change, moving to another city, going back to college, or starting a new business, you will likely experience a better outcome by listening to godly counsel. "Where no counsel *is*, the people fall: but in the multitude of counsellors *there is* safety" (Proverbs 11:14 KJV).

> Before going into debt, making a career change, moving to another city, going back to college, or starting a new business, you will likely experience a better outcome by listening to godly counsel.

Jesus told a parable of four different kinds of hearers and described them as four different kinds of soil. (See Matthew 13:4–8, 18–23.) He described the first kind of hearer as a path alongside the field. This kind of person cannot hear the instruction because no preparation has been made to receive instruction. Therefore, it could be said the instruction fell on deaf ears.

The second kind of soil was described as full of stones. These individuals may get excited to hear truth, but they quickly wilt when encountering any opposition. They value friendship and peace more than truth and wisdom. Stony-ground hearers have no real commitment to truth, and the cost of discipleship is too high for them. "They fall away as soon as they have problems or are persecuted for believing God's word" (Matthew 13:21 NLT). This kind of hearer often shows up for revival meetings and "immediately with joy" expresses great future plans for serving the Lord, but something will soon come along that causes him or her to fall away because the stones prevent any depth of commitment.

Then there are those who express a desire for truth, but they are more interested in money and pleasure. They are absorbed with work, hobbies, or amusements; they cannot find the time, or are not willing to put forth the effort, to zealously pursue the kingdom of God. The love of money and pleasure ruins them. The apostle Paul wrote, "Some people, eager for money, have wandered from the faith" (1 Timothy 6:10). This person's focus is earthly, so "the deceitfulness of riches, choke the word, and he becometh unfruitful" (Matthew 13:22 KJV). Paul wrote of one of his colaborers, "Demas hath forsaken me, having loved this present world" (2 Timothy 4:10 KJV). The rest is left unsaid but understood.

Then there is the one who hears the Word, understands it, and builds their life on it. "He indeed bears fruit and yields, in one case a hundredfold, in another sixty, and in another thirty" (Matthew 13:23 ESV). This kind of hearer is committed and diligent, as the proverb describes. Therefore, they will hear and keep His Word and receive God's favor. The Bereans stand out as an example of this kind of hearer, "They received the word with all readiness of mind, and searched the scriptures daily, whether those things were so" (Acts 17:11 KJV). They approached hearing the Word of God like hunting for treasure—with great zeal.

WATCHING AND WAITING

"Blessed is the man who listens to me, watching daily at my doors, waiting at my doors" (Proverbs 8:34). This speaks not only of desire for the things of God but of an expectation. Do you wait with excited anticipation for any opportunity to learn more of the things of God?

"For those who find me find life and receive favor from the LORD" (Proverbs 8:35).

These words bring to mind the theme of the Olivet discourse. This kind of hearer not only waits expectantly for more of the Word of God, but their eyes are fixed on the eastern horizon to see if the dawn yet appears. They wait expectantly, looking for the return of Christ. Throughout the Olivet discourse, Jesus emphasized the importance of watching and waiting expectantly, "because the Son of Man will return when you least expect him. (Matthew 24:42–44 GWT).

In His teaching on the Mount of Olives, Jesus utilized a series of parables to emphasize this theme. In one of those parables, He described ten virgins—five wise and five foolish. It was the expectancy—watching and waiting—that resulted in them meeting their bridegroom: "At midnight there was a cry made, Behold, the bridegroom cometh; go ye out to meet him ... And they that were ready went in with him to the marriage: and the door was shut" (Matthew 25:6, 10 KJV).

That bridegroom is none other than the Lord Jesus, and no more important guest than He will ever come to your house. But you don't have to wait for the cry of the bridegroom's entourage to welcome Him into your house. For He declares, "Behold, I stand at the door, and knock: if any man hear my voice, and open the door, I will come in to him, and will sup with him, and he with me" (Revelation 3:20 KJV). Do not delay in responding to His knock.

> You don't have to wait for the cry of the bridegroom's entourage to welcome Him into your house.

It would be foolish to miss the return of our Lord by failing to *expect* and to *watch*. "Blessed are those who listen to me, watching daily at my doors, waiting at my doorway" (Proverbs 8:34).

No one is turned away because of race, ethnicity, or national origin. "For who find me find life and receive favor from the LORD" (Proverbs 8:35). Heaven will be filled with souls from every nation and language group that has ever existed. (See Revelation 5:9.) For God is no respecter of persons. He has no favorites. (See Acts 10:34.) The wonderful promise of salvation is available to everyone.

LIFE IS FOUND IN JESUS CHRIST

When the disciples discovered Jesus was the Messiah, they recognized they had found life, and they were compelled to share what they had found. "The first thing Andrew did was to find his brother Simon and tell him, 'We have found the Messiah'" (John 1:41 ESV). The word was then passed on, and Philip was introduced to him. In turn, "Philip findeth Nathanael, and saith unto him, We have found him, of whom Moses in the law, and the prophets, did write, Jesus of Nazareth, the son of Joseph" (John 1:45 KJV). Wisdom points us in the direction of life, and that life is found in Jesus Christ.

> Sir James Simpson discovered chloroform. ... His discovery of chloroform revolutionized medicine. Before his day, surgery was a nightmare.
>
> One day a newspaper reporter interviewed the famous researcher. The journalist asked his first question: "Sir James, would you please tell me what you consider to be your most important discovery?"
>
> The scientist promptly replied, "My most important discovery was when I found out that I was a sinner in the sight of a holy God."
>
> The startled newsman did not think that answer would get his article on the front page, so he tried again. "Thank you, Sir James," he said. "Now would you tell me what you consider to be your second most important discovery?"
>
> The famous scientist replied, "Young man, my second most important discovery was when I found that Jesus died for a sinner like me." Sir James had found wisdom, he had found life, and he had obtained favor of the Lord. (Phillips 1995, p. 214)

Consider the value of receiving the favor of the Lord—Wisdom's blessings! When Christians look at the wonderful life they now enjoy in Christ Jesus, they must remember that nothing in it is the product of their own effort or goodness, other than the willingness to allow God to work in their lives. What can be seen is the ongoing handiwork of the Savior. One writer described it this way:

> With skillful hands, the Master creates joy where sorrow existed. With patient strokes, He paints peace in a life that sin had colored with turmoil. He daily works righteous practices, righteous thoughts, and righteous motives into this new creation. When He completes the process, He will welcome His bride home, "a glorious church not having spot, or wrinkle, or any such thing" (Ephesians 5:27). It is His finest work—His signature creation that bears His name. The Christian is truly His ultimate masterpiece! (Johnson 2004 spring, p. 17)

When Christians look at the wonderful life they now enjoy in Christ Jesus, they must remember that nothing in it is the product of their own effort or goodness, other than the willingness to allow God to work in their lives.

"For we are his workmanship, created in Christ Jesus unto good works, which God hath before ordained that we should walk in them" (Ephesians 2:10 KJV).

WHEN WISDOM IS NOT VALUED

"But those who fail to find me harm themselves; all who hate me love death" (Proverbs 8:36). Not valuing wisdom was a characteristic of the nation of Israel from the time of their deliverance out of Egypt to the crossing of the Jordan River and beyond. The LORD was continually providing direction, but Israel was quick to reject the wisdom of God. Consider the times they panicked when faced with an opportunity for a miracle. Was not the Red Sea and Pharaoh's army an opportunity to see the miracle-working hand of God? God's wisdom—God's plan—was a corridor through the Red Sea with a wall of water on each side as an escape route for the Israelites and a tomb for the Egyptians:

> So as the sun began to rise, Moses raised his hand over the sea, and the water rushed back into its usual place. The Egyptians tried to escape, but the LORD swept them into the sea. Then the waters returned and covered all the chariots and charioteers—the entire army of Pharaoh. Of all the Egyptians who had chased the Israelites into the sea, not a single one survived. (Exodus 14:27–28 NLT)

God's wisdom—God's plan—was a corridor through the Red Sea with a wall of water on each side as an escape route for the Israelites and a tomb for the Egyptians.

Again and again, Israel would fail to see Wisdom's blessings. The LORD gave them bread from heaven, but they cried for flesh. Instead of seeing Wisdom's blessings in the moment, when times got tough, they fondly remembered the land of bondage: "We remember the fish we ate in Egypt at no cost—also the cucumbers, melons, leeks, onions and garlic" (Numbers 11:5).

Leap forward. When the wisdom of God is not valued, grace also is not valued. Time and again, Jesus tried to point out Judas's sin but to no avail. When anyone rejects the words of our Lord, they reject Wisdom. At the Last Supper, when Jesus informed the apostles He would be betrayed by someone reclining with Him around the table, one inquired as to who it might be. "Jesus answered, He it is, to whom I shall give a sop, when I have dipped *it*. And when he had dipped the sop, he gave *it* to Judas Iscariot, *the son* of Simon" (John 13:26 KJV). No doubt, that was an offer of grace.

> When the wisdom of God is not valued, grace also is not valued.

When wisdom is not valued and grace is rejected, tragic consequences follow. "And when he had dipped the sop, he gave *it* to Judas Iscariot, *the son* of Simon. And after the sop Satan entered into him" (John 13:26–27 KJV). It is unclear when Jesus last offered Judas grace, but it may have been when he spoke questioningly, "Judas, are you betraying the Son of Man with a kiss?" (Luke 22:48). Or maybe when Jesus asked, "Do what you came for, friend?" (Matthew 26:50). What we do know is when grace is rejected, wisdom is not valued, and the end result is destruction. Though he expressed regret, there's no indication that he truly repented. Instead, "he cast down the pieces of silver in the temple, and departed, and went and hanged himself" (Matthew 27:3–5 KJV).

IN CLOSING

How tragic! How terrible to reject the offer of grace, to reject Wisdom's blessings. Jesus is concerned about your future, and He is whispering in muted tones, encouraging you to make the right decision at every turn. Like the five wise virgins, we need to keep our eyes on the eastern horizon. "Watch therefore: for ye know not what hour your Lord doth come" (Matthew 24:42 KJV). But equally, we need to be aware of the offer of grace by our Lord on a daily basis. "Blessed are those who listen to me, watching daily at my doors, waiting at my doorway" (Proverbs 8:34).

> Jesus is concerned about your future, and He is whispering in muted tones, encouraging you to make the right decision at every turn.

How often we fail to connect the grace of God with the wisdom of God. How often we fail to see the bigger picture. When life gets tough, we may want to curse the day of our birth and withdraw from life, but the man Christ Jesus, feeling the full weight of humanity, facing the crucifixion the next day, demonstrated a different reaction: "Now is my soul troubled; and what shall I say? Father, save me from this hour: but for this cause came I unto this hour" (John 12:27 KJV). "But for this cause came I unto this hour." At that moment, as a man, he trusted the wisdom of God and submitted to the bigger picture—the purpose for which He came. "Who for the joy that was set before him endured the cross, despising the shame, and is set down at the right hand of the throne of God" (Hebrews 12:2 KJV). Without that, none of us could experience the grace of God under a new covenant. None of us would know the blessings of Wisdom!

LESSON 48

COME

PROVERBS 9:1-6

¹ *Wisdom has built her house; she has set up its seven pillars.* ² *She has prepared her meat and mixed her wine; she has also set her table.* ³ *She has sent out her servants, and she calls from the highest point of the city.* ⁴ *"Let all who are simple come to my house!" To those who have no sense she says,* ⁵ *"Come, eat my food and drink the wine I have mixed.* ⁶ *Leave your simple ways and you will live; walk in the way of insight.*

Wisdom is introduced here as a magnificent and beneficent queen. She has built a house with seven pillars. What is so significant about seven pillars? In the scriptures, the number seven represents perfection. Though we may see imperfection when we look at the people that make up God's house, God's house is a place of perfection. Charles Spurgeon beautifully described how this is possible:

> The church is not perfect, but woe to the man who finds pleasure in pointing out her imperfections. Christ loved his church, and let us do the same. I have no doubt that the Lord can see more fault in his church than I can; and I have equal confidence that he sees no fault at all. Because he covers her faults with his own love—that love which covers a

multitude of sins; and he removes all her defilement with that precious blood which washes away all the transgressions of his people. (cited in Jordan 2012)

> Though we may see imperfection when we look at the people that make up God's house, God's house is a place of perfection.

A PLACE OF PERFECTION

It is easy to see imperfection in one another, but covered by the blood, God's house is perfect. By making that statement, in no way is sin condoned. Jesus raised the bar for everyone: "Be ye therefore perfect, even as your Father which is in heaven is perfect" (Matthew 5:48 KJV). In fact, this perfect place—God's house—with imperfect people is the place where God's people are made perfect. It's the place where anyone can come, fall down on their knees, and plead, "What must I do to inherit eternal life?" And what is the Lord's response to that question? "If you want to be perfect, go, sell your possessions and give to the poor, and you will have treasure in heaven. Then come, follow me" (Matthew 19:21). Jesus is not telling everyone to sell everything they own and be destitute, but if there is anything you are not willing to give up for Him, you are not perfect and not fit for the kingdom. "You cannot serve both God and worldly riches" (Luke 16:13 NCV).

A WEDDING BANQUET PREPARED

Though Wisdom is introduced as a queen in this chapter of Proverbs, in previous lessons we discovered that wisdom is a characteristic of God and is inseparable from God. As a queen, "she has prepared her meat and mixed her wine; she has also set her table" (Proverbs 9:2). The description is reminiscent of a parable Jesus told His disciples, "The kingdom of heaven is like a king who prepared a wedding banquet for his son" (Matthew 22:2). I suspect that if a king (or a queen) were preparing a wedding banquet for a son, nothing would be left out. Put your imagination to work. What would the feast be like? You probably picture tables spread with sumptuous dishes. Now consider the meal our Lord would prepare. The table He has spread will feed the spirit of humans and not the flesh. When Jesus talked with the Samaritan woman at the well, He spoke of water that would quench her thirst forever. "Whosoever drinketh of the water that I shall give him shall never thirst; but the water that I shall give him shall be in him a well of water springing up into everlasting life" (John 4:14 KJV). In the same way, Jesus told His hearers that He is the Bread of Life that came down from heaven. Just as the we will thirst again if we partake only of natural water, we will hunger again if we partake only of natural food. Instead, if we partake of His meal, it is "food that endures to eternal life, which the Son of Man will give you" (John 6:27). Wisdom's sumptuous meal is a picture of the kingdom of God.

FOOD THAT WILL SATISFY THE SOUL

Paul went on to write, "In the kingdom of God, eating and drinking are not important. The important things are living right with God, peace, and joy in the Holy Spirit" (Romans 14:17 NCV). And Jesus instructed his hearers to hunger and thirst after righteousness. (See Matthew 5:6.) Only that can satisfy a hungry soul. In fact, Jesus put a stamp of guarantee on His meal by stating, "They shall be filled" (Matthew 5:6 KJV). And just as the food He prepares for us is beyond the physical realm, so is His kingdom, which is not some place. It's not even a church building; it is in us, and when we come together as "lively stones," we are the kingdom of God. (See Luke 17:20–21.)

> The kingdom of God is not some place. It's not even a church building; it is in us, and when we come together as "lively stones," we are the kingdom of God.

The kingdom of God is beyond measure, and when we recognize the value of it, we ought to treasure it. In Matthew 13, Jesus gave us two parables describing what our action should be when we find it:

- The kingdom of heaven is like unto treasure hid in a field; the which when a man hath found, he hideth, and for joy thereof goeth and selleth all that he hath, and buyeth that field. (Matthew 13:44 KJV)
- The kingdom of heaven is like unto a merchant man, seeking goodly pearls: Who, when he had found one pearl of great price, went and sold all that he had, and bought it. (Matthew 13:45–46 KJV)

In each parable, the one who found the treasured item sold everything he owned to obtain it. It may have seemed like a tremendously high price to pay, but it was the only thing each could do to obtain the treasure. And the reason was quite simple: they knew the value of the treasure in the field and the pearl of great price. The first man apparently sold his home and all of his belongings and purchased that piece a land. The second, likewise, sold everything he had to purchase something of greater value. When the first man walked away with a deed in his hand, his family and friends may have thought him to be the most foolish man in the entire world. What good is that old piece of land going to do for your family? How is commitment to that church going to improve your status in life? How is giving away a tenth of everything you make going to pay your bills? And when the second man stood with his destitute family on the street with an oyster's growth in his hand, he could have been the perfect target of ridicule. It's true that many times family, friends, and associates do not understand the value of the church—the kingdom of God. But I cannot emphasize enough the value of the church while upon the earth and of our eternal home in heaven. Jesus made it clear: "Every one that hath forsaken houses, or brethren, or sisters, or father, or mother, or wife, or children, or lands, for my name's sake, shall receive an hundredfold, and shall inherit everlasting life" (Matthew 19:29 KJV).

INVITATIONS SENT TO WHOSOEVER WILL

After Wisdom described the sumptuous meal prepared, she issued a call to whosoever will:

> She has sent out her servants, and she calls from the highest point of the city. "Let all who are simple come to my house!" To those who have no sense she says, "Come, eat my food and drink the wine I have mixed." (Proverbs 9:3–5)

The call is not to only a few; the call is to all. Jesus, likewise, spoke of a great banquet. The servant was instructed, "Go out into the highways and hedges, and compel *them* to come in, that my house may be filled" (Luke 14:23 KJV). His call was and is to whosoever will come.

Wisdom's message was to whosoever was willing, but there was and is a requirement if you want to join in around the banquet table: "Leave your simple ways and you will live; walk in the way of insight" (Proverbs 9:6). The call is the same today—you must leave the life of sin and walk in the way of righteousness and holiness. Paul issued a call to the Corinthians to leave behind a world of sin and live a life separated unto the Lord. In doing so, he used the Lord's words from the Old Testament:

> Come out from among them, and be ye separate, saith the Lord, and touch not the unclean *thing*; and I will receive you, And will be a Father unto you, and ye shall be my sons and daughters, saith the Lord Almighty. (2 Corinthians 6:17–18 KJV)

In order to partake of the wonderful promise to become sons and daughters of our heavenly Father, it is our responsibility to take whatever steps necessary to cleanse ourselves and perfect holiness out of reverence for Him. Some seem to be waiting for the Lord to force change in their lives, but notice, "Having therefore these promises, dearly beloved, let us cleanse ourselves from all filthiness of the flesh and spirit, perfecting holiness in the fear of God" (2 Corinthians 7:1 KJV). The responsibility lies with the individual believer. It is a choice. Jesus is a gentleman, and as such, He doesn't force His will on anyone. He has both authority and power, but when it comes to the call, we are granted the opportunity to accept or reject. For now, Jesus simply invites us to "Come:"

> Come unto me, all *ye* that labour and are heavy laden, and I will give you rest. Take my yoke upon you, and learn of me; for I am meek and lowly in heart: and ye shall find rest unto your souls. (Matthew 11:28–29 KJV)

As a result of the wonderful promise to become sons and daughters of the heavenly Father, it is our responsibility to take whatever steps necessary to cleanse ourselves and perfect holiness out of reverence for Him.

IN CLOSING

Near the end of the exilic period in Babylon, the LORD spoke through Isaiah to come home. At this point in time, the people and descendants of those who had been exiled were living a good life. King Cyrus of Persia had defeated the Babylonians. The Jewish exiles were granted land to stay in Babylon, and they were also allowed to be part of Commerce. Enough time had passed that other than a few, like Nehemiah, gave little thought as to what was happening in the Old Country. Though the LORD told their fathers to settle down in the land of captivity, obtain employment, and raise families, he did not intend for them to stay forever. So, like Wisdom, the LORD put forth a call through Isaiah for them to come home:

Come, all you who are thirsty, come to the waters; and you who have no money, come, buy and eat! Come, buy wine and milk without money and without cost. Why spend money on what is not bread, and your labor on what does not satisfy? Listen, listen to me, and eat what is good, and you will delight in the richest of fare. (Isaiah 55:1–2)

That sounds a lot like the call of Lady Wisdom, the queen of this chapter. And it sounds a lot like the call of our Lord Jesus to come and partake of the banquet He has prepared for whosoever will in the kingdom of God. Notice the meal has been purchased and prepared. It is without cost to the one who partakes, though a great expense to Him. Further, notice that it is soul food. "Eat what is good, and you will delight in the richest of fare" (Isaiah 55:2). The only expense to the hearer is to leave behind their sins and everything of this world that might separate them from the kingdom of God. The fare has been paid. Wisdom has built her house, the table has been set, and the food has been prepared. Come!

LESSON 49

CORRECTING AND ACCEPTING CORRECTION

PROVERBS 9:7-9

⁷ "Whoever corrects a mocker invites insults; whoever rebukes the wicked incurs abuse. ⁸ Do not rebuke mockers or they will hate you; rebuke the wise and they will love you. ⁹ Instruct the wise and they will be wiser still; teach the righteous and they will add to their learning.

The goal of reproof, or correction, must never be to rule over someone but to save that person from sin, hurt, or heartache. The scriptures speak of the importance of the man of God in your life, but many people never place themselves under pastoral authority because to do so would require submitting to correction. The scriptures emphasize that correction is essential to spiritual growth.

> The goal of reproof, or correction, must never be to rule over someone but to save that person from sin, hurt, or heartache.

Paul instructed Timothy that, when necessary, "correct, rebuke and encourage—with great patience and careful instruction" (2 Timothy 4:2). The purpose of godly discipline is to mold every child of God into a vessel that can be useful to the work of God.

THE SHIELD OF PRIDE

Why would Solomon write that whoever corrects a mocker can expect to receive an insult in return? What is in the hearts of those who resist correction? Probably pride. Pride is often found in concert with feelings of inferiority. When taken aside and corrected, the person with an inferiority complex believes others will perceive him or her as less of a person as a result of being corrected. Therefore, pride raises its ugly head as a defense mechanism. But is pride worth saving? Pride is of no value to other people; it is valued only by the one who possesses it.

> Pride is of no value to other people; it is valued only by the one who possesses it.

Being open to correction means making oneself vulnerable. Pride attempts to protect against vulnerability, but it's a very poor shield. When you take away the shield of pride and become vulnerable to correction, particularly if that correction is by the Word of God, spiritual development can occur. Ralph Waldo Emerson (1982) once stated, "Let me never fall into the vulgar mistake of dreaming that I am persecuted whenever I am contradicted" (p. 206). Take the risk and be vulnerable. Allow others to show you your blind spots.

THE FEAR OF TRUTH

Then there are those who close their eyes to truth. They are afraid of the truth because if they were to accept truth, they would have to change their ways. Often, you hear fear in the voices of those who try to prevent truth from being spoken. Recently, a group of scientists sought federal legislation to require the teaching of evolution in high schools because so many of their colleagues were defecting from the theory of evolution due to lack of evidence. The National Science Teachers Association (NSTA 2013) put forth the following statement:

> Some legislators and policy makers continue attempts to distort the teaching of evolution through mandates that would require teachers to teach evolution as "only a theory" or that would require a textbook or lesson on evolution to be preceded by a disclaimer. Regardless of the legal status of these mandates, they are bad educational policy. Such policies have the effect of intimidating teachers, which may result in the de-emphasis or omission of evolution. As a consequence, the public will only be further confused about the nature of scientific theories. Furthermore, if students learn less about evolution, science literacy itself will suffer.

Those who close their eyes to truth are afraid of the truth because if they were to accept truth, they would have to change their ways.

The possibility that God created everything is frightening to those who advocate evolution as the process by which all things came into existence. If there's a creator, they might have to acknowledge the existence of an afterlife. Further, they might have to acknowledge a tangible heaven, requirements to get there, and consequences for sin. Ironically, those who claim to seek truth but eliminate the possibility of a creator have closed their eyes to truth, and they will do whatever is necessary to keep God out of the classroom, even if it requires legislation.

Once, Jehoshaphat, king of Judah, foolishly went to visit Ahab, king of Israel. The scriptures state, "Jehoshaphat the king of Judah came down to the king of Israel" (1 Kings 22:2 KJV). It's interesting to note that Israel was north of Judah, but it says he went "down" to visit Ahab. When he went "down" to visit Ahab, he ended up joining himself to Ahab. You may believe you are moving up in the world by leaving the security of God's church to find fame among the stars, but any time you leave the safety of God's kingdom, you go *down*. You might believe wealth will take you to the top, but if that is your goal, more than likely, the love of money will take you down to the pit. Listen to the conversation between a king who still desired to hear from God and one who had closed his eyes to truth:

> Jehoshaphat said, *Is there* not here a prophet of the LORD besides, that we might enquire of him? And the king of Israel said unto Jehoshaphat, *There is* yet one man, Micaiah the son of Imlah, by whom we may enquire of the LORD: but I hate him; for he doth not prophesy good concerning me, but evil. (1 Kings 22:7–8 KJV)

> You may believe you are moving up in the world by leaving the security of God's church to find fame among the stars, but any time you leave the safety of God's kingdom, you go down.

Ahab knew that truth was in the mouth of the prophet of the LORD, but he didn't like what he heard when the prophet spoke. Reluctantly, Ahab called for the prophet, but when he arrived, Micaiah taunted Ahab by encouraging him to go into battle and assuring him a great victory. Ahab demanded that Micaiah tell him the truth, which he proceeded to do. Micaiah declared, "I saw all Israel scattered upon the hills, as sheep that have not a shepherd" (1 Kings 22:17 KJV). Closing his eyes to truth, Ahab had the prophet thrown into prison. Ahab recognized when the prophet didn't tell him the truth but put him in prison when he did tell him the truth. Closing his eyes to truth, he plunged headlong toward his death.

On another occasion in the history of backslidden Israel, not just the king but the religious leaders became upset at hearing the Word of the LORD: "Then Amaziah the priest of Bethel sent to Jeroboam king of Israel, saying, Amos hath conspired against thee in the midst of the house of Israel: the land is not able to bear all his words" (Amos 7:10 KJV). The words the land could not bear were the words of God. Truth sometimes upsets the status quo.

Truth sometimes upsets the status quo.

There are times when speaking the truth results in suffering. Regardless, we must "have nothing to do with the fruitless deeds of darkness, but rather expose them" (Ephesians 5:11). During the transition period between the Old and New Testaments, John the Baptist was not afraid to confront and rebuke King Herod for taking his brother Philip's wife from him and marrying her. John declared to his face, "It is not lawful for thee to have her" (Matthew 14:4 KJV). This truth did not sit well with Herod, and he imprisoned him. He would have put him to death, except he feared the people regarded John as a prophet. (See Matthew 14:1–5.) John the Baptist stands out as one who was willing to stand for truth, even when it resulted in suffering and eventually death. We too must be willing to suffer for truth because there is a day coming when we will stand in judgment alongside those who "did not love their lives but were willing to die" (Revelation 12:11 NLV).

WISE PEOPLE ACCEPT CORRECTION

Wise people recognize they are fallible and in need of guidance and correction. It's not always convenient to make those corrections, but as long as humans live upon the earth, corrections will be necessary. Being confronted for wrongdoing can be uncomfortable, but corrective action is what turns a sinner into a saint. In his first letter to the Corinthians, the apostle Paul strongly rebuked the church for sin in their midst—sin that that they laughed and boasted about. When he wrote his second letter to that church, he was able to commend their repentant response to his rebuke:

> See what this godly sorrow has produced in you: what earnestness, what eagerness to clear yourselves, what indignation, what alarm, what longing, what concern, what readiness to see justice done. At every point you have proved yourselves to be innocent in this matter. (2 Corinthians 7:11)

When rebuked, the Corinthians accepted correction and made the necessary changes. As a result, their sinful lives became past tense, and they became new creatures in Christ Jesus.

> Wise people recognize they are fallible and need guidance and correction.

Thus, it is essential that we accept correction and rebuke. Unfortunately, sometimes we allow our inferiority to get in the way. The little person within rises up, becomes recalcitrant, and allows pride to dominate, resisting correction at all cost. Peter was a great man and could have allowed his greatness to go to his head. His position of authority granted by Jesus could have led him to believe he was infallible, yet he stands out as one of the greatest examples of how to accept rebuke and correction. Paul described a time he confronted Peter:

> But when Peter came to Antioch, I had to oppose him to his face, for what he did was very wrong. When he first arrived, he ate with the Gentile believers, who were not circumcised. But afterward, when some friends of James came, Peter wouldn't eat with the Gentiles anymore. He was afraid of criticism from these people who insisted on the necessity of

circumcision. As a result, other Jewish believers followed Peter's hypocrisy, and even Barnabas was led astray by their hypocrisy.

When I saw that they were not following the truth of the gospel message, I said to Peter in front of all the others, "Since you, a Jew by birth, have discarded the Jewish laws and are living like a Gentile, why are you now trying to make these Gentiles follow the Jewish traditions?" (Galatians 2:11–14 NLT)

> The little person within rises up, becomes recalcitrant, and allows pride to dominate, resisting correction at all cost.

What did Peter do as a result of this rebuke? Go off in a huff? Exercise his authority as the man with the keys? Have Paul stripped of his apostleship? From all appearances, Peter acknowledged his error, repented, and went on without denigrating Paul. This is supported by what he had to say about Paul in his second epistle: "Our beloved brother Paul also according to the wisdom given unto him hath written unto you" (2 Peter 3:15 KJV). "Beloved brother Paul"—that's how we ought to feel toward the person who corrects our wayward ways.

THE POWER OF THE WORD

The Word of God has power to correct our erring ways. It is "quick, and powerful, and sharper than any twoedged sword, piercing even to the dividing asunder of soul and spirit, and of the joints and marrow, and *is* a discerner of the thoughts and intents of the heart" (Hebrews 4:12 KJV). If we are to grow in God, it is essential that we recognize corrective authority of God in the preached Word. We need to be like the Thessalonian church. When they heard the Word of God preached, they "received *it* not *as* the word of men, but as it is in truth, the word of God" (1 Thessalonians 2:13 KJV).

Paul encouraged Timothy, "Preach the word; be instant in season, out of season; reprove, rebuke, exhort with all longsuffering and doctrine" (2 Timothy 4:2 KJV). Return to the Old Testament, and you see the impact of the Word of God when spoken into the life of David after he had gone astray. That living active Word of God stopped the king in his tracks and caused him to run for an altar: "And Nathan said to David, Thou art the man ... And David said unto Nathan, I have sinned against the Lord" (2 Samuel 12:7, 13 KJV).

It is so much better to be rebuked, whether by the Word of God or by a friend, than to continue down a path toward destruction. At some point in David's life, possibly years after Nathan rebuked him, he wrote, "Let a righteous man strike me—that is kindness; let him rebuke me—that is oil on my head" (Psalm 141:5). And Solomon acknowledged, "Faithful *are* the wounds of a friend; but the kisses of an enemy *are* deceitful" (Proverbs 27:6 KJV).

> It is so much better to be rebuked, whether by the Word of God or by a friend, than to continue down a path toward destruction.

WHEN AND HOW TO CORRECT

Considering what we have learned up to this point, there must be a time to correct and a time to refrain from correcting. "Whoever corrects a mocker invites insult; whoever rebukes the wicked incurs abuse. Do not rebuke mockers or they will hate you" (Proverbs 9:7–8). Who wants to take the risk of correcting someone who is going to insult you? Who wants to be hated for lovingly correcting someone? On the other hand, those who are wise will love you for caring enough to correct them. "Rebuke the wise and they will love you" (Proverbs 9:8).

A good rule of thumb is to not rebuke when an explanation will do. "Instruct the wise and they will be wiser still; teach the righteous and they will add to their learning" (Proverbs 9:9). An excellent example of this was Priscilla and Aquila's approach to Apollos: "[Apollos] began to speak boldly in the synagogue. When Priscilla and Aquila heard him, they invited him to their home and explained to him the way of God more adequately" (Acts 18:26). This instruction amounted to correction. Apollos added to what he already knew and went on to become great worker in the harvest field of the Lord. Almost immediately, Apollos was inducted into Christian ministry and became a close cohort of Peter and Paul. (See 1 Corinthians 3:6, 3:22, 4:6.)

> A good rule of thumb is to not rebuke when an explanation will do.

When administering correction, love must prevail— "Reprove, rebuke, exhort with all longsuffering and doctrine" (2 Timothy 4:2 KJV). And when we need correction, our love for the Lord will help us to be grateful toward the one caring enough to correct us.

IN CLOSING

If you are a man, and your pastor calls you aside to speak to you about the way he saw you mistreat your wife, and he corrects you using the Word of God as a guide, are you going to accept it? If you are a lady, and the preacher delivers a sermon or Bible study on the application of modesty from the scriptures, are you going to go away in a huff, or are you willing to submit to the Word of God? If you are a young person, do you mock the prophet, or are you thankful someone cares enough to tell you the truth?

Everyone needs correction. Pray that God will send people into your life who will correct you and keep you on the path of righteousness. If you have a tendency to get offended when someone points out your mistakes, make a conscious choice to repent and to forgive. Recognize that they are sent by God to keep you on the highway of holiness—the narrow path to the celestial city. Purposefully pray the following prayer: "Create in me a clean heart, O God; and renew a right spirit within me" (Psalm 51:10 KJV).

LESSON 50

A LONG LIFE

PROVERBS 9:10-12

¹⁰ "The fear of the LORD is the beginning of wisdom, and knowledge of the Holy One is understanding. ¹¹ For through wisdom your days will be many, and years will be added to your life. ¹² If you are wise, your wisdom will reward you; if you are a mocker, you alone will suffer."

"The Fear of the LORD is the Beginning of Wisdom" (Proverbs 9:10). The definition of the fear of the LORD is "reverence" or "a deep respect or awe." The scriptures teach that there are rewards for reverence:

- In the fear of the LORD *is* strong confidence: and his children shall have a place of refuge. (Proverbs 14:26 KJV)
- The fear of the LORD *is* a fountain of life, to depart from the snares of death. (Proverbs 14:27 KJV)
- By the fear of the LORD *men* depart from evil. (Proverbs 16:6 KJV)
- The LORD is exalted, for he dwells on high; he will fill Zion with justice and righteousness. He will be the sure foundation for your times, a rich store of salvation and wisdom and knowledge; the fear of the LORD is the key to this treasure. (Isaiah 33:5–6)

Reverence for God should grow with your knowledge of Him. It has been said that familiarity breeds contempt, but that should not be true concerning your relationship with God. Familiarity with the Lord should increase your awe of the holy, rather than reduce it. However, over the last century, there has been a significant decrease in respect for the sacred. In the past, no man would have considered entering a house of worship without first removing his hat. And arriving late for service with coffee in hand as though attending a business meeting would not have been tolerated. But this is not the result of familiarity with our heavenly Father; it's ignorance of the expectations of a holy God. Church members need to regain a reverence for the sacred. It's one thing for those who do not claim to know the Lord to lack reverence for holy things, but that should not be true for God's people. Lack of respect for the sacred by the world is not nearly as bad as irreverence by the church. Irreverence shows a disregard for God and His kingdom.

> Familiarity with God should increase our awe for the holy, not reduce it.

Unfortunately, many have lost out with God because they never had, or did not maintain, a proper respect for the sacred. The sons of Aaron provide an example:

> Aaron's sons Nadab and Abihu each took an incense burner and put burning coals and incense in it. Then in the LORD's presence they offered this unauthorized fire. A fire flashed from the LORD and burned them, and they died in the presence of the LORD. (Leviticus 10:1–2 GW)

DIMINISHED RESPECT

Abraham Lincoln (1838) noted that diminished respect leads to anarchy:

Let every man remember that to violate the law is to trample on the blood of his father and to tear the character of his own and his children's liberty ... Bad laws, if they exist, should be repealed as soon as possible; still, while they continue in force, they should be religiously observed.

The year was 1979, and East High School in Madison, Wisconsin, probably was not the place where you would have wanted your kids to go to school. That was the year Milton McPike, former pro-football player with the San Francisco 49ers, became school principal. With discipline and compassion, he turned a chaotic environment into a place of learning. Under his leadership, East High gained a reputation for academic achievement, and in 1989, it was recognized as a National School of Excellence. Just as the fear of the LORD is the beginning of wisdom and knowledge, McPike believed that respect is where learning begins.

His first day, he was greeted by five fire trucks and an ambulance at the school's entrance. "False alarm," explained a firefighter. "We get these all the time here."

Inside, McPike found boarded-up windows, and floors covered with garbage and spit from kids who chewed tobacco. Students hung out in the stairwells, verbally harassing anyone who walked past.

McPike immediately prohibited chewing tobacco and personal stereos, closed off certain stairwells and forbade the wearing of hats in the building. "Manners are where learning starts."

At first, students didn't believe McPike would enforce his rules. Ten of them were in for a surprise when he found them spitting tobacco on the floor. "Gentlemen, you've got a choice," he said. "You can mop these floors or face suspensions."

"You don't have enough mops for ten of us," one teenager replied smugly. Minutes later, McPike and several custodians returned with ten mops—and ten buckets too.

But the next time McPike saw the ten young men during a class break, he greeted them warmly, learned their names and asked about their girlfriends. McPike, the kids began to see, wasn't just a rule-maker in a suit; he was more like a father. For many of them, he was the only father figure they had. (Chazen 1992, p. 90)

DEVELOPING RESPECT FOR THE THINGS OF GOD

Songwriter Ira F. Stanphill (1968) wrote the following:

> Happiness is to know the Savior,
> Living a life within His favor,
> Having a change in my behavior,
> Happiness is the Lord.

Truly, to know the Savior produces happiness, and to know the Savior will result in a change in your behavior. Unfortunately, we are living in a day of convenient Christianity. If your coworkers do not know that you are a Christian, your Christianity may be too comfortable. To be a disciple of Jesus is to deny yourself and take up the cross (Matthew 16:24), to endure persecution (John 15:20), and to be willing to give up the comforts of home and family (Luke 9:58–62) rather than to deny the Word of God. It is a willingness to give up anything that stands between you and serving the Lord (Matthew 19:21) and a willingness to be crucified with Christ (Galatians 2:20).

> If your coworkers do not know that you are a Christian, your Christianity may be too comfortable.

LORIN BRADBURY, PH.D.

Solomon reminded us, "The fear of the LORD is the beginning of wisdom, and knowledge of the Holy One is understanding" (Proverbs 9:10). It is the beginning of wisdom. Developing an understanding of the fear of the LORD doesn't just happen. It requires instruction in the ways of the Holy One; it requires consistent maintenance of those teachings and mores; and it requires discipline and correction when those teachings and mores are violated. It is an ongoing process.

IN CLOSING

Do you want to live a long life? Wisdom offers a free life extension. Here is a general rule from the God of heaven—"Through wisdom your days will be many, and years will be added to your life" (Proverbs 9:11). The Lord extends life for showing respect for authority, honoring parents (Ephesians 6:1–3), and even for dispensing mercy to other creatures in His kingdom:

> If you come across a bird's nest beside the road, either in a tree or on the ground, and the mother is sitting on the young or on the eggs, do not take the mother with the young. You may take the young, but be sure to let the mother go, so that it may go well with you and you may have a long life. (Deuteronomy 22:6–7)

> The Lord extends life for showing respect for authority, honoring parents (Ephesians 6:1–3), and even for dispensing mercy to other creatures in His kingdom.

Therefore, if you fear and love God and you walk in the ways of wisdom, you will live longer. It is only reasonable that by avoiding the hard life and risky behaviors of sinners, by avoiding the sword of justice-avenging crimes, by avoiding the accidents that often claim the foolish, and by avoiding diseases associated with certain sins, your life span will be extended.

But there is another factor in shortening one's life beyond the natural consequences of folly; there is the sovereign judgment of God—the right of God to determine your life span. It will not matter how well you eat, your daily exercise routine, or the skill of your physicians; God can shorten your life upon this earth as punishment for ungodliness. Solomon wrote, "The lamp of the wicked shall be put out" (Proverbs 13:9 KJV). Who shall put it out? The LORD shall put it out.

So be wise. Fear the LORD and exercise wisdom. You will certainly live better, you will live longer, and eventually you will get to spend eternity with your heavenly Father.

LESSON 51

DECEPTION

PROVERBS 9:13-18

¹³ Folly is an unruly woman; she is simple and knows nothing. ¹⁴ She sits at the door of her house, on a seat at the highest point of the city, ¹⁵ calling out to those who pass by, who go straight on their way, ¹⁶ "Let all who are simple come to my house!" To those who have no sense she says, ¹⁷ "Stolen water is sweet; food eaten in secret is delicious!" ¹⁸ But little do they know that the dead are there, that her guests are deep in the realm of the dead.

The ninth chapter of Proverbs describes two women—Wisdom and Folly. It should be noted they both sit in high places. R. F. Horton (1903) entitled the chapter he wrote on this text, "Two Voices in the High Places in the City" (p. 122). This lesson focuses on the evil woman, Folly. Folly deceitfully propositions, "Stolen water is sweet; food eaten in secret is delicious!" (Proverbs 9:17). As one writer described it, "She suggests that secrecy and illicitness will lend a charm to what in itself is a sorry delight" (Horton 1903, p. 132).

Folly always attempts to make sin appear glamorous. Adam and Eve were deceived when they listened to the serpent, and their life was never again the same. David was deceived when he yielded to the lust of the flesh and the lust of the eyes. The fruit of his deception plagued him the rest of his life. The son born of that illicit relationship died, some of his children rebelled against him, and he lived with the knowledge that "my sin is always before me" (Psalm 51:3).

> Folly always attempts to make sin appear glamorous.

There was an unknown prophet who listened to humans instead of God. He is simply known as, "The man of God who was disobedient unto the word of the LORD" (1 Kings 13:26 KJV). And the Word of God describes the fruit of his deception, "The LORD hath delivered him unto the lion, which hath torn him, and slain him, according to the word of the LORD" (1 Kings 13:26 KJV).

Then there was the failure to ask God concerning important decisions. Joshua, as great a man as he was, listened to the wrong voices, and he and his colleagues were deceived into making a covenant with long-term consequences. The Word of God describes how easily they were deceived, "The Israelites sampled their provisions but did not inquire of the LORD. Then Joshua made a treaty of peace with them to let them live, and the leaders of the assembly ratified it by oath" (Joshua 9:14–15). The LORD was waiting, and He would have exposed this lie if Joshua and his men had just taken time to ask Him. Failing to pray before signing an agreement, they compromised with the enemy—a failure with long-term consequences.

A MATTER OF THE HEART

Deception is much more a matter of the heart than of the mind. Josh McDowell (1979) described how he was counseling a person who said she could not believe in Christianity because it was not historical or factual. "She had convinced everyone that she had searched and found profound intellectual problems [with Christianity] as a result of her university studies. One after another would try to persuade her intellectually and to answer her many accusations" (p. 11). Professor McDowell (1979) listened and then asked her several questions. "Within 30 minutes she admitted she had fooled everyone, and that she developed these intellectual doubts in order to excuse her moral life" (p. 11).

> Deception is much more a matter of the heart than of the mind.

A student at a New England university claimed that intellectually he had problems with Christianity and therefore would not acknowledge Jesus as his Savior. McDowell (1979) then asked, "If I demonstrate to you that the New Testament is one of the most reliable pieces of literature of antiquity, will you believe?" (p. 11). The student retorted, "No!" His problem was not with his head but with his heart.

A young lawyer asserted that if anyone could show him that Jesus Christ arose from the dead; he would believe in Him. A minister gathered all of the evidence together and presented it to him.

A week later when the young lawyer returned the material, the minister asked, "What is your conclusion?"

"I'm convinced that Jesus Christ arose; the evidence is indisputable," was his reply.

"Will you put your trust in Him then?" the minister asked.

"No, sir!" the young man answered. "You see, I discovered that the problems I have with Christ are not in my head but in my heart. My moral life would have to be altered if I trusted Christ."

MAKING EXCUSES FOR SIN

Excuses for not serving God are varied and abundant. When I lived in Anchorage, I conducted nursing home services at Glenmore Nursing Home. Prior to each service, my wife and I would go around the home and ask patients if they would like us to wheel them to the room were the service would be conducted. It was interesting to hear the excuses some made:

- I'm too tired.
- I think I have company coming tonight.
- I'm too busy.
- Not tonight. Maybe next time.

None of the residents had anything else productive going on at that moment. Others who did attend the services were easily found by family members who came to visit while they were attending services, and often they would join in worship. In truth, many had been making excuses all of their lives for not going to church and not serving God, and it had become a habit. Jesus taught a parable in Luke 14:16–20 that included three lame excuses:

- I just bought a field, and I must go and check it out. Please excuse me.
- I just bought five yoke of oxen, and I'm on my way to try them out. Please excuse me.
- I just got married, so I can't come.

And just as people make excuses for not serving God, some who claim to serve God make all kinds of excuses for not living a righteous life. Below are some of the more common excuses for infidelity:

- God wants me to be happy. I can't be happy married to her. So I'm leaving … and I know He'll understand.
- There was a time when this might have been considered immoral. But not today. The Lord gave me this desire and he wants me to enjoy it.
- Look, nobody's perfect. So I got in deeper than I planned. Sure it's a little shady, but what's grace all about anyway?
- Me? Ask forgiveness? That's ridiculous! My relationship with God is much deeper than shallow techniques like that.
- Hey, if it feels good, have at it! Life's too short to sweat small stuff. We're not under law, you know.
- So what if a little hanky-panky … a little fun 'n' games goes on? What's life about without some spice and risk? All those 'thou shalt nots' are unrealistic. (Swindoll 1983, p. 245)

If any of those statements are true, then what does it mean to be holy? Israel was called to live as a distinctively separate people. At the core of holiness is the fundamental premise that not all human behavior is acceptable to God. We must restrain ourselves from behaviors and attitudes that God deems unholy, including how we live, act, dress, think, or speak. He is interested in everything about us, and His Word communicates how we can live to please Him. The LORD is emphatic, "Ye shall be holy; for I *am* holy" (Leviticus 11:44 KJV).

> At the core of holiness is the fundamental premise that not all human behavior is acceptable to God.

If any of those excuses justifying infidelity are true, what does it mean to be pure? Dinesh D'Souza (2007), author of the best seller *What's So Great about Christianity*, put forth the following statement concerning purity of heart:

> Christ says in the Sermon on the Mount, "Blessed are the pure in heart, for they shall see God." What counts for God is not only our external conduct but also our inward disposition. Holiness does not mean merely performing the obligatory rituals on the outside; it means staying pure on the inside. (p. 304)

The issue of grace is often raised when people want to justify their sin, but what do the scriptures say about grace? Does God turn a blind eye to sin? What about the excuse noted above, "Look, nobody's perfect. So I got in deeper than I planned. Sure, it's a little shady, but what's grace all about anyway?" If grace doesn't cover us when we are less than perfect, than what does it do?

Paul answers that question with a couple of rhetorical questions: "What shall we say then? Shall we continue in sin, that grace may abound? God forbid" (Romans 6:1-2 KJV). God forbid that we use grace as a coverup for sin. Before you sin and before you use grace as an excuse for sinning, look to the cross! Grace wasn't cheap; we must not cheapen it by using it to excuse our sins.

TURNING A BLIND EYE TO SIN

Open your Bible to Revelation 23:1 and read along. "Thus, it matters not what ye do as long as it affects only thy self. Therefore, if it feels good do it." Well, if you opened your Bible to Revelation 23:1, you found it doesn't exist, and neither do many of today's doctrines that are soft on sin. In fact,

> If any man shall take away from the words of the book of this prophecy, God shall take away his part out of the book of life, and out of the holy city, and *from* the things which are written in this book. (Revelation 22:19 KJV)

If a preacher turns a blind eye to sin in his preaching and teaching, he is committing the sin of taking words away from the Book.

If a preacher turns a blind eye to sin in his preaching and teaching, he is committing the sin of taking words away from the Book.

Where have all the sinners gone? Today, we seem to have the hope or feeling that when someone dies, death will somehow make a transformation of that person. Even though the deceased lived an overtly sinful life, people seek comfort in acting as if that person will end up in heaven with God for all eternity. The following story illustrates this well:

> There was a preacher who was called very early one Sunday morning by a member of his church, asking

him to go and tell his sister that her husband had just been killed in an auto accident.

The man who had died and his wife were not members of his church, but her brother couldn't get hold of their minister, so he asked his own preacher to go and break the news to her. So, at around 2:00 in the morning this preacher went to tell her of her husband's death. It was not until the next day that the preacher learned that the accident had occurred while the man was rushing home from having spent most of the night with his current mistress.

Well, the preacher went to the funeral, and heard the man's minister preach him right into heaven. He lifted him up as a pillar in the community, a man of integrity and honesty and with great faith. He said he was just sure that this man was now walking side by side with Jesus on the streets of gold. (cited in Wimpey 2015)

In writing to the Corinthians, Paul warned them, "Do not be deceived" (1 Corinthians 6:9). And his reason is simply this: "Wrongdoers will not inherit the kingdom of God" (1 Corinthians 6:9). And then he proceeds to define what he means by the wicked: "Those who indulge in sexual sin, or who worship idols, or commit adultery, or are male prostitutes, or practice homosexuality, or are thieves, or greedy people, or drunkards, or are abusive, or cheat people" (1 Corinthians 6:9–10 NLT). Consider the man in our illustration above. Did he have time to repent of his sins and make things right with his wife? Probably not. In fact, repentance is more than being sorry we were caught in our sin. It describes a change in lifestyle.

AMEND YOUR LIFE!

The Geneva Bible captures this sense of repenting as more than being sorry but of requiring a demonstration of a change in lifestyle. For example, after John the Baptist was put in prison, "Jesus began to preach, and to say, Amend your lives, for the kingdom of heaven is at hand" (Matthew 4:17 GNV). Similarly, when Paul was testifying before King Agrippa, he explained how the Lord Jesus had called him to preach the Gospel, and to whomever he went, he was to preach "that they should repent and turn to God, and do works worthy amendment of life" (Acts 26:20 GNV).

It's unfortunate that the ministry all too often turns a blind eye to sin and in the process leads people down the dark path toward eternal damnation. Consider someone who dies, obviously involved in one of the sins listed by Paul in 1 Corinthians 6. How does the minister conduct a funeral under such conditions? To talk about how that person is now walking on the streets of gold or to assure loved ones they will see that person again in heaven is to disregard the Word of God and substitute wishful thinking for God's words. I'm not advocating being so callous as to add to the suffering of parents, spouses, and other loved ones by judging the person and putting him or her in hell. But neither should we turn our back on God and give a false assurance to those same loved ones.

> It's unfortunate that the ministry all too often turns a blind eye to sin and in the process leads people down the dark path toward eternal damnation.

IN CLOSING

A prime example of modern deception is the acceptance of LGBTQ lifestyles as alternate lifestyles, rather than recognizing them as sins. However, deception is not limited to those who put their stamp of approval on such behaviors. All too commonly, husbands justify cheating on their wives, wives justify leaving their husbands, and singles justify living together unmarried.

Deception has filled the modern Christian church. Christianity has moved in the direction of accepting all doctrines as equal. But all doctrines are not created equal. Truth is not based on society's likes and dislikes. Truth is a constant.

It only makes sense that not all religious teachings can be true. They could all be wrong, but they cannot all be right. Man-made doctrines are equivalent to fig leaves when it comes to covering sin. The songwriter wrote, "What can wash away my sins? Nothing but the blood of Jesus." And Jesus stated emphatically, "He that entereth not by the door into the sheepfold, but climbeth up some other way, the same is a thief and a robber" (John 10:1 KJV). No thieves or robbers makes it into the kingdom of God unless, or until, the blood of the Lamb has cleansed them. And that is the key!

Paul warned the Corinthian believers about deceiving themselves into thinking that everyone goes to heaven. He gave a list of relatively common sins and then declared, "Do you not know that wrongdoers will not inherit the kingdom of God? Do not be deceived" (1 Corinthians 6:9–10). So, who will be in heaven? Those who have been born again— those who have been washed, sanctified, and justified in the name of the Lord Jesus Christ. (See 1 Corinthians 6:11.)

There is no need to be deceived. Jesus will save your soul and transform your life, if you will allow Him. The deceiver would like you to believe the lie that you can go to heaven just as you are. If that doesn't work, he will attempt to make you believe you cannot change. That also is a lie from the pit of hell. Do not be deceived, because "by his divine power, God has given us everything we need for living a godly life" (2 Peter 1:3 NLT).

Instead of listening to the voice of Folly, pay attention to the cry of Wisdom. She calls from the highest point in the city, "Come to my house; I have a delicious satisfying meal prepared for you." (See Proverbs 9:5.) And when you get up from her table, there will be no regrets.

REFERENCES

Anonymous. 1976. "Seven years later." *Pentecostal Herald,* 51, no. 2, February 1976, 16–17.

Ballmann, R. E. 1991. *How Your Family Can Flourish: A Guide to Christian Living in a Post-Christian Culture.* Wheaton, IL: Crossway Books.

Barnes, A. 1872. *Notes, Explanatory and Practical on the First Epistle of Paul to the Corinthians.* New York: Harper & Brothers, Publishers.

Barton, F. M. 1914. *The Expositor and Current Anecdotes* 16, no. 1, 454.

Bell, R. J. 2012. *Your Pastor Needs This Book: 5 Huge Mistakes You Can Help Your Pastor Avoid.* Four Bells Publishing.

Bennett, W. J., ed. 1993. *The Book of Virtues.* Norwalk, CT: Easton Press.

Bonhoeffer, D. 1955. *Temptation.* London: SCM Press LTD.

Bounds, E. M. 1990. *The Complete Works of E. M. Bounds on Prayer.* Grand Rapids, MI: Baker Books.

Bridges, C. 1846/1968. *A Commentary on Proverbs.* Carlisle, PA: Banner of Truth Trust.

Brown, G. ed. "True mother's love." *The Vision,* May 8, 1977, 1–2.

Brown, G. ed. 1976. *Word Aflame Adult Teacher: A Seven Year through the Bible Series.* Hazelwood, MO: Pentecostal Publishing House.

Center for Disease Control. 2013. *Incidence, Prevalence, and Cost of Sexually Transmitted Infections in the United States.* CDC, http://www.cdc.gov/std/stats/sti-estimates-fact-sheet-feb-2013.pdf

Center for Disease Control. 2014. *Unmarried Childbearing.* CDC, http://www.cdc.gov/nchs/fastats/unmarried-childbearing.htm

Chazin, S. "One Kid at a Time." *Reader's Digest,* 140, No. 841, May 1992, 89–93.

Davis, R.M. ed. 2013. *Word Aflame Adult Teacher: Celebration Series.* Hazelwood, MO: Pentecostal Publishing House.

Davis, R.M. ed. 2012. *Word Aflame Adult Teacher: Celebration Series.* Hazelwood, MO: Pentecostal Publishing House.

Davis, R. M. ed. 1995. *Word Aflame Adult Teacher: Century Series.* Hazelwood, MO: Pentecostal Publishing House

Davis, R. M. ed. 1990. *Word Aflame Adult Teacher: Silver Scripture Series.* Hazelwood, MO: Pentecostal Publishing House.

Doan, E. 1968. *The New Speaker's Sourcebook.* Grand Rapids, MI: Zondervan.

Dobson, J. C. 1980. *Straight Talk to Men and Their Wives.* Waco, TX: Word Books.

Dobson, J. 1975. *What Wives Wish Their Husbands Knew about Women.* Wheaton, IL: Tyndale Publishers, Inc.

Dowland, S. "The Modesto Manifesto." *Christian History,* no. 111, 2014, 40.

Drummond, H. 2007. *The Greatest Thing in the World: Walking in Love.* Mechanicsburg, PA: Executive Books.

D'Souza, D. 2007. *What's So Great about Christianity.* Washington, D. C.: Regnery Publishing, Inc.

Duvall, L. 1989. "When the Spirit of the Lord." *Petra Praise: The Rock Cries Out.* DaySpring Records. 1989. track 9. https://www. metrolyrics.com/i-will-celebrate-when-the-spirit-of-the-lord-lyrics-petra.html

Eisenhower, William D. "Fearing God: Those Who Have Never Trembled from Head to Toe Will Never Know God's Perfect Love." *Christianity Today,* 30, No. 2, March 7, 1986, pp 32–34.

Elliot, E. 2001. *Keeping the Peace.* Accessed July 11, 2001. http://www. gospelcom.net/bttb/gateway/printer.htm

Emerson, R. W. 1982. *Emerson in His Journals.* Cambridge, MA: Harvard University Press.

Eyre, L. & Eyre, R. 1984. *Teaching Your Children Responsibility.* New York, NY: Simon and Shuster.

Farmer, K. A. 1991. *Proverbs and Ecclesiastes: Who Knows What Is Good?* Grand Rapids, MI: Eerdmans Publishing.

Finney, C. G. 2005. *Skeletons of a Course of Theological Lectures: Volume 3.* Fenwick, MI: Alethea in Heart.

Guttmacher Institute. 2013. *Unintended Pregnancy in the United States.* Guttmacher Institute, http://www.guttmacher.org/pubs/ FB-Unintended-Pregnancy-US.html

Hall, J. L. ed. 1980. *Word Aflame Adult Teacher.* Hazelwood, MO: Word Aflame Publications.

Hall, J. L. ed. 1977. *Word Aflame Adult Teacher.* Hazelwood, MO: Word Aflame Publications.

Harney, K. G. 2005. *Seismic Shifts.* Grand Rapids, MI: Zondervan.

Henry, M. n.d. *Matthew Henry's Commentary: vol. 1.* Old Tappan, NJ: Fleming H. Revell

Henry, M. n.d. *Matthew Henry's Commentary: vol. 3*. Old Tappan, NJ: Fleming H. Revell

Henry, M. n.d. *Matthew Henry's Commentary: vol. 6*. Old Tappan, NJ: Fleming H. Revell

Hester, D. J. 1985. *The Vance Havner Quote Book: Sparking Gems from the Most Quoted Preacher in America*. Grand Rapids, MI: Baker Book House.

Horton, R. F. 1903. *The Expositor's Bible: The Book of Proverbs*. New York: A. C. Armstrong and Son.

Hubbard, D. A. 1989. *The Communicator's Commentary: Proverbs*. Dallas: Word.

Hughes, R. K. 1991. *Disciplines of a Godly Man*. Wheaton, IL: Crossway Books.

Ingersoll, R. G. 1888. *Selections from His Oratory and Writings*. Accessed May 27, 2019. https://www.bartleby.com/400/prose/1827.html

Ironside, H. A. 1908. *Proverbs*. Neptune, NJ: Loizeaux Brothers.

Johnson, D. G. ed. 2011. *Word Aflame Adult Teacher: Celebration Series*. Hazelwood, MO: Word Aflame Publications.

Johnson, D. G. ed. 2010. *Word Aflame Adult Teacher: Celebration Series*. Hazelwood, MO: Word Aflame Publications.

Johnson, D. G. ed. 2009. *Word Aflame Adult Teacher: Church Alive Series*. Hazelwood, MO: Word Aflame Publications.

Johnson, D. G. ed. 2004. *Word Aflame Adult Teacher: Expository Series*. Hazelwood, MO: Word Aflame Publications.

Jordan, C. 2013. *New Life Blog. Charles Spurgeon Quotes—On the Church*. Accessed July 15, 2014. http://pastorchrisjordan.wordpress.com/2013/01/10/charles-spurgeon-quotes-on-the-church/

Kidner, D. 1964. *Proverbs: An Introduction and Commentary.* Downers Grove, IL: Inter-varsity Press.

Kloepper, R. P. ed. 1972. *Adult Teacher's Manual,* 37, no. 4. Hazelwood, MO: Word Aflame Publications.

Knight, W. B. 1956. *Knight's Master Book of New Illustrations.* Grand Rapids, MI: Wm. B. Eerdmans Publishing Company.

Krell, K. 2006. *A Tale of Two Men.* Accessed August 20, 2016. https://bible.org/seriespage/17-tale-two-men-genesis-135-18

Lavin, C. A Down-Home Look at Ross Perot—He's A Man of Norman Rockwell Values. *Seattle Times.* June 3, 1992. Accessed November 24, 2017. http://community.seattletimes.nwsource.com/archive/?date=19920603&slug=1495191

Leak, M. n.d. *Do You Really Desire Wisdom.* Accessed May 20, 2013. http://www.lifeway.com/ArticleView?storeId=10054&catalogId=10001&langId=-1&article=sermon-do-you-really-desire-wisdom-proverbs-james

Lewis, C. S. 1961. *Screwtape letters.* New York: MacMillan.

Lincoln, A. 1838. *The Perpetuation of Our Political Institutions: Address Before the Young Men's Lyceum of Springfield, Illinois.* January 28, 1838. Accessed January 5, 2015. http://www.abrahamlincolnonline.org/lincoln/speeches/lyceum.htm

Macarthur, J. 1979. *The Power of the Word in the Believer's Life, Part I.* July 1, 1979. Accessed December 25, 2016. http://www.gty.org/resources/sermons/1379/the-power-of-the-word-in-the-believers-life-part-1

Maynard, J. 1977. "Dolly." *Good Housekeeping,* 185, no. 3, September 1977, 54, 56, 58, 60.

Massengale, T. W. ed. 2002. "Whatever Feels Right." *IBC Perspectives,* *12, no. 4, 9.*

McCaghy, C. 1985. *Deviant Behavior: Crime, Conflict, and Interest Groups.* 2nd ed. New York: Macmillan Publishing Company.

McDowell, J. 1979. *Evidence That Demands a Verdict, vol. 1: Historical Evidence for the Christian Faith.* Nashville, TN: Thomas Nelson Publishers.

Mooney, P. 2016. "Eyes of Your Understanding." *IBC Perspectives,* 26, no. 4, 2.

Morgan, G. C. 2015. *The Ten Commandments.* New York: Scriptura Press.

Morley, P. M. 1992. *The man in the mirror: Solving the 24 Problems Men Face.* Nashville: Thomas Nelson.

Morris, E. & A. n.d. *Dating vs Courtship.* Accessed June 15, 2019. http://LiveTheExtremeLife.org

Murphy, R. E. 1998. *Word Biblical Commentary.* Nashville: Thomas Nelson.

National Aeronautics and Space Administration. 2014. *Galaxies.* NASA. http://science.nasa.gov/astrophysics/focus-areas/what-are-galaxies/

National Aeronautics and Space Administration. 2009. *How Big Is Our Universe?* NASA. http://www.nasa.gov/audience/foreducators/5-8/features/F_How_Big_is_Our_Universe.html

National Science Teachers' Association. 2013. *NSTA Position Statement: The Teaching of Evolution.* NTSA. http://www.nsta.org/about/positions/evolution.aspx

Native Family Studies. 1985. "Dealing with Everyday Problems." *Native Family Studies.* Dryden Ontario: Native Youth Ministries.

Patterson, J. & Kim, P. 1991. *The Day America told the Truth.* New York: Prentice Hall.

Peacock, R. n.d. *The Probability of Life.* Accessed November 1, 2014. http://evolutionfaq.com/articles/probability-life

Peterson, J. A. 1983. *The Myth of the Greener Grass.* Wheaton, IL: Tyndale House.

Phillips, J. 1995. *Exploring Proverbs: vol. 1.* Neptune, NJ: Loizeaux.

Phillips, J. B. 1972. *The New Testament in Modern English.* rev. ed. New York: Simon & Shuster.

Pius XII. 1950. *Encyclical humani generis of the holy father Pius XII to our venerable brethren, patriarchs, primates, archbishops, bishops, and other local ordinaries enjoying peace and communion with the holy see concerning some false opinions threatening to undermine the foundations of catholic doctrine.* Accessed October 9, 2019. http://w2.vatican.va/content/pius-xii/en/encyclicals/documents/hf_p-xii_enc_12081950_humani-generis.html

Popenoe, D. & Whitehead, B. D. 1999. "Should we live together? What young adults need to know about cohabitation before marriage: A comprehensive review of recent research." *The National Marriage Project Rutgers,* New Brunswick, NJ: The State University of New Jersey.

Random House Dictionary of the English Language. New York: Random House. 1968.

Roberts, W. & Wright, H. N. 1978. *Before You Say "I Do".* Eugene, OR: Harvest House

Rhodes, R. 2011. *1001 Unforgettable Quotes about God, Faith, and the Bible.* Eugene, OR: Harvest House

Sanders, J. O. 1965. *Bible Men of Faith.* Chicago, IL: Moody Press.

Schmidt, K. ed. 1975. *Encounter with Emotions: Senior High Teacher's Manual.* Hazelwood, MO: Word Aflame.

Segraves, D. L. 1990. *Proverbs: Ancient Wisdom for Today's World.* Hazelwood, MO: Word Aflame.

Segraves, K. L. 1973. *Jesus Christ Creator.* San Diego, CA: Creation–Science Research Center

Showalter, S. L. 2017. *Escaping Fantasyland: Overcoming Pornography One Decision at a Time.* Weldon Springs, MO: Word Aflame Press.

Sing unto the Lord. 1978. Hazelwood, MO: Word Aflame Press.

Spurgeon, C. H. 1988. *The Treasury of David: vol. 1, part 1.* McLean, VA: MacDonald Publishing Company.

Spurgeon, C. H. 1988. *The Treasury of David: vol. 2, part 2.* McLean, VA: MacDonald Publishing Company.

Spurgeon, C. H. 1976. "Words of Expostulation." *The Metropolitan Tabernacle pulpit: 1861,* 65–72.

Stanphill, I. F. 1968. "Happiness is the Lord." Accessed November 5, 2016. http://hymnal.calvarybaptistsv.org/188.html

Strong, J. 1990. *The New Strong's Exhaustive Concordance of the Bible.* Nashville, TN: Thomas Nelson Publishers.

Swindoll, C. R. 1985. *Come before Winter … and Share My Hope.* Portland, OR: Multnomah Press.

Swindoll, C.R. 1983. *Growing Strong in the Seasons of Life.* Portland, OR: Multnomah Press.

Tan, P. L. 1979. *Encyclopedia of 7700 Illustrations.* Garland, TX: Assurance Publishers.

Tanner, I. J. 1973. *Loneliness: The Fear of Love.* New York: Harper & Row.

Tenney, T. F. n.d. "The Home: God's Heaven on Earth." *Pentecostal Homelife.*

Toy, C. H. 1999. *A Critical and Exegetical Commentary on the Book of Proverbs*. Edinburgh: T & T Clark.

Tozer, A. W. 2017. *The Pursuit of God.* Cooper & Hudson.

Trupin, S. R., Spandorfer, S. D., Talavera, F., Barnes, A.D., Gaupp, F. B., Rivlin, M. E. 2014. *Elective Abortion.* http://emedicine. medscape.com/article/252560-overview

Unwin, J. D. 1940. *Hopousia: The Sexual and Economic Foundations of a New Society.* London: George Allen & Unwin.

Wangerin, W. 1984. *Ragman and Other Cries of Faith.* New York: Harper & Row.

Webster's New World College Dictionary, 4th ed. 1999. New York: MacMillan.

Webster's Seventh New Collegiate Dictionary. 1970. Springfield, MA: G. & C. Merriam Co.

Wiersbe, W. 1988. *Be Faithful: How to Be Faithful to the Word, Your Tasks, and People Who Need You.* Wheaton, IL: Chariot Victor Books.

Wiersbe, Warren W. 1977. *Treasury of the World's Great Sermons.* Grand Rapids, MI: Kregel

Wildmon, D. E. 1985. *The Home Invaders.* Wheaton, IL: Victor Books.

Wimpey, H. *Deception.* November 13, 2015. Accessed October 24, 2019. https://www.sermoncentral.com/sermons/deception-horace-wimpey-sermon-on-deception-198064?page=2&wc=800

Wright, H. N. 1975. *The Living Marriage: Lessons from the Living Bible.* Old Tappan, NJ: Fleming H. Revell.

Yonts, J. 1980. "Family Finance." *My Father's house discipleship course, teacher's manual III.* 1–9. Hazelwood, MO: General Home Missions Division, United Pentecostal Church, International.

Zietlow, A. 2013. "Religion Runs in the Family." *Christianity Today.* September 20, 2013. http://www.christianitytoday.com/ct/2013/august-web-only/religion-runs-in-family.html?share=HGLkuGHIkvQaBi6Bw6SqzemZLB8TcJFm

SUBJECT INDEX

SCRIPTURE INDEX

ABOUT THE AUTHOR

Lorin Bradbury has served as pastor of the United Pentecostal Church in Bethel, Alaska since 1993. During that time, the church has grown from a fledgling mission work to a thriving church impacting the region. Prior to moving to Bethel, he pastored United Pentecostal Churches in Hoonah (1976-1982) and Juneau (1982-1988), Alaska.

He earned a Bachelor of Liberal Arts Degree from the University of Alaska Southeast, a Master of Science Degree in Counselor Education from the University of Wisconsin-Madison, and a Ph.D. in Educational Psychology from the University of Mississippi. Additionally, Dr. Bradbury completed post-graduate work in Clinical and Counseling Psychology at Region III Mental Health Center in Tupelo, Mississippi.

Dr. Bradbury is licensed to practice psychology in the State of Alaska. Currently, he has an established private practice in Clinical and Forensic Psychology in Bethel, Alaska.

He has published articles in the Pentecostal Homelife Magazine, Preserving Christian Homes, Pentecostal Herald, Pentecostal Life, Alaska-Yukon Witness, and the Forward. For Eight years, he wrote adult Sunday school lessons for Word Aflame Press. In 2013, he published his first book, *Starting Points: A Balanced Diet for Your Church* and a sequel, *Starting Points for Revival* in 2017. In addition to writing Christian literature, Dr. Bradbury writes a weekly newspaper column in the Delta Discovery titled *Ask Dr. Bradbury* answering questions on mental health.

Dr. Bradbury and his wife, Bonnie, have been married since 1971. They have five children and twelve grandchildren.

CPSIA information can be obtained
at www.ICGtesting.com
Printed in the USA
BVHW030953180820
586612BV00023B/14